TEACHING THE
Best Practice
WAY

TEACHING THE Best Practice WAY

Methods That Matter, K-12

HARVEY DANIELS
MARILYN BIZAR

Stenhouse Publishers
Portland, Maine

Stenhouse Publishers
www.stenhouse.com

Library of Congress Cataloging-in-Publication Data
Daniels, Harvey, 1947-
    Teaching the best practice way : methods that matter, K–12 / Harvey Daniels, Marilyn Bizar.
        p. cm.
        Includes bibliographical references and index.
        ISBN 1-57110-405-4 (alk. paper)
        1. Teaching. 2. Interdisciplinary approach in education. 3. Group work in education. 4. Educational tests and measurements. I. Bizar, Marilyn. II. Title.
LB1027.D245 2004
371.3—dc22   2004056575

Cover and interior design by Martha Drury
Manufactured in the United States of America on acid-free paper
12 11 10 09 08 07   15 14 13 12 11 10 9 8 7 6 5 4

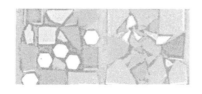  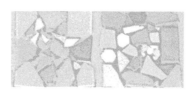

CONTENTS

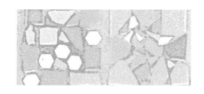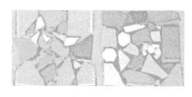

CONTRIBUTED PIECES

(in order of appearance)

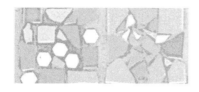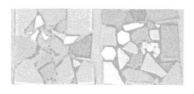

ACKNOWLEDGMENTS

We have the best jobs in the world. Our work takes us to classrooms, schools, and professional conferences all over the country, where we meet creative and innovative teachers all year long. And these colleagues, generous as ever, contribute the ideas, stories, and articles that give life to our books. Whatever credibility and usefulness this volume has is owed to the thoughtful, frank, and practical accounts of classroom instruction these professionals have shared. To all these treasured colleagues, our deepest thanks.

As you read this book, you'll notice that three particular schools—Waters Arts Academy, Baker Demonstration School, and Best Practice High School—have provided more than their share of stories and articles. Tomas Revollo and the teachers at Waters School have shown what true "Best Practice" believers can achieve in an unassuming urban neighborhood. Over ten years of steady and steadfast commitment, they have turned a drab and ordinary school into an extraordinary environment for children, filled with art, books, nature, ideas, writing, music, achievement, and delight. They have energized the parent community, enlisted local artists, planted a beautiful community garden, stewarded eight nearby nature areas—and raised their test scores. The school slogan really fits: "Waters School, where fresh ideas flow."

Since 1936, Baker Demonstration School has been an integral part of National-Louis University, where we both serve as professors of education. Baker's goal is to live out the progressive vision of Elizabeth Harrison, a colleague of John Dewey and the founder of our university. As you'll learn in several sections of this book, the Baker curriculum is built around kids' experience and expression, and fueled by the passions of extraordinary teachers who are given free rein to create and innovate. Harvey's two children were fortunate enough to spend most of their pre-K through eighth-grade years at Baker; he and Elaine credit much of their kids' later success to the foundation of curiosity, thoughtfulness, and self-respect built there. Over the next few years, Baker is going to become an independent school, to be run by its talented and powerful parent body, and we look forward to helping that transition (and afterward) in any way we can.

One of our most ambitious and character-building projects has been helping start a new, small Chicago public (not private, not charter) high school on the city's nearby West Side. In 1996, Best Practice High School opened with 132 pioneer students in a newly rehabbed building across from Michael Jordan's United Center. Now we have 400 kids in grades 9–12, and have been sending 80 percent of our graduates on to college in a school system with a 60 percent drop-out rate. Not bad for a "nonselective magnet" school that enrolls a regular assortment of city kids.

But BPHS has problems, too. When you operate a small, intentionally different institution within a vast bureaucracy like the Chicago Public Schools, you always feel as if you are an invading body that has activated the immune system, like a virus being attacked by swarming white cells. The administrators who fear the school's progressive vision may finally win their ceaseless battle to close us down, and the school we know may not exist next year. If that happens, the great teachers who have made BPHS a beacon in the city and a must-visit stop for educators from around the country, will scatter to other, more stable schools, where they will carry on and become even stronger educators and leaders. The kids who would have enrolled with us will find other high schools to attend. But they may never have the personal relationships with teachers they would have found at BPHS, they probably won't be co-planning the curriculum with the faculty, and those full-ride scholarships to colleges like USC, Grinnell, or the University of Illinois may or may not await them upon graduation. One small consolation is that the faculty's stories, plans, and teaching units have been recorded in this and other professional books. The two of us are proud to be a part of the BPHS story, as long as it lasts and wherever it leads from here.

The secondary education department at NLU is our home base. Our stellar colleagues Jerry Ligon, Connie Keiffer, Marilyn Halliday, Harry Ross, Mary Ann Corley, Scott Sullivan, Cynthia Robinson, Anna Silberg, Jean Ann Hunt, new kid Greg Michie, and our assistant (who pretty much runs the department), Connie Lohman-Huey, create a community where sharing and learning are the bedrock on which we stand. Our students, mostly midlife career changers, give us renewed hope for the high quality of our country's future teachers.

We are also part of a long-running family of teachers, authors, and consultants who have worked together in assorted guises for twenty years. Whether through the Illinois Writing Project, the Center for City Schools, the Walloon Institute, or a dozen grant-funded school improvement projects, we keep gathering the same cast of characters to do the work. Members of this lively team are Steve Zemelman, Nancy Doda, Jim Vopat, Nancy Steineke, Lynette Emmons, Yolanda Simmons, Linda Bailey, Barbara Morris, Barbara Dress, Mary Hausner, Kathy Daniels, Pat Bearden, Toni Murff, Marianne Flanagan, Jessica Swanson, Sara Nordlund, Melissa Woodbury, Alice Perry, and gofers extraordinaire Marny Daniels, Mary Perry, and Kyle Doda.

Among this group of indispensable people, we have to send an extra thanks to Pete Leki, our friend and colleague, the music and ecology guru of our workshops, and one of the most amazing teachers we've ever known. Astute readers will notice that Pete has made *three* contributions to this book (in Chapters 1, 3, and 6), each showing a different way that schools can draw upon their natural surroundings to build best practice learning across the curriculum. Thanks, Pete, for keeping us connected to community, music, and Mother Earth.

For the past fifteen summers, these people (and many of this volume's contributors) have been gathering at our Walloon Institute. There, in an energizing north-woods atmosphere, we spend a week with other teachers, parents, and principals from around the country, all of whom are trying to bring Best Practice teaching and learning to life in their schools. We don't know whether it's the provocative speakers, the respite from back-home pressures, the late-night debates, or the goofy sing-alongs, but we always come back from Walloon smarter, stronger, and more committed than ever to progressive principles. Our thanks go to the thirty-member staff who make Walloon possible each summer, and so does our invitation to interested readers to join us up north next summer—we'll be there.

When we faced the necessity of doing this second edition, we knew that the fun part would be working with everyone at Stenhouse again. As usual, Philippa Stratton went far beyond the call of editorial duty in helping this book live up to our dreams for it. Early on, she sat patiently through several *Groundhog Day*–style meetings during which we had the exact same conversations with no resulting action. Later, she sat in Harvey's living room helping us sift through an increasingly promising tangle of ingredients. To nudge the process along, she recruited several established Stenhouse teacher-authors to contribute key stories to the book. And when we finally produced a manuscript, Philippa abandoned her precious garden for another kind of weeding and pruning.

Everyone at Stenhouse lent a helpful hand on this book. The peerless Brenda Power, our favorite book doctor, helped develop the new reading chapter through many phone calls, e-mails, and hands-on rewrites. Bill Varner gave us a page of unerringly helpful suggestions; we'll probably rue the few we didn't take. Martha Drury helped us deal with files from thirty-four different contributors using every conceivable word-processing program from Appleworks to Word for Aliens. We know that Martha will now take this seven-pound stack of paper and turn it into a beautiful object that we'll hold in our hands six months from now and say: wow! And finally, we have learned to trust that Tom Seavey will find plenty of readers for this book; the final consummation, devoutly wished.

Teaching the Best Practice Way was one of the most complicated manuscripts we have ever worked on, with drafts, artwork, photos, references, and correspondence swapping back and forth between more than fifty people. To make things worse, Harvey suddenly discovered the joys of handwriting text on airplanes, which meant that we had to find someone who could read hieroglyphics. Diane Kessler answered the call, somehow decoding all these ciphers, and handling the 550-page manuscript with aplomb and stunning timeliness. Without her careful and accurate work along the way, and her urgent last-minute entry of all changes, this book would still be unpublishable chicken scratches.

Between us, we have written sixteen books, and we used to be amazed that our families would support us through the long psychological absences that writers' kin typically endure. Now we're starting to think *maybe they like it* when we go and write a book. Maybe for our spouses and kids, it's their favorite time of year. "Whew, we thought they'd never leave," they probably confide to each other when we get out of their hair for a few months. Or maybe not. Still, our families do inspire us.

Harvey's children, Marny and Nick, have grown into two creative, independent, and completely different young people. Nick's career in pathology continues its remarkable route from forensic to surgical work, and soon, from Minnesota to points west. Marny works two jobs in Santa Fe while growing her "wearable art" business and reading many of the same books as her bibliovore mother. Elaine Daniels teaches, advises, and supervises student teachers at National-Louis University and is the sweetest companion one could ever wish for in a newly empty nest. Elaine put plenty of sweat equity into this particular volume, serving as the final and sharpest-eyed reader of the manuscript. Smokey would also like to thank the people who worked alongside him all the way through this project: Steve Perry, Joe Tyler, Tom Hamilton, Joey Kramer, Brad Whitford, Mick Jagger, Keith Richards, Ronnie Wood, Charlie Watts, Jimmy Buffet, and, for the live albums only, Brian Adams, Rod Stewart, Sheryl Crowe, and the BoDeans.

Marilyn would like to thank her husband, Michael Koch, for his support, his pride, and for always making her laugh. His unique brand of craziness helps to make life and work doable. The many young adults in her life—Josh, Michael, Stacy, Jeffrey, Gigi, Marc, Cheryl, Liza, Dina, Laurie, and Mark—continue the ongoing task of teaching her to talk less and listen more. And now her grandchildren, Noah, Sydney, Koryn, and Kaleb, provide yet another reason to help teachers make learning authentic, challenging, and collaborative.

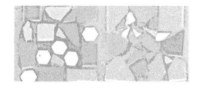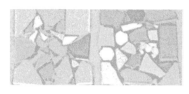

PROLOGUE

Who Do We Think We Are?

So, this book is called *Teaching the Best Practice Way*? Now that's a pretty ambitious topic. Those two authors must be pretty fabulous teachers themselves, or maybe they just think they are the best. Come to think of it, who are these guys to define how other people—students in certification programs, new teachers just starting out, journeyman educators at midcareer, even the savvy veterans—ought to teach? Who do they think they are?

Good questions, we admit.

When we decided on the title for this book, our publisher, with characteristic British understatement, advised: "Well, I suppose you'll have to deal with the hubris factor rather early on." That's for sure, Philippa, so here goes.

No, we do not think we are the "best" teachers in the world. We have plenty of former students running around who'd probably be delighted to tell you about our lessons that bombed, units that flopped, and every classroom crash and burn along the way. No, we certainly don't know everything about the incredibly complex art, craft, science, journey, and roller coaster called teaching young people. And yes, we're acutely aware that our title may convey more expertise than anyone can fairly claim.

But we're not just aw shucks folks, either. Between us, we have taught for seventy-four years, from elementary grades through high school and college. We've worked in city schools with poor, underserved kids, and in elite suburban schools with every conceivable resource. We've guest-taught in classrooms across the country, where curious colleagues have invited us to trade practices with them. We've helped start a brand-new public school on Chicago's West Side and guided it through nine years of development. For the past year, we have been regularly teaching in a small school in southeastern Ohio, which has opened up a new perspective on the joys and challenges of rural education. Between us, we've also written sixteen previous books, each one focused on some aspect of literacy, learning, or school reform. These days, we mostly earn our keep as teacher-educators at National-Louis University in Chicago, where we are working with adult students who are leaving careers in nursing, technology, public relations, dentistry, social work, advertising, and law to become teachers. So, while there's plenty we still don't know about teaching, we have done a lot of it, watched a lot of it, and have been studying this mysterious craft for quite a while.

This Stuff Works

This book began its life in 1998 as *Methods that Matter: Six Structures for Best Practice Classrooms*. Since that time, the practices described in our first edition have grown and spread in American classrooms. The book club model we described can fairly be said to have swept the schools, with millions of students from kindergarten through high school now engaging in peer-led literature circles patterned after adult reading groups. Collaborative activities, broadly endorsed by curriculum and subject-matter organizations, such as the National Council of Teachers of English and the National Board for Professional Teaching Standards, continue to grow in use and in refinement. Thematic, integrative units are the hallmark of the country's highest-achieving schools; visit award-winning public or private schools in any American city and you'll see students engaged in extended, interdisciplinary studies of fairy tales, global warming, the future, and more. Strategic reading, or reading-as-thinking, has become a major focus in today's schools, one of the highest priorities for staff development and a key theme of accreditation visits. Thousands of teachers across the curriculum are implementing the new reading-as-thinking strategies to make sure students understand and remember what they read, especially nonfiction text in math, science, and history. And reflective, student-driven forms of assessment are replacing traditional tests and quizzes, while conferences, rubrics, and portfolios are becoming new standard forms of evaluation.

While it is gratifying to see the spread of Best Practices among working teachers, not everything has been sunshine and lollipops since this book first appeared.

First, the term *educational standards* has taken on some new and worrisome meanings. Back in the early 1990s, the two of us were happy to be part of the standards movement, which at that time involved educational organizations (like the International Reading Association and the American Association for the Advancement of Science) defining what good teaching and learning looked like in each school subject field. The documents these groups developed, many with federal funding, focused on "opportunity to learn" standards—defining what kind of instruction, experiences, and materials kids should be offered. In other words, we were working on the "inputs," making sure there would be equity and excellence for all.

But a second, and increasingly contrary, standards movement arose, focused not on supporting the development of individual learners, but on testing and comparing numerical outputs, under the banner of "accountability." Backed with the political muscle of state legislatures, governors, business groups, Washington think tanks, and presidents from both parties, the accountability branch of the standards movement pretty much hijacked the school reform conversation. Resources were shifted away from providing instruction to children and toward ranking students with standardized tests and dealing out punishments to kids, teachers, and schools deemed to have failed. States developed thousands of new outcome-based standards, and backed them with batteries of high-stakes tests that could land noncompliant schools or teachers in trouble fast.

How do all these politics affect you, as a reader of *Teaching the Best Practice Way*? Not much, we hope. It depends on how the accountability movement impinges upon your teaching life. The main thing you need to know is that the seven methods featured in this book have a long record of validation, in both qualitative and quantitative studies of rigorous design. We have abundant proof that, for example, well-structured small-group projects, or strategic reading activities, or authentic experiences, or thematic teaching units are linked to improved achievement on valid measures of student performance.

In other words, students taught with these methods typically score very well on high-stakes tests, even though the methods aren't intentionally aligned to such measures. Best Practice kids, if we can call them that, do better on the customary measures of educational achievement as a natural consequence of good teaching— or as a side effect of it. They become powerful learners, proficient readers and writers and thinkers; they are accustomed to taking responsibility for themselves, experienced at solving problems, full of confidence, and sensitive to situations in which they are being evaluated. Now, that doesn't mean we take high scores for granted. In schools where we work, we also do some very focused coaching when the standardized testing season comes along. It's vital that the students know the format, the rules, and best angles of attack when they sit down in front of that test booklet. Hey, we don't like all this testing, but we're not going to let our kids get busted while we bask in our own orthodoxy. We have a motto for our forty-week school calendar in Chicago: "thirty-six weeks of pure Best Practice teaching and four weeks of savvy, well-timed test-prep."

A recurrent theme of the accountability movement is to demand "scientific proof"—evidence, usually in statistical form, showing that certain educational practices really do work. Seems reasonable to us. After all, if we are going to devote millions of dollars and zillions of classroom hours to a particular activity, it certainly ought to be worthwhile. That's why we're happy to report that the seven key practices described in this book, sometimes under different names, have bodies of research going back sixty years or more, some of which we have documented in our own previous work (Zemelman, Daniels, and Hyde 1998; Zemelman, Daniels, and Bizar 1999).

But there's much more research that validates progressive practices, enough to fill a whole book, leaving little room for the practical instructions, classroom vignettes, and materials we really want to share. So, at the end of each chapter, we will direct you to further readings where you can learn about the heritage, theory, and research base behind each of these important methods. But before we move on, we want to introduce you to one line of research that's especially illuminating.

Fred Newmann and a number of his colleagues at the University of Wisconsin have been working for twenty years on the idea of "authentic instruction." This is their name for a model of teaching that diverges from the traditional paradigm in a number of ways. In authentic lessons:

> Students draw conclusions, elaborate on their understanding, or make and
> support arguments.
> Students construct knowledge, by interpreting, analyzing, and evaluating,
> and not merely reciting information.
> Students connect topics to their own lives or similar situations in daily life
> outside school.

For many years, Newmann (1996) has documented that students taught "the authentic way" score far better on challenging subject-matter tests than kids taught through standard lectures and solitary seatwork.

But the lingering question has been: What about high-stakes state or national standardized tests that are not necessarily aligned with the curriculum being taught? How would kids score on these increasingly prevalent exams? Using a large sample of Chicago public school students, Newmann's group looked at the quality of assignments given by teachers, as measured by their embodiment of these three elements of authenticity (Newmann, Bryk, and Nagaoka 2001). The study found that

- classrooms with high-quality assignments make gains that are 20 percent greater than the average, on the Iowa Test of Basic Skills in reading, over one year;
- classrooms with low-quality assignments make gains that are only 70 percent of the average, on the ITBS in reading, over one year.

Newmann's team also looked at whether classroom instruction was more teacher-centered, featuring extensive lecturing and relatively passive student roles, or more interactive, featuring more social and exploratory activities for students. Studying another selection of Chicago schools, the researchers found that

- with high didactic instruction, students gain 3.4 percent *less* than the city average on reading achievement tests, over one year;
- with low didactic instruction, students gain 3.7 percent *more* than the city average on reading, over one year.

Finally, Newmann looked at interaction levels, comparing outcomes in classrooms that feature extensive collaborative, small-group work with those of students who mostly worked quietly and alone. Their findings showed that

- with *high* use of interactive instruction, students gain 5.2 percent *more* than the city average on reading, over one year;
- with *low* use of interactive instruction, students gain 4.5 percent *less* than the city average on reading, over one year.

While some of these effects may seem modest, Newmann points out that the difference in achievement is cumulative, multiplying over the years.

What Newmann calls "authentic instruction" is what many educators, including us, call Best Practice. And the seven "methods that matter" in this book are the tools teachers need to create classrooms that are thoughtful, authentic, interactive, rooted in real life, and engaged in exploration.

The Design of This Book

Each of the next seven chapters gives a detailed and practical picture of one good teaching structure. We start each section with a descriptive essay, outlining the method, tracing its history and roots, acknowledging its pioneers, and listing the structure's vital features. Next, several teachers representing different grade levels and school communities will explain how they adopted the basic model, adapted it to their students, and made it their own. That means you'll be getting the inside story from working teachers—professionals who are bringing Best Practice to life in their classrooms every day and now sharing their best ideas with you. Because we are lucky enough to visit a variety of regions and schools every year, we can be matchmakers, introducing you to thirty-four wonderful colleagues, people who face the same challenges that you do every day. There's no more credible source of expertise and advice.

We've asked each teacher-author to share a story of good teaching in their own style and voice. These master teachers take you behind the scenes of their practice, explaining how they got started, planned their innovations, equipped their classrooms, prepared students, managed their activities, solved problems, sustained their energy when things got tough, and found colleagues for sharing and support. We've asked the writers to be practical and specific, not just inspirational. While it is always fun to hear how someone else succeeded—it's even more useful to learn how to replicate their success in your own classroom.

In each chapter, you'll find teacher stories for every grade range—primary, elementary, middle, and high school; these stories come from a variety of school types in six different states. (OK, there are rather a lot of Chicagoans—please forgive our hometown boosterism.) While many of these reports come to us from skillful veteran teachers, the oldsters haven't cornered the market on excellence; there are plenty of younger educators here, even some first- and second-year teachers. And while the reports differ in style and language, you'll notice the shared underlying assumptions about student-centered, progressive, Best Practice teaching.

Many of the stories are detailed enough that other teachers can use them as the basis for their own classroom experiments. But no one here is bragging or trying to make it sound easy. Nobody thinks they have perfected themselves as teachers. Indeed, many of this book's contributors describe themselves as being in process, on the road, partway there, or even taking baby steps. All these teacher-authors know firsthand that change is hard, and many have written about their frustrations as well as their triumphs. For most of us who teach, change comes in small, hard-earned increments, not in one sudden, dramatic transformation.

Taken together, these sets of descriptions and stories provide a basic understanding of the seven Best Practice classroom structures, but they probably won't answer every question that a teacher contemplating a classroom implementation might raise. This book occupies a kind of middle level in the pyramid of resources about any one of these activities. For example, many books and standards reports endorse the workshop model, but without explaining it. In this book, we explain the basic structure of workshop and offer four stories of teacher variations. Readers who want even more detail about workshop can then turn to whole books that focus closely on this single structure. That's one reason we provide reading suggestions at the end of each chapter.

As you read along, you'll also notice that these teacher stories aren't just about strategies and practices, but also about theories and ideas: the articles mention developmental stage models, cognitive processes, thinking taxonomies, process-writing research, reader-response theory, and other large concepts about learning. That's because teaching is idea-driven work; educators who are in charge of their own professional growth want to know where innovative strategies come from, how activities can be translated up and down the grades, and what research supports them. Teachers want to know how their own daily experiences and experiments fit in with those of colleagues around the country; they are eager to become part of the wider professional conversation that constantly bounces between the concrete and the conceptual. Teachers want activities that will work with real kids on Monday, but they also want to understand *why* things work so they can answer their own questions and make their own choices down the line.

Though these contributors range from kindergarten through high school, we think that every single story has value for all teachers, not only for people who happen to teach at the same grade level. The seven Best Practice methods are truly generic, meaning that vital tips or translatable stories about management, organization, materials, scheduling, evaluation, or record keeping can come from colleagues at any grade level.

We like the fact that this book speaks to all teachers. In both editions, we've violated the conventional wisdom that says you must aim professional books at the same grade-level spans we use for school buildings: K–5, 6–8, 9–12, etc. For some topics that may be a sensible segregation. But for the biggest ideas, the ones that genuinely apply to all grade levels, we need everyone to join the conversation. Indeed, while we think this book will be helpful to individual readers, our dream audience is a whole school faculty, a whole *district* faculty, coming together to talk about the really big ideas in teaching, from kindergarten through senior year, from beginning reading to AP physics.

What's New in This Edition?

The big news is, we have "discovered" a seventh method that matters. Can you imagine? The missing method was a true case of something being right under our noses, something so fundamental and pervasive that we forgot to mention it: reading. But we don't mean same-old school reading lessons or activities. We are talking about something distinct and special here. Teachers who nurture strategic readers have a repertoire of activities that help kids deeply understand not just typical school print (textbooks, novels, math problems) but also art, film, dance—they learn to "read" the world. And this special kind of reading goes far beyond merely decoding letters or comprehending facts. Strategic readers deploy a sophisticated repertoire of cognitive strategies that allow them to understand, remember, and even challenge the material and experiences in the curriculum. We'll talk much more about this in Chapter 2.

We also discovered, or at least decided, that in the previous edition we got the order of things wrong. Last time, we opened the book by talking about integrative units, which may be the most challenging of the seven methods to implement. Indeed, there is a sense in which these big, extended, often interdisciplinary inquiries are the culmination, the "payoff" of all Best Practice teaching, since they tend to include all six of the other methods as they unfold over a period of days. So this time, we've put our seven structures into a more stepwise sequence, culminating rather than commencing with the most ambitious one.

Of course, we've done everything else you'd expect for a new edition: we have revised everything; plugged in new stories, examples, and handouts; and brought the references up to date with some exciting new research and teacher accounts. But the main change is the addition of thirteen wonderful new teacher voices to the book, and the practical classroom stories they are sharing here for the first time. From these expert educators, and from the nineteen "old-timers" held over from the first edition, *Teaching the Best Practice Way* gets its life.

We've created a little community while writing this book, which has brought joy as well as knowledge. Sadly, that feeling of fellowship is rare in this field. For too long, teaching has been an isolating profession where colleagues can work just a few steps apart but feel miles away. Today, progressive reform is opening up the old, cellular organization of schools, bringing groups of teachers together to plan, share, reflect, and build the kind of vibrant professional community that teaching has never quite enjoyed. Teachers are helping each other grow, whether in official peer-led workshops, by passing along classroom materials, through casual faculty-lounge dialogue, or by discussing professional publications. Just as we are rediscovering the power of peer tutoring—of kids teaching kids—so, too, are we rediscovering the professional energy that is unleashed when teachers teach teachers.

That's what we are trying to do here, in book form. So join the thirty-four of us, your newfound colleagues, as we explore the meaning of Best Practice, the nature of good teaching, and the methods that really matter.

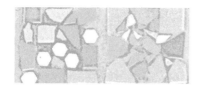

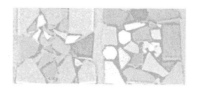

ONE

HOW TO TEACH

How do you teach well? How do you create a thinking community that's focused on inquiry, powered by curiosity, and cradled with caring? How do you instruct children and young adults with impact, respect, and grace? What classroom experiences best help young people to understand and remember valuable information, concepts, and procedures? As a grown-up, a subject-matter expert, and a veteran learner, what roles should you take in relationship to students? Exactly what do we mean when we give that highest of compliments, "good teacher"?

Three factors determine how any of us go about teaching:

1. our personality, background, tastes, and attitudes;
2. our own experiences as a student in school; and
3. what we learn as a student of teaching.

The first influence we can't change—and we wouldn't want to. Teaching is a deeply personal trade, and many different personalities—performer, introvert, coach, scholar—can make effective educators. Next, our experience in school, for sixteen or more years, fills our heads with models, assumptions, scripts, and stereotypes out of which we build, mostly unconsciously, a model of teaching that's comfortable for us.

The third, and often weakest, influence on how we teach is our conscious study of the craft, including ideas and practices that don't immediately feel natural to our personal styles, or that haven't been repeatedly demonstrated to us during our own schooling. This book focuses—of necessity—on this latter domain: What can we learn when we study teaching carefully? How can our repertoire grow when we don't just re-create, but question our experience as kids in school? And what unfamiliar classroom styles can we actually grow into, if we stretch our personalities beyond the everyday comfort zone?

The best teachers are not the ones trying to channel a favorite teacher from their school days or build a classroom solely around their personal enthusiasms, as productive as those strategies can be. Having thousands of lesson plans in your head doesn't make you a master teacher, either, though it is a common side effect of excellent teaching. Nor do the really top teachers study state curriculum standards as they drive to school each day, stopping at every red light to review a few more benchmarks, targets, or outcomes. No, what truly accomplished teachers possess is a small repertoire of powerful structures that help them organize subject matter, time, space, materials, students, and themselves to make learning happen. These few "methods that matter" are recurrent, complex, and generative. Some very accomplished teachers may not even be fully aware that they own and use these patterns.

These key structures, these building blocks of good instruction, can be named in many ways, but based on our research and observation, we use these seven descriptors:

reading-as-thinking
representing-to-learn
small-group activities
classroom workshop
authentic experiences
reflective assessment
integrative units

Some of these terms are self-explanatory, while others may sound more obscure. Our job is to explain them as this book unfolds.

Defining Best Practice Teaching

There are many names for good teaching. Some are descriptive: exemplary, state-of-the-art, research-based, proficient, standards-based. Others bear a heavier conceptual load: instructional efficacy, teaching for engagement, and the like. We prefer the label *Best Practice,* partly because it is a well-understood term in other professions, and partly because it is clearly defined with reference to specific documents, research, and standards. Or it *was* well-defined, until "terminology drift," the bane of our professional language, set in.

Today the term *Best Practice* has entered the daily vocabulary of teachers, administrators, board members, policy makers, education reporters, and everyday citizens. This once-venerable phrase, borrowed from medicine, law, and architecture, was meant to clarify what we mean by good teaching. Now there's more cloudiness than clarity, as promiscuous and nonspecific use of the term proliferates. School district mission statements and curriculum guides trumpet their institutional allegiance to Best Practice. Blue-ribbon committees bestow golden apples on teachers who manifest Best Practice. Conference programs glibly promise their attendees templates for Best Practice classrooms, and slap the slogan on the free tote bags, ballpoints, and key chains. Aspiring politicians pledge to bring Best Practices to the schools of their districts, should they be elected. The U.S. Department of Education scatters the term *Best Practice* through its Web pages, grant applications, and brochures, even though it actively opposes the same practices in other venues.

The one common feature of all these utterances is that hardly anyone who uses the term *Best Practice* knows what it means. These days, it's simply what you are supposed to embrace, a phrase that vaguely substitutes for "good," "with-it," "mainstream." Best Practice has become a generic, ceremonial seal of approval, a fuzzy pledge of okayness, a genuflection to whatever everyone else is doing or claims to be doing. Sometimes it seems as though Best Practice is about to take the place of the term *quality education,* a blessing that of course everyone wants for their children, but that has no shared definition whatsoever.

We think the term *Best Practice* does mean something, something very concrete and particular, and something well worth defending. It is not at all vague. Genuine Best Practice embraces certain educational ideas and activities while clearly ruling others out. It has a deep basis in research, in the study of child development and learning, in the history and philosophy of American (and world) education. Best Practice, under other, older names, has a long and distinguished pedigree and is manifested through a limited and distinctive set of classroom practices.

So what do we mean by Best Practice teaching? The definition, as well as the theoretical and research base, for today's best educational practices can be found in the standards documents published by the nation's mainline professional associations, subject-matter organizations, research centers, and curriculum groups, including:

American Association for the Advancement of Science
International Reading Association
National Board for Professional Teaching Standards

Center for Civic Education
Consortium of National Arts Organizations
Geography Education Standards Project
National Council of Teachers of English
National Council for Education and the Economy
National Council of Teachers of Mathematics
National Association for the Education of Young Children
Joint Committee on National Health Education Standards
National Research Council
National Center for History in the Schools

In spite of their diverse subject specialties and discipline loyalties, groups as disparate as the National Council of Teachers of Mathematics and the International Reading Association have endorsed a very similar model of teaching and learning. In their various reports, all these organizations call for classrooms that are

- student-centered
- experiential
- reflective
- authentic
- holistic
- social
- collaborative
- democratic
- cognitive
- developmental
- constructivist
- challenging.

Since these diverse groups affirmed these shared principles, it was not surprising that their official recommendations looked so much alike.

Most of the standards documents called for similar shifts in the ways classrooms were organized and run. They called for a rebalancing of the ingredients of schooling—students, time, space, materials, experiences, and assistance. Some of the key changes suggested that Best Practice teaching means

LESS
whole-class-directed instruction, e.g., lecturing;
student passivity: sitting, listening, receiving, and absorbing information;
prizing and rewarding of silence in the classroom;

classroom time devoted to fill-in-the-blank worksheets, dittos, workbooks, and other "seatwork";

student time spent reading textbooks and basal readers;

time spent thinly "covering" large amounts of material in every subject area;

rote memorization of facts and details;

stress on competition and grades;

tracking or leveling students into "ability groups";

use of pull-out special programs;

use of and reliance on standardized tests.

MORE

experiential, inductive, hands-on learning;

active learning in the classroom, with all the attendant noise and movement of students doing, talking, and collaborating;

emphasis on higher-order thinking; learning a field's key concepts and principles;

penetrating study of fewer topics, so that students internalize the field's way of inquiry;

time devoted to reading whole, original, real books and nonfiction materials;

responsibility transferred to students for their work: goal setting, record keeping, monitoring, evaluation;

choice for students—picking their own books, writing topics, team partners, research projects;

enacting and modeling of the principles of democracy in school;

attention to varying cognitive and affective styles of individual students;

cooperative, collaborative activity; developing the classroom as an interdependent community;

heterogeneously grouped classrooms where individual needs are met through individualized activities, not segregation of bodies;

delivery of special help to students in regular classrooms;

varied and cooperative roles for teachers, parents, and administrators;

reliance on teachers' descriptive evaluation of student growth, including qualitative/anecdotal observations (Zemelman, Daniels, and Hyde 1998).

Now, if you're feeling provoked, please keep in mind that this list says "more" not "all," and "less" not "none." The standards don't repudiate traditional schooling; they simply call for a rebalancing between the predominant teacher-directed activities and other structures that give students more responsibility and challenge.

In the various standards reports, the general instructional advice was backed up with scores, and often hundreds, of specific recommendations concerning different bodies of content and grade levels. But behind the details lay a consistent and surprising commitment to the shared, underlying principles. The National Council of Teachers of Mathematics led the way, describing math as a special kind of thinking instead of a body of content; calling for the integration of more writing, talking, and artwork into math; and arguing for the importance of estimation and real-world problem solving. The American Association for the Advancement of Science forswore the ancient tradition of curriculum coverage, arguing instead that students should delve more deeply into a smaller number of topics. Though highly politicized and subject to demagogic attack, even the social studies standards called for students to *do* history, to take multiple perspectives, and not merely absorb the official ingredients of cultural literacy.

However bold the standards projects sometimes seemed, most of these principles and recommendations were nothing particularly new. As one of our longtime teacher-reformer friends sighed when we put this list of principles on an overhead projector at a recent workshop, "Well, duuhhhh!" At least some educators have been calling for American schooling to be more experiential, reflective, and democratic throughout the whole history of this country and back through the ages. John Dewey would have recognized and embraced these principles, though he might have asked someone to explain constructivism to him. The legacy reaches back thousands of years and across the world, to figures like Marcus Fabius Quintilianus, Johann Pestalozzi, Friedrich Wilhelm Froebel, Maria Montessori, Jean Piaget, John Dewey, Eric Ericson, Carl Rogers, Elizabeth Harrison, and, more recently, figures like Jonathan Kozol, James Beane, Paolo Friere, Deborah Meier, Maxine Greene, and Howard Gardner. In other words, today's Best Practice teachers are heirs to what is commonly called the *student-centered* or *progressive* paradigm of teaching.

There are other paradigms of teaching, of course, each with its own pantheon of thinkers and lines of research. Some of these other paradigms are contrary or even hostile toward the progressive model. In fact, there's a highly acrimonious clash of educational paradigms happening right now in our country. But here's the important thing: the progressive paradigm, the student-centered, Best Practice model, is the one endorsed by our contemporary professional standards documents. That is, the authoritative national professional standards, the ones developed by our colleagues in each of the subject-matter fields, say: teach the student-centered way, extend the progressive tradition.

What Does It Look Like?

So we have a firm definition of Best Practice: there's a set of clear and interlocking principles, some relative valuings of different classroom activities, and, within particular subject areas, scores of authoritative recommendations guided by these ideas and values. But these are mostly abstractions. What does this look like in practice, in real life, with real kids? How can a teacher—or a whole school—grow toward, enact, and live out the meaning of Best Practice in real, workaday classrooms?

Let's take a tour of Waters School in the spring. Your guide is Pete Leki, a naturalist, teacher, and parent who, along with principal Tomas Revollo, has led Waters's transformation from an ordinary K–8 school in Chicago to something very different and special.

Waters School: Where Fresh Ideas Flow

PETE LEKI

The field house is low and blue. Blue from the sky of the mural that wraps around its weathered siding. There are elephants and butterflies standing in jungles of green plantlike things. Mr. Javier supervised this beautiful mural. I pleaded for prairies and buffalo. But the kids painted a fantasy landscape from some primeval *Star Trek* set. Now I like it a lot.

From inside there comes a sound like a semi truckload of ice chests being dumped down three flights of stairs. It is Ms. Z's drumming class. Kids are whaling away at inverted five-gallon plastic buckets, bungeed to milk crates. Ms. V, the art teacher, is standing before me with her mouth moving. She motions with her head to come with her to the art side of the building, insulated behind two doors, where we can talk.

Ms. V says, "Hey, Mr. W says he wants to do butterflies in science, so I told him I'd talk to you about how we could pull in the garden and Mighty Acorns work."

"Yes, I had heard that," I tell her. "I just forgot." I forget about a lot of things on my list. Usually I can't even find the list. "OK. Butterflies fit into a bigger picture. We have lots of butterflies that evolved here in our region over millennia. Many have developed close relationships with larval host plants and adult nectar preferences."

"I know that!" says Ms. V. "I'm a country girl. So Mr. W and I got a list of natives, and some reading materials for the kids, and I asked Ms. T [the computer teacher] to help the kids access color photos and information about the ones the kids picked out. Each child got one. So what else do you think they should learn?"

"Maybe . . . life history. Larval plant and adult nectar preferences. Then we compile the list and let the kids match it against the plant list we have for our garden. We could see which plant families we are lacking and which we might be able to get. You know checkerspot butterflies need turtleheads. And monarch caterpillars like all the Asclepias. And . . ."

"And what I'd like to do is get them working on some real detailed paintings of their choice butterfly and use that time to talk about symmetry and the basics of butterfly anatomy. Maybe we could laminate and post them around the garden near their butterfly's favorite plants."

"Well, you know, Mr. W was wondering what to plant in their classroom plot. I have a whole tray of butterfly weed seedlings that need transplanting. And some dill. And rattlesnake master. Their whole plot could be used to raise unrepresented host species."

"Which would increase plant biodiversity?"

"Which would increase butterfly biodiversity."

"They could lead groups from other classrooms around the garden to tell them about interdependency and stuff."

"Uh-oh, quick. Hide. Here come Ms. Z—she's gonna want to do a butterfly opera or something. . . ."

So goes life in the little, run-down field house at Waters School, where the art, music, and ecology teachers are headquartered, here at the entrance to the grand garden area, watched over by four ancient bur oak sentinels. We meet every Wednesday to discuss how we can integrate our specialties into the teaching goals of our classroom colleagues in the big building across the playground.

Integration has become so much the normal thing in our school that it seems there are nonstop performances, field trips, culminating activities, and meetings, meetings, meetings. Ms. Z and Ms. V have pioneered a great new idea: Down with big, schoolwide, auditorium assemblies! Up with repeated, smaller touring performances. No mikes, no echoes. I recently heard Ms. G's second-grade class put on a first-rate show in the classroom, for parents, about the water cycle. Beautiful costumes; well-spoken, easy-to-hear lines; funny songs and movement; and time for comments and questions. A real, human-dimension performance that they took up and down the second-floor hall. By the end of that day those kids knew their water cycle, and kids in their audiences did, too.

Ms. Z; Ms. V; Ms. R, the librarian; and Ms. T, the computer teacher, are always finding ways to work their way into our ecology strand, a program that stretches from pre-K through eighth grade. Ms. Z heard that we had taken our third graders on their first of nine Mighty Acorns journeys to Sauganash Prairie Grove, in the Cook County Forest Preserves. On that fine fall morning their first task was to familiarize themselves with the thirty-five-acre site and the five distinct ecosystems that I tell them exist there: slough, floodplain woods, oak woods, oak savanna, and wet prairie. They have maps and journals and are supposed to visit each place and sketch something from each one to remember it by. At a pre-trip workshop they were given a custom-written (by me) nonfiction piece to read and paste into their journal, that describes the history of the land, pre- and post-settlement, and that gives the basic vocabulary that they should start to use.

Well, Ms. Z hears about all this vocabulary and decides that she has to have them write songs about their new discoveries, to a rhumba rhythm no less:

We went to the savanna
But we didn't see no bananas
We saw squirrels everywhere
But we didn't see no bears

Chorus:
The grassy prairie had beautiful flowers
The wetland slough had frogs and fish
The oak woodland had rabbits and deer
The savanna had bur oak trees

In the floodplain woods
A big maple tree stood
We saw mushrooms there
And some pieces of rabbit hair

In the oak woodlands
There were some Joe Pye weeds
We saw some poison ivy
And alien invader species

We went to the slough
And we saw something new
Arrow leaf and duckweed, too
And the big turkey vulture flew

Fuimos a la pradera
Y las flores alcanzaban a la cadera
Habia plantas con los espinas
Y vimos venados en todas esquinas

The kids sing these silly songs on the bus to and from the preserve, reading from their journals, verse after endless verse. The science words enter deep crannies of the mind and reemerge during journal freewrites in the woods. The trusty journal follows them throughout their Mighty Acorn experience, packed with reading materials about history and invasive species and biodiversity and stewardship responsibilities. For us, drawing and writing are very similar activities and we expect our students to draw what they can't write and write what they can't draw. We expect their journals to look like da Vinci sketch/field notebooks. Sometimes they approach that.

There is no ecology class at Waters. Instead, we strive to integrate all subjects and all teaching staff. Ms. V uses her art time to teach kids how to sketch the identifying features of European buckthorn, an aggressive alien species invading our oak woodlands. Ms. W uses math time to teach the tabulation, averaging, graphing, and percentages kids need to complete our fifth-grade Mighty Acorns winter survey of woody plants. Ms. H uses her science class to prepare for flower studies in the spring woods. PE time is used to run school-yard simulations of habitat loss and predator prey games. The scheduling and planning of this cooperative work happens on Wednesday mornings, which have been freed by the school administration for integration meetings. It also goes on in hallways, stairwells, in parking lots, and no doubt in coffee shops and bars. It's very athletic—dancelike—in the flexiblity that is needed to make it work.

The Waters ecology strand, which began in 1994 with a third-through-fifth-grade Mighty Acorn exploration of our homeland natural areas, has expanded over the years. Its main features are repeated visits to natural areas to explore, study, and care for them. Over the years other natural areas were added, so that starting in 2003–2004 the strand was extended from pre-K through eighth grade. Now it looks like this:

Grade	Natural Area	Partner Organization
pre-K through first	Waters School Garden	School staff, Chicago Botanic Gardens
second	Chicago River riverbank between Berteau and Montrose	Friends of the Chicago River
third through fifth	Sauganash Prairie Grove	Cook County Forest Preserves
sixth	Chicago River at Ronan Park	Friends of the Chicago River
seventh	Montrose Point, Lake Michigan	Friends of the Parks, Nature Along the Lake
eighth	Waters School Garden	School staff, Chicago Botanic Gardens

All these site visits to natural areas are preceded with readings, from the simplest picture books in pre-K to quite involved descriptions of the Great Lakes watershed, geology, and human water uses in seventh grade. All students come to the sites armed with some prior knowledge and their journal and pencil. All classes are broken up into small subunits for the explorations. I don't want to lead a class like a herd of straggling buffalo through a natural area or like tourists through a museum. I don't want to have to shout to a line of thirty kids, "Look. That's a flicker on that red oak. That's a FLICKER ON . . . THAT WAS A FLICK . . ." I couldn't stand it.

So on all of our field trips our students are in small exploratory groups of five to eight, led by a volunteer parent or community member. The Mighty Acorns are encouraged to develop *wood craft*: a way of behaving in the woods that is respectful of the place and its creatures, and mindful of each thing done. "Noise scares away animals. And screams tell me that someone is hurt and needs help right away. Don't do that. Be silent in the woods, like a fox," I tell them. When groups come upon each other in the woods they are taught to freeze, hide, or turn away. We explain that these are wild places, not parks. They are homes to animals and plants that are rare, precious and can be dangerous. The very reiteration of these warnings helps students to feel the faith and confidence we have in them. The small groups help the experience to be more intimate, with more surprises. Our students have, over the past ten years, single-handedly controlled the invasion of garlic mustard in our floodplain woods. They have read about it in the classroom. They have drawn it in art. And in the woods they learn quickly to identify the weed, to avoid stinging nettles, and to avoid stomping and uprooting green dragon and trillium and wild ginger. Last year they carried out 480 pounds of garlic mustard and its seed, and composted it at the school. They do important work, highly valued by the professional staff of the Forest Preserves.

None of this would be possible without a corps of volunteers who feel comfortable leading groups of students in this way. During the last school year, forty-eight volunteers were honored for their work. We have veteran leaders and newcomers. All are invited for coffee and a briefing in the field house before every trip. We explain the trip goals and activities. Group leaders, or guides, as they are called, are encouraged to step up to the job of teacher, building group cooperation, making sure tasks are accomplished, and modeling for the students their own curiosity, their eagerness to draw and write and learn from the place. This job is very different from the typical chaperone tasks allocated to parents during most trips. At Waters our cadre of parents comes directly from our use for the past thirteen years of the Parent Project, a workshop approach to bringing parents into the vision of progressive education (Vopat 1994) that is enshrined in the School Improvement

Plan. In the Parent Project, participants do the same stuff that their kids are doing in the classroom: literature circles, group work, journal writing, publishing, site-based exploration, integration of the subject areas. These parents also find their way onto the Local School Council, helping to strengthen the political will to recognize and support the good work going on in our classrooms.

Partner organizations like Friends of the Chicago River, the Cook County Forest Preserves, the Botanic Gardens, and others often help us financially by paying for buses, but also provide a source for top-notch scientific expertise and a chance for our kids to see possible future job opportunities for themselves.

Journals are the main way that I am able to know what students are learning. In addition to freewriting and drawing in natural areas, students are asked to synthesize what they have read, been told, and experienced in a post-trip journaling session. I try to look through each child's journal and respond to their writing with a note of my own. Occasionally a student's journal is an awful mess, where I can't even tell which side is up. This gives me an opportunity to confer with the child and talk with the classroom teacher about what extra help the student might need.

One time I sat with a fourth-grade boy on the stairway outside his class and questioned him about the largely blank page where he was supposed to have responded to the pre-trip lesson I had given his class. There was almost nothing. "So, don't you know why we are going to find buckthorn in the woods?" He looked blankly. "You don't remember the pictures I drew on the board about the way buckthorn shades out other plants?" He shook his head slowly. "Well, no wonder you didn't write anything. Listen, Jorge, the reason that I want you to write, to tell me the story, is so that I can see if you understand what I was teaching. If you don't know, it means that I didn't do a good job teaching."

He brightened up. "No, Mr. Lucky, you did a good job."

I laughed. "But the way that I know that I did a good job is if you can explain it back to me. Tell me what you do remember." So we sat and pieced together the story of the invasion of buckthorn into the millennia-old rich woodlands of Illinois, the loss of biodiversity, the sad poorness of the lost community. "Do you think you can finish?"

"Yes, Mr. Lucky, I can finish it." And he did.

I give quizzes, too. I like these quizzes because if you don't "pass" you get to take it again. And if you still don't pass you get to have a conference with me. Two good things come from this. By the end, all the students can answer the questions and have some basic grasp of the subject matter and vocabulary. And I get an opportunity to spend extra time with the most needy kids. Often, I will ask them the question that they got wrong, and they will tell me the correct answer. There may be reading problems there, or other cognitive or learning style problems. In the end they all pass, as I expected from the beginning they would.

My job can be a real delight because I get to spend this extra time with these students. And I get to lead them in learning in wild places, in small groups. Positions like mine are not common. My work is funded piecemeal through grants captured by our school principal, Tomas Revollo, or myself. This is a pain in the neck. But the payback is extraordinary in other ways. At our recent Spring Garden Day 150 kids, teachers, and parents showed up in the freezing, pouring rain to haul compost, weed, till the classroom's raised beds, and cover them with mulch to await the spring planting. Eighth graders dug through gravel and mud to create a new, 2,000-square-foot crescent flower bed that will surround their graduation gift to the school: an outdoor classroom made out of nine electrical spool tables and thirty-six tree-stump seats. A place wrapped in the arms of the garden where a whole class can do its business under the brilliant sky. Where staff can take lunch, or families can picnic after hours.

Everyone worked very hard. Under the dripping eaves of the field house, parents cooked quesadillas over the grill and served them with mounds of refried beans and pico de gallo salsa, chased with lemonade. The place smelled of tortillas and rain. And when we called a halt to the freezing work and gathered to thank everyone, to share some words and song, I couldn't help but think that this is a very special kind of learning. And a very beautiful place. On any particular day there may be catastrophes going on, cops in the office, problems. We, for sure, fall short in many ways. Writing an account like this maybe encourages a little extra glow. But we are trying.

■　■　■

Thanks, Pete.

Sounds like a great school, doesn't it? Kind of makes you want to find your own woods to steward. But did you also notice that these teachers are using the seven fundamental Best Practice structures, over and over again? At Waters, students range far beyond the textbook: *reading thoughtfully and strategically* about stacks of challenging nonfiction material, studying big ideas from butterflies to biodiversity. Teachers coach kids to think carefully as they read, giving them tools like journals and sketchbooks, and hold one-to-one conferences to make sure kids understand and remember. As they work, students *represent their learning* in a multitude of genres: constant writing and drawing, songs on the bus, rhumba rhymes, bucket drumming, murals, traveling classroom performances, and more. The work of the ecology strand is deeply *authentic*: kids are engaged with real ecosystems, living things, the powers of nature—and real problems, too, since each of these wild places is in some way endangered and in need of stewardship.

Classes often shift into *workshop* mode, where kids don't just hear about subjects, they *do* them. With adults serving as coaches and mentors, kids pull weeds, collect specimens, replant with native species, create their own classroom gardens, choose and conduct their own inquiries. To unleash the social power of learning, students are organized into various well-structured *small groups*—in the woods, in the garden, and in the classroom. Doing important work with a team of friends leverages knowledge, makes the work light, and unleashes the joy of communal effort. All along the way, students and teachers regularly take time for *reflective assessment*, talking and writing about progress, problems, and achievements, and setting new goals. Sure, there are quizzes and requirements, but everything leads back to conversations like Pete's one-to-one conference with Jorge. At Waters, assessment is caring adults asking kids, "Where are you in this work? What's the next step for you? And how can I help?" And finally, of course, the whole nine-year ecology experience is one big *integrative inquiry*, something that pulls together all the school's efforts, and provides students with coherence and meaning throughout their school life. Just imagine: in ten or twenty or thirty years, what do you think these children will remember from their elementary school days? It's our guess that Waters alumni will include a large number of passionate and environmentally aware citizens, along with a host of lifelong readers, fearless artists, and careful thinkers.

Waters' K–8 urban ecology program shows Best Practice teaching at its most comprehensive. Because the teachers have internalized and mastered seven fundamental ways of organizing instruction, they consistently create genuine student-centered experiences, follow the recommendations of the national curriculum standards, and enact the principles of progressive education. With those big ideas in mind, with the repertoire they possess, these teachers don't have to sort through thousands of state standards to create powerful lessons every day.

But the commitment is also very official. If you look at the cover of Waters's School Improvement Plan, a document that guides the program, budget, and staffing all year long, it says, "Waters: A Best Practice School." For ten years, Principal Revollo and the teachers have stuck with their commitment to Best Practice pedagogy in spite of districtwide pressures for more traditional teaching. Over that time, the school's standardized test scores have risen significantly in reading, math, science, and social studies. With a population of mostly poor and Hispanic kids, including many newly arrived immigrants, other schools might have played it safe with textbooks, worksheets, and seatwork. But the people at Waters would never settle for education as usual. They want their school to be as vibrant, beautiful, creative, and multidimensional as the community around it. As a result of this professional wisdom and courage, Waters has become one of the showplace schools in Chicago's seven-hundred-building district.

■ ■ ■

In the chapters to come, we will explain each of the seven Methods That Matter in detail, showing the history and development of each, acknowledging the teachers and authors who developed strong and replicable versions of them. And most important, we'll share several examples of each structure, written by teachers who have implemented them in real, diverse classrooms around the country.

These seven structures or patterns are applicable to all grade levels and subject areas, from early childhood through college. Waters happens to be a K–8 school, but we can take you to high schools with equally exciting programs—indeed, we'll do that many times in the pages of this book. The seven structures act as templates that allow teachers to organize the ingredients of schooling: students, time, space, materials, experiences, and assistance. We sometimes call these structures the *fundamental, recurrent activities.* By this we mean that once teachers have mastered their management and students have internalized their norms, these seven structures become the palette from which teachers and kids together can paint rich, vibrant cycles of learning during which these key activities alternate, interweave, and are cycled through the curriculum for days, weeks, or years.

These activities are processes, not bodies of knowledge. They are broad generic strategies or, simply, *teaching methods.* Today, the term *methods* is often scoffed at by school critics like E. D. Hirsch (1996) as irrelevant education-school fluff. But the fact is that the way we teach school subjects is tremendously important to whether and how much students learn. These seven structures work. They are validated by decades of practitioner reports, documented in educational literature and research, and richly supported by the principles of group dynamics, the field of study that describes the ways groups of people can be organized to maximize their efforts. To be concerned with pedagogy is not, as Hirsch accuses, to be "anti-knowledge" or "anti-fact." On the contrary, giving serious attention to the structures and processes of learning reflects a deep respect for the importance of facts and knowledge. We don't want to raise yet another generation of Americans who laugh proudly, "I forgot everything they taught me in school." We experiment with methodology because we want students to embrace, internalize, and recall far more of the curriculum than has traditionally been the case.

Though they are process-oriented and adaptable to all disciplines, these structures are also highly *rigorous*, specific, and tightly organized. They require considerable teacher skill to implement properly. Far from being loosey-goosey or touchy-feely (it's interesting to note how often progressive practices are demeaned by cutesy epithets), these structures demand more management from teachers and more discipline among students than traditional presentational methods. They require that both teachers and students play a much wider range of roles throughout the school day, shift smoothly among them, and manage and monitor their own work across many dimensions. In short: It's not just sit-'n'-git anymore.

These structures are *recurrent*. They are not one-shot lesson plans that get used up, but can be used over and over, phasing in and out of the schedule throughout a school year, and from year to year as teachers orchestrate a healthful balance of activities. Before they can be put into the rotation, of course, every structure requires that teachers invest time in preparing students. But once oriented, kids can operate within and use the structure throughout a year and throughout their school lives, with periodic refreshers and updates.

These structures are *overlapping*. Authentic experiences will be at the core of any well-designed integrative unit or small-group project. Representing-to-learn happens across all the other structures as students plan inquiries, keep notes, record findings, initiate and answer correspondence, and share their learnings. Reflective assessment is also braided through all the other structures, as evaluation becomes an integral part of instruction. The teacher-student conferences held during a workshop session will be both a form of assessment and a part of instruction, while the peer conferences that are a regular feature of such workshops are an important kind of collaborative small group. Indeed, most broad classroom projects will embody many of these structures at once. For the purposes of this book, we have needed to separate the seven structures, highlighting their individual ingredients and features. But back in any real classroom, teachers will reassemble them into unique hybrids and seamless combinations.

These structures are also *conceptually asymmetrical*. That is, the list of seven structures isn't quite apples and apples. There are valuable representing-to-learn activities that take no more than a few minutes of class time, while a typical integrative unit will probably occupy whole days or weeks. Some structures, like reading and writing workshops, have clear-cut, codified pedagogies already in print, while others, like centers or learning stations, have a much sparser professional literature littered with misleading corruptions. Some of the structures are clearly stepwise pedagogies, while others, most notably authentic experiences, aren't methods at all, but rather types (or even locations) of experience. We have tried to probe and resolve these discrepancies, but every time we attempt to delete one element or combine it with another, something urgently important is lost. We appear to need all seven ingredients in order to describe the Best Practice paradigm.

Sadly, as these activities have increasingly become recognized, adopted, and applied across the country, they have also been opened to more misunderstanding and misapplication. At worst, the methods become platitudes, undergoing the same degenerative process that afflicts the term *Best Practice* itself. We recently saw booklets full of "best practice worksheets" prominently for sale at the International Reading Association's annual conference. *Classroom workshop* offers another cautionary example. In the early 1980s, this highly structured method of literacy instruction was described by such authors as Donald Graves (1983), Lucy

Calkins (1986), and Nancie Atwell (1998). They outlined a very complex but nontraditional approach to developing children's reading and writing—a holistic, developmental process featuring student choice of books and writing topics, strong teacher modeling, extended student practice, guided peer feedback, and a portfolio assessment system.

Within a few years' time, however, the term *workshop* had drifted away from the careful and narrow definition of its inventors, until by the late 1990s almost any activity involving student reading or writing, including methods totally contradictory to the original model, were being blithely labeled *workshop*. Some of this deterioration was caused by textbook publishers who willfully appropriated and corrupted the term, but the rest owes to teachers' characteristic failure to defend our own professional culture.

Which is to say that, in order to work properly, the seven structures must be implemented roughly the way they were designed. While adapting and personalizing are necessary elements of good teaching, a reasonable degree of adherence to the original model is also required. Assigning writing activities that mostly involve copying or regurgitating correct answers, conducting conferences where students have no voice, designing collaborative activities that are really just competitive memorization games, or implementing integrative units in which students have no interest—these are not Best Practices, whatever they are named.

Common Features of All Seven Methods

Within all seven of these classroom structures, and across them as a set, several important values are threaded. On the surface, these structures are simply organized delivery systems that allow students to engage important curricular content and academic skills. But at a deeper level, they also work to develop the rich, supportive psychological and intellectual climate that young learners need and deserve. Among the vital ingredients of this "Best Practice climate" are choice, responsibility, expression, community, diversity, and technology.

Choice

Student ownership and initiation of learning have always been tenets of progressive education. In recent years, Deborah Meier (2003), Pedro Noguera (2004), William Glasser (1986), Alfie Kohn (1995), and others have made critiques that are both familiar and irrefutable. The thirteen years of submission and passivity customarily provided to young people by American schools is an exceedingly poor preparation for resourceful, self-initiating problem solvers, not to mention free and critical citizens. Indeed, the bland but unrelenting authoritarianism of American schools discourages and alienates so many children as it unwittingly channels them toward long-abolished assembly-line jobs and a mentality to match. If we really want to raise the kind of young people we claim to treasure, we have to start inviting them, from preschool onward, to make meaningful decisions and choices, living with all the consequences that choice entails.

Each of the seven key activities inherently gives students a real voice and some meaningful choices. In workshop, students choose, from an approved range of options, what to write, read, or investigate. As a part of reflective assessment, teachers help students write and talk about their learning, set academic goals, reflect on their progress, review their own work and records. As they *represent* their learning through writing or art, students are often invited to decide for themselves what mode, style, genre, or medium of expression will best show their thinking.

Responsibility

The other side of the coin of choice is *responsibility*. If we are to restructure big parts of the school day for students to make decisions about their learning, select and explore alternatives, and pursue some of their own interests and goals, then we have to hold them accountable for finishing the jobs they start, monitoring their own performance, submitting their learnings to public exhibition, critically appraising their own work or artifacts, and making even better choices the next time, as their understanding of the process of inquiry grows.

These seven key structures invite just such responsibility. In the workshop, students have regular conferences with the teacher to review progress, assess work samples, and set goals. In well-structured *integrative units* or *small-group* investigations, students must select topics, find resources, identify targets, build schedules, make contributions to the wider group, create required tangible products, and regularly report to the teacher as they proceed. In reflective assessment, we ask students to set academic goals, save their work in folders, track and discuss their progress, keep their own records, and join with the teacher in creating reports for parents and other interested audiences.

Expression

In her remarkable 1969 book, *Young Lives at Stake*, the English educator Charity James passionately reminded teachers of a simple fact about human beings: people need to make stuff. It comes with our genes. We are driven to shape and decorate and act upon our environment, whether that means painting the walls of our caves, grinding grain into flour, spinning stories around the fire, forging tools, or creating performances with our violins. Expression, in all of its manifold forms, is a key to learning and thinking. And yet, more than ever today, the expressive arts are being marginalized in public education, systematically pushed out of school schedules, curriculum, and budgets. In spite of their manifest capacity to captivate children and ignite the curriculum, the arts have become a bystander in the current school reform movement.

Thus, as you look into the structure of the seven key activities featured here, you see that each one carries many opportunities for students to find a wide range of *expression* for their ideas and feelings. Amid all these activities, kids make real stuff—artwork, writing, stories, performances, exhibitions, posters, research reports, semester goals, book reviews, sculptures, and bar graphs. And they don't just create these products in solitude for their own satisfaction, but for interaction with real audiences of peers, teachers, families, and communities—people with whom these products and performances can be shared, discussed, and used.

Harvey: My two children have had an extraordinary education at the Baker Demonstration School at National-Louis University. For years I have tried to explain to curious teachers what makes Baker different and special. Although the school is equipped with all the usual progressive declarations and pedigrees, something beyond the letter of the official mission statement always seemed to be going on. Finally, after we'd had children in the school for almost ten years, it dawned on my wife (who later explained it to me) that, along with all the other things that Baker teachers so consciously and carefully do, there is also a deep, abiding focus on children's *expression*.

Though Baker is not officially an arts-centered school, the teachers are attuned and committed to nurturing children's expression in every possible medium: writing, singing, storytelling, painting, hypermedia, dance, dialogue journaling, drama, poetry, fashion design, conversation, or photography. You can always pick out a Baker student because they are much more likely than "normal" kids to suddenly burst into song, dance, writing, or to drag you over to the computer to see their portfolio. They expect you to pay attention and take them seriously. And you always know a Baker teacher, because when a kid starts to express, they drop everything and attend. They stop and they listen and they smile and you can see their wheels start to turn as they think, "Wow. This is interesting. I wonder where this came from. How can I sustain this? Where does it fit in? What might be this kid's next step?"

How powerful and formative to have your early, tentative expressions met with this kind of fascinated and respectful response from the adults at your school—not just from doting parents at home. It implies that you are a part of the human conversation and are expected to have something unique and worthwhile to contribute.

It invites you to express more, to attend to others' expressions, to learn how grown-ups shape and hone and improve their own expressions. It affirms that your personal search through the different media and art forms is part of a serious lifelong quest to know more and communicate better. All children deserve to meet this kind of response in school, to have their expressions cherished.

Community

Traditional schooling, with its silent and solitary seatwork, tracking and ability grouping, and competitive grading, is highly individualistic. In its most toxic forms, education becomes a zero-sum game that pits students against each other. Classmates become enemies. The implicit motto is: I cannot win unless others lose. In this setting, the idea of classroom community is anathema; indeed, if students come together at all as a group, they are more likely to coalesce against a teacher than to join with him as a community of learners.

On the other hand, the seven structures we focus on here are social and cooperative by nature. As part of their inherent design, they contribute to building community. They invite the expression of the individual, yet they also offer ways for students to connect, to team, to collaborate. These structures tend to create a group esprit, the sense that there is a commonality of interest and purpose, that we are *in this thing together.* Looked at in terms of group dynamics theory, these activities invite students to participate in the development of classroom expectations and norms, to develop widely dispersed friendship patterns, to shoulder some leadership and responsibility, to communicate with others through a broad array of communication channels, and to negotiate and resolve conflicts.

Diversity

Pundits often speak—sometimes with alarm—about the tremendous range of students arriving in today's classrooms. This is supposed to be new? Diversity isn't just a modern phenomenon; America has been a nation of immigrants, a symphony of languages, a host of religions, and a tangle of social classes for centuries, not just the past couple of years. Student diversity used to be viewed as a problem to be solved: students of supposedly varying abilities were segregated by tracking. Minority, Special Education, or ELL students were shunted off to separate rooms and programs. Then the teacher aimed instruction at "the middle" of the remaining class. The result was that many kids were left behind academically and disrespected as people.

Now smart schools see differences as assets in the classroom, not as troubles to divest. Not only are we more accepting of ethnic, racial, and religious diversity, but we are recognizing that all students are distinctive and different in a variety of ways. For just one example, Howard Gardner's work on multiple intelligences has shown us that there are "many kinds of smart" among human beings, not one unitary trait called "intelligence" (1983). We recognize that each of us has learning styles and habits of mind that hold great influence over how we learn—and that also, if properly tapped, offer a rich sharing of talents, views, and voices.

All seven Best Practice structures open the door to a decentralized classroom where learners of all talents, personalities, learning styles, cultural backgrounds, races, and languages can find meaningful opportunities to explore and excel. Teachers who have mastered these methods have ways to differentiate instruction, create flexible grouping patterns, make accommodations in lessons, address language differences, find "just-right" materials. They know to teach to varied learning styles, create appropriate assessment tools, and develop genuine choices for students.

Technology

Today's technology offers some powerful tools with potential school applications. But there's nothing automatically "Best Practice" about using any electronic device in the classroom. A video camera can be an adjunct to excellent teaching or a total waste of time. Kids can use a graphing calculator for open-ended explorations of mathematical concepts—or merely to finish the odd-numbered problems at the end of the chapter. Some schools are filled with shiny new computers running nothing but mundane drill programs—a $3,000 delivery system for flash cards! As our friend and computer consultant Jeff Flynn says, "You shouldn't be asking, 'Can we do it on a computer?' But, 'Is a computer the right tool for the job?' And, 'Is the job worth doing?'"

We believe that technology can leverage some of our very best teaching if we use it wisely. Once a student has done algebra problems on a Web-based "balance beam" program, he can understand equations at a bone-deep level. When a child publishes a poem on the Internet and gets responses from kids all around the country, writing can take on a whole new level of seriousness. When a teenager is offered choices of media through which to "show what you know," instead of just passing a Scantron test, not only is school more engaging, but the student is building valuable real-life skills.

In each of the seven methods that matter, technology can play a supporting or a lead role, as you'll discover in the stories from our thirty-four teacher colleagues. You'll also notice that all these Best Practice teachers are technologically literate themselves. They use the Web in school assignments, have their own classroom and/or personal Web sites, are in touch with students, families, and colleagues by e-mail. They can support their students' inquiry and authoring in a wide range of media. But don't get intimidated. You don't have to be a wirehead or a geek; you just need to demonstrate and coach skillful and critical technology use for your students. The saving grace for the technophobic educator is that you will always have several kids in any class who will be pleased to teach you how to run any machine or software.

Harvey and Marilyn: Can we speak frankly? The two of us have been teachers (and now professors) since the 1960s. We have spent a huge chunk of our professional lives in libraries, among librarians, whom we adore. We have read hundreds of dusty volumes in the stacks, copied important passages by hand, and waited in line to read (but never to check out) the precious back issues of key journals. We typed our dissertations on manual typewriters (with one carbon-paper copy). We used reel-to-reel audiotape for our interviews, and filmed classroom vignettes on three-quarter-inch black-and-white videotape, using cameras the size of a compact car. We "edited" by splicing segments together with Scotch tape. We published our early research on a medium called microfiche, which no one, to our knowledge, has ever looked at.

While writing this chapter, Harvey called up Marilyn and asked, "When was the last time you set foot in a library?" We don't want to shock you with her actual answer, but let's just say library-visits-per-week are down—way down—for both of us. Even as academic researchers and writers, we can find almost anything we need on-line, immediately. What an amazing change. It stuns us how the whole process of knowledge storage (and creation) has changed in the past few years of our lifetimes. The kids we are teaching are growing up with all this, of course, and if there are any libraries left when they get to be our age, they're going to look very different.

But Can I Still Teach? Time Sharing in Best Practice Schools

How much of the time do we actually use these Best Practice methods? All day, every day? Once a week, for an hour? What's the balance?

The seven Methods That Matter do not take up the whole day. But in genuinely progressive schools and classrooms, these seven featured activities provide structure for *the majority of the school day, week, or year*—more than half (and maybe more like three-fourths) of the time kids spend in school. After all, these structures allow students rich exploration and active practice in subject areas, in a context of teacher guidance and peer interaction, with plenty of coaching and feedback.

Still, the big seven structures are not the only activities that need to occur during a school day, year, or in a student's career. Obviously, there are some ingredients on the "less" list that still have merit and value. There remains a significant place for traditional, teacher-directed, presentational activities. For example, reading good literature aloud to children is one teacher performance that should never be curtailed; kids of all ages should have continuous opportunities to hear the sounds of great literature. And hey, a little lecturing is OK, in brief and memorable bursts, especially for older kids. A whole class can sometimes read the same book together, and be guided by the teacher in interpreting the text. Memorizing some dates, state capitals, poems, or math facts might not be such a bad idea, either. And teachers should definitely make sure that primary children know the sounds that letters make, so that they can decode and comprehend text. These traditional school activities aren't wrong—they've just been vastly overemphasized, and need to be put back into reasonable balance with all the other ways of spending children's precious school time.

The problem has been that these old teacher-centered activities have gobbled up whole days, whole years, so that kids never got a chance to digest, consolidate, and most important to *use* the ideas that teachers presented. Kids don't get enough practice moving concepts from the pale and passive world of something that was mentioned into the robust world of personal application. After all, every contemporary learning theory—behaviorist, cognitive, information processing—has one common feature in its paradigm of learning: for human beings to assimilate information they must somehow *act on it*.

But acting on information takes time and support, and that's exactly where the seven key structures come in. They help to rebalance the school schedule, providing large, well-structured periods of time during which students can act upon the ideas and information that teachers have presented in their now more proportionate fraction of the school day. The Best Practice structures help us create a new mix of presentation, demonstration, practice, application, coaching, and reflection that is far more likely to help students remember what they read, hear what their teachers say, understand ideas that are discussed, grasp concepts that are introduced, master skills that are modeled, care about the process, and value their place in it.

Still, we must be careful not to let the old teacher-centered fox back into the henhouse. Ancient pedagogical habits die hard, and teachers probably wouldn't have originally chosen this vocation if we didn't crave the spotlight on some deep psychological level. The hunger to "really teach something" has probably derailed more student-centered innovations than administrative timidity and textbook company co-option combined.

Luckily, there are ways to strike and defend a balance. Many of the Best Practice structures can be infused with small doses of traditional, teacher-directed activities. A great example of this blending is mini-lessons in reading-writing workshops, an idea now well-developed in the professional literature (see Daniels and Steineke 2004; Calkins 1986, 2000; Harwayne 1992; Atwell 1998; Fletcher and Portalupi 1998; Hindley 1996) whereby the teacher designs short, pointed, and well-timed presentations and embeds them in the context of a long chunk of student practice time. This kind of teacher-directed lesson offers the greatest possibility that the information will actually transfer into the work of students, since it can be applied and practiced promptly.

There's one other category of time expenditure in school that's separate, not exactly a method or a structure, but rather a diffuse pursuit using many structures: community building and maintenance. Even though, as we've argued, the seven Best Practice structures do inherently nourish relationships and groups, some of this development often needs to occur separately. Depending on the age of the students and the goals of the teacher, such community building may involve periodic and structured class meetings, acquaintance-building activities, conflict resolution or mediation programs, advisory periods, and the like. Some systemic reform efforts, like the Comer Project, make individual and group relationships an especially significant part of the school calendar. "The Responsive Classroom" is another model of school-as-community development built around carefully structured and thoughtful daily class meetings. At the high school we helped to start in Chicago, the faculty gives big chunks of time to special group-building activities early in the year, commits two-and-one-half hours per week all year to an advisory period, and runs an active peer mediation program to deal with problems that arise (Hoverstein, Doda, and Lounsbury 1998; Daniels, Bizar, and Zemelman 2001). Happily there has been a recent burst of research and writing on the topic of community-building in the classroom, with an especially valuable contribution from Nancy Steineke (2002).

■　■　■

Now we turn to describing the methods themselves. The next seven chapters explain how each of these big teaching ideas works across the curriculum, from kindergarten through high school. For each structure, the two of us will first lay the groundwork and then turn the conversation over to several teacher-colleagues who'll tell you how it works in their own classrooms. That means you are about to hear from thirty-four colleagues, teachers who are creating powerful, memorable learning experiences for their students every day. These are the people who really know how to teach the Best Practice way.

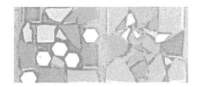  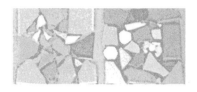

T W O

READING-AS-THINKING

What is the best way to teach reading? That is the perennial Big Question of American public schooling—and the "third rail" of many educational debates. Everyone from politicians to evangelists to television commentators seems to have a preferred method of teaching reading to kids. It's rather amazing when you think about it. Reading is the only school subject about which so many citizens have an opinion (often a strong one) and a preferred pedagogy. And so these never-ending "reading wars" are fought out on talk radio, in magazines, and in letters to the editor of every local newspaper in the nation. Mostly, the debates boil down to one narrow question: how much phonics instruction should kids get in the early grades? Certainly, effective phonics instruction is necessary, but it's far from sufficient for raising smart, lifelong readers. There's much more to this task, and it sure doesn't help when pundits on both sides dumb down the complexity of reading by lobbing sound-bite grenades at each other's dug-in positions.

All these commentators should spend some time in schools. If they did, they'd find that reading instruction really *is* a hot topic, but not in the polarized and limited way they've framed it. Today, the teaching of reading is being transformed from the primary grades up through high school. Teachers now realize that reading is not an accumulation of "subskills," but a complex and specialized form of *thinking*. Once we see reading as thinking, we transcend debates about phonics, synthetic alphabets, and phonemic awareness. Learning to read is a much deeper, broader, and more complex cognitive task, one that extends from preschool through college.

Young Readers at Work

At Francis Parker School, Ann Angel is a teaching intern in Alison Abbot's second-grade classroom. This week, the children are beginning a three-month study of Japan, its history, culture, and people. The children gather on the rug in front of her rocking chair as Ann begins today's read-aloud. The book is *Grass Sandals,* an illustrated biography of the famed seventeenth-century haiku poet Basho (Spivak 1997). Ann wants to be sure that the kids think carefully about the ideas in the book, so she stops often while she reads to think out loud about her own connections to the text. ("This reminds me of the mountains in Colorado I've visited.") She invites kids to pose questions about the book ("What would you ask the author if he were here?"), and lingers over passages with strong visual or sensory images ("What were you seeing while I was reading that?"). Ann talks very explicitly about the ways good readers think: making pictures in your head, connecting the book to your own life, predicting what might happen next, and noticing the questions that pop into your mind along the way.

As the Japan unit unfolds, kids read many different books, some as a whole class and others chosen individually. Everyone reads two books about tsunamis, using Venn diagrams to represent the similarities and differences between tidal waves and the impact they have had on human populations. When kids go to select their own books, there's a large collection of relevant fiction and nonfiction around the classroom and down the hall in the school library. There are single copies for individual readers, as well as multiple-copy sets, so kids can form book discussion groups around chosen titles. There are also several excellent Japan-for-kids Web sites bookmarked on the classroom computers.

Each child selects and pursues a personal research topic (calligraphy, origami, martial arts, baseball, clothing, architecture) and investigates it over a period of weeks. Ann shows kids how to jot "interesting and important ideas" on note cards as they read, saving them in a decorated binder. There's always an abundance of facts, so Ann offers ongoing mini-lessons about how smart readers determine what's more and less important. At the end of the unit, each child dons a kimono, presents a poster session detailing eight to ten really important facts they have learned about their chosen topic, and answers questions from their well-informed classmates.

Finally, the children read about and join in the Japanese tradition of "worry dolls." Each child makes a small human figure out of paper (much easier if you have already done some origami, as these kids have). Next they make a separate cover—a kimono—out of wrapping or other decorative paper. The children write their own worries or concerns on the inside of the kimono, and wrap it over the doll. Then, with great ceremony, the class marches outside to the courtyard pond where, one by one, each child gently floats away his or her doll, sending their worries across the sea in the traditional Japanese way. Janine confides to a visitor, "I feel better already."

Twenty blocks west, at Best Practice High School, seventy-five seniors have just begun a four-week study of the fast food industry and its economic, social, and nutritional implications. Today, in their nonfiction book club, Tyrell, Kira, James, and Tiffany are discussing the national best-seller *Fast Food Nation: The Dark Side of the All-American Meal* by Eric Schlosser. They've just finished reading a grisly chapter about the slaughterhouses where ground beef is processed, and James asserts: "Well, I still like the way the burgers taste, even if the slaughterhouses are sickening. If I want to eat fast food I'm going to buy it and enjoy it." Others nod, but after a pause, Kira mentions quietly, "You know, before I started reading this book, I had already stopped eating beef and pork, and this book just makes you wanna quit meat altogether." The rest of the kids look dubious. After all, fast food burgers are a staple of teenage life. Tyrell rejoins, "Well, this book won't really change the way I buy food, but it might change the way I think about it. Sure, it makes me nauseous, but that don't stop me." The kids laugh and continue with their discussion. But just a few weeks later, more than a third of these students will have changed their eating habits, and two will have been tossed out of a McDonald's restaurant for leafleting the place about its unhealthful food.

To support this interdisciplinary unit, the teachers on the senior team have gathered a rich array of reading materials about every aspect of the fast food industry. In addition to Schlosser's hard-core exposé, there are newspaper, magazine, and Web site articles representing widely different points of view, including the National Restaurant Association's sizzling press release "The Truth About *Fast Food Nation*." All students will read some of this material together, including a *Harper's* magazine article about how fast food companies target poor communities, and another from *The Atlantic*, which argues that the dangers of fat consumption are a myth. At other times, kids select their own readings, as when they choose from twelve articles about animal exploitation on the People for the Ethical Treatment of Animals (PETA) Web site. In addition to all this trade nonfiction and journalism, students also study the chapters on nutrition, digestion, bacteria, and viruses in their biology textbook. Not only is this material required by the citywide curriculum guide but it also helps students sort out the many controversial health and nutrition issues raised in other readings.

To help students dig deep into all this grown-up reading material, the teachers repeatedly offer lessons about the ways smart readers think, especially when dealing with footnote-laden yet highly polemical materials. They show the kids how to get beneath the surface of the text, demanding clarity, questioning the author, challenging conclusions, separating opinion from fact. And the teachers provide kids with practical tools that embody these kinds of reading-as-thinking skills. One such device is a bookmark, a folded piece of notebook paper on which kids jot notes in four categories (my responses, my questions, memorable passages, and important statistics) either during or just after reading a section of the book. These notes become the seedbed of conversation topics when kids meet in their book clubs every few days. But that's not all. In the students' copies of *Fast Food Nation*, you find evidence of other active-reading strategies the teachers have shared. The pages are strewn with codes (? = something puzzling, * = an important section); there are marginal notes and comments throughout ("This hurts just reading it"); and Post-it notes stick out from many page edges, flagging topics for later discussion.

The fast food unit culminates with "social service" projects that require each student to investigate one aspect of the fast food world in more detail, and share their findings with the wider community. All of these projects must have both a written product and an action step. One group created an educational picture book for young children titled "What's in Your Happy Meal," which showed the dark side of fast food so explicitly that second graders were deemed the youngest appropriate audience. Others created anti-junk-food petitions and circulated them through the neighborhood; some wrote letters to their congresspersons or to FDA officials, demanding more supervision of fast food joints, and one team created a graphic exposé of the execrable, fast-food-like meals served in the school's own cafeteria. Two groups of kids made informational pamphlets and handed them out to patrons at nearby fast food places. The restaurant manager thought their flyer, which graphically depicted the consequences of *E. coli* poisoning, was a little over the top. But the kids had a point: fifteen Americans die every month from hamburger-borne illness.

These two schools show us what Best Practice reading lessons look like. Yes, there is plenty of skill instruction going on, but the skills go far beyond phonics and word study. These teachers are teaching *thinking*. They are helping kids develop and refine a repertoire of cognitive strategies for reading, a set of "mind moves" that helps them actively visualize, question, connect, infer, evaluate, and synthesize as they move through text. This work begins in the primary grades, but it is never done. As students encounter steadily more complex and technical materials, they need increasingly sophisticated thinking strategies to make sense of them.

Good teachers don't simply assign ever more challenging texts, say, "Read this for Friday," and follow it up with a pop quiz. Now they work with the students all along the way, providing explicit demonstrations and tangible tools for working into, through, and beyond tough text. No longer do teachers depend on one basal reader or textbook as the sole authority on a subject. Instead, they provide kids a balanced diet of reading materials: fiction and nonfiction, short and long, easy and hard, assigned and kid-chosen, in a variety of genres and representing different points of view. And, as we have just seen, they conduct this reading instruction not in workbooks and drills, but amid meaty topics of real-life interest to students.

Indeed, these two brief vignettes reveal far more than state-of-the-art reading instruction. The other six Methods That Matter, the focus of the rest of this book, are also implicitly at work here. The exemplary schools we have just visited embed their reading instruction in a context of broad and interesting *integrative units*. The kids work in a variety of *small groups* along the way, including peer-led book clubs and other collaborative structures. Students are constantly *representing learning* in writing, art, and performance. Classrooms often shift into *workshop* mode, where kids pursue individual reading projects with teacher coaching and guidance. Teachers consistently find ways to bring *authentic experience* to school work, making even far-off nations, neighborhood restaurants, and big, thick textbooks come alive. And all along the way, students are learning to self-evaluate, as they learn the tools of *reflective assessment*.

New Perspectives on Teaching Reading

So reading is thinking. That's not so hard to accept. As teachers, we know a little about thinking. In college, we learned about Bloom's taxonomy, which classifies levels of thinking as literal, inferential, and critical-creative. Indeed, many school textbooks label questions at the end of the chapter according to Bloom's taxonomy. But do our students know that reading is thinking? Hey, if a student wasn't thinking *before* he started reading, and he wasn't thinking *while* he was reading, why would he be able to think *after* reading? Those questions at the end of the chapter don't "teach reading," as the publishers want us to believe. At best, they assess comprehension after it is too late to assist it. If we want students to understand what they read, they must enter the text thinking, demanding sense and clarity from the material. Since reading is thinking, we must provide our young readers with rich text worth thinking about, strategies to help them think, and others with whom to think.

What Is Reading?

We used to think of reading as a "black box" phenomenon, a mysterious and invisible process by which a reader decodes the message on a page. In this view, the reader receives "the correct meaning," the one that the author intended. But today, researchers have helped us to see that meaning does not reside in the ink on a page, nor is it simply received by a reader. Proficient readers are cocreators of meaning, and most texts don't have just one intended meaning or interpretation. Instead, readers constantly build meaning for themselves as they think along with an author's words. Skillful readers actually *construct* meaning from print, in a far more complex and active process than we had previously imagined.

The old assumption that reading is an accumulation of subskills doesn't hold up very well against modern cognitive models of reading as thinking—nor does the bottom-up, bit-by-bit pedagogy traditionally associated with it. Instead, teaching young readers should be more like teaching a child to ride a bicycle. We don't have the kid sit on a chair and practice raising his right leg and lowering his left. We don't have him practice squeezing imaginary hand brakes. Instead, we place the emerging rider on a bike, run alongside, and let go when the time is right.

Now, we can approach reading the same way. We can invite the learner to practice the whole activity, orchestrating all the elements with reasonable expectations for her developmental level. We can put kids in books and run alongside, giving support when it's needed and letting go when the time is right. What do we do if a bike rider rides into a tree? We dry his eyes, and then we teach him explicitly about using the brakes. The same with reading: we carefully observe the learner at work, and then teach focused lessons on one element of the process at a time.

Once we understand that reading is meaning making, not message receiving, we can begin to align our teaching with the cognitive realities. We can act on three key insights about the reading process: reading is interactive, constructive, and strategic.

Reading Is Interactive

Reading is an interaction between the reader and the author in which the reader's prior knowledge is a prime determinant of comprehension. What we readers bring to the text in terms of knowledge of content, structure, and vocabulary is what enables us to make meaning. If we cannot understand a passage, it's not necessarily because we can't decode well or missed learning a subskill in elementary school. Often, we simply lack the prior knowledge needed to enter the text, or we may even have good knowledge but not be able to access it. Try this example:

The notes were sour because the seams split.

As we read this sentence, we can decode all the words, which are part of our reading and our speaking vocabulary, but we can't make sense of the sentence. Clearly this is not just a problem of phonics or vocabulary; the meaning exists on some level that we can't immediately construct. Of course we're not completely lost.

With our knowledge of words and syntax, we can imagine that "notes" and "sour" might somehow relate to music. We can make other plausible guesses, too: maybe "notes" and "sour" come from some kind of wine-tasting lingo.

But the context is everything. When we tell you that the passage is about bagpipes, you can immediately access your prior knowledge and even create a rich visual image. Oh, bagpipes. The notes were sour because the seams split!

Reading Is Constructive

Reading is the construction of meaning from text. Fluent reading is a constant back-and-forth process of inferences, filling in the blanks, testing hypotheses, and constructing meaning on the fly. Try this:

> The man went to the window and asked what time the feature began. The cashier answered him. He handed her $16 and rushed into the dark room with his companion.

There's not a word in this passage about movie theaters, but we'll bet our next paychecks that you were just visualizing one, marquee and all. You inferred that the man asked his question of a cashier in a movie theater. You inferred that each ticket cost $8. You inferred that the movie had just begun or was just about to start. How did you figure out all those smart things? Because you know a good deal about going to the movies, and you used your life experience to make the inferences necessary to understand this passage. Going back and forth between your own knowledge and these thirty words, you constructed the meaning of the passage, which, as you can now see, is not entirely on the page.

Reading Is Strategic

Ideally, these examples are surfacing your awareness, reminding you of the strategies you use every day as a reader, mostly unconsciously and maybe without ever being directly taught them in school. Proficient readers like you must orchestrate multiple ingredients: the words on the page, your own prior knowledge and purposes for reading, the difficulty of the material, what's given and what's implicit. And to do such complex work, you utilize a repertoire of specific mental tools or patterns you have developed through years of reading experience. While there are different ways to label these components of reading-as-thinking, these are the main ones:

visualizing (making mental pictures or sensory images)
connecting (connecting to one's own experience, to events in the world, to other readings)

questioning (actively wondering, surfacing uncertainties, interrogating text
and author)

inferring (predicting, hypothesizing, interpreting, drawing conclusions)

evaluating (determining importance, making judgments)

analyzing (noticing text structures, author's craft, vocabulary, purpose,
theme, point of view)

recalling (retelling, summarizing, remembering information)

self-monitoring (recognizing and acting on confusion, uncertainty, attention
problems)

These are the tools of strategic reading, the ones that you have acquired through a lifetime of reading, and that your students need to make sense of the printed material they encounter in school.

How do we give this gift of thinking to kids? We teach these strategies explicitly and bring the mental process of reading into the light. We open up our own heads for students, showing them how veteran readers operate with text. We make thinking visible by showing students tools like highlighters, sticky notes, bookmarks, role sheets, and response logs that help them monitor and reveal their thinking as they read. And then we use these "tracks of thinking" in small-group and whole-class discussions about reading.

Reading and Learning

We often talk as if schools had two separate reading tasks to complete: helping young children learn to read, and then later, helping older kids read to learn content. This dichotomy has often been enshrined in teacher-education course titles that label primary-level reading methods classes "beginning reading" or even "decoding," while the intermediate-grade course is called "comprehension." This makes it sound as though little kids just deal with sounds, and only from third grade up start noticing what those letters can mean!

There's a grain of truth in the dichotomy, of course. Five- and six- and seven-year-olds do have a special task, which is to make the fundamental sound-symbol connection of written language. And without belittling the significance of this challenge, it's important to recognize that for the great majority of American children, this process is straightforward, often quite pleasant, and typically completed by the end of second grade. Every year, hundreds of thousands of American kids come to school already reading; most others arrive knowing the alphabet, having heard enough language, and having played enough with writing to be ready to break the code in short order.

But the dichotomy between learning to read versus reading to learn is still a false one, even for the youngest children. After all, five- and six-year-olds are constantly hearing and looking at real stories. Sure, teachers may draw kids' attention to words and their sounds, but there's also tons of meaning, information, narrative, characters, and interesting facts in the text being used. Picture books may be used to teach phonics, but they also offer young students real stories and engaging information. Indeed, except in the most rigid behavior-modification programs, where meaning is intentionally excluded from classroom materials, children are always reading to learn even as they are mastering the skills of decoding. The kids are comprehending all the way.

You don't just learn how to read once in primary grades and then you're set for life. As students grow older, they meet new reading challenges and need to continually develop new and more refined reading skills. Just look at the growing sophistication of texts—how could eight-year-olds possibly have acquired all the skills they would need to plow through a series of graphs and text on population extrapolations for the next century? How can a middle schooler understand the shifting point of view in a novel like *Yellow Raft in Blue Water*? How do older students handle whole new genres, like contemporary narrative poetry, that require solid knowledge of how both novels and poems work?

In every school subject from science to history to mathematics, the text gets more complex and the cognitive demands of reading get heavier and heavier. That's why teachers at all grade levels across the curriculum must help their students develop new levels and kinds of reading strategies. They design activities, experiences, materials, and tools that help kids dig meaning out of tough text and put it to work in memorable, authentic ways. They help kids get ready, move through, and apply information. Since they understand that prior knowledge is a key to comprehension, they make sure that students have the knowledge they need *before* they read. Sometimes this just means reminding kids to use knowledge they have. But often, teachers must take action to help students build the knowledge they need. They *frontload* the instruction, making sure that students discuss, predict, question, and/or brainstorm about the topic before they read.

What does this frontloading look like in practice? Let's say a middle school class is about to study taxation in a social studies course. Reading-savvy teachers don't just send the kids off to read the textbook, even though it may have a good chapter on the topic. They know that unless kids are ready to connect the material to their prior knowledge, they will not understand or remember the chapter for very long. So, using a strategy like K-W-L (described on pages 63–71), the teacher helps students surface their prior knowledge (including misconceptions) about taxation and then pose specific questions to be investigated or clarified.

Only after carefully building a list of reading goals and purposes does the teacher turn kids loose on a textbook selection.

During reading, the teacher provides more support, helping students monitor their comprehension, consciously capture responses and connections, and cope effectively if they get lost. Because they know that reading is a social act, and that truly engaged readers always want to talk about what they read, teachers use collaborative classroom structures to support both conversation and comprehension. They use strategies like Say Something, in which students pause after reading short sections of text, turn to a partner, and make a comment or pose a question in response to the reading just completed. And to make sure these active, collaborative activities work, savvy teachers explicitly train students in the social skills of small-group interaction. (For more on this see Chapter 4.)

We're All in This Together

You may have the heebie-jeebies right now, after what we have just said about strategy instruction being a never-ending process involving all teachers. When the battle cry "Everyone a teacher of reading!" goes up, it may sound fine to people in self-contained elementary classrooms, but many math, history, and science teachers want to scurry for the exits. They're usually too polite to shout out, "Hey, I am a teacher of chemistry [or music or algebra]. I have all I can handle just teaching my subject. I don't have time to help the reading teachers do their job!" They don't say that, but they think it.

Our colleague Donna Ogle puts this dilemma plainly.

Many middle and high school teachers think of themselves as content experts. When I started teaching, I thought of myself as a historian. I wanted to teach history, and I really didn't think much about how students learn. I always focused on content. A lot of secondary teachers enter the field because of their passion for what they are teaching. It's an unusual teacher who comes into secondary education wanting to teach students how to learn. Yet, if we're going to be good teachers, that's really essential.

If you are a so-called "content-area" teacher, let us be the first to let you off the hook. You are *not* primarily a teacher of reading. You are primarily a teacher of the ideas and concepts and procedures and traditions of your chosen subject-matter field. Which is to say, you are teaching your students to *think* mathematically, historically, artistically, scientifically. But the road to thinking in any of these disciplines goes through text, whether that means print, artwork, or images. And if kids aren't thinking effectively while they read, they aren't going to understand or remember vital math or social studies or art or science content. It's really the *thinking skills* that allow kids to master content, to care about a field, even to understand the unique quirks or distinctive ways of thinking in different subject areas.

So how do you get kids to think like historians, scientists, mathematicians? We can't leave students to guess how experts in the field think, as probably happened to some of us old-timers in school. The key is naming and practicing specific cognitive strategies and using appropriate tools in the context of the discipline. For the younger ones, of course, we keep it simple. When Terrie Bridgman's first graders study insects by reading a series of Eric Carle picture books, she shows them three big ways of thinking. Terrie explains that some ideas about bugs will be "right there" in the book (recalling); others require "the-author-and-me" (inferring, analyzing), and others kids can pursue "on my own" (connecting, evaluating, synthesizing). Terrie uses three-column charts on the classroom easel to reinforce kids' awareness of smart-reader thinking. By later elementary grades, we're talking straightforwardly about the whole inventory of strategies and helping students practice each one in fiction and nonfiction text. As you'll soon hear about, Franki Sibberson helps her fifth graders delve deeply into literature and nonfiction by integrating talk about texts with independent writing and reading tasks.

In our high school in Chicago we're still working on content-area thinking strategies all the time even though the kids are teenagers. When her juniors are forming small, peer-led book discussion groups, Tina Peano always begins by reviewing the ways proficient readers can look at a book. After that discussion, Tina has kids copy the strategies list (connecting, questioning, visualizing, inferring, evaluating) on the inside cover of their reading logs to remind them of the different lenses smart readers can look through. Then, Tina gives kids "roles" for their first few weeks of note taking and small-group discussion. These job sheets encourage kids to range among all the strategies as they read and discuss. Sure, these high school students have been hearing about reading strategies for years, but we are never done with them. Teachers are always helping them go deeper, constantly expanding and refining their thinking repertoires.

A Variety of Texts for a Variety of Purposes

In school, there's a great premium on hard reading. We don't want to "baby" the students or underchallenge them. So it's considered good, rigorous teaching to assign materials (like most content-area textbooks) that kids cannot read independently and that require extensive teacher translation. Sometimes this is called "keeping students on grade level." But studies of standard grade-level ratings

(Allington 2000) show that many commonly used textbooks are actually much harder than their scores indicate. As a result, in the name of rigor, we too often put kids in books they cannot understand or remember—which means they will continue to struggle with the subject.

What kids really need is more assistance in *understanding hard concepts*. Instead of a constant stream of super-hard texts, students need a mix of materials, ranging from easy to hard. We already have textbooks in the classroom; what we need to add, in all content areas, is more material that's relatively easy, so students can concentrate on absorbing challenging content. This may sound counterintuitive, but evidence shows that students, including struggling readers, progress faster when given opportunities to read books that make sense to them (Allington 2002). We probably shouldn't need research to convince us of this simple reality: when kids read stuff they *can read*, they make more sense of what they *do read*. Just as important, Allington reports that when given interesting materials that they can read without too much difficulty, students *will* read. If we believe that our job is to help students enter the subject fields, dig into the big ideas, and grapple with increasingly complex concepts, then we must add accessible books to the reading mix.

So how are we supposed to assemble a balanced diet of materials in classrooms that are equipped only with thick, bone-dry textbooks? First of all, we should take a deep breath and remind ourselves: you cannot do this all at once. Building a rich and varied classroom library is the work of years—of a career, really. But we can jump-start our collections by gathering newspaper and magazine articles, Web site pages, trade books, and text sets right now. We can take advantage of the high-interest, content-rich materials published by *Time for Kids*, *National Geographic*, and other high-quality publishers. We can be on the lookout for materials that show different sides of a question (global warming, Hiroshima, etc.), so students can jigsaw information from different sources, authors, and viewpoints. We can also give students more choices of what to read, so they can find sources that are just right for them. If we find it hard to let go of assigning all the reading, we need to remember that if the teacher selects every single thing a child reads all the way through school, it encourages dependence, prevents the child from developing personal reading tastes, and fails to allow for different reading rates, styles, and interests.

So what does this balanced reading diet look like, with young kids or older ones? In her kindergarten classroom in San Diego, Linda Hamilton has assembled a collection of book baskets, each one filled with six to ten books on a particular subject: whales, dinosaurs, insects, holidays, and more. Some contain mostly pictures while others have plenty of text; the publishers would probably say each basket runs from preschool to third-grade level or higher. As part of every day's routine, pairs of children select a basket that interests them, sit down together on the rug, and go through a "text set," looking at the similarities among the books. Then they pick one book to "read" together, which means they page through the book, talking about the pictures as they go, along with any text they can decipher.

At Andrew High School in Tinley Park, Illinois, Jeff Janes's science students are reading selections from the current adult nonfiction title $E=MC^2$: *A Biography of the World's Most Famous Equation* by David Bodanis, which explains Einstein's famous equation by sharing the biographies of a dozen people, including several as yet unsung women, who contributed key ideas over several centuries. Why has Jeff assigned the book, which is far longer and more detailed than the related sections in the physics textbook? Simple, Jeff explains: "It is written at an easier reading level, it's much more interesting, and it does a much better job of explaining the equation than our physics textbook. I think kids who read this book will really understand the concepts."

In *Mosaic of Thought,* Ellin Keene and Susan Zimmermann show how skilled, accomplished readers can easily get lost in articles from technical journals, floundering in ways that simulate their students' experience. We've always thought that a most illuminating faculty experience for middle and high school teachers is to swap textbooks with each other. When an English teacher finds herself unable to comprehend the science book her students are grappling with every day, it sheds a lot of light on what reading really entails. You can create a similar experience yourself by simply picking up the latest *Time* or *Newsweek* and purposely reading the most alien or "uninteresting" article, one you would normally skip over. As you find yourself awash in strange terminology, short on prior knowledge, and confronted with unstated assumptions, you'll be empathizing with your students.

Teachers who read regularly, and who often challenge their own thinking with hard text, come to the classroom with vital extra tools. They bring enthusiasm and energy for reading; they can model for kids how to get meaning out of tough texts; they can talk about specific books and make appropriate recommendations to young readers. But most important, teachers with fresh reading experience understand what goes on in their own minds when they read. Once they become aware of their own proficient-reader strategies—visualizing, connecting, questioning, inferring, analyzing, noticing an author's craft, and more—then teachers can better teach this repertoire of cognitive moves to kids directly and clearly.

Into the Classroom

What we have just described is a tall order, that's for sure. But now we'll turn the conversation over to five remarkable educators who are growing thoughtful, strategic readers in their classrooms every day. Kathleen Fay, coauthor of *Becoming One*

Community: Reading and Writing with English Language Learners, invites us into her first-grade classroom as she confers with students during reading workshop. Kath's one-to-one conferences help her understand and develop the strategies her students use to unlock meaning and decode words. Next, Marilyn reports on some important before-reading strategies she has used with third graders, "frontloading" instruction so that students have the information they need to tackle the text. Franki Sibberson, coauthor of *Still Learning to Read: Teaching Students in Grades 3–6*, shows us how she helps young readers use a variety of practical tools—Post-it notes, highlighters, message boards, and more—to drive and record their thinking.

Next, our colleague Donna Ogle, who developed the widely used K-W-L strategy, shows how K-W-L+ works with middle and high school kids, in both science and English. Donna is the author of many books and articles, and one that we love is *Reading Comprehension: Strategies for Independent Learners*, written with Camille Blachowicz (2001). Our final story comes from Connie Kieffer, who has worked on uncovering and preserving WPA murals in many Chicagoland schools, as well as being an art department chairperson. Connie tells how she and her colleagues at Highland Park High School built an extensive interdisciplinary unit for their ELL students around New Deal murals. Her story reminds us that students can (and should) be "reading" visual images and works of art, as well as print.

Further Reading

Allen, Janet. 2000. *Yellow Brick Roads: Shared and Guided Paths to Independent Reading 4–12.* Portland, ME: Stenhouse.

Allington, Richard L. 2000. *What Really Matters for Struggling Readers: Designing Research-Based Programs.* New York: Addison-Wesley Longman.

Beers, Kylene. 2002. *When Kids Can't Read, What Teachers Can Do: A Guide for Teachers 6–12.* Portsmouth, NH: Heinemann.

Blachowicz, Camille, and Peter Fisher. 1996. *Teaching Vocabulary in All Classrooms.* Englewood Cliffs, NJ: Merrill.

Blachowicz, Camille, and Donna Ogle. 2001. *Reading Comprehension: Strategies for Independent Learners.* New York: Guilford Press.

Burke, Jim. 2000. *Reading Reminders: Tools, Tips and Techniques.* Portsmouth, NH: Boynton/Cook.

Daniels, Harvey. 2002. *Literature Circles: Voice and Choice in Book Clubs and Reading Groups,* 2nd ed. Portland, ME: Stenhouse.

Daniels, Harvey, and Steven Zemelman. 2004. *Subjects Matter: Every Teacher's Guide to Content-Area Reading.* Portsmouth, NH: Heinemann.

Davidson, Judith, and David Koppenhaver. 1993. *Adolescent Literacy: What Works and Why.* New York: Garland.

Diller, Debbie. 2003. *Literacy Work Stations: Making Centers Work.* Portland, ME: Stenhouse.

Fay, Kathleen, and Suzanne Whaley. 2004. *Becoming One Community: Reading and Writing with English Language Learners.* Portland, ME: Stenhouse.

Fountas, Irene C., and Gay Su Pinnell. 1996. *Guided Reading: Good First Teaching for All Children.* Portsmouth, NH: Heinemann.

Harvey, Stephanie, and Anne Goudvis. 2000. *Strategies That Work: Teaching Comprehension to Enhance Understanding.* Portland, ME: Stenhouse.

Hindley, Joanne. 1996. *In the Company of Children.* Portland, ME: Stenhouse.

Keene, Ellin Oliver, and Susan Zimmermann. 1997. *Mosaic of Thought: Teaching Reading Comprehension in a Reader's Workshop.* Portsmouth, NH: Heinemann.

Mantione, Roberta D., and Sabine Smead. 2003. *Weaving Through Words: Using the Arts to Teach Reading Comprehension Strategies.* Newark, DE: International Reading Association.

Miller, Debbie. 2002. *Reading with Meaning: Teaching Comprehension in the Primary Grades.* Portland, ME: Stenhouse.

Ogle, Donna. 1986. "K-W-L: A Teaching Model That Develops Active Reading of Expository Text." *Reading Teacher* 39: 564–70.

Reynolds, Marilyn. 2004. *I Won't Read and You Can't Make Me: Reaching Reluctant Teen Readers.* Portsmouth, NH: Heinemann.

Sibberson, Franki, and Karen Szymusiak. 2003. *Still Learning to Read: Teaching Students in Grades 3–6.* Portland, ME: Stenhouse.

Smith, Michael, and Jeffrey Wilhelm. 2002. *Reading Don't Fix No Chevys: Literacy Lives of Young Men.* Portsmouth, NH: Heinemann.

Szymusiak, Karen, and Franki Sibberson. 2001. *Beyond Leveled Books: Supporting Transitional Readers in Grades 2–5.* Portland, ME: Stenhouse.

Tovani, Cris. 2000. *I Read It, but I Don't Get It: Comprehension Strategies for Adolescent Readers.* Portland, ME: Stenhouse.

———. 2004. *Do I Really Have to Teach Reading? Content Comprehension, Grades 6–12.* Portland, ME: Stenhouse.

Walker, Barbara. 2003. *Supporting Struggling Readers.* Portsmouth, NH: Heinemann.

Wilhelm, Jeffrey D., Tanya N. Baker, and Julie Dube. 2001. *Strategic Reading: Guiding Students to Lifelong Literacy 6–12.* Portsmouth: NH: Heinemann.

Thinking About Our Reading in First Grade

KATHLEEN FAY

Edwin was almost finished reading *Mushrooms for Dinner* when I sat down next to him. The last page had a picture of a frying pan full of fish and mushrooms. Edwin turned to me and asked, "Do bears really eat mushrooms?"

When reading new texts, Edwin often appeals for help or wants me to confirm his attempts to read unknown words. I had been teaching him ways to check for himself. Today I was glad he shared his question about bears, but my concern was the same: I did not want him to consider me the one with all the answers. I wanted him to know he could think through an idea for himself so I said, "What do you think?"

Edwin: I think, no.
Kath: Why do you think that?
Edwin: Because they're not real bears?
Kath: Tell me how you know they're not real bears.
Edwin: Real bears don't talk. But I kind of think they eat fish.
Kath: Oh. (*waiting*)
Edwin: I think they do. (*looks up and stares into space*) Oh, they do [eat fish].
    They do because in the other book, *Father Bear Goes Fishing* . . . And I saw
    it on TV.
Kath: Oh yeah? Tell me what you saw.

He described a TV show where he saw real bears catching fish with their paws. Then I said, "Let's look for more clues that this story isn't true, that it's fiction." Edwin happily ticked off a number of human attributes: "They don't wear that [a kerchief], they don't wear glasses, they don't do that, putting the hands like Mother Bear does. They do walk, though, but on four legs . . ."

The answer to Edwin's question, "Do bears eat mushrooms?" did not make or break his comprehension of this story; he was still able to read and understand Baby Bear's adventure. On another day, however, his question might impact his understanding of the story line. I encouraged him to pursue possible answers to his question, hoping that it would become a strategy he could use with other texts.

Every day during reading workshop the children spend some time reading out of their book boxes, which contain books that have been introduced during guided reading lessons. Sometimes children also include library books or storybooks or nonfiction texts from the classroom library in their book boxes (some of these books might be too difficult to read independently, but they hold a student's interest with familiar content or supportive illustrations). After my conversation with Edwin I decided to spend the rest of the day's workshop listening to students reread their familiar books instead of calling students over to introduce new texts in guided reading lessons. Today I wanted to check in on their connections and understanding with the texts they were rereading independently.

Next I sat with Melissa, an English language learner who was rereading a book called *Down by the Sea*. The story is about a grandmother looking for shells at the shore with her granddaughter. A boat rides by behind them and leaves a wave in its wake, which eventually surprises the grandmother and the girl. Melissa quickly read the first page but hesitated after reading the following sentence: "They did not see the big wave that it made." She mumbled the last word, as if she wasn't sure she was correct. She has read those words in other contexts so I took a guess that the structure of the sentence was confusing her—she wasn't sure what *it* referred to in the phrase *that it made.*

I asked, "You read it right. Does it make sense?" She shook her head. "Then I'm glad you stopped. It's good to stop and think when you're confused. Let's see if I can help. Grandma and the girl were facing the other way and did not see the wave that the boat made. See the wave?" She stared silently as I pointed to the picture; she still seemed confused. "Do you understand how a boat can make a wave?" She thought and then shook her head again. Annoyed with myself for not checking on this the first time she read the book, I tried to explain, "Have you ever noticed when you get into the tub the water moves a little? It makes tiny waves. Or when you move your hand back and forth through the water it makes little waves, too? This boat is doing the same thing because it's so big and heavy. When the boat goes along, it makes waves in the sea." I wanted to make sure she understood me so I asked, "Have you ever been to the ocean or to the sea?"

Melissa: No.
Kath: Have you ever been somewhere where there are waves?
Melissa: The pond . . . They were little.
Kath: Little waves . . . How do you think waves are made in the pond?
Melissa: You could get the thing . . . the thing for the sand and get it and put it back in and make it move.
Kath: A shovel? Or a bucket?
Melissa: A bucket. And you could get it . . .
Kath: Get the water . . .
Melissa: You could get the water and put it back in the pond.
Kath: I see. When you pour the water into the pond, that makes waves. You're right! In this story this big heavy boat makes a very big wave and then you know what happens to Grandma, right? Let's read this part again and see if it makes sense now . . ."

The story has to make sense to Melissa if she's going to be able to confirm for herself that she's reading the words correctly. She was, in fact, reading the words correctly but a significant aspect of the story wasn't clear to her. Melissa's gap in prior knowledge, like Edwin's question, needed to be cleared up for her to fully understand the story (and in her case to be able to read it independently with confidence). Taking the time to listen to children rereading familiar text is as important as introducing new books because I can praise them for strategies they are using. And for a more passive student, such as Melissa, it creates space to talk about what she is reading. I want her to be comfortable enough to say so when she does not understand.

As we moved into buddy reading time I sat with Christopher and Jenny, who were reading *A Friend for Little White Rabbit*. Little White Rabbit asks a few animals to be her friend and each tells her to go away—the duck honking at her and the lamb attempting to charge her. The next illustration shows the rabbit up on her hind legs with a lost look on her face. The text says, "'Who will play with me?' said the little white rabbit. 'Oh, who will play with me?'" When the kids finished reading I turned back to this picture and asked, "How is the little white rabbit feeling?" Jenny said, "She's sad." At the same time Christopher leaned over and said, "Mad." So Jenny changed her mind and her tone of voice and asked, "Mad?" Again, I wanted them to decide for themselves so I encouraged the children to explain their respective responses.

Kath: Well, let's see. Maybe it could be either. Jenny, look at the picture. Why do you think she is sad?

Jenny: He don't play with her.

Kath: That would be sad. Christopher, why is she mad?

Christopher: Because they won't play with him. They're mean. See, he's mean. It could be both.

Jenny: I'm right? Sad?

Kath: You are right, and so is Christopher. Listen to how I read it when she's sad (*with a breathy, whiney voice*). "Ooooooooooh, who will play with me?"
Now see if this sounds mad (*faster and more clipped, trying to sound annoyed*). "Oh, who will play with me?" Do you want to try it? Jenny, you read it and we'll see if we can tell how you feel, then Christopher can take a turn . . .

Next I met with Ronaldo and Elisa. Ronaldo had a picture-book version of *The Little Red Hen* in his book box. I had read it aloud to the class a few times and Ronaldo asked to keep it in his book box. Ronaldo needs a variety of instruction: he needs explicit instruction while reading very simple text and he needs to interact with rich stories as well. It is taking him longer to learn concepts about print, and I worry that if I instruct Ronaldo only with low-level text (simple patterns with little or no story line), we'll lose opportunities to develop his ability to tell and to understand complex stories in English. Ronaldo and Elisa were taking turns: Elisa was reading the text on her page and Ronaldo was retelling the story by looking at the pictures when it was his turn.

Elisa: "'Who will help me take the wheat to the mill?' asked the little red hen . . . 'Then I'll do it myself . . .'"

Kath: What did she do next after she made flour? (*I thought aloud for Ronaldo so that he could more easily predict what would happen next.*)

Ronaldo: "Who gonna help me . . . do . . . the . . . *pan*? Br . . .?" [*Pan* = bread in Spanish.]

Kath: Yes, *pan*. Or bread.

Ronaldo: Br . . . "I do all myself."

Elisa (*continuing to read*): "Soon it was time to eat the bread."

Ronaldo (*pointing to the loaf of bread*): You know this? *Pan. Pan.*

Kath: Yes. *Pan* is the same as bread. What else could we call this? (*They say nothing.*) It looks like a roll. What else could we call it?

Ronaldo: Look it, look it (*pointing to the sliced bread on the next page*). He cut it.

Kath: What do you call it there, when you see it like that?

Elisa: Butter toast.

Kath: That's what you could say. What else could you say?

Ronaldo: Sandwich?

Kath: It does look like that . . . you could call bread *pan*, you could call it sandwich, you could call it toast, all those things . . .

It was worthwhile to spend the morning talking and thinking with children; perhaps they will become more flexible readers and will learn to value their own (and each other's) opinions. I felt a little freedom from the constant pressure to quickly push children into more difficult text. Listening to children's side comments and encouraging them to follow through with ideas and toss around their questions, I recognized the value in doing this regularly and purposefully. And with children such as Ronaldo, I am reminded that whatever difficulties he may have remembering vocabulary or learning to look at print, he is smart. He understands the stories he hears and he has his own opinions. I need to keep giving him multiple opportunities to share what he's thinking.

Ronaldo: "I eat it all myself."

Kath: Why did she eat it all herself?

Ronaldo: Um . . . "Nobody help me."

Kath: What would you do if you did all the work? You planted it. You watered it. You made the bread . . . And nobody helped you. Would you share?

Elisa: No.

Ronaldo: Yeah. I gonna share this (*pointing to the toast*).

Kath: You're going to share the toast?

Ronaldo: Yeah, for Elisa.

Kath: Oh, you would share with Elisa?

Ronaldo: Yeah.

Kath: Even if Elisa didn't help you, you would share?

Ronaldo: . . . No . . .

And he giggled and we all burst out laughing.

Frontloading Instruction: Helping Children Think Through Expository Text

MARILYN BIZAR

Students are generally introduced to reading through stories or *narrative text*. Lucky children have stories read to them at home, and good primary teachers tap the power of reading aloud to kids. As they move along through the grades, students typically spend most of their time in basals and anthologies that are mostly fiction, so they are constantly immersed in narrative, getting invited into language, and learning how stories can move them. We have known for decades that if students understand the structure of narrative text, it helps them better understand the stories they read. Knowing that narrative text uses characters, a setting, and problems and resolutions helps young readers make sense of the story.

Expository text has structures, too, but they are different from the ones used in stories. Because expository material is usually written to convey factual information or explain ideas, it uses structures like description, cause and effect, problem and solution, and comparison and contrast, to name a few. If we look at real expository text in the world, we often find that it uses more than one structure, even on the same page. An expository piece about an animal might begin with description, go on to comparing and contrasting the animal to another, and end with problem and solution. Even more worrisome, expository text is sometimes poorly organized, which throws students another curve.

So, for kids who have cut their teeth almost exclusively on narratives, expository, nonfiction, or informational text can pose quite a challenge. But the same underlying principle applies: students who know what patterns of organization to expect will have better control over the text they encounter. When students can foresee certain categories of information, they can impose order on the text as they go, making it easier to make sense of even the most "inconsiderate" material, like many school textbooks.

In my third-grade class at Carpenter School in Chicago, my students had very disparate reading abilities and levels of prior knowledge. Half the children were African American and had been in Chicago their whole lives, and the other half were recent immigrants from Mexico. To help the kids understand expository material and to make sure they had all the information needed to cope effectively with the text, I had to really emphasize before-reading activities. Jeff Wilhelm (2001) has given the name "frontloading" to this instructional emphasis, which simply means helping kids activate their prior knowledge and set purposes before they read, so that they enter the text thinking.

When we brainstormed our prior knowledge before reading, I was usually pleasantly surprised at how much the kids knew. Before reading a short expository piece about catfish, the kids generated this list of characteristics:

- They taste good.
- They have whiskers like cats.
- They are caught in ponds.
- They are cooked in frying pans.
- They have big heads.
- They are ugly.
- They are easy to catch.
- You can catch them with worms.
- You catch them with bugs.

There were several steps in our brainstorming process. First, I elicited what students knew, and then I asked them to think about how they knew it. Students who had eaten or fished for catfish had some pretty good information to share. Kids who had specific knowledge about the subject got a chance to share it with the group. Even some of my apparently poor readers were excellent thinkers when given a forum in which to expound. All this time spent brainstorming before reading is important because students won't necessarily use the knowledge they have unless they can access and activate it.

After the initial brainstorming, I asked the group to figure out what categories of information they would expect to find in the upcoming reading. I posed this question: "In an article about catfish, what kinds of questions would you expect the author to answer?" I wanted students to anticipate the categories of knowledge that would probably be found in the article about catfish—just as they might foresee the categories in any informational text. My third graders were equal to the task. With a little prompting, the students generated this list of questions.

What do they look like? (appearance)
How did they get the name catfish?

Where are they found? (habitat)
What do they eat? (food)
How do they make babies? (reproduction)
Who are their enemies? (predators)
How do they protect themselves?

These content-based questions give structure to what kids are reading and help them notice important information as they encounter it. After they generated the list of questions, I asked students to read part of the text to see if the author answered some of their predicted questions. The kids were excited to see that some of their personal questions were being answered by the author, as if by magic!

Another way to help kids visually categorize brainstormed ideas—and later, to inventory their after-reading knowledge—is semantic mapping. This valuable variation is simply an arrangement of words (and hence the concepts that the words represent) around a topic. When we construct a semantic map with students before they read, we provide a vehicle for connecting known to new knowledge. Later when the reading is done, we map again to show all we have learned. Here's how it goes step by step, using the catfish lesson as an example.

STEP 1: *Brainstorming.* The teacher asks the students to think of words or phrases that come to mind when they think of catfish.

STEP 2: *Mapping Categories.* The teacher and students construct a map on the board, by grouping the words into their categories. Figure 2.1 was devised by the same third-grade class before reading the article.

STEP 3: *Revision of the map.* After reading the selection, students revise the map in response to the text. Categories are added, and information is added or moved around the map (see Figure 2.2).

These frontloading processes show children that in different types of expository text, we can anticipate certain categories of information. For example, authors of articles about animals usually include the kinds of information that the students predicted. Students need to know that they can generalize these categories to similar texts. A few days after the catfish lesson, I might say: "Today we are going to read an article about spiders. Remember the questions that we asked about catfish? This article about spiders will talk about many of those same categories."

In my class, we used this same strategy—brainstorming and categorizing—with many other kinds of expository texts. When we read a biography of Susan B. Anthony, the students generated this list of categories that they expected to find:

Figure 2.1: Third graders' prereading map.

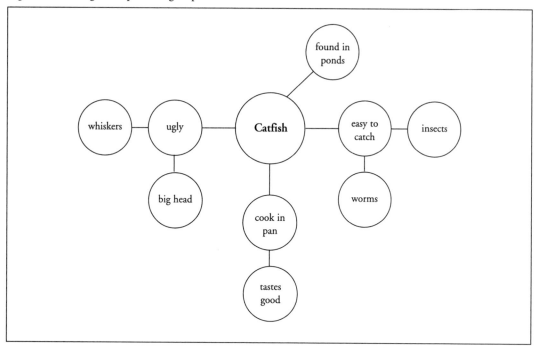

Figure 2.2: Third graders' after-reading map.

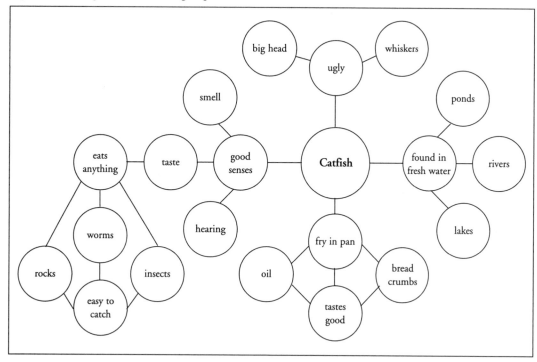

1. What did she do?
2. Why was a biography written about her?
3. When did she live?
4. Where did she live?
5. What was her childhood like?
6. What kind of education did she have?
7. What was her family like?
8. Did she have children?

After reading the biography together, the students went to the library to read biographies of their own choice. They found that the same categories of information were also used in the biographies they had selected, and that recognition helped to power the kids' comprehension.

In beginning a unit about the Civil War, we brainstormed what we knew about that time in history, and then I asked the kids to generate the categories of information that the author was likely to cover. Here is their list:

1. When did the war take place?
2. Where was it fought?
3. What was it about?
4. Who won?
5. What happened after the war?
6. What were the important battles?
7. Who were the important people?

Once again, the kids were able to predict many of the key categories of information that exist in any history text.

All these frontloading activities are simple, and yet so powerful. In the old days, we would assign reading and then stand back, watching many kids struggle with expository text. Now, when we take the time to get kids really ready to read, they can think through text eagerly and successfully.

Thinking Tools and Talkworthy Texts

FRANKI SIBBERSON

It's easy to get carried away with using new tools and materials for holding thinking when I teach reading. I am amazed and a little overwhelmed every time I go to the office supply store. Sticky notes come in so many more sizes, shapes, and colors than they did not too long ago. Highlighters are also available in every color of the rainbow. I love to try out a new style of sticky note or a new color pen when I am marking ideas and questions in text. I know that my students do, too. But I am often hesitant to buy the new, expensive sticky notes because I know that they will disappear in minutes. What ten-year-old can resist the opportunity to use a see-through arrow, after all?

With all of these options for marking thinking while reading, the hurdle for me as a teacher is to help students become more sophisticated in choosing tools to use for understanding texts. I know that the novelty of new sticky notes, highlighters, or labels really helps encourage kids to slow down and mark thinking in text, even if they hate to write or interrupt their reading, but I can't let the fun of testing out new materials become more important than the thinking the tool can provoke. A set of highlighters in a neon color can do wonders for engagement on the first day they are introduced, but the initial excitement will wear off quickly.

I am really honest with my students about the variety of tools available. I want to introduce them to lots of ways to think about text, and we do a great deal of talking about tools for thinking. What tools do we use in our reading that really help us understand more deeply? More important, which tools work best for you? Which tools work best for your classmates? Which tools cause problems? Which tools are right for which purposes?

Recently, Sam came into school with the book *Flags of Our Fathers* by James Bradley. He and his father were reading and discussing this book each night. As Sam read the book during reading workshop, he highlighted those places in the text that he wanted to discuss. Sam had decided to use a highlighter because it was an easy way to let his father know which lines he wanted to discuss. He knew that his father would pay more attention to those lines during his reading and that they would be easy to find when they started to chat.

Shea told me he was using sticky tabs to think through current issues in Iraq and the United States. Shea chose a tab rather than a sticky note because he knew they were sturdier and would last for the entire year as he found new articles. The tab also gave him just enough room to write a word or two to summarize some of his thinking about the article. My students keep a binder that includes all of the issues of *Time for Kids* for the year. This allows them to go to back issues whenever they need new information, have a question, or make a new connection to an article. Shea let me know that he is tabbing and rereading all of the articles about Iraq to decide whether or not he thinks our president is making good decisions.

Questions to Ask When Evaluating Students' Uses of Tools
Which tools do I provide to support students' understanding of text (sticky notes, charts, boards, highlighters, notebooks)?

How can I make tools available to students throughout the day?

When and how do I talk to students about the reasons that people use the tools?

How do I value students' processes for understanding—even when they differ from my own?

How do I model the use of different tools?

How do I provide opportunities for students to reflect on their use of certain tools?

How do I provide time for students to share their innovative uses of tools?

How do I celebrate the times that students find new ways to use tools successfully?

What do I do to make sure that boards, word walls, etc., are anchors for conversation?

How do I help students get out of ruts if they overuse certain tools?

One of the ways I try to validate student use of tools is to create a board in the classroom to share tools that work, titled "Tools for Thinking." The board starts out blank, but as I conference with kids and meet with small groups, I monitor the use of tools and suggest that students share new uses as they emerge. Often the tools are created for a specific purpose based on the needs of the readers. The board helps students to see that I want them to use and design tools that work to help them understand their reading. It also helps me realize how well students use tools when the goal is understanding.

For example, Emily and Karynn were in a book group discussing Margaret Peterson Haddix's book *Takeoffs and Landings*. The girls wanted to track the characters' feelings and changes as they related to the title. They decided that the title was a metaphor for the characters' emotions, which changed over the course of the book. Because they had never encountered a situation like this one, they designed their own tool—a chart marking the emotional highs and lows each of the three main characters experienced throughout the book.

Another great use of multiple tools was a poster that a group of three girls made to help them with their discussion of *Coraline* by Neil Gaiman. Prior to the reading, the girls decided to use sticky notes to mark passages in the text and to write short notes on the sticky notes so they would be ready to talk. When they got together, they decided that their talk would be more meaningful if they took the time to sort the sticky notes into categories. They created a poster of sticky notes in various categories and then chose their talk topics based on those that all three girls had marked repeatedly in the text. It was a great tool to actually see where their thinking overlapped and where it differed.

While reading *Touching Spirit Bear* by Ben Mikaelsen, a few students discussed the quote at the beginning of the book and what it told them about the

"Tools for Thinking" is the place where students post the innovative ways they track their ideas and responses to a variety of text.

book. The quote was a Chinese proverb that read, "Fall down seven times, stand up eight." They decided to use an easel and chart paper to track the times in the book that Cole, the main character "fell" and the times that he "got back up" to see if there were actually seven falls. During their discussion and charting, they decided that the number of times that Cole fell wasn't what the author meant to emphasize. They thought that the author wanted readers to realize that you had to get stronger every time bad things happened, no matter how many times.

"Talkworthy" Novels for Readers

In the past, I haven't had a lot of success with small book groups. Kids participated, but I never felt like they understood the book any better because of these chats. Most of the time, they quickly went through the motions of sharing their thinking. This year, I started to think about book groups differently. I had students invite adult readers to come in and talk to us about the book clubs they belonged to. Students took notes about each reader in their reader's notebooks. By having the notes in one place, the students could easily reflect on their comments and refer to readers who had visited previously.

As we listened to each reader share his or her experiences, it became clear that joining a book club is a very personal decision for many adults. Some readers belonged to one book club, others belonged to three or four a month, while others only joined once in a while for work-related learning. There are mother-daughter book clubs, and each month they read books about a strong female character. There are work-related book clubs, mom clubs, clubs that read books on healthful living, neighborhood clubs, and invitation-only clubs. We learned that most book clubs meet after everyone has finished the book and that some groups are a bit more serious than others. We learned that some readers keep notebooks of things they want to discuss while others use sticky notes and others just think about the things they want to say. So, how could we make our classroom book talks authentic now that we knew how real book clubs work?

I realized if I wanted students to talk deeply about text, I needed to help them focus their thinking with tools in ways that would help them dig deeper than they would on their own. The adult readers who visited our classroom had keen interests in the books they read and in the book-group members. This was in contrast to how book discussion groups had worked in the past in my room. When kids responded to books, they usually focused on whether they liked or disliked the book. They often quickly listed lots of shallow responses to the book without developing a greater understanding.

A key concept I started using this year that I learned from my colleague Karen Szymusiak is the notion of "talkworthy" texts. "Talkworthy" means a book worth talking about. Not all texts require conversations for deeper understanding. We've all read books that are great fun to read but are also forgotten as soon we've read the last page. And then we've read books that we can't forget and are dying to talk with someone about.

When I introduced the concept of "talkworthy" texts to my students this year, the class brainstormed the kind of reading that is best supported through conversation. Their collective ideas formed an anchor chart that stayed up on the walls for weeks and was revised as students participated in groups and developed new links between talk and texts. Here are some of their ideas:

What Makes a Text Talkworthy?
an interesting topic
a good plot (looking for clues/suspenseful)
good characters (interesting/mysterious/funny)
characters who change
threads/focus through the entire book
interesting writing

details in the writing (craft)

topic that encourages personal opinion (controversial)

series/author/genre—books in same category to compare and discuss

At the same time, we brainstormed ways to extend and deepen our discussions of novels. For example, students often struggle with the comprehension strategy of questioning the text. A big question for them may simply be one that confuses them, and not one that is necessarily "talkworthy." Students in the upper elementary grades need to learn that some questions can be answered quickly once evidence is found. Other questions need mulling over.

Most questions that are "thinkworthy" are also "talkworthy." After reading books to the whole class as part of read-aloud, I usually ask students to choose questions that would be worthy of talk: Which questions can you talk about for a long time? Many children's books now come with questions in the back for literature circles. After we've read the book, I often ask my students to evaluate those questions in the back for talkworthiness. Which are worth talking about and why? Which are not really worthy of good talk?

Here is another anchor chart we developed soon after the "talkworthy" discussion:

Ways We Dig Deeper into Books

Look at the author. Think about other books he/she has written; his/her style of writing.

List the characters and descriptions. Follow certain characters throughout the book. Pay attention to changes.

Look for and follow a thread—something that comes up over and over.

What does the title mean? Connect to the book, look for clues, look for words in the title throughout the book.

Preview the book—keep going back to those first thoughts.

Find a big question and build on it by finding things that are important to that question.

These whole-class discussions about deep thinking and talk with texts helped prepare my students for work on their own in small-group book clubs. Once students had determined what makes a book worth talking about and had some idea of what they might want to talk about, the next step was building in opportunities to write in preparation for these book discussions. I needed to find ways to help students bridge books worth talking about with others with different strategies for tracking thinking in text and the best tools to use to mark this thinking.

Tracking Thinking Before Reading Group Meetings

As our class was just beginning to organize small-group discussions of books, I knew that many of the groups had decided to read the entire book before meeting. Because we had learned from adult readers that many book groups worked that way, we decided to give it a try. But I worried that without support and preparation before the meetings, the students would all come to the conversation with different things to discuss and then spend their time round-robin sharing. I suspected that instead of getting into a good conversation, the talk would be superficial.

So I mounted a board on our cabinets to support these groups-in-progress. For each group that was reading a book and planning on discussing it together, I created a space. The group put a sign up designating the space as theirs with the title of the book and the date they planned to meet. They also included the names or photos of the members of the group. Then I put a basket holding a variety of sticky notes near the area. I told the students that this could serve as their communication tool as they were reading. If during their reading they had something they wanted to discuss with others, they could put a little note up on their space.

By writing and posting these notes, the group would come together knowing what others in the group were thinking and focusing on during the reading. I reminded kids to check the board frequently so that they kept up with others' thinking. I knew that this small display would change the reading experience for all.

As always, the students took this further than I ever imagined. Early on, Chris decided that they couldn't just put sticky notes up there—"Mrs. Sibberson, what if I just started the book and someone else puts a note up that tells me too much about something I haven't read yet?" I hadn't thought that far. Chris decided to use arrow-shaped sticky notes to separate the space for his book talk by page numbers. One arrow pointed to space below in case you wanted to comment on pages 1–50. Another arrow pointed down for sticky notes for pages 51–100 and so on. In this way, readers could look at those notes written only about the pages they had already read.

Another unexpected benefit of the book club board was the surprising dialogue it sparked. For many of the groups, the board notes became an ongoing conversation. One reader would post a question or an idea and another reader would connect his sticky note to the first one to show that he was responding. They might agree, disagree, or share a new thought. The way they connected the sticky notes showed how the thoughts were connected.

The board also served as a great resource for me. I could read the postings every few days to see the kinds of talking and thinking that were happening in the groups. As their teacher, I was also more prepared when the groups met because I

Displays of book group members, book covers, and spaces for posting notes, questions, and responses to ideas from classmates prepare students for more thoughtful conversations around books.

had already seen thinking during individual readings and I could anticipate some of the conversation.

Helping students use different tools to prepare for group book talks is essential for fostering deeper, more interesting conversations and thinking around texts. This is especially true when students are encountering longer, more sophisticated reading in the upper elementary grades. One of my most important roles is to provide many reading and writing tools, as well as opportunities to make book talk more thoughtful.

K-W-L+ in Action

DONNA M. OGLE

Henry David Thoreau said: "Knowledge that becomes ours is knowledge that we construct." And that's especially true of the special thinking activity called *reading*. Both teachers and students need models and opportunities to construct meaning around text. As teachers we need to employ classroom instructional strategies that facilitate students' construction of their own meanings. Current research has made quite clear the importance of the active, constructive nature of reading and learning; good learners link their prior knowledge to new information, reorganize it, and create their own meanings. The K-W-L+ strategy, described in this article, is designed to help readers do just that. K-W-L+ provides a framework for learning that can be used across content areas to help students become active constructors of meaning.

The K-W-L+ Strategy Explained

The letters in the initialism K-W-L+ stand for the process of making meaning that begins with what students *Know*, moves to the articulation of questions of what they *Want to Know*, and continues as students record what they *Learn*. The strategy is designed to be used by a teacher and group of students working together. It is then easily transferred into a method for students' independent study. In using the strategy the teacher first leads the group through an oral discussion of each of the components and then turns the process over to students to individually write their own ideas and questions on a personal worksheet (see Figure 2.3a). The intent of the strategy is to involve students actively: First, the connection between their prior knowledge and the information that will be presented in the texts is made real, both by eliciting what they know about the specific information and the ways that information is likely to be structured. Second, teachers guide the students to think of questions they need and want to have answered, and third, students make notes and then organize the old and new information in graphic and elaborated written form (Figure 2.3b).

As teachers initiate a new topic or prepare students to read an article or chapter, they explain the strategy that is being used. They might say:

> It is important to first find out what we think we know about this topic. Then we want to anticipate how an author is likely to present and organize the information. From this assessment we can generate good questions to focus our reading and study. Our level of knowledge will determine to some extent how we will study. Then as we read we will make notes of questions that get answered and other new and important information we learn. During this process some new questions will probably occur to us; these we should also note so we can get clarification later.

After a brief explanation the teacher and students identify what they think they know about the topic; the teacher writes student-brainstormed ideas on the board or an overhead transparency. All ideas should be recorded—it is not the

Figure 2.3a: K-W-L+ strategy sheet.

K-W-L+ Strategy Sheet
(from Ogle [1986])

Name ——————————————————————— Subject ———————————

Date ———————————————————————————

1. K—What We Know	W—What We Want to Know	L—What We Learned and Still Need to Learn

2. Categories of Information We Expect to Use

A	E
B	F
C	G
D	H

teacher's role at this time to correct misconceptions, but simply to let students first articulate the associations they have with the topic, right or wrong. As students engage in this brainstorming, some questions should begin to emerge. Not everyone should have the same ideas; some disagreements and misconceptions begin to surface. The teacher notes these differences and helps students frame them into questions. These then become the beginning of the second column, What We Want to Know.

As the teacher facilitates the brainstorming of ideas and elicits questions that will guide the reading, she is modeling the writing of ideas and framing of questions for students who have a difficult time taking risks and composing their own questions. As soon as the teacher thinks students are ready, she suggests that each now write on their own sheet what they individually think they know in the Know column and the two or three questions that are of most interest to them in the second column, Want to Know. With less motivated students, selecting questions from those modeled by the teacher may provide a basic level of commitment to the learning.

Another important component of the prereading preparation is anticipating the organization and structure of ideas that authors are most likely to use. This aspect of prereading taps a different kind of knowledge that is important for learn-

Figure 2.3b: Completed K-W-L+ strategy sheet.

K-W-L+ Strategy Sheet
(from Ogle [1986])

Name ————————————————————— Subject ————————————————
Date ————————————————————————————————

1. K—What We Know	W—What We Want to Know	L—What We Learned and Still Need to Learn
A plant used to make cigarettes Can cause cancer to lips, mouth, and lungs Causes emphysema Addictive Smokeless, chewing Surgeon General says don't use	1. Where is tobacco grown? 2. How does it cause cancer? 3. Why is it a legal substance? 4. Is tobacco used for anything worthwhile? 5. Is the tocacco you chew and the kind you smoke the same? 6. What is smokeless tobacco?	1. Tobacco is a drug 2. 350,000 Americans die from tobacco-related diseases 3. Nicotiana-tocabum = name of plant 4. Tobacco smoke is inhaled nicotime; it is absorbed through lining of mouth and lungs into bloodstream 5. Transported to brain in 7.5 seconds 6. 90% of all lung cancer from smoking 7. Average smoker spends $10,000-$20,000 on cigarettes in a lifetime

2. Categories of Information We Expect to Use

A Harms/Effects	E Odors
B Types	F Growth
C Uses	G
D Composition	H

ing. The bottom of the first column on the worksheet provides space for students to list anticipated categories or topics. If students are not familiar with categorizing and structuring information, teachers can model this kind of thinking from the initial brainstorming students do by asking, "How do you think the author of a text or article on _____ is likely to organize the information? What categories or topics would you expect to find?" If no ideas are forthcoming, the teacher can direct students' attention to the list of information they generated. This list can then be used to help students identify like ideas that could be chunked into a single category. For example: during a prereading discussion of coelenterates (corals and jellyfish) students may have suggested information like the following: live in salt water, have soft bodies, eat small creatures, wait for food to come to them, and are simple animals. The teacher can help students identify the more general categories represented by this information: habitat, physical characteristics, eating, and scientific classification. These categories should not be difficult for secondary students to generate once they are attuned to thinking of organization of knowledge. Yet, it is surprising how few students will use these organizers if not led to do so by teachers.

The time spent focusing students on thinking about likely structure is important, whether the K-W-L+ is used as a framework for reading a chapter or to initiate a broader unit of exploration and study. Too often content teachers assume students know how to use larger organizing structures for learning; asking students to anticipate most likely structures assures that we don't overlook gaps in students' strategic thinking and provides us a naturally occurring occasion to teach these structures. These structures also have tremendous value when students come to study and write. Having organizing frames consciously available empowers students to chunk together discrete pieces of information in meaningful and, thus, memorable ways.

After students have accessed their ideas about content and structure and have identified key questions, they then read and make notes in the third, Learned, column of their worksheet. They will write answers to their questions and note new and interesting information. This note making can occur as an ongoing reading-note-making recursive activity. Other students may wait until they have read through a whole section of text before stopping to check what they have learned and make notes. Teachers can model making notes and then checking questions against the text information; this can provide a good opportunity to demonstrate the need for multiple sources of information if some basic questions are overlooked or not answered adequately.

Content Teachers Make K-W-L+ Their Own

Eighth-grade science teacher Katherine Walker uses K-W-L+ regularly with her students. She says that she likes the framework because it helps her find out what her students bring to their study of different topics and motivates some students to become involved in learning who would not normally do so. She has also found improved test scores, something that pleases her.

Katherine shares how the process works from a textbook section she taught on tobacco. Her objective for the selection was to familiarize students with the effects of tobacco on the human body. As Katherine put it: "The lesson must build on the students' knowledge of how a healthy body functions so that the information learned about the composition of tobacco and its physical effects and the diseases caused by and attributed to its use show how the body systems are impaired from normal function when tobacco is used."

Katherine introduced the topic by asking students what they already knew about tobacco and its effects. As students volunteered information she also helped them frame questions like, "Why is it a legal substance?" and "How does it cause cancer?" As students got involved in thinking about what section in a text could help them learn, she asked what topics or categories of information about tobacco they could anticipate finding in the textbook. Again, she guided their thinking as they suggested characteristics such as harm, effects, types, uses, composition, odors, and growth. After all the students had written their own notes in the first two columns on worksheets or notebook paper divided into thirds, she gave them time in class to begin reading and filling in the third column, What We Learned. The text section and note making were completed as homework. The next day the students discussed the information they had gained and checked to see if their questions had been answered. Then they moved on to the "+" step of the K-W-L+ strategy and constructed semantic maps of their knowledge, and from these, each student wrote a summary. An example of one student's work is included to illustrate the personal nature of the learning and construction of meaning (see Figure 2.4).

In her own written reflections, Katherine explored the effectiveness of the strategy for this lesson. She wrote:

1. It allowed me to learn what students knew about tobacco.
2. It provided me with a means of getting more oral participation from nontalkative students when discussion occurs in my classroom.
3. It motivated some inactive students to become involved in both writing and talking.
4. It allowed my students to become cooperative in their learning while brainstorming.
5. It provided a means of additional research generated by student responses rather than teacher-mandated demands.
6. It provided a better test base for my students to comprehend information about tobacco. The students answered more questions correctly after having worked with the strategy than they usually do.

Beverly Shand, a ninth-grade English teacher, used K-W-L+ in a somewhat different way while she was teaching a unit on author Richard Wright. Rather than begin with the strategy, she first had students read Wright's novel *Black Boy*. Then, before students read his biographical sketch and two additional short stories, she engaged the students in doing a K-W-L+. The object of her lesson was to prepare students to respond to the two short stories by identifying Wright's strengths and to understand how his personal struggle affected his point of view and purpose for writing.

As she began the lesson she asked each class what they knew about Wright, what questions they had, and what they wanted to find out. By giving students the opportunity to read some of Wright's own writing she had ensured some prior knowledge about his youth. Students were able to draw on their reading and make good inferences about his character and future as they worked in small groups using the worksheet as a guide (see Figure 2.5). They were motivated by reading *Black Boy* and wanted to know more about Wright. Because she knew the classes

Figure 2.4: Semantic map and summary.

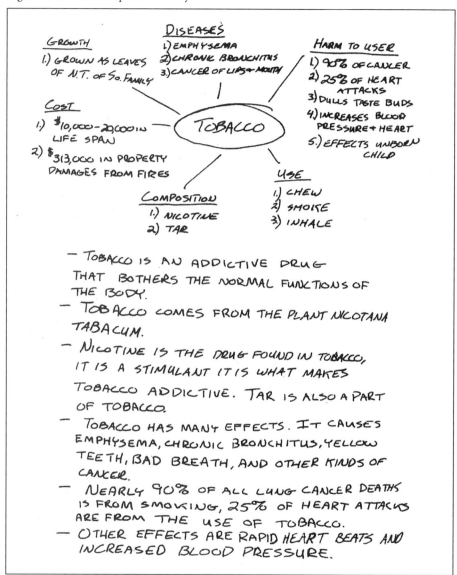

had some knowledge, she felt comfortable having them work in small groups to brainstorm and form questions to guide their reading.

In her own reflections, Beverly added that

1. students are able to connect their prior knowledge, or schema, to new information that they themselves identify as desired-to-know facts, and to

Figure 2.5: K-W-L+ on Richard Wright.

K-W-L+ Strategy Sheet
(from Ogle [1986])

Name ———————————————— Subject ————————————————

Date ————————————————

1. K—What We Know	W—What We Want to Know	L—What We Learned and Still Need to Learn
Writer/American	What other books did he write?	The book <u>Black Boy</u> would have
Black/Author Black Boy	What family life was like?	been named <u>American Hunger</u>.
Intelligent	Is he alive now?	Born near Nachez, Miss.
Bad child/killed cat	What was his life like in	Lived in France for 13 yrs.
Drunkard at 6	U.S.A.?	Great writer
Father left family	How old would he be?	Wife Ellan, 2 daughters
Mother had severe breakdown	Was he married?	Father illiterate sharecropper
Brother	How did he die?	Mom—schoolteacher
Leg hit by wagon	Did he get any awards?	Valedictorian, May 1925
	Why did he write?	Married
	What was his goal?	Wrote poetry and short stories

2. Categories of Information We Expect to Use

A   Profession   E

B   Works   F

C   Personal life   G

D   H

Won prize with <u>Uncle Tom's Children</u>
Wrote <u>Native Son</u>
Bigger was violent
Then <u>Black Boy</u>—Direct
Went to France—Exiled self
Wrote 8 books there
Died young 1960

    use this new information in a synthesis that increases their level of critical thinking and ability to synthesize in the future;

2.   the small-group setting used in brainstorming provides a more secure, less threatening environment for student interactions as effective brainstorming is done;

3.   the making of graphic organizers, including the K-W-L+ sheet, gives students valuable practice in an activity that lends them strength in organizing material into meaningful, easier to remember chunks both now and in future lessons. For visual learners, as our students mostly are, this is an important tool for successful learning;

4.   K-W-L+ allows students to address the idea of learning as a metacognitive process. If students know how they learn best they will be more successful learners.

    Often students are confronted with a great deal of information they are expected to internalize in short periods of time. When it is important to retain the information, the two postreading components of the strategy, mapping and summarizing, are valuable. These "plus" activities were added after the original K-W-L was developed because teachers found that students still needed help rehearsing new information in ways that would make it memorable (Carr and Ogle 1987). Once students have completed their reading and note making, they go back and create a graphic map or diagram of the ideas. This map should include both what the student knew prior to reading and the important information that has been gained. Some teachers suggest students use two colors of pen or pencil to make even clearer the weaving together of new and old information. As students create a map of their ideas they should be using some of the basic structures or frames inherent to the content presentation. When the map is completed it is easy for students to write summaries; they simply use the category labels on their maps as main ideas and the subsumed information as details or illustrations. Research (Carr and Ogle 1987) has demonstrated the value of the postreading mapping and summarizing for long-term content retention.

Having each student involved in writing her own ideas before, during, and after reading is central to the K-W-L+ strategy. It provides a means for students to retain the information they are learning. The writing also helps students continually monitor their own thinking and learning on the worksheet. Even if they do not contribute orally to the class discussions their writing provides a way for students and teacher to dialogue about their learning. This writing component is valuable to teachers, too, for several reasons. First, because so much content-area instruction is conducted with whole classes, oral discussion often misses just those students who most need the time spent in focusing and calling up prior knowledge. The writing task provides a concrete way for all students to participate in the thinking about the topic even when not talking. Second, since they need to write out their ideas, there is a more personal commitment to the content. Third, written knowledge and questions provide teachers a window on students' thinking and interaction with the text information. Finally, those written sheets provide a good working copy of students' knowledge building that can serve teachers and students when they read and learn from multiple sources of information.

Reading a Work of Art

CONNIE KIEFFER

At Highland Park High School, students who are brand-new immigrants to the United States are offered an immersion program that integrates the study of English with content from other disciplines. One of these special classes is a combined U.S. history and English course taught by Mary Schwartz (English) and

Phil Koulentes (social studies). I worked with the team in my capacity as the school's art department chairperson. This course meets for three periods per day instead of two, so students have more time to study English and apply their growing language skills to U.S. history content. All four aspects of language—reading, writing, speaking, and listening—are included in every lesson. In addition, technology is regularly used to support and extend kids' work. This year's class had sixteen students, most of them from Mexico, with one student from Guatemala and one from Bosnia.

A big topic in our social studies curriculum is the Great Depression, and we try to involve kids in a unit that encompasses reading, writing, speaking, listening, U.S. history, and visual arts. We began this three-week study by asking students to list some questions they had about the 1930s in the United States. Some of the questions that students raised were the following:

- How was life in 1930s United States similar to life in the United States today?
- How was life different?
- What were the causes of the Great Depression?
- What kinds of jobs did people lose during the Depression era?
- What did the president, Franklin Delano Roosevelt, do about the bad economy?

We teachers knew that the answers to the kids' questions could be found in some very special "texts"—the beautiful New Deal murals that hang in our own school's library and in several other nearby locations. Since these American artworks draw their roots from the Mexican muralist tradition, and since so many of the students in the class were from Mexico, we thought these local murals would make great "readings" for our Depression unit.

After recording the kids' initial questions, we introduced works by three prominent Mexican muralists, Diego Rivera, David Siqueiros, and José Clemente Orozco. As the students (like any viewer) first looked at these works of art, they developed an initial emotional response. They began talking about whether they "liked it" or "didn't like it." Of course, we wanted kids to look more closely, read more carefully.

Next, in small groups, we showed students more ways to "read a work of art," to deepen their observations, to look through different cognitive lenses, and to dig below the surface for meaning. To help kids take these thinking stances, we gave them the following tool to aid comprehension:

1. What kind of lines do you see in the art? Straight? Horizontal? Vertical? Diagonal? Curved?

2. What kinds of shapes or forms do you see in the art? Square? Round? Hexagonal? Are any forms taken from nature? Are there forms from geometry?
3. Are there people in the art? If so, what are they doing? What is their relationship? Where are they looking? Do they face toward or away from each other?
4. What colors are utilized in the art? Are they warm or cool colors?
5. When you look at the art, where does your eye go first?
6. What kind of music do you think of when you look at the art?
7. What emotion do you feel when you look at the art?

By looking more closely at the mural, students got a feel for subject matter most important to the artist. Is he painting a quiet, serene landscape, a passive portrait, or a work with dynamic, human interaction? Do the lines of the mural depict a quiet environment (soft and circular) or an angry, action-filled milieu?

Soon, the students began to connect their knowledge of Mexican history to the artists and their paintings. It was a time of political upheaval when these muralists were painting. The Mexican government was funding the work of artists to create public works of art, but the murals were also social and political commentary about the times. When these painters later worked in the United States, their work continued to reflect contemporary issues and turmoil.

Another tool we introduced to guide and record the kids' thinking was a variation on a Venn diagram. We asked students to put common features of all three painters in the center circle, and unique features of each individual artist around the side (see Figure 2.6).

On the diagram, students identified Rivera's work with a greater number of curved lines, while both Orozco and Siqueiros utilized active, often diagonal and angular lines suggesting anger. Students identified Rivera's shapes as more rounded and more often drawn from nature, while the other two artists made greater use of geometric shapes, again depicting dynamic action. Students saw the use of colors as extremely important in all three of the Mexican muralists' work. Rivera and Orozco used colors across the palette, while rich, red earth tones dominated Siqueiros's work. Students saw all three of the artists using a great variety of patterns and intricate detail related to the often violent, revolutionary times when they were painted.

Now we asked students working in pairs to create their own stories inspired by the viewing of one mural. In this way, we invited them to connect what they had learned from "reading a work of art" to their own life experiences. Some of the resulting stories connected the murals to the arduous and sometimes dangerous entry into another country as illegal immigrants with few relatives, little food, and

Figure 2.6: Venn diagram

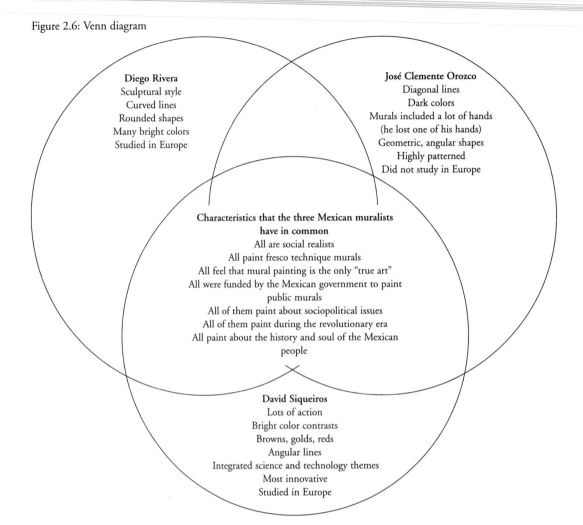

Diego Rivera
Sculptural style
Curved lines
Rounded shapes
Many bright colors
Studied in Europe

José Clemente Orozco
Diagonal lines
Dark colors
Murals included a lot of hands
(he lost one of his hands)
Geometric, angular shapes
Highly patterned
Did not study in Europe

**Characteristics that the three Mexican muralists
have in common**
All are social realists
All paint fresco technique murals
All feel that mural painting is the only "true art"
All were funded by the Mexican government to paint
public murals
All of them paint about sociopolitical issues
All of them paint during the revolutionary era
All paint about the history and soul of the Mexican
people

David Siqueiros
Lots of action
Bright color contrasts
Browns, golds, reds
Angular lines
Integrated science and technology themes
Most innovative
Studied in Europe

no money. Other stories revealed the pride that Mexican students felt about their heritage and the rich artistic traditions that were brought to America.

During the next class period, students took an in-school field trip to study both the 1934 Edgar Britton New Deal murals in the school library and the Hector Duarte (a contemporary Mexican artist) mural in the school's auditorium foyer. They could see Diego Rivera's influence in Britton's work and David Siqueiros's influence in Hector Duarte's mural. They saw the graceful curved lines in Britton's work similar to Diego Rivera's. They identified the sharp, angular lines in Hector Duarte's mural as similar to the diagonal and rectilinear lines in Siqueiros's murals.

Now we broke kids up into six groups to study one particular mural in depth. Each team was given a large photograph of a different New Deal mural housed in schools in the greater Chicago area. Kids were asked to use the murals as one text in a wider study of the Great Depression and its impact on 1930s Americans, and to compare life in the 1930s with their own lives today.

We introduced students to a wide range of research sources and tools. Of course we used art reference books from the school library to see more examples of the artists' paintings and learn what galleries displayed their work. The Internet also proved very helpful, and many teams began their investigation by Googling terms like *Illinois New Deal Murals*. Then they branched out, writing letters to their artist's surviving relatives, to government agencies connected to the New Deal murals such as the U.S. Postal Service and the General Services Administration (GSA), and to foundations related to these muralists.

All the information that students gathered was kept in careful notes, including a bibliography of references. Among the sources were letters received from two artists' widows, one artist's foundation, and the GSA. Finally, following an outline we provided, the groups prepared speeches about their assigned mural and muralist to be presented during an upcoming field trip. A few days later, students traveled to stand in front of the murals they had seen only in photographs, and gave videotaped, oral presentations about their mural, the artist who created it, and what the mural taught them about the Depression era.

One stop on the field trip was Lane Tech High School in Chicago, a school with sixty-six murals. Flora Doody, a special education teacher, and her students had raised over one million dollars (through bake sales and dance marathons) to clean and restore all of the school's murals. She also started a student docent program where visitors learn firsthand from students about the mural tradition. Lane Tech's student docents met our students and took them on a tour of murals at their school. Our kids especially enjoyed the 1933 Century of Progress murals painted by Miklos Gaspar that lined the halls, and the auditorium stage curtain by John Walley, which was recently restored through the removal of several coats of paint.

Next, our Highland Park students completed their presentations in front of the two sets of murals that they studied. The first speech centered on the auditorium foyer murals by Mitchell Siporin titled "Arts" and the second covered the "Epochs of History" murals in the cafeteria, painted by Edgar Britton, the same artist who completed our own murals back at Highland Park.

As the teacher team looked back, we saw many benefits of the New Deal mural unit for this special group of ESL kids. All the students

improved their English skills throughout the unit;
learned how to read a work of art and connect it to their own lives;
improved their observational and visual literacy skills;
read text in various genres about the artists and their murals;

used the Internet as a research tool;

wrote letters and speeches and gave oral presentations that were videotaped;

interacted socially with students from other high schools;

got to know each other working in collaborative groups;

connected the learning to their own lives in Highland Park; and

saw what a significant contribution Mexican culture has made to American art.

The unit also brought us plenty of valuable sidebars and great conversations. Toward the end of the unit, the kids noticed that all the artists they were studying were male! (There were a few female New Deal muralists, but this group did not study any of their work.) The Edgar Britton murals at Highland Park depict nine different industrial jobs, all being done by men. A heated discussion about jobs and gender ensued after the kids viewed those murals. This conversation emerged again when students studied the Edward Millman murals at Lucy Flower High School in Chicago. Millman's murals depict nine women significant during the 1930s, including Lucy Flower, Grace Abbott, Frances Perkins, Jane Addams, Susan B. Anthony, Harriet Tubman, Harriet Beecher Stowe, and Clara Barton. However, students found out that one year after these murals were painted, the all-male Chicago Board of Education had them painted over (whitewashed) because they didn't like the way they portrayed women! An interchange about the role of men and women in the 1930s and today followed this field trip.

For our kids, who are newcomers to America, the mural-reading project was deeply engaging, even as it delivered strong content and literacy development. The students learned that many of the New Deal muralists were also recent immigrants to the United States and shared similar experiences to the students today. Like our students' families, the muralists struggled with the language, finding jobs, getting an education, and making ends meet. This became a strong common bond between students and the 1930s artists they studied. In turn, it gave them a clear understanding of what it was like to live during the Great Depression.

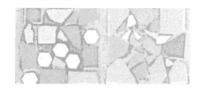  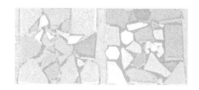

T H R E E

REPRESENTING-
TO-LEARN

Our second method has a slightly artificial-sounding name, and we're sorry about that. We prefer to use everyday language wherever possible, but for this special set of activities, no other term quite does the job. Here's why:

Think of cave paintings, made by ancient peoples, going back thousands of years. Since the very beginning of humankind, our species has manifested an impulse to represent experience—our adventures, our worship, our sensual tastes, our grain harvests—in artistic and (for the past 2,000 years) written form. Representing our world seems to help us engage and enjoy life more deeply, to keep better records, to pass along ideas to our young, to celebrate and decorate our life spaces. In American schools over the past twenty-five years, a teaching movement called *writing-to-learn* has built upon this insight into the species. Figuring that human beings have probably used writing to understand the world ever since the first alphabet, clay tablet, and stylus were invented, these smart teachers invite kids to use writing not just as a performance to be graded for grammar and mechanics, but as a tool for thinking, a "crescent wrench of the mind" that allows a learner to both explore and show what she knows. Developed and elaborated by teachers like Peter Elbow (1973) and Toby Fulwiler (1987), writing-to-learn has become a minimovement with a broad literature and a wide following, especially among interdisciplinary college programs.

More recently, we have begun to see that jotting down *words* is not the only way for students to seek, engage, construct, probe, and store knowledge and share ideas. Many other representational strategies that are commonly classified as art—drawing, sketching, mapping, drama, movement, dance, song—turn out to be equally powerful cognitive levers, used either alone or in combination with words.

We can hear you thinking: "I know where this is headed. Me draw? Dance? Act?" The minute we invite teachers to have their students engage ideas artistically, we run into rampant instructor art phobia. While we can agree that writing is a normal and necessary school undertaking, art seems like an extra, and a nervous-making one at that. So in this chapter, let's talk about writing as a tool of learning first. Later, we'll see how the arts add another constellation of representing activities that students can use in any subject across the curriculum.

Writing is not just one of the "language arts." It is also a form of thinking, a way of engaging and acting on information. As we discussed in Chapter 1, all contemporary learning theories share one precept: in order for students to remember information, they must act on it. Writing can be a way of acting on information, manipulating, challenging, exploring, and storing it. However, for writing to have this cognitive power, the words students write must be original. Copying isn't exploration. Filling in worksheets does not count as writing-to-learn. Even taking notes in class can be mere transcription, with the transcriber's brain idling in neutral. Such closed-ended, right-answer exercises are more like obedience rituals, and rarely involve constructing any meaning. Unfortunately much of the writing done in American schools still does not tap the higher-order uses of writing. Writing even continues to be used as a punishment in some classrooms. On the floor of a Milwaukee school, a colleague recently found a sheet of notebook paper with the richly ironic phrase "I will not talk in art class" written one hundred times.

Sometimes teachers outside of language arts are a bit suspicious about the exhortation that they should use more writing in their history, biology, or physical education classes. They suspect that English teachers are trying to invade their subjects, conscripting them to teach stuff that should have been covered during English. Well, the skepticism is understandable, but we can pledge that writing-to-learn really isn't a camouflaged turf grab by wily language artists. Rather, it is a real gift—a gift of pedagogy.

That's because writing can also be seen as a teaching method. Writing activities provide instructional options that all teachers enjoy, just as they may elect to have students read a book, listen to a presentation, conduct an experiment, watch a video, or join in a discussion. Of course, inviting students to write does not exactly seem like a radical new choice on the pedagogical menu—after all, book reports, term papers, and written exams have long been a staple of many classrooms, grade levels, and subjects. But these traditional kinds of writing assignments offer tightly convergent, and solitary, tasks—and writing-to-learn points at something quite different.

Instead, students need more open-ended, well-coached, and sociable writing experiences. If writing can actually help people think—sort through, weigh, comprehend, and save information—it should be used *during* class, while information is flowing. And if writing can be used to share learnings, to represent and embody ideas, we need to involve the class as collaborators and as audiences for each other's writings. Again, we need to rebalance, cutting down on lockstep writing assignments done alone at home with no coaching and submitted to no audience other than the teacher's in-box. In their place, teachers need to tap the tool of writing to help students connect with the content of the curriculum, and with each other, here and now.

Now, let's add art to the picture; in fact, let's notice that art is already present. As teachers have explored and used the repertoire of WTL strategies, they notice that many of the most powerful "writing" variants—like clustering, mapping, or webbing—actually combine words with some kind of drawing or graphic element. When you divide a journal page into two columns, or array ideas in two overlapping circles, or begin to draw arrows between concepts, you are using spatial and artistic, as well as linguistic, strategies to help you think. From there, it is a short step to recognizing the value of purely graphic forms of journaling and other writing/drawing combinations.

There are two main types of representing-to-learn, one especially useful for constructing meaning and the other for sharing it. The first, *journaling*, involves short writings or drawings that help students move into, through, and beyond the content of the curriculum in any subject. While they needn't be literally contained within an official journal, notebook, sketchbook, or learning log, these entries have several features in common: they are short, spontaneous, exploratory, expressive, informal, personal, unedited, and ungraded. Typically these drawings/writings are completed in two- to five-minute bursts before, during, or at the end of a lesson or class session.

While these entries are typically not collected or graded by the teacher, they are systematically *used* during class as a springboard to activity. At the start of class, students may jot down questions on the topic of the day; these can be shared aloud and then become part of the official agenda. Or the teacher can begin the class by reading aloud a few "admit slips," in which students have offered their open-ended reactions to the previous night's reading assignment. Often, whole-class discussion can be sparked by the varying responses. In the middle of a presentation, the teacher can stop and ask students to sketch a graphic or picture that represents their understanding of the topic, sharing these with a partner. Or at the end of class, students can write "exit slips" explaining what from the day's lesson has been most important or most difficult, and the teacher can then draw on these writings to plan the next day's class. For homework, students may exchange their dialogue

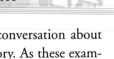

journals with their partners, continuing an ongoing written conversation about the subject of the class, whether it is science, literature, or history. As these examples suggest, journaling can truly be a teaching method, not an invasion by English teachers trying to impose their world on you. The prompts and structures for journaling are genuinely generic, and can be applied to any subject.

Representing in *genres* is more formal and extensive. In writing, we invite students to use the whole range of conventional forms (mysteries, sonnets, laboratory reports, editorials) to embody and share their thinking about the content of the curriculum. In contrast to journaling, which is quick and unedited, genre writing is substantial, considered, and polished. While in journals, we don't worry about inconsistencies or informality, in genre writing we work hard to meet the norms and requirements of the form we have chosen. While journaling is mainly a tool that helps us think, genre writing is also for sharing with others. It's not just for finding out what we know, but for offering what we know to some kind of audience by embedding our ideas within the conventions of a carefully crafted form.

Most teachers are already familiar with the range of options for genre writing. But, when we move into artistic genres, very few of us possess a repertoire of activities to help kids represent their learning. Indeed, many teachers feel reluctant and unsure about the process, or the validity, of bringing art from the margins of schooling to the center. This reticence runs deep. As Arnold Aprill, director of the Chicago Arts Partnerships in Education (CAPE), explains, most Americans (including schoolteachers) have had their expressive impulses shamed and silenced in school, stunted by scores of prescriptive, do-it-right "art" assignments: "Here's a doily and a sheet of red construction paper. Make a heart just like the one on the board." While we know that very few teachers had good experiences with writing in school, even fewer had their artistic sensibilities nurtured and developed. Clearly, if a teacher is a wounded artist (or writer), she is highly unlikely to devote much classroom time to activities personally connected with uncertainty, discomfort, embarrassment, and failure.

Beyond their own fears, teachers also raise sincere questions about the legitimacy of arts activities. Is acting out a story really a valid representation of understanding? Wouldn't writing an essay be more meaningful? Isn't a poem about using the microscope a little less academic than a well-organized list of directions? And isn't drawing your response to a historical figure just the easy way out, compared with composing a reasoned argument and supporting your interpretation?

Questions like these reflect a couple of issues. For one, they reveal the pressure teachers feel about grading, about finding ways to score and rate and classify their students. Perhaps because they have more practice at it, many teachers are capable of assigning and defending grades on student writing, but feel at a loss when required to hand out grades for a reader's theater performance or a mosaic mural.

But even more important, teachers' reluctance about the artistic representation of learning shows us how little the idea of "multiple intelligences" has actually penetrated our school culture. In recent years, practically everyone working in education has enthusiastically genuflected to Howard Gardner's (1983) concept that human beings don't have just a single type of intelligence, but rather a combination of eight different kinds of "smarts": linguistic, mathematical, musical, spatial, kinesthetic, interpersonal, intrapersonal, and environmental. The key implication of this reasonable and well-supported theory is that schools must extend kids' existing areas of intelligence, while helping them develop their weaker ones. Pedagogically, this means students should be encountering, processing, and representing ideas through a dramatically widened range of instructional activities. The connection with the arts is apparent: they offer established practices, media, materials, and conventions for making learning more kinesthetic, more spatial, more musical, and in many ways, more inter- and intrapersonal.

At the Center for City Schools in Chicago, we and our teacher-consultants have been working hard to become more multiply intelligent, to grow our own repertoires of classroom arts activities. Many of us came to this as reading and writing specialists, graduates of the Illinois Writing Project who are now supposed to help other teachers develop integrated curriculum in their Chicago schools. As we have tried to get past our own insecurities and learn new strategies, we have worked with several CAPE artists, people who divide their time between doing art and working with teachers and kids in school. We have also worked with technology gurus who have enabled us to see the art of making and demonstrating meaning through the creative use of computers. For now, we'll share just two of the promising activities we've learned from these special colleagues.

Two-Minute Videos

Virtually every American school, and many individual classrooms, now possesses video cameras. Unfortunately, not everyone seems to know what to do with them. Camcorders can be hard to work with: they're breakable; the kids push buttons before they know what they do; it's hard to get good sound in noisy classrooms. But video artist Dierdre Searcy has taught us a truly simple structure she calls "Two-Minute Videos," which neatly solves these problems and potentially applies to any subject in the curriculum. All you need to make two-minute videos is a subject (the solar system, racism, photosynthesis—what's in your curriculum?), some old magazines and scissors, and a video camera on a tripod.

Working in pairs or small groups, students first review and discuss the ideas they want to represent. Then they leaf through some magazines, seeking images

that can somehow convey their big ideas and main points. They cut out these pictures or graphics, and then start arranging them on a tabletop, seeking a good
sequence. Next they write a script, essentially a caption to go with each image.
Usually this script will include words to be read into the camera microphone by
one or more students, but it can also include sound effects or bits of music. When
they are ready, each group brings their pictures and script to the stationary camera "studio." They hang the first image on the wall, focus in, push the camera shut-
ter, and read the script segment. Then they stop the camera (this is called *pause
editing* in the video business), put up the next visual, get ready, turn the camera
on again, and read the second script segment. And so on. When they are done,
students have a smoothly edited, professional-looking, two-minute video that can
be as solid, informative, entertaining, or provocative as their script and images
allow. Some of the veteran teachers who routinely use two-minute videos enhance
kids' chances of creating great pieces by building extensive classroom collections
of images, photos, and other visuals. Over the years of steady collecting, kids have
more and more powerful images to work with. The really hard-core devotees also
collect sound bites—segments of CDs with music and words that enhance the stories kids seek to tell.

Multimedia

Classroom computers obviously provide us with other artistic representing activities—if we know how to use them for this purpose. But we need a little help.
While school boards are relatively quick to invest in hardware, software purchases
and teacher training tend to lag behind, so computers end up being used mostly
for mundane drill programs and grade-book records, and teachers don't use them
to invite kids' expression and develop their multiple intelligences. But at their best,
computers can be used for sophisticated forms of multimedia authoring—a new
and exciting genre of art.

Among such programs are iMovie and Premiere, which allow students to create nonlinear, audience-directed multimedia presentations. In other words, kids
can create something like a Web site, where their audience is offered text, sound,
graphics, music, photos, and video clips in combinations and sequences that visitors select for themselves as they make choices, following forks and branches
designed by the author. Working with our computer-guru colleague Jeff Flynn,
elementary and secondary students around the Midwest have developed a wide
array of multimedia documents on a wide variety of topics. At Lincoln Park High
School in Chicago, each of Madame Breen's foreign language students created a
series of images about a chosen French artist, reading the text aloud in English, in

their own first language (including Polish and Spanish in this class), and, of course, in their very best French. Sharon Flynn's middle school class in Dexter, Michigan, read Felice Holman's novel *Slake's Limbo*, about a homeless teenager living in a subway tunnel. Moved by the book, the kids created a multimedia presentation that included artwork, music, and kid-written and -performed raps addressing issues of urban fear, violence, and loneliness. In Lisa Hahn's first-grade room at Gifford School in Elgin, Illinois, her Reading Recovery students use simple hypermedia programs to document their own reading, while teachers use theirs to conduct miscue analysis. Across town at Eastview Middle School, John Case has his science students creating programs that explain angles of measurement using graphs, sound, and visuals.

Multimedia authoring stands at the other end of the complexity spectrum from the two-minute videos described above. While kids can be up and running with Dierdre's videos in ten minutes, some computer programs are tricky and require training and experience. Creating multimedia projects can be a demanding artistic challenge. Unlike traditional writing, which uses only words, multimedia authors may select from words or pictures or video clips or sounds in creating a text. Even more complex is the fact that the order is not fixed; the author must provide for a "reader" who can jump through the ingredients in any sequence. Indeed, one of the special responsibilities of a multimedia author is to offer the audience lots of genuine and attractive choices. There may be a steep learning curve for us grown-ups, but you can be sure of this: there will be several kids in any classroom who can teach the program to you in one day.

These two strategies are emblematic of a whole range of arts genres and forms that teachers can adopt and use, provided that they experience them personally first and have a chance to get past their old "I'm not an artist" thinking. When art-shamed adults make their own two-minute videos or mini–Web sites, it can be a truly transformative experience. Teachers are often stunned to hear themselves saying: "I can do this!" Many pull a pedagogical U-turn; they can't wait to bring the arts activity that terrified them an hour ago into their own classrooms.

Into the Classroom

First Steve Zemelman shows how very young writers can produce an example of their own favorite genre: the big book. With careful teacher guidance, the whole class coauthors and produces its own volume, even as the kids are learning how to read from other, "real" big books every day. Next we tune in to station WGST-TV at Hubbard Woods School, where David Wartik and Joe Mazza are getting their fourth- and fifth-grade students ready to broadcast their daily morning newscast.

Students at Hubbard Woods have produced and anchored hundreds of television broadcasts where they have opportunities to represent their learning in real and meaningful ways.

In Chapter 1, we met Pete Leki, the teacher, ecologist, parent, and school board member from Waters School. Here, Pete tells how he shared his fascination with the Chicago River with students at Waters. Pete visited a few classrooms and simply invited young people to write and draw their experiences with rivers, either the one in the neighborhood's backyard, or ones they had grown up with back in Mexico, Bosnia, or Mississippi. Beginning with a book collecting these special stories and artworks, the children, the teacher, and Pete gradually developed a commitment to ecological studies that has since become the official schoolwide theme (see pages 15–31).

At Stevenson High School in Buffalo Grove, Illinois, Kim Lubeke has a unique way for students to learn about mitosis, the complex process by which cells divide; she has them dancing to learn. Kim's students become parts of the cell—centrosomes, ribosomes, chromosomes, and all—and physically move through the stages of mitosis. Last, Harvey offers an inventory of twenty-three notebook-entry prompts, brief activities that invite students to use drawing, writing, or combinations of the two to engage ideas and connect with content. These strategies are generic in the proudest sense: they are adaptable to any almost subject matter or age level.

Further Reading

Anson, Chris, and Richard Beach. 1995. *Journals in the Classroom: Writing to Learn.* Norwood, MA: Christopher-Gordon.

Blecher, Sharon, and Kathy Jaffee. 1998. *Weaving in the Arts: Widening the Learning Circle.* Portsmouth, NH: Heinemann.

Cohen, Elaine Pear, and Ruth Strauss Gainer. 1995. *Art: Another Language for Learning.* 3rd ed. Portsmouth, NH: Heinemann.

Countryman, Joan. 1992. *Writing to Learn Mathematics: Strategies That Work, K–12.* Portsmouth, NH: Heinemann.

Ehrenworth, Mary. 2003. *Looking to Write: Students Writing Through the Visual Arts.* Portsmouth, NH: Heinemann.

Ernst, Karen. 1994. *Picturing Learning: Artists and Writers in the Classroom.* Portsmouth, NH: Heinemann.

Fineberg, Carol. 2004. *Creating Islands of Excellence: Arts Education as a Partner in School Reform.* Portsmouth, NH: Heinemann.

Gee, Karolynne. 1999. *Visual Arts as a Way of Knowing.* Portland, ME: Stenhouse.

Gilmore, Barry. 1999. *Creative Writing Through the Visual and Performing Arts.* Portsmouth, NH: Heinemann.

Heller, Paul G. 1995. *Drama as a Way of Knowing.* Portland, ME: Stenhouse.

Hubbard, Ruth Shagoury, and Karen Ernst, eds. 1996. *New Entries: Learning by Writing and Drawing.* Portsmouth, NH: Heinemann.

Isaacs, Judith Ann, and Janine Brodine. 1994. *Journals in the Classroom: A Complete Guide for the Elementary Teacher.* Winnipeg: Peguis.

Lambert, Joe. 2002. *Digital Storytelling: Capturing Lives, Creating Community.* Berkeley: Digital Diner.

Mantione, Roberta D., and Sabine Smead. 2003. *Weaving Through Words: Using the Arts to Teach Reading Comprehension Strategies.* Newark, DE: International Reading Association.

Miller, Carole, S., and Juliana Saxton. 2004. *Into the Story: Language in Action Through Drama.* Portsmouth, NH: Heinemann.

Moline, Steve. 1995. *I See What You Mean: Children at Work with Visual Information.* Portland, ME: Stenhouse.

Noppi Brandon, Gail. 2004. *Finding Your Voice: A Methodology for Enhancing Literacy Through Re-Writing and Re-Acting.* Portsmouth, NH: Heinemann.

Page, Nick. 1996. *Music as a Way of Knowing.* Portland, ME: Stenhouse.

Parsons, Les. 1994. *Expanding Response Journals in All Subject Areas.* Portsmouth, NH: Heinemann.

Robinson, Gillian. 1996. *Sketch-Books: Explore and Store.* Portsmouth, NH: Heinemann.

Romano, Tom. 2000. *Blending Genre, Altering Style: Writing Multigenre Papers.* Portsmouth, NH: Boynton/Cook.

Swartz, Larry. 2002. *The New Dramathemes.* Markham, ON: Pembroke.

Whitin, Phyllis. 1996. *Sketching Stories, Stretching Minds: Responding Visually to Literature.* Portsmouth, NH: Heinemann.

Zakkai, Jennifer. 1997. *Dance as a Way of Knowing.* Portland, ME: Stenhouse.

How to Help Your Kids Compose and Publish a Whole-Class Big Book

STEVEN ZEMELMAN

The favorite literary genre of many early primary children is the "big book." These huge, two-by-three-foot books are designed to help teachers re-create the intense closeness of reading on a parent's lap. Big books are so large that the teacher can hold one up to a group of children who are sitting on the rug in front of her and, metaphorically, put every one of them in her lap as she reads aloud. The best big books include plenty of rhyme, big illustrations, predictable stories, and language patterns that young children can follow and pick up. Some are simply enlarged versions of established classics (*Goodnight Moon, Who Is the Beast?*), while others have been written specifically to be big books (*Mrs. Wishy-Washy, The Best Book for Terry Lee*). Once kids get into big books, they usually want to write (and read) their own, and so, along with some teachers from the Disney Magnet School in Chicago, I developed the following pattern for helping primary kids create and "publish" their own big books.

1. *Introduce a mini-lesson.* Introduce to children the concept that every story includes a problem or conflict. Use a read-aloud or two to illustrate this—*Wilfred Gordon McDonald Partridge, Thundercake, Owl Moon*—just about any of your favorite picture books will work just fine. Because this is a powerful concept that students can use throughout their schooling to think about literature, it's well worth taking time to help them become comfortable with it over a period of days or weeks.

2. *Brainstorm possible problems for the class big book to focus on.* Ask the kids to think about problems they might like to write stories about. Then go around the circle several times and record all the ideas on a chalkboard or flip chart. Often, kids who don't volunteer right away have an idea by the second or third round. You might wish to star the ideas that are mentioned more than once, to spread the recognition and begin to focus on the topics held in common in the class.

3. *The group votes to choose one idea for the class book.* Several rounds of voting may be required for narrowing down the list since, especially with younger kids, each person will at first tend to vote for his or her own suggestion. This process can be challenging, because some children will be disappointed their idea wasn't chosen. It's good to reassure the class that this is really a list of excellent story ideas for the whole year, and that everyone will also get a chance to write his or her very own piece for the next project.

4. *Identify a variable and a refrain for the predictable pages.* Most big books for early readers are built around repetition, so the book can be structured by figuring out what event or aspect can be repeated with variations on a number of pages. For example, in a story about a lost pet, the variable might be the numerous places where the children search for the animal. Depending on the age level, the kids may need your help determining this variable. Once it's set, they'll have no trouble brainstorming lots of choices and then deciding on an appropriate refrain. For the pet story, our class listed lots of places to look: up a tree, under the bed, in the cafeteria, and so on. The refrain on each page was then easily created: "But he wasn't there!" The group also wanted to identify the pet, so it became Green Star, the dog.

5. *Small groups go to work to create the middle pages.* Even though there's more to plan, it's good to do some concrete work at this point. Divide the class into groups of three, so each group can create one page. If possible, each group should have at least one strong writer. The tasks for the groups are as follows:

1. Choose one of the variable options.
2. Decide what the words will be for the page.
3. Pick one writer to draft the words on a half-sheet of butcher paper or chart paper.
4. Assign the other two kids to draw and color the illustration on the upper half of a full sheet of paper (this allows all to work simultaneously without getting in each other's way).

Depending on the children's age, writing experience, and purpose for the book, you may decide to use the children's writing as is or to prepare a large-size, computer-printed, teacher-spelled version of the words. If it's just for the class and the children are beginning writers, the most encouraging approach is to use the children's own spelling. If the book will be used for other children to practice their reading, it's legitimate to create a "publisher's" version. To honor the children's efforts, their original versions can be included on the pages as well.

6. *Brainstorm a beginning and an ending.* We still need some parts for our story, so it's time for the group to brainstorm some more. How will the story start? What initiates the problem? And how will it end? For our example, the children creating the lost pet big book decided the dog ran away because his owners weren't taking good care of him. Then they brainstormed where he would be found, for the ending. It helped the thinking to point out to the kids that the dog's hiding place would relate to why he ran away in the first place. Our group overwhelmingly chose the principal's office for the ending—a revealing insight into first graders' need for order and authority—or their idea of a "good home."

7. *Groups draft the beginning, ending, and other needed pages.* Divide the class into groups of three again. Assign (or help kids choose) one group to create the first page, one for the last page, and other groups to create a title page, an "about the author" page, a back page "advertisement" for the book, and so on, to involve as many groups as you have as well as to acquaint them with the various elements of a published text.

8. *Put it all together.* Tape the wording sheets onto the picture sheets. Bind the pages together at the top or sides, using individual notebook rings or other flexi-

ble fasteners. Then include the rereading of the big book as a regular option during sustained silent reading and other open choice work times. Finally, inspire other classes to create their own books and trade them around the building for reading practice. The children will all be extremely proud that their books are being regularly used to help others learn to read.

Some Helpful Mini-lessons for Getting Started

1. Have kids develop a list of their own topics for writing. Do your own first to demonstrate.

2. Guide students in using journals to develop good topics. For example, events, people, or issues that come up repeatedly over a period of time can be given separate sections in the journal and the student can go to that section whenever an additional thought on the topic comes to mind. Once a number of entries have been collected, it will probably be easy to use some of them, or parts of them, as the core of a more formal written piece.

3. Help the class to set some work-time behavior rules—and state them as positives. For example, "Use your twelve-inch voice when conferring with a partner," rather than "Don't talk loudly." Ask the class to make a list of things a student can do if he or she is finished with a draft, or stuck, or waiting for a conference—this will help keep kids productive. Put these lists up on posters, so it will be easy to refer to them when students need reminding.

4. Help kids to develop their own list of goals for improvement, which will go into their folders and will be consulted during assessment conferences. Then demonstrate how a writer can use the list to self-evaluate his or her own work and continue working on it before submitting it to the teacher.

5. Teach kids how to respond with a brief description of what they're working on (the topic, what stage they're at, and whether they need help today) during "status of the class" meetings so that you can get a quick read on how students will be using their time during the workshop period, and who will be needing help from you.

6. Teach kids how to work with you when having a teacher-student conference. They should be prepared to respond to three questions that you'll ask them before you read anything they've written: (1) What is your piece about? (2) What stage are you at in the work? and (3) What help do you want from me? Help them to pick out one important thing in the writing that they'd like to improve—and to ask for a conference after they've done this preparatory thinking.

WGST-TV Is on the Air

DAVID WARTIK

"Good morning and welcome to WGST Morning News. It's Wednesday, December 12. I'm Grace, your news anchor for today."

So begins another school day at Hubbard Woods School.

All through the building, classes sit with their teachers (and usually a few lingering parents who have just dropped off their children) and watch our program on closed-circuit TVs.

In the makeshift basement studio, our crew of ten fourth graders is hard at work, performing their jobs and producing that morning's TV show. Just about four short minutes later, Grace wraps things up and we've completed another virtually flawless show. Even though we've been on the air for over a year, it takes a good deal of teamwork to get the show up and running every morning. Let's travel back in time a bit.

It's 7:50 on a typical morning, fifty minutes before school starts. Third-grade teacher Joe Mazza and I head down the hallway of school and toward the steps that lead to the "garden level." This floor used to contain one fourth-grade classroom, the school psychologist's office, and a large storage room. But now, due to the generous grants provided by the Winnetka Public Schools Foundation and the Hubbard Woods PTA, the garden level has also become the home of the newest and most exciting feature at Hubbard Woods School—WGST 6, the school's TV station.

It's just ten minutes before this week's crew arrives to begin work at WGST, so Joe and I quickly go through our normal preshow checklist of tasks. I make sure that the Macintosh computer that doubles as a teleprompter has that day's script skeleton already loaded on—complete with the correct anchor and meteorologist names, any necessary school announcements, and any student birthdays in the school. Joe, meanwhile, checks over the character generator (CG)—the small computer that will put the names and birthdays on the TV screen as we broadcast.

I check to make sure that all the videotapes we'll need for that day are ready and racked up. We have one for the meteorologist's report, which gets pretaped. We have another tape with the show's opening and closing montages. Finally, we have the master tape for recording each week's episodes. About five minutes before 8:00, we start hearing the quiet whispers of the students outside, anxious to get inside and prepare the day's broadcast.

Will, Anchor Two for the day, and Austin, our special reporter, knock and enter the control room. They hand me the stories they've written for the day's show. We make sure the stories are OK, make necessary edits, and I type them into the teleprompter. Joe and I really have only three requirements for the news stories: they must be written by the student; they must be school appropriate; and they may not be about sports. When our school used to do morning announcements over the loudspeaker, almost all of the "news" stories were sports stories. While Joe and I are big sports fans, we wanted to have actual news stories every day—as did the other teachers in the school. We added a "sports report" to our Friday broadcasts, so the student assigned that job gets to broadcast our one sports story of the week.

We tell the kids they can use any type of news story—in-school, local, regional, national, or international—as long as it's appropriate and positive. Considering all that's going on in our world, we decide not to cover stories about terrorism, war, or crime. (This has been the right decision for us, but we know other schools and teachers might choose to include the tougher topics.) With kindergartners and first graders watching every morning, we know we have to be responsible broadcasters and consider our audience. Very often, kids complain to us about how hard it is to find a positive news story, and they're very correct. And that's quite sad.

With everything set, we open the door and welcome the kids in. They immediately announce—for our benefit, as well as each other's—what their jobs are for that day. Will and Austin head into the studio, followed by Grace, who is Anchor One. Julie, the meteorologist, follows her in. The student director, cameraperson, and lighting technician head in, too. Joe heads into the studio with that portion of the crew. Meanwhile, in the control room, I'm getting the day's video switcher, audio mixer, and teleprompter operator situated.

In the studio, Joe is getting Julie ready for her spot. Julie has written her weather report ahead of time. Joe and Julie touch base on her "numbers"—the temperatures for that day. He'll type those into the CG and they'll appear on-screen when she's on. Sometimes, the meteorologist will also have sunrise and sunset times or some other useful weather data and we'll get that on-screen, too.

Tim, our lighting and security technician, has turned on the studio lights and placed them in the right position for shooting the weather report. He then grabs one of the official navy blue WGST blazers and hands it to Julie. She is now standing off to the side of the studio, in front of a green backdrop. This allows us to "chroma key" the image of the newspaper's weather map behind her. We have chroma keyed many different backdrops for many different stories during our first year. Some favorites included putting a student's head in the middle of a doughnut for a story on Krispy Kremes and having another student inside a coffee cup for a story on a man who was trying to go to every Starbucks in the world. Our cameraperson, Scott, makes sure we have a good shot of Julie with Camera Two. Then, Scott goes over to Camera One to check how the morning newspaper—propped on the easel—looks.

Back in the control room, I'm working with that day's video switcher, Greg, to make sure our chroma key is set up properly. The image of the newspaper is perfect behind the meteorologist. Joe is now in there with me, working with our audio mixer, Catherine, to make sure we've got the microphone on in the studio and running through our audio board.

With all systems go, we do one rehearsal with everyone in place. Tim, fulfilling the "security" part of his title, goes out in the hall to stop anyone from coming in or making noise while we tape. We hit "record" on our main VCR and signal Lindsay, the student director, who's standing by in the studio. She counts down from 5 (silent after "3") and then Julie is on. We normally need only one take. Julie does well and we pop the tape out, checking it to make sure we've got both picture and sound (from time to time, something will go wrong). We've got it—the weather report is all done, ready for broadcast in a few minutes.

The second big movement now occurs. Tim comes back from the hall and adjusts the studio lights so that they're facing our news desk. Grace, Will, and Austin get their blazers from Tim and get ready to practice the script. Scott moves the cameras so that Camera One now has a nice shot of the kids at the anchor desk. Camera Two is zoomed in on the American flag that hangs on a separate backdrop. Austin has brought in a picture to go with his story, so that gets placed on the easel. After the Pledge of Allegiance, Scott will have to switch Camera Two's shot from the flag to the picture on the easel. He practices a few times and gets a thumbs-up from the control room when he's got it down pat.

Madeline, working the teleprompter, gets the day's script cued up and ready to go. I make sure the weather report, in VCR C, and the opening and closing montages, in VCR D, are cued up. At this point, our news anchors normally need only one run-through. Grace, even though she doesn't have a news story, has a mouthful to say. She starts off the show, leads us in the Pledge of Allegiance, and "throws it" to the meteorologist. After the tape of the weather has played, Will thanks Julie for the weather report and then reads his news story. He then sends it to Austin for his special report. Scott has framed a nice shot of Austin's picture on the easel and Greg switches to it while Austin reads.

After that, it's back to Grace. Since it's a Wednesday, she now announces the "Wednesday Word of the Day." This word is sometimes submitted by our "viewers" and is sometimes selected by Joe and me or other teachers. Today, however, in honor of Noah Webster's birthday, our school librarian has suggested *dictionary*. For the Word of the Day, our anchor will define the word, describe part of its origin, and then ask a multiple choice question about it for our audience.

Today, the question asks which state Webster was born in. After Grace reads the four choices, Catherine, on the audio board, mutes the studio mike and turns on the CD player line, where Joe has the *Who Wants to Be a Millionaire* music cued up. The four answer choices, on the screen, are slowly removed until only the correct one remains. Catherine turns off the CD, puts the mike back on, Madeline advances the teleprompter (which had been on hold as the music played), and Grace continues. After the Word of the Day, Will announces the names of the two students who are celebrating their birthdays that day—a first grader and a fourth grader. We put the names on the screen and play birthday music in the background. Catherine keeps the studio mike on, but boosts the CD line so that we can hear Will reading the name and the birthday song at the same time. Austin makes an announcement about that day's student council meeting and then Grace closes the show.

Rehearsals have finished and now we're about ready to do it for real. Will has a tough name to pronounce on the birthday list, so we make him repeat it a few times until it sounds right. Out goes Tim to monitor the hallway; we pop the master tape into the VCR and get ready. I've got all the tapes cued, Joe's got the CG ready, and everyone else checks in to say they're ready to go. I hit "record" and then cue Catherine to turn on the audio for VCR D, where the opening montage is located, and I have Greg go to VCR D on the video switcher. The opening music plays and we're under way.

The kids, as always, do a marvelous job. Grace, Will, and Austin read fluently, and the teleprompter keeps up with them pretty well. Lindsay, the student director, cues the anchors at all the proper spots. Greg is on top of everything, deftly switching between the four video sources—our two cameras and our two VCRs. Catherine is just as swift with the four audio sources. The show goes smoothly, the end credits roll, the closing music fades out, and we stop recording.

We check the tape just to be sure it recorded all right. This time, it did. Most days are like that. A few times, we've actually forgotten to record the show! Or, we've gotten sound and a jumpy picture. With the show "in the can" at 8:27 and set to air at 8:40, we're in great shape. Tim turns off the lights, Scott turns off the camera, the WGST blazers get returned to their spots, and we send the kids off. We tell them they did a great job and look forward to seeing them the next morning, when they'll each have a new job and a new role in our crew. We're sure to remind everyone to be at the studio at 8:00 and that the meteorologist, Anchor Two, and special reporter need to have stories ready to go. They head up to their classrooms, which will officially open at 8:30, and get ready to watch their work at 8:40.

There are many things about WGST that have made this ongoing project a worthwhile experience for students, teachers, and the whole school. First of all, the kids care so much about it. They're excited when it's their turn to come down at

8:00 every morning for a week. They enjoy writing stories and doing the more technical jobs. Of course, they love to watch themselves on TV. It's thrilling to walk down the halls of our school at 8:40 and hear the show's theme music blasting out of every room. It's exciting to hear the kids root for their answer choice with the Wednesday Word of the Day. It's satisfying to hear the kids cheer when their name is announced as part of the WGST crew for the next week, as we do every Thursday. You can see the smiles on the faces of children as their birthday (or half-birthday for many of our June, July, and August birthdays) is announced and their classmates break into applause.

We strive to give the students as full an experience as possible. In our first full year of running the studio, each fourth grader was able to work for three weeks in the studio, crewing the news from September to March. Then, a small group of fourth graders who've proved especially responsible, patient, and helpful are chosen as mentors. These mentors help out the third graders, who take over the WGST controls from spring break until summer vacation.

WGST transcends the morning announcements and has not only become a part of our school's life, but also has created even more community among us. It's something we share, as a school, as a student body, as a faculty. Many parents gather together every morning to watch the broadcast. On days when their child is on the air, they head to the classroom to watch it with them. Students from all grade levels can be seen in the opening and closing montages, which are shot and changed every three to four weeks. We often see first and second graders on the playground acting out their own WGST news shows, using some of the familiar tag lines they hear on the morning news.

We'll shoot "special reports" around the school, when the kindergarten is doing a play, the second grade is in the Star Lab, or the third grade is hosting a Medieval Fair. We've had special guests down in the studio—teachers popping in to make a special announcement or just a fun surprise appearance. Needless to say, we always present a funny and spooky Halloween episode. A great highlight from last year was when ABC news anchor Peter Jennings made a taped appearance on our show, complimenting the WGST team for its broadcasting skills!

WGST is now a fully integrated part of our school—something unique and special. In under two years' time, WGST (which stands for "World's Greatest School Television"—we're nothing if not modest) went from a pie in the sky idea to a regular, daily program that begins every school day and has already logged over 220 episodes. Countless parents have sought us out to say how wonderful they think it is and how good it has been for their kids. The studio has done amazing things for kids who normally refuse to write, who are afraid to get up in front of their classmates, or who have trouble reading or writing. No matter who the child is or what he or she may struggle with, *everyone* shines when they're down in the studio.

That, right there, is why we do it. As teachers, Joe and I strive every day to provide our students with meaningful, memorable learning experiences. WGST has proven to be an amazing venue for us and for the students. Talk about an authentic experience! It would be one thing for students to learn *how* a TV show is put together. Interesting? Maybe. Memorable? Probably not. But, put them *in a real studio*, give them the tools to work with, and watch them create a TV show—that's learning. That's educational. Valuable. Memorable.

"That's all the news for today. Be sure to tune in tomorrow morning for our next broadcast. On behalf of Will, Austin, Julie, and everyone else here at WGST, have a wonderful Wednesday!"

A River of Miracles by Waters School

PETE LEKI

In the city, standing on a school playground carpeted with black asphalt, it's hard to picture the wetlands of the Chicago River that used to linger and sprawl here, under what is now the foundation of Waters Elementary School. Hard to picture cormorants and herons nesting in the reeds; bears foraging the shallows for spawning sturgeon; wolves, elk, and buffalo searching among the little blue stem grasses for a place to nap under the broad canopy of savanna oaks; and the music and prattle of human voices coming from the camps and villages of the Illinois and Potawatomi peoples for whom these grounds were sacred.

This was my son's school. It was my neighborhood. I chaired the Local School Council. I had taken a leave of absence from my job as a water plant operator to finish up a long dormant college degree in interdisciplinary studies, ecology, education, and neighborhood studies. In the winter of 1994, I asked seventh graders at Waters to share their perceptions of and experiences on the Chicago River, which runs through our neighborhood. I asked them to ask their parents for river memories from their own youths and homelands. The students jotted down several possible ideas for stories and finally selected one to work on. I visited their classrooms once a week over about a six-week period, and sat with them in the hall, conferencing on their drafts. The students seemed to enjoy the one-on-one conferencing as much as I did. They read their work to me. Although the quality varied widely, every story had some unique charm to it. April wrote two pieces, one softly poetic with an eerie edge to it. This companion piece, an interview with her father, is staccato, Chicago, a historic artifact:

Stinky Hole
by April Weisgerber
AW: Where did you grow up at?
WW: Armitage and Seminary.
AW: Where did you hang out at?
WW: Adam's Park.
AW: Did you ever hang out at a river?
WW: Yes.
AW: What was its name?
WW: The Chicago River.
AW: What other name did you call it?
WW: The Stinky Hole.
AW: What did you used to do down there?
WW: Sit and have a couple of beers.
AW: What kind of beer?
WW: Budweiser.
AW: Do you remember anything in or around the river?
WW: Around there was a paint factory on Cortland. There was a tire fac-
       tory on Cortland and Southport. And a shrimp house on Cortland
       and Southport on the opposite side. And that's still standing now
       till this day.
AW: Did you ever see any animals?
WW: Rats and birds.

Peaches was a big girl, always smiling and eating candy. She struggled with her
piece. In the end we decided to format it as a poem, full of redundant longing:

So Nice Over There (Eight Mile Rock, Bahamas)
by Peaches Rahming
The sea is so nice over in the Bahamas.
I wish I was there now.
There is nothing in the water.
Nothing.
It is so blue, it looks like the sky.
There is all kind of fish and nice stuff.
Like the pearl conch shell.
It is so nice.
The sand is so nice over in the Bahamas.
The people is so nice over there.
There is no pollution in the water.

I love over there.

That's why I wish I was over there now.

Valeria, a small, quiet girl, surprised me with this vivid piece:

Piranas Came (Michoacan, Mexico)
by Valeria Guiterrez

One day we went to the river and there were other people at the river. And the people there were in the water. And the paranas came where the people were. And the paranas eat the people. And it was so ugly because they take the people's eyes and fingers. The people were crying and yelling for help. And the police came and the people were with blood and so disgusting and were ugly. My family went to the car and brought our stuff back and went to the other river. But the paranas were there too, eating other people. So we went to help the people get out of the water.

Santos was just learning English and had a learning disorder as well. But he shared a real piece of life with us. Notice the pattern of word repetition: *river* in the first paragraph, *mother* in the second:

Washing Clothes (Cuspala, Mexico)
by Santos Covarrubias

My mother washed the clothes in the river. Me and my friends played in the river. The river was in the back of my house. The river was clean. There were rocks in the river. I could walk to the river. I went to the river almost every day. The river was in Cuspala, Mexico. I took a bath in the river.

My mother goes there when she is mad. She was mad because her mother screamed at her. Her mother was mad at my mother because she didn't like her cleaning. That's why my mother went to the river.

Once we were satisfied with the text, we copyedited and I entered the stories into the computer. We asked the students to illustrate their stories or to bring in photographs. I showed them photos from the Ravenswood historical archives of the river in our neighborhood. We looked for their rivers on maps, in atlases, on globes.

Later on, with the help of the Chicago Teachers Center, the collection was published as *Sipi*, the Algonquian word for *river*. The book is anchored in our little stretch of the Chicago River, which the native peoples called the Stinking Onion River, but it branches and commingles with waters from around the planet, the headwaters of our community.

The goal of this volume was to introduce our stories, our rivers, and our lives to one another. The river represents the natural world, its diversity and bounty. The clear flowing stream stories told by some of our writers help us to envision our own river, restored and healthy. This is the birthright of every child: to drink, swim, fish, and meditate in clear waters along with all of creation.

I would like to say that the best time to go to the river is to get anger out and think. It's the best place to be alone. I go there when I'm mad. Like when me and my Dad would get into a fight I would just blow it off. Instead of taking it out on my loved ones, I would go down to the river and let the sunshine and the wind soothe my mind and soul. I go there to think. Though it's all dirty and messed up, I think it's a beautiful place. I could get my anger out just by looking at the green water. It looks like my Dad. It's peaceful and wonderful.
by April Weisgerber

The Beginning of Time
by Jerry Caldwell
The river was from the beginning of time
It is so muddy and mucky
But it is so beautiful in so much time
Thou shalt think the true beauty of it
is the parasites, bugs, and slime.

All these things I've told you, happened in the river. Me and my family all thought that there was something bad about that river. So we decided to get out of that river. We were on our way out of the river, to another pool, when we saw a sign in the sand close, like two feet away from the river. We read the sign. It said River of Miracles.
by Janet Pineda

Once we started telling river stories, we were hooked. Our curiosity about the river inevitably connected us up with the Friends of the Chicago River, an advocacy group just gearing up for elementary school outreach work. Friends took members of our staff and a group of teachers from Amundsen High School (the local environmentally focused high school most of our graduates attend) on a walking tour of the river in our neighborhood. A trio of teachers—in art, journalism, and biology—invited me to work on river writing with their high school students. The artwork of one high school student, Davy Bulba, depicting the history of the river, was used to illustrate *Sipi*.

Friends of the Chicago River put us in contact with the Illinois Rivers Project, which coordinates a statewide interdisciplinary river study and protection effort at the high school level. They publish a yearly collection of student writing from the Mississippi watershed called *Meanderings*. The Chicago Academy of Sciences also looked to the school for a partnership as it opened its Water Wonder exhibit that spring. Along with the Friends of the Chicago River, they were networking with agencies, advocacy groups, and schools to do watershed protection and organize summer conferences to develop an elementary school rivers studies curriculum.

The Nature Conservancy's Mighty Acorns project, a joint venture with the Cook County Forest Preserves, came to us like some fairy godmother and offered to take classrooms of students out to prairie restoration sites (five students to one Acorn volunteer), to explore, learn, and perform stewardship tasks like pulling weeds, cutting brush, and collecting seed. Jullietta Thornton, an art consultant hired by the school, received a grant to try out her Potawatomi project, a hands-on study of native plants, wigwams, dream catchers, medicine pouches, and our ancestor people who lived here for centuries.

Finally, the governmental agency charged with control of the Chicago River system, the Metropolitan Water Reclamation District, answered our inquiries about support and cooperation by saying, "This is the phone call we've been waiting for." At a get-acquainted meeting we discussed the whole realm of possibilities for river exploration and study at the middle school level: water quality monitoring and testing on their barge-lab, fish surveys, river trips to scout out illegal dumping, and neighborhood campaigns to stop the disposal of oil, toxins, and antifreeze in street sewers.

Since then we've written and received grants from the City's Urban Greening program to re-create a savanna oak community at the south end of our school ground, an area that somehow escaped entombment in asphalt. Our newly made log circle is in place for storytelling. Raised planting beds arranged in two circles are reserved, one for each class, another set for families. This sacred space makes it easier for teachers to access nature. The beauty and vigor of the place has discouraged vandalism.

So the river theme was only the beginning of a vision of land and community-based learning. It seemed to me that the river and the nearby prairie lands were calling out to our school for a meeting. We were lucky to have such a rich place to study history, ecology, social issues, math, and science. We seemed blessed to have nearby resource institutions ready and willing to offer staff development and technical and material resources to our faculty. Waters Local School Council embraced this opportunity for community-based, experiential, meaningful, hands-on learning. Our marriage to the river and prairie were officially written into our school improvement plan.

But that doesn't mean teachers could immediately implement programs and use all the resources offered. Sometimes we construct enormous possibilities in our minds, while the people who have the responsibility of carrying them out are busy thrashing through the big and small traumas of daily school life in the city and the cascades of changes brought on by citywide reform and local/neighborhood politics.

But the call seemed too strong to ignore. We in the council were slowly learning the importance of focusing on a few changes at a time: to allow change itself necessitates adequate time and resources and an honorable title in school renewal. Our link-up with the Best Practice network of the Center for City Schools has convinced me of the primacy of the process. The power of Best Practice methods for teaching, writing, and reading are modeled in staff and parent development sessions. Reading and writing workshop formats and collaborative experiences allow students, parents, and staff time to discover themselves, the person next to them, their community, and their place in the world.

I know that rivers and prairies will have a place in that discovery because they are speaking to us so clearly and insistently. The mighty bur oaks that guard the south end of the playground, the night heron cruising over the river against the western sky, the rogue carp thrashing and spawning in the weedy shallows. Discovering, maybe inventing, our community is the reason I came to Waters with my son Jamal in the first place.

> Then, later on, we were sitting in the dry dirt, our butts were crushing some leaves. One of my friends told us to "Look. Look at the seagull." It took me a few seconds to realize that the seagull held a fish in its claw. Then it dropped it. Another seagull swooped down and stole the floating fish. I was so surprised. I didn't know that these birds hunted. I thought they just eat junk food that we litter on the streets and sidewalks.
> *by Albert Vo*

> Q: How did the Mississippi affect your thinking pattern?
> A: It didn't really have much effect on me other than when looking into the water I seemed to be able to think more clearly.
> *by Vincent Crowder*

Spending some time with the children in their classrooms, producing this modest but beautiful piece of community self-reflection, our book, called *Sipi*, is both process and end all in one.

The Dance of Mitosis

KIM LUBEKE

One reason I love teaching biology is that it lends itself to great hands-on activities that incorporate art. Before I became a teacher, I was a medical illustrator, and I know the power of art to bring ideas to life. In my classroom, students draw time lines that stretch across the room while they investigate man's relationship to time. They design Eco-Trails outside the school when they study small animals and plants indigenous to our area of Illinois. And when we study cell division, they learn and practice the mitosis dance. Here is the lesson that makes sure students understand and can represent mitosis, the process of cell division, using the performing arts. My students learn about mitosis by dancing to learn.

Introduction
In this activity, students will transform themselves into various intercellular organelles and walk through the stages of mitosis.

Objectives
At the end of the lesson students should have a basic understanding of

- vocabulary terms used in mitosis
- the stages of mitosis
- the chronology of the stages
- events that occur in each stage.

Previous Knowledge
Students should be familiar with the organelles listed below and their functions.

- Cell membrane
- Cytoplasm
- Nucleus
- Nuclear membrane
- Chromosome
- Duplicated chromosome
- Centromere
- Spindle fiber
- Centrioles

Materials
This list is geared for twenty-four students. If you have more or fewer than twenty-four, add to or subtract from the cell membrane group.

1. Mitosis name tags (one per student)
   - sixteen cell membrane name tags
   - three chromosome name tags (one red, one blue, and one yellow)
   - three duplicated chromosome name tags (one red, one blue, and one yellow)
   - one centriole name tag
   - one duplicated centriole name tag
2. Twenty-four safety pins (to fasten name tags)
3. Six pieces of rope approximately five feet in length (jump ropes work well)
4. Overhead projector with transparencies of mitosis (optional)

Preparation

You will need a large open space. If you plan to perform this in the classroom, then you will need to push all the desks to the perimeter of the room. If possible, perform this in an alternate setting, such as an auditorium. If weather permits, this could be performed outside on the school's lawn. If the dance is performed in the classroom, have an illustration of each mitotic stage projected on the overhead. Students can then refer to this as they move through the various stages.

Procedure

Distribute one name tag to each student and have them fasten it on. You may want to give any student(s) who will have difficulties following along a cell membrane name tag (there are fewer steps involved). The following procedures are organized by the various mitotic stages (see Figure 3.1).

Interphase Have the three students who are wearing the "chromosome" name tags form a huddle in the middle of the classroom. This huddle formation represents chromosomes located in the nucleus. Have the student wearing the "centriole" name tag stand a few feet away.

Next, have the students who are wearing the "cell membrane" name tags stand in a circle formation around the chromosomes and centriole. The students who represent the cell membrane should hold hands and spread out. Make this circle as large as possible. The "dance" is going to take place inside the circle. The student wearing the centriole name tag may wander freely around the cell in the cytoplasm. The class is now ready to begin the mitosis dance.

The first event in the process of mitosis is the duplication of materials required for cell division. Have the students wearing the "duplicated chromosome" name tags walk inside the cell and stand next to the student who is wearing the same-color chromosome name tag. Each colored pair (red, blue, and yellow) now rep-

Figure 3.1: Stages of cell division acted out in mitosis dance.

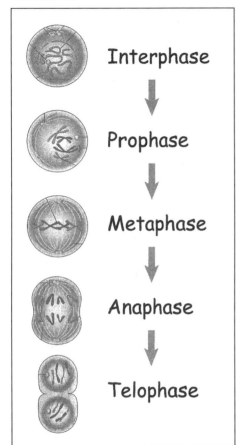

resents a "doubled chromosome." All six of these students should be standing in a tight huddle formation in the middle of the cell that represents the nucleus. Next, the student wearing the "duplicated centriole" should stand next to the centriole in the cytoplasm.

Prophase During this stage, each centriole should begin to migrate toward opposite ends of the cell. Late in prophase, the nuclear membrane lysis open. The doubled chromosomes (colored pairs) may spread out a little to signify the breakdown of the nuclear membrane. Students in a doubled chromosome formation should stand with their backs to each other and face the centriole at the poles. At this time, hand each centriole three jump ropes. Have them hold the jump ropes at one end only. Take the opposite end of each rope and hand it to a student in a doubled chromosome. These jump ropes represent the spindle fibers.

Metaphase At this time, the six students representing doubled chromosomes (still with their backs to each other and paired by color) should line up in the middle of the cell at the metaphase plate. A red, blue, and yellow chromosome should be facing a centriole at the pole. The centriole should be holding on to the ends of three ropes. Meanwhile, the chromosomes facing the centriole should be holding on to the opposite end of the ropes. This formation should be mirrored in the other half of the cell. Now, the spindle formation is complete.

Anaphase The centrioles should begin to pull on the ropes, slowly causing the doubled chromosomes to separate and move toward the poles of the cell (near the centrioles).

Telophase The chromosomes are now separate and near the poles. The students who represent the cell membrane located near the middle of the cell (where the metaphase plate was located) should start to walk inward. Have them walk inward until students from opposite sides of the cell meet. Then, split them up. Half the students should form the cell membrane for one new cell while the other half form the cell membrane for the other new cell. Mitosis is complete! Where there was one cell, there are now two separate but identical cells. Each cell should contain the same organelles. One cell should contain three chromosomes (red, blue, and yellow) and a centriole. The other cell has the duplicated chromosomes and centriole.

Other Possible Activities

In addition to the choreographed dance, students can perform related activities: they can create a flip book or a storyboard, where each cell includes a different step in the cell division process.

■ ■ ■

Not only have I done this activity with kids, but I have also taught this lesson to other teachers. Just like the students, teachers put on their name tags and walk through the dance from interphase through cytokinesis or telophase. My colleagues report that they had never understood mitosis in such a basic, organic way until they did the mitosis dance for themselves.

Jotting and Sketching: Twenty-Three Ways to Use a Notebook

HARVEY DANIELS

Old-time, pre–Best Practice schooling emphasized the *reception* of ideas. Teachers told, delivered, explained, lectured, presented, demonstrated, and talked. The job of students, by and large, was to receive, hear, listen, watch, catch, or somehow absorb ideas teachers expressed. Education embodied the popular T-shirt slogan: "Don't just do something—sit there!" Not uncommonly, school days consisted of a nonstop stream of teacher expression and student reception. Of course, the process of student reception was notoriously imperfect, leading to endless control battles and elaborate punishment/reward systems of extrinsic motivation.

Today, modern learning theory, the mandates of subject matter experts, and common sense tell us how backward this paradigm was. Students, not just teachers, need to express ideas, act on information and knowledge, and construct meaning. Passivity isn't wrong just because it's boring; it is wrong because it doesn't work. All the major learning theories—behaviorism, information-processing, cognitivism—agree: for learners to internalize ideas, they must act upon them. Knowledge cannot remain external, inert, untouched. Learners must do something with information: connect it, draw it, weigh it, dance it, manipulate it. They need to grab ideas by the throat and demand that they make sense.

Happily, there are plenty of writing and drawing activities that can help students to engage and explore subject matter in just this way. The best of these activities translate across subject fields and grade levels, helping students to move into, through, and beyond the content of the curriculum. In a moment, we'll review an inventory of twenty-three such activities. But first, a bit of definition. We want to be clear that journaling or notebook activities are different from genre writing and formal art assignments in several important ways. Here are eight key contrasts:

spontaneous versus planned
short versus lengthy
exploratory versus authoritative
expressive versus transactional
informal versus formal
personal versus audience-centered
unedited versus polished
ungraded versus graded

Journaling or notebooking involves short, spontaneous, exploratory writings, often done amid or between other activities. This form of representing is tool-like: we use jotting or sketching as a device that organizes, channels, and gives extra leverage to thinking. These thinking tools work best when students can be informal, tentative, colloquial, loose, and personal; when experimentation and risk taking are invited; when the demands for revising and the risks of grading are eliminated; and when the products are frequently *used* in class, as contributions to an ongoing exploration of content.

We stress these contrasts to make it clear that the two types of representing-to-learn—journaling and genres—are quite different, though equally important. Elsewhere in this book we honor the value and importance of students' producing artworks and writings that are carefully planned, substantial, and polished; products that speak effectively to others, that observe the conventions of their genre, and that are ready to compete in the public arena of ideas. For now, though, we are talking about another category of representing—much more personal and transient—that is also vital to the development of powerful thinkers.

Sample Activities

1. *Start-Up or Warm-Up.* The first three to five minutes of class time each day are regularly set aside for students to do a quick segment of writing on the topic of the

upcoming lesson. This can be the same question each day (reflections on my reading, questions I have this morning, highlights from the homework, etc.) or may be in response to a specific daily question or quote put on the board by the teacher. This activity works especially well to begin a class, since it causes students to break social contact, look down at their writing, tune in to the lesson, gather thoughts, and get centered. The "investment" of a few minutes of class time helps students clear their minds of previous issues, activate their prior knowledge, and prepare to join in the upcoming topic.

2. *Freewriting.* In "focused freewriting," students simply write as fast as they can on a given topic for two to three minutes, to tune in to what they know, to surface their knowledge. The teacher's instructions must expressly invite sentences, phrases, notes, jottings—whatever helps you to get thoughts down quickly. Because the goal of freewriting is spontaneous, quick jottings, teachers are careful not to say, "Write a paragraph." For many kids, that command is rooted in detached, unengaged writing. This and the next three activities are variants of brainstorming that are especially useful for introducing new topics or units.

3. *Listing or List-Storming.* This is the written version of brainstorming. Here, the student quickly jots a list of words or phrases reflecting whatever they know—or think they know—about a given subject, without editing or second-guessing themselves. Later, lists can be used in many ways: pairs or teams can compare and discuss their lists, frequency tallies for certain items can be totaled and announced, and so on.

4. *Fact/Values Lists.* When a new topic with a strong values dimension (e.g., AIDS, nuclear war, slavery) is being introduced, students begin by making two lists side by side: on the left, facts about the topic, and on the right, attitudes, beliefs, values, or opinions they have about it. As the lesson proceeds, students can validate their facts and explore their values.

5. *K-W-L.* When a topic is being introduced and investigated, students make and use three lists that guide the inquiry. At the start of the unit, each kid divides a piece of paper into three columns, sideways (see Figure 3.2). In the left column, each student lists all the things they *K*now, or think they know, about the topic. Then these are shared aloud and a whole-group list of "Knows" is compiled. Next, in the middle column, everyone writes down some things they *W*ant to know. Then these are shared aloud and a whole-group list of "Want to Knows" is also compiled. Then the class pursues its questions as the unit unfolds. Toward the end of the unit (perhaps days later) kids return to fill in their third columns with things

Figure 3.2: One student's K-W-L brainstorming on the topic of taxation.

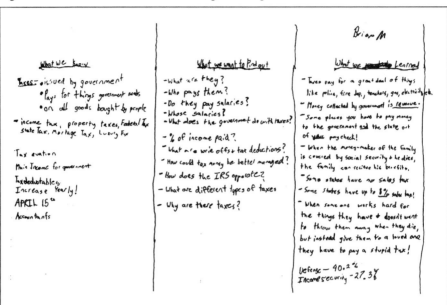

they *Learned*, and these are again the subject of a wider class discussion and review (Ogle 1986). (For a full description of this highly powerful and expandable strategy, see pages 63–71.)

6. *Graphic Responses.* Drawing and writing are branches of the same cognitive tree, and for many students the graphic mode better fits their learning style. There's always room for doodling ideas, cartooning the subject being studied, making sketches, maps, or diagrams of important concepts. Below are a batch of graphic/drawing strategies, all of which combine words with pictures.

> *Clustering:* A special form of representing-to-learn using a kind of right-brained outlining developed by Gabrielle Rico in *Writing the Natural Way* (1985). Students put a key concept, term, or name in a circle at the center of a page and then free-associate, jotting down all the words that occur to them in circles arrayed around the kernel term, in whatever pattern "seems right" (see Figure 3.3). Often, clustering reveals unrecognized connections and relationships, and is great for surfacing prior knowledge or recollecting "lost" information.

> *Semantic Maps:* Maps or diagrams of ideas that help us to remember terms, concepts, ingredients, or relationships. These maps help kids to chart

Figure 3.3: Clustering can help students to map and remember key concepts.

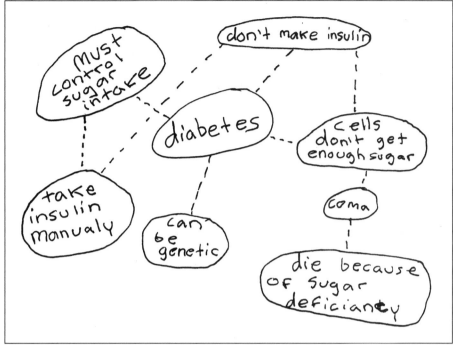

content or knowledge in order to plug it into their brain, or memorize it. Clustering is helpful for retrieving the map later on.

Story Maps: Diagrams or maps of the events in a story or narrative, often done chronologically. This can apply to both literature and to historical narrative.

Venn Diagrams: When subjects—books, concepts, people, countries, and so on—have certain attributes that are *alike* and others that are *different*, kids can use two or three interlocking circles to display the contrasts and similarities.

Time Lines: Another familiar combination of graphics and writing, applied to chronology. Works best when cartoons or other illustrations are added.

Drawing/Sketching: This is the graphic equivalent of freewriting. Students do original drawings to illustrate ideas found in their reading, discussion, and inquiry. Drawing can be used to probe passages or quotations in reading materials, and labels or captions can be mixed with lines and forms (see Figure 3.4).

Figure 3.4: Drawing helps students visualize ideas, even in Latin class.

Cartoons: Another combination of words and drawings, cartooning can either be a quick response or a fine-art form, depending on the time devoted to it. This can be a key strategy to help get reluctant writers to put words on a page—in balloons or captions.

Mindmapping: This raises the idea of mapping to the level of art. The principle: if you really want to remember something—like a set of terminologies or a complex concept—it helps to make a careful, craftsmanlike, artful illustration of it. This strategy can involve considerable time making a unique and personal map.

7. *Written Conversation/Dialogue Journals.* Legalize note passing (hey, the kids are doing it anyway) and bring it into your curriculum. When students talk infor-

mally in writing about course content with the teacher and/or other students, it provides a private, two-way channel of communication, and invites an exchange of information about both academic and interpersonal issues. If written conversation is to stand alone as a regular class activity, the teacher will have to make significant efforts to institutionalize it (perhaps by initiating the first notes, by installing a mailbox, by doing much modeling, and by responding promptly and fully, etc.). As this gets to be a regular activity, it blends into learning logs (see below). Either the teacher or another student must respond to each letter/entry; Post-it notes limit the burden and also save the surface of students' work from markings.

8. *Learning Logs.* Learning logs could appear anywhere on the list, and in a sense are the natural culmination of doing lots of notebooking/journaling activities. You've got to save all this stuff somewhere! As teachers become committed to journaling, they want to make it an official, regular, consistent, and predictable part of their courses. They also need a place for students to store all their drawings, lists, clusters, admit slips, and freewrites. Many teachers have formalized this approach by asking each student to keep a continuous notebook or learning log throughout the class. While some specific topics may be set by the teacher, the essential idea is for students to be making regular journal entries on a variety of class-related topics—three, four, or five entries per week, some in school and some at home. This document becomes a special place where the subject-matter learning of the course is both accomplished and reflected on. We prefer a loose-leaf format, so that students can remove and share one entry without having to hand over their whole spiral notebook to someone else. Index cards, admit slips, and any other odd-sized entries can simply be pasted or stapled on a loose-leaf page and added to the notebook.

9. *Exit Slips.* Instead of teaching "bell to bell," teachers save the last three to five minutes of class for students to do a short piece of writing or drawing representing their response, summary, or questions about the day's session. The teacher may collect and study these herself, and use them to plan future lessons. Exit slips can be a great diagnostic tool for the teacher, and a natural source of quick-review highlights during the next class—the teacher can read a few sample exit slips from the previous day aloud (without names, probably) to commence the lesson.

10. *Admit Slips.* Upon entering class, students hand over their "tickets of admission"—short writings on a preassigned topic, such as three suggested discussion questions for today's class, a sketch of a character or historical figure appearing in our reading, or a summary of the previous night's reading assignment. To begin class, the teacher may share some or all (with or without names attached), or admit

Figure 3.5: Admit slips are used at the beginning of class to start discussion or group work.

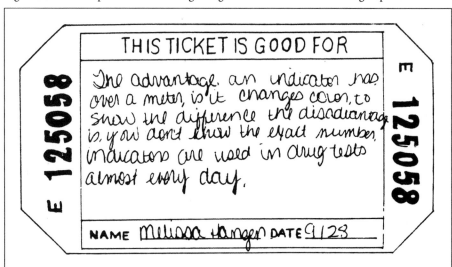

THIS TICKET IS GOOD FOR

The advantage an indicator has over a meter, is it changes color, to show the difference the disadvantage is, you don't know the exact number, indicators are used in drug tests almost every day.

NAME Melissa Hangen DATE 9/23

E 125058

E 125058

slips may be passed out randomly among students to be discussed in pairs or groups (see Figure 3.5).

11. *"Stop-n-Write."* Too often in presentations, teachers feel a need to plunge on and "cover the material," when in fact, students would benefit greatly from an occasional pause for them to reflect on their thoughts. Some possible focusing suggestions: what I'm thinking right now; what I grasp up to this moment; questions that are bugging me. This pausing to draw or write provides kids a chance to consolidate what's been learned so far and prepare to go on (see Figure 3.6).

12. *Poetry.* Many different genres of verse are adaptable to quick-draft or content-area writing: haiku, limericks, bio poems, diamantes, and the like. The ones with simple and clear-cut formulas seem to work best.

13. *Dialogues.* A good way to ensure that students grasp both sides of complex issues is to have them write dramatic dialogues between opposing characters, personages, historical figures, points of view, scientific traditions, and so on, giving students practice articulating ideas with two sides or varied interpretations.

14. *"Faction."* Students can create a piece of fiction that depends upon a solid understanding of facts studied in a course. Examples: writing imaginary scenes from history or from novels. You cannot create a "missing chapter" of *Huckleberry Finn* or write plausible corridor gossip from the Constitutional Convention unless

Figure 3.6: When teachers give students time to stop and write, they can reflect, consolidate, and predict.

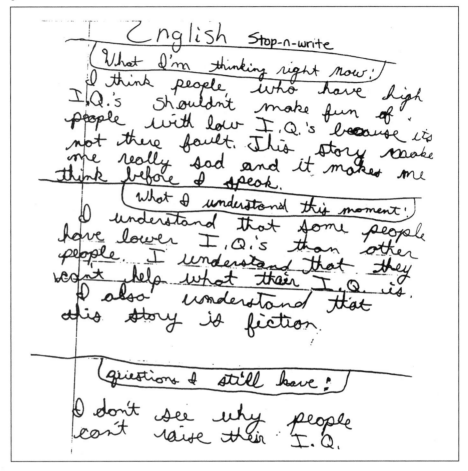

you know the material. Roving reporters can interview Pythagoras, Madam Curie, Hitler, and so on. All these "factions" invite illustration, of course.

15. *Definitions.* Sometimes it is valuable to focus on certain key words in vocabulary-heavy content areas. Some basic approaches: freewriting on the key word or key term; predicting definitions of the central vocabulary of a lesson; drawing with concrete poetry using key words from the subject matter.

16. *Paraphrases.* Paraphrasing means writing precise summaries of key ideas, concepts, procedures, processes, events, quotations, demonstrations, or scenes. Yes, you can even have kids write summaries of textbook sections. Though this activity is drier than others, it can be more palatable if done in pairs or teams rather

Figure 3.7: Even paraphrasing the textbook can be energizing when your personal cartoon character speaks for you.

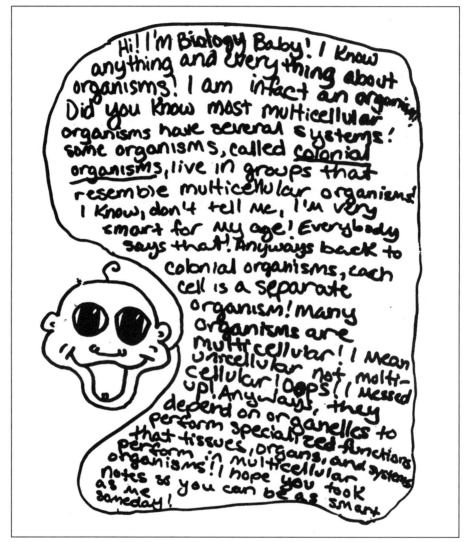

than solo. The "side talk" that goes on while kids try to boil a chunk of text down to its elements is often worthwhile. One of our teacher friends has each student create their own cartoon character (e.g., "Biology Baby") who "writes" each summary (see Figure 3.7).

17. *Predictions.* The teacher stops students at a key point in a reading, an activity, or a lecture and invites them to quickly write or draw what they think will happen next, and then discuss their predictions in small- or whole-group settings.

Figure 3.8: Dialectic journals invite students to work problems both in mathematical symbols and everyday language.

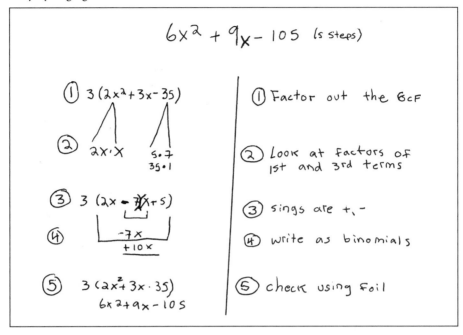

18. *Dialectics/Double-Entries.* Students divide note cards or journal pages in half, thirds, or quarters, and then use each space for a different kind of writing or drawing. In one kind of double-entry journal, the left side is used for factual note taking during reading, lecture, or activity, and the right side is used for personal reactions and questions. In mathematics, one side can be used for doing calculations and the other for explaining in words how the student attacked them. Many math teachers report that if students can explain a concept in these two languages— symbolic and English—they really grasp the ideas (see Figure 3.8).

19. *Metacognitive Analysis.* In metacognitive analysis, the student writes to describe her or his own thinking process in the subject, perhaps until difficulties are encountered—for example, showing how a math problem is tackled and worked through up to the point where the student becomes stumped. One teacher we know gives full credit if the student can explain clearly in prose "what I would need to be able to do to complete this problem successfully."

20. *Instructions/Directions.* The "how-to" is one of the most primitive and inherently engaging forms of writing. Classroom possibilities: how to conduct a science experiment, how to build a birdhouse, how to hem a skirt, how to plan a battle

strategy, how to solve a quadratic equation. Notice the natural audience possibilities. A realistic performance assessment would be: can a reader do this task, based upon the instructions given?

21. *Observation Reports.* Science labs have always offered a special and valuable kind of composing experience: reporting data from the close observation of physical objects, processes, phenomena, and events. This sort of writing can be extended to data gathering and observational reports in a number of other subject areas and formats. Social observation (ethnography) and interviewing are subtypes useful in social studies classes, for example.

22. *Class Minutes.* One student is elected (or serves on a rotating schedule) as minutes taker for each daily class session, and must produce a set of official "minutes" by the following class. Minutes are either posted in a regular spot or are copied for distribution to the group. Reading and amending these minutes provides an excellent focusing activity for the start of each day's class; having everyone's captive attention gives each student author a chance to shine. In practice, authors usually try to infuse the minutes with as much personality as accuracy will permit.

23. *Problems, Questions, Exercises.* OK, it's the oldest one in the book, and potentially deadly if mishandled, but . . . students can write their own discussion, study, essay, or even exam questions, mathematics word problems, or science experiments on the material being covered. This can replace dull, rote, end-of-the-chapter questions or workbook banalities with questions that students originate because *they* identify them to be worth considering.

Variations and Extensions

Any of these twenty-three activities can be made collaborative. One of the best ways to help students to externalize, verbalize, and further organize their thinking is to work with one or two other students in actually creating writings or drawings together. This may be done by pairs or small teams, and it works especially well on a quick paragraph, short observation report, or a simple diagram.

Any of these short notebook entries can be treated as rough drafts, as first steps toward longer, more polished genre writings or artworks. Sometimes we call these second echelon products "upgrades." Any piece begun in one of the above activities can be pushed toward a more formal, audience-centered product. In fact, this program of frequent, exploratory daily journaling is almost guaranteed to create an inventory of seed ideas, some of which students will be eager to develop further.

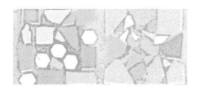  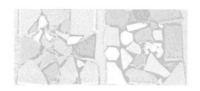

F O U R

SMALL-GROUP ACTIVITIES

The progressive paradigm of schooling has long been guided and inspired by the work of John Dewey, who argued that schools should be working, authentic communities. He emphasized the social aspects of learning and described school as a place where students should practice democracy and work together to identify and solve problems. He envisioned a curriculum in which students would bring democracy to life by making choices and teaming up to develop and carry out inquiries. Dewey emphasized the methods as well as the content of education, believing that students would learn more about themselves, about the world, and about valuable subject matter by working collaboratively with others (Dewey [1938] 1963).

It seems that the world is finally catching on to Dewey's ideas. In businesses and factories, workers who once toiled alone have been reorganized into teams, task forces, and quality circles. Across the country, corporations are flattening their organizations, offering more input, participation, decision making, and ownership to once-silenced workers. Businesses are spinning off autonomous boutique micro-companies, where, freed from the hierarchical constraints of corporate culture as usual, small creative groups think outside the box. While these nascent forms of capitalistic cooperation are obviously aimed more at the maximization of profit than at the perfecting of democracy, they also underscore one pragmatic and unromantic conclusion: small-group collaboration works.

Many American schools, on the other hand, still cling to the factory model of organization, with each worker harnessed to a solitary spot on the assembly line of education—a desk bolted to the floor. Students continue to do much of their work alone; indeed, consulting with others, in many school circumstances, is still considered to be cheating and can be severely punished. In many classrooms, learning is often limited to the memorization and practice of those ingredients called the basic skills. Well, we guess if memorization is the goal, then asking others for help may indeed be cheating. But we set an abysmally low standard of education when we reduce reading, writing, math, even thinking itself, to "skills" used mainly to memorize and regurgitate facts.

The predominance of competition in American classrooms obviously reflects our school system's role as a socioeconomic screening mechanism, which apportions rewards and opportunities to selected students on sometimes questionable pretexts. There are some complex and distasteful issues here that individual classroom teachers are unlikely to conquer or transform. But we can clearly see that putting kids in constant individual opposition is both archaic and impractical. While there may be some benefits to occasionally matching yourself *against* others, individual conquest is not the only life skill. Indeed, the world keeps telling us that young people need much more experience working *with* groups of people. Students already get plenty of dog-eat-dog contention in school; now they need more chances to work in small teams with common purposes just like most adults do every day, in their offices, hospitals, law firms, gas stations, departments, insurance agencies, grocery stores, city councils, and ad agencies.

We think collaboration is here to stay in American business and in education. Working with others is not a passing fad that will soon be out of favor. Many adults, when asked to identify their most meaningful learning experiences in school, warmly remember working with friends to address difficult problems that would have been hard to solve on their own.

Marilyn: As I look back over my very traditional education in the Chicago Public Schools, the only content that stands out in my mind are the few topics we were allowed to attack in groups. In eighth-grade math, which had very few highlights for me, we were put in groups of three, given an income, expenses, and income tax forms, and told to figure our taxes. Possibly, this experience is memorable because these kinds of semi-authentic activities were a rare burst of sunlight in my rather dreary schooling; here, we were asked to do something real and to work with others to accomplish it. This group activity enabled me to learn and understand this material deeply, to learn from and teach my classmates.

In order to understand the tax forms, compute the necessary figures, and complete the paperwork, we had to constantly talk to each other, clarifying concepts, asking questions, reviewing the directions, checking our reasoning, challenging each other's ideas. We had to externalize our thinking, get it out on the table. We had to explicitly talk through ideas that, if we were working alone, probably would have remained internal and implicit—and possibly unconsidered and wrong. Many heads really are better than one. Plenty of discussion beats solitary assumptions any time. To this day, I am the one person in my family who understands and figures out the taxes. That eighth-grade collaborative learning experience actually prepared me for a real-world task and has been valuable to me throughout my life.

When typical American grown-ups are asked to reach back into their pasts and think of something that they learned easily, in or out of school, they usually recall some kind of social-collaborative learning—a knitting circle, a basketball team, a book discussion group, a tennis club. They think of groups where they worked and practiced, where there was always someone to be coached by, where others were at different levels of proficiency, where diversity was an advantage rather than a liability, and where learners were cooperating rather than competing.

Adult citizens and business leaders aren't the only ones to recognize the value of cooperative activity. The educational standards reports issued by our major subject-matter organizations have underscored the need for teamwork and cooperation in school. Most of these documents agree that the memorization of isolated facts and skills should be replaced with attention to the intellectual processes, the major ideas and distinctive conceptions addressed. Teachers who value this kind of thinking curriculum structure their classrooms to give students time to think, problems that are worth thinking about, and other students with whom to think (Hyde and Bizar 1989). Collaboration is the mainstay of these classrooms, where small-group projects are often substituted for workbooks and worksheets, and where questions and inquiry (rather than textbooks and rote learning) become the guideposts of learning.

More and more "thinking schools" are popping up every day. In *Schools that Work* (1993), George Wood describes a number of the most promising schools and classrooms around the country—our most exciting, stimulating, and rigorous learning communities. As Wood testifies, these classrooms are easy to spot, and we all recognize them the moment we step inside. The walls are generally filled with varied examples of student artwork and writing. Books and materials are everywhere, and students are working (often noisily) around the room. And one nearly universal feature is their frequent use of collaborative, task-oriented student groups, working at the heart of the learning process, not at the periphery.

In the schools that Wood features, "it's hard to find a room with desks lined up in straight rows, presided over by a lectern and a chalkboard full of notes.

Instead, desks, or just as likely tables, are arranged in small groups throughout the room. There is a delightful sense of purposeful clutter to these classrooms and schools. They are places to do things in, not places to sit and watch" (p. xiii). Upon entering one of these settings, it is often hard to spot the teacher, who is typically sitting down, working with one or another of the small groups. Children welcome visitors and are eager to tour them through the interesting projects in which they are engaged. The classrooms are decentralized and student-centered, which is to say that students' work, very often deployed in pairs and teams, partnerships and task forces, is the center of attention.

Models of Collaboration

There are many structures for implementing cooperative, students-as-partners work in elementary and secondary schools. Some have been around American classrooms for ages, though used sparingly, while others have been devised only in the last few years. David and Roger Johnson have been the modern pioneers in this effort, offering particularly helpful structures, variations, rationales, and research findings. Whatever the vintage or source, however, all effective models of collaborative work have one thing in common: solid procedures for keeping groups productive. If a teacher is going to turn kids loose in several simultaneously meeting groups, he by definition cannot be managing and guiding everywhere at once, which means the group activities must have enough inherent structure to operate autonomously, to remain engaging, on-task, and relevant. Some of the simplest models are designed for pairs of students, while other, more complex structures help groups of three to five students work effectively together.

Partner Reading and Listening
Primary students pair up and take turns reading aloud to each other, each holding a copy of the same story or article. Whether reading or listening, kids pay close attention to the written text and can question each other's readings. In the "buddy" variation, an older child reads or writes with a younger one, modeling more grown-up strategies.

Lab Partners
In any class that involves experimenting or making, teachers can put students in pairs and give them interlocking assignments that require joint observing, writing, reading, discussion, problem solving, or making. Though lab partners are already common in science classes, too often they are filling out convergent, right-answer lab workbooks rather than genuinely exploring and constructing meaning.

Dialogue Journaling

Pairs of students engage in written conversations about the content of the curriculum, which might be a book both are reading, a scientific process they are exploring, or a historical period under study. On a regular schedule, students write and exchange notes with one another (and occasionally the teacher), carrying on a discussion that might otherwise have been done orally. Written conversations can be held during class time, so that, contrary to an out-loud discussion where most people silently await a turn that never comes, everyone "talks" at once, in writing.

Say Something

Reading highly conceptual content-area text requires that students stop at various points in their reading to demand clarity, sort out confusion, and discuss ideas, issues, and/or vocabulary. In this strategy, students are invited to read with a partner, and agree on a place to stop reading and "Say Something." At this point, the partners take just a minute to talk about what seems important, to make connections and predictions, and to react to ideas. "Say Something" helps students make sense out of difficult material and value their own thinking and insights.

Peer Response and Editing Groups

Ongoing groups of three to five students regularly meet and offer feedback, guidance, and advice to each other as fellow authors. Some peer writing groups meet regularly, while others gather only when convened by a member with a draft ready for response. Some jot comments and edits right on photocopies of classmates' drafts; others stick to verbal feedback.

Group Investigations

Multiple student-research teams investigate different aspects of a larger topic, which can be either a student interest or a curriculum mandate. The process starts when the whole class discusses, responds to, and divides up a large topic, jigsawing the pieces out to smaller task groups for investigation. This model is a direct descendant of John Dewey's, with an assist by Herbert Thelan (1967).

Literature Circles

In this school equivalent of adult book discussion groups, students choose their own books and discussion partners, set their own reading and meeting schedule, and share their reading with others. Students use structured note taking or journaling strategies to capture their responses as they read and to guide their discussions while they meet.

These models are formal, tried-and-true structures, each with its own history and professional literature. But there are countless other collaborative learning structures, informal homegrown ways that teachers put students together to learn. What these teachers have found (once they got used to the noise) is that students have a great deal to learn from each other. Collaboration can even turn the taking of a multiple choice test into a learning experience where students are able to debate the correct answer, support their answers to their peers, teach others what they know, and learn much about themselves as teachers and learners.

Once the power of peer collaboration is recognized, teachers want to harness it to all kinds of previously solitary activities. At the Best Practice High School in Chicago, one of our design features is a school-to-work internship program where each student goes to an apprenticeship one morning a week. Our internship coordinator has placed students in seventy-nine different sites around the city, including museums, hospitals, community organizations, and schools. During the first year, some students attended their internships in groups, while others worked alone. We were powerfully struck by the difference. The kids' real-world job experiences were far more meaningful when they shared and processed the experience with classmates, on the bus coming and going, in dialogue journals, and back at their advisory groups. We were reminded that kids learn best when they have other people with whom to debrief and reflect upon the challenges they face together. We felt so strongly about the shared experience that we decided to make no future solo placements—everyone now has at least one fellow intern to think and talk with.

Making Collaboration Work: Community and Structure

All these models of collaborative grouping, formal and informal, can work in a variety of classrooms, but each requires preparation, troubleshooting, and management. The activities grow faster and stronger in classrooms where community is already valued and nurtured, and they in turn contribute to the development of more interpersonal connections and closeness. Teachers who want to build their curriculum around small-group experiences know that the process of collaboration cannot be left to chance. These teachers carefully grow classroom cultures that support cooperation, where students are powerfully encouraged and rewarded for helping each other to learn.

In a second-grade classroom in one of Chicago's toughest housing projects, Angie Bynum's students understand that working together and helping each other is everyone's most important responsibility. Students' desks are arranged in sets of four, and these small groups work together in literature circles, in peer editing, and in all other work of the day. Ms. Bynum reminds students to go to each other when they are stumped. Her motto is "see three before me." She'll interrupt nearly any classroom activity to announce: "Everyone, I want you to give James a big hand, because he just helped Vivian finish her math project!"

Cooperation, not competition, is the glue that holds this classroom community together. The hand-built culture of respect permeates Ms. Bynum's classroom, enabling students to work and learn collaboratively. These seven-year-olds run their own thirty-minute book discussion groups every day (not to mention other group activities) with little or no direct supervision from Ms. Bynum. They constantly surprise visitors who assume that "these kids" can't handle the responsibility of working in autonomous small groups.

Cooperation also requires structure. Classrooms with effective subgroups are usually well-structured places where students follow carefully developed norms and routines, and where working together is not a disruptive departure but rather business as usual. The activities in which students engage are often authentic and include some form of demonstration of knowledge and competence. Students learn to depend on one another and, in addition to receiving grades and evaluating themselves, are often asked to reflect on how well their groups worked together.

At Addison Trails High School in Addison, Illinois, the culminating activity for an interdisciplinary course that combined English, social studies, and biology was an Education Fair. Groups of freshmen demonstrated their knowledge in projects set up around the gym; the projects dealt with the rain forest, the effects of drugs, recycling, the Vietnam War, and many other real-world topics. Students, parents, and judges were invited to ask each of the presenters questions and listen to their presentations. In this exciting (and noisy) setting, it was obvious to see how much could be accomplished by students when they work together. Student teams had conducted interviews, performed experiments, gathered data, developed videotapes, written reports, and built exhibits to demonstrate their expertise. The gym was filled with the exciting products of learning. In this room, the power of collaboration was palpable.

We think John Dewey was right. Students do need to work and think together, because well-structured collaborative experiences help young people to learn deeply, to really understand, to share knowledge, to ask important questions, and in some cases to take action. If we believe that learning is thinking, then students need to have rich experiences, interesting questions to pursue, large blocks of time in which to pursue them, and others with whom to think.

Into the Classroom

Now five teachers show us how they organize just such collaborative experiences for their students. Steve Zemelman tells how eight kindergarten teachers at Chicago's Disney Magnet School designed a set of "hands-on" experiences with the moon. With their Moon Passport in hand, groups of five-year-olds circulated through stations that simulated different scientific aspects of the lunar environment. Next, we visit Baker Demonstration School to see how Theresa Kubasak uses literature circles with third graders. These small, peer-led book discussion groups meet regularly in her classroom, and Theresa offers a variety of targeted mini-lessons to both groups and the whole class before, during, and after book club meetings.

Steve Wolk describes an extended team research project that began with some mathematics content, and got his middle schoolers really involved in thinking critically about their world. Next, we hear from Sara Kajder, who readers may know of from her book, *The Tech-Savvy English Classroom* (2003). Sara's high school students in Alexandria, Virginia, work in inquiry groups using state-of-the-art technology to get answers to questions they pose. And finally, Harvey writes about how centers or learning stations fit into the larger picture of small-group activities, both as a structural alternative to whole-class teaching and as a way of grouping clusters of kids around particular materials or experiences.

Further Reading

Beverly, T. 2003. *Small-Group Reading Instruction: A Differentiated Teaching Model for Beginning and Struggling Readers.* Newark, DE: International Reading Association.

Caldwell, Jo Anne, and Michael P. Ford. 2002. *Where Have All the Bluebirds Gone? How to Soar with Flexible Grouping.* Portsmouth, NH: Heinemann.

Cohen, Elizabeth. 1986. *Designing Groupwork: Strategies for the Heterogeneous Classroom.* New York: Teachers College Press.

Daniels, Harvey. 2002. *Literature Circles: Voice and Choice in Book Clubs and Reading Groups.* 2nd ed. Portland, ME: Stenhouse.

Diffily, Deborah, and Charlotte Sassman. 2002. *Project-Based Learning with Young Children.* Portsmouth, NH: Heinemann.

Girard, Suzanne, and Kathlene Willing. 1996. *Partnerships for Classroom Learning: From Reading Buddies to Pen Pals to the Community and the World Beyond.* Portsmouth, NH: Heinemann.

Hill, Bonnie Campbell, and Nancy Johnson. 1995. *Literature Circles and Response.* Norwood, MA: Christopher-Gordon.

Hill, Susan, and Tim Hill. 1990. *The Collaborative Classroom: A Guide to Cooperative Learning.* Portsmouth, NH: Heinemann.

Johnson, David, Roger Johnson, Edythe Holubec, and Patricia Roy. 1991. *Cooperation in the Classroom.* Edina, MN: Interaction Book.

Kajder, Sara B. 2003. *The Tech-Savvy English Classroom.* Portland, ME: Stenhouse.

Mariott, Donna. 2002. *Comprehension Right from the Start: How to Organize and Manage Book Clubs for Young Readers.* Portsmouth, NH: Heinemann.

Samway, Katharine, Gail Whang, and Mary Pippitt. 1995. *Buddy Reading: Cross-Age Tutoring in a Multicultural School.* Portsmouth, NH: Heinemann.

Schlick-Noe, Katherine, and Nancy J. Johnson. 1999. *Getting Started with Literature Circles.* Norwood, MA: Christopher-Gordon.

Schmidt, Laurel. 2004. *The 12 Secrets of Great Teachers.* Portsmouth, NH: Heinemann.

Schmuck, Richard, and Patricia Schmuck. 2000. *Group Processes in the Classroom.* New York: McGraw-Hill.

Sharan, Yael, and Shlomo Sharan. 1992. *Expanding Cooperative Learning Through Group Investigation.* New York: Teachers College Press.

Steineke, Nancy. 2002. *Reading and Writing Together: Collaborative Literacy in Action.* Portsmouth, NH: Heinemann.

Thousand, Jacqueline, et al. 2002. *Creativity and Collaborative Learning.* Baltimore, MD: Brookes.

Small-Group Tours of the Moon

STEVEN ZEMELMAN

How do teachers create opportunities for experiential, hands-on learning, particularly when they're working with primary-age children who need lots of guidance as they do things? The kindergarten teachers at Disney Magnet School in Chicago asked if I would help create such an activity, and we agreed to design and run the unit together. Disney is a big school, with eight kindergarten teachers, so two willing risk takers, Audrey Laufman and Liz Ostman, volunteered to work with me as a planning committee.

The teachers had already chosen a topic: the moon. They wanted to see what could be done with science, and weren't entirely happy with the existing curriculum. Looking back, we would have done better to consult the children on this, but we're still learning what it means to integrate subjects in a meaningful way. Fortunately, just as this request came up, I was reading a lively manuscript submitted to the National Council of Teachers of English called *Empowering Ourselves to Inquire: Preservice Teacher Education as a Collaborative Enterprise* by Wayne Serebrin. It described a yearlong effort with a class of prospective primary-grade teachers to help them view teaching as a constructive response to kids' needs rather than as a mechanized routine. A high point was the creation of "playscapes" for the children in their student-teaching classrooms—settings that worked with children's real questions and invited learning through play. I recommended the manuscript for publication and borrowed the approach immediately!

Taking Serebrin's lead, I first went to the children. Audrey gathered her energetic troop on the floor one morning and I asked, "Do you ever wonder about the moon? Do you have questions about it, or wish you understood more about it?" The kids responded immediately—not with questions, but with answers. Kindergartners are wonderfully confident human beings, not yet beaten down by the judgments of schools. They told me plenty, and when anyone did have a question, someone else supplied an answer. But adults are persistent. We explained to the kids about asking questions. We cheated and turned some of their statements into questions. And of course not everyone was so sure about the assertions some kids made. Here's what emerged:

> How does an eclipse work?
> Are there people or aliens living on the moon?
> Why are there little circles on the moon?
> Why does the moon follow you when you're riding in a car? (Try explaining that one!)
> The moon looks little, but it's really big—why?
> How does the moon change from a little slice to a half to a whole?
> Why is the moon a cold-looking color?
> How do astronauts get to the moon?
> Why do astronauts put American flags on the moon?
> How do astronauts carry things on their back? And what's in those packs?
> Is there a car on the moon?

Now the challenge: what activities could address some of these questions and involve active play at the same time? The following letter, sent to the rest of the kindergarten teachers, describes what we ultimately planned for the children:

Dear Friends:

Audrey Laufman, Liz Ostman, and I have planned a special integrated-learning science project on the moon for kindergarten children, which will be available to your classes during the week of May 1–5. Learning will be centered in a moon playscape, to be located in the first-floor commons area, featuring centers for exploring concepts and information connected with the moon. The activities are based on actual questions Audrey's children have asked. These stations and their learning areas within the fields of science, math, language arts, and physical development are as follows:

1. Astronaut backpacks. Children select and pack objects in backpacks and weigh the packs to ensure the total is under five pounds. They mark their selections on a graph to compare preferences for items chosen, and then write, draw, or dictate reasons for these selections. Learning areas: problem solving, measuring, graphing, and speaking or writing to explain ideas.

2. Lunar vehicles. Children make model vehicles using wood, pipe cleaners, and glue, and record on a graph the size wheels they choose for navigating lunar terrain. The vehicles can be taken home. Learning areas: problem solving, small-motor coordination, and graphing.

3. Moon-phase box. The children take turns looking into a large, darkened box and moving a Styrofoam ball to various positions to see how light from a hole in the box forms crescent, half-circle, and whole-circle shapes like those seen on the moon. They draw what they observed and write or dictate explanations about why the shape changes and how this might relate to the moon. Learning areas: observing, drawing inferences, and speaking or writing to explain ideas.

4. Clay moonscapes. Children make models of moon surface features, based on photographs of the lunar landscape that are displayed on a bulletin board. The clay is then returned to its holder for others to use. Learning areas: observing and small-motor coordination.

5. Appearance of differing size. In pairs, children look through a tube to observe a large ball at different distances to see how distance affects the appearance of size. One child observes while the other carries the ball, standing at various spots marked on the floor. They then trade places so each gets to observe. They draw, write, and/or dictate explanations of what they observed and how it might relate to the moon. Learning areas: observing, drawing inferences, and speaking or writing to explain ideas.

There will be brief tape-recorded instructions at each activity to guide the children. Please feel free to organize your kids' visit(s) to the moon playscape as you see fit. You may wish to explain the basic steps in the centers at the start of your children's visit. We'll have construction paper, crayons, and other materials at each station for children to record their observations and ideas; and you can choose one or two stations to monitor, or move about to help children with the tasks, take dictation, guide them as they mark on the charts, etc. I will be available at various times throughout the week to help out as well.

How Did It Go?

We learned a tremendous amount as we ran the playscape over an exhausting but fascinating four days. First, the nitty-gritty: kindergarten kids need an older guide at each station if they are to get the most out of it. The taped instructions were a clever idea, but got lost in the shuffle. To solve this we drafted and trained a very willing group of sixth graders. The older kids saved the day, had fun, and learned about younger children, but they unfortunately also acted like overly efficient border guards, stamping passports (see Figure 4.1) and moving children along briskly. This shows the training school actually provides for students!

A handy trick also helped bring order to the near chaos. After the first round of confusion, I found Liz Ostman on the floor marking out a large square with colored tape next to each play station. This allowed teachers and sixth graders to send kids who had finished one activity on to the next in a clear and positive way. It provided just enough order so the project could proceed.

As for the activities, some proved better than others. Observing a ball through a tube actually did the best job of answering one of the questions on the kids' list. Everyone could see that up close the ball filled the whole viewing space, and as it moved farther away it appeared to shrink. This didn't capture imaginations too strongly, however. The moon phase box was popular because children could crawl inside, where it was dark. However, sometimes the sixth graders rushed them through, so they hadn't fully grasped what might be learned. The lunar vehicles were the greatest hit. We ultimately used chunks of pink Styrofoam, Styrofoam cups for radio antennae, coffee cup lids for wheels, and pipe cleaners as axles (solving a big worry about kids extracting nails to jab each other on the bus). The result was tables full of little pink and white fluffs of cloud. The kids got some good small-motor exercise and lessons in patient handiwork out of this, although not much science.

Still, everyone had a grand time. However, finally, what was needed was a fuller involvement of the children both before and after their actual visit to the moonscape. According to Jim Beane's levels of curriculum integration, we were somewhere between "fusing subjects" and "student-concern-centered curriculum." We weren't yet fully engaging student choice or achieving sufficient depth to call our effort an "integrated" one. Of course, some of the teachers conducted additional activities on their own. But next year, we'll expand the unit to help each group ask questions and connect the questions with the activities. We'll provide lots of picture books and information for kids to look over and have read to them, offer choices of follow-up activities and nighttime observations, and debrief afterward to discover what they learned. The core event, playing at the moonscape, is just a beginning. And oh, yes we're really going to train those sixth graders in

Figure 4.1: Moon passports were stamped as students entered each of five stations.

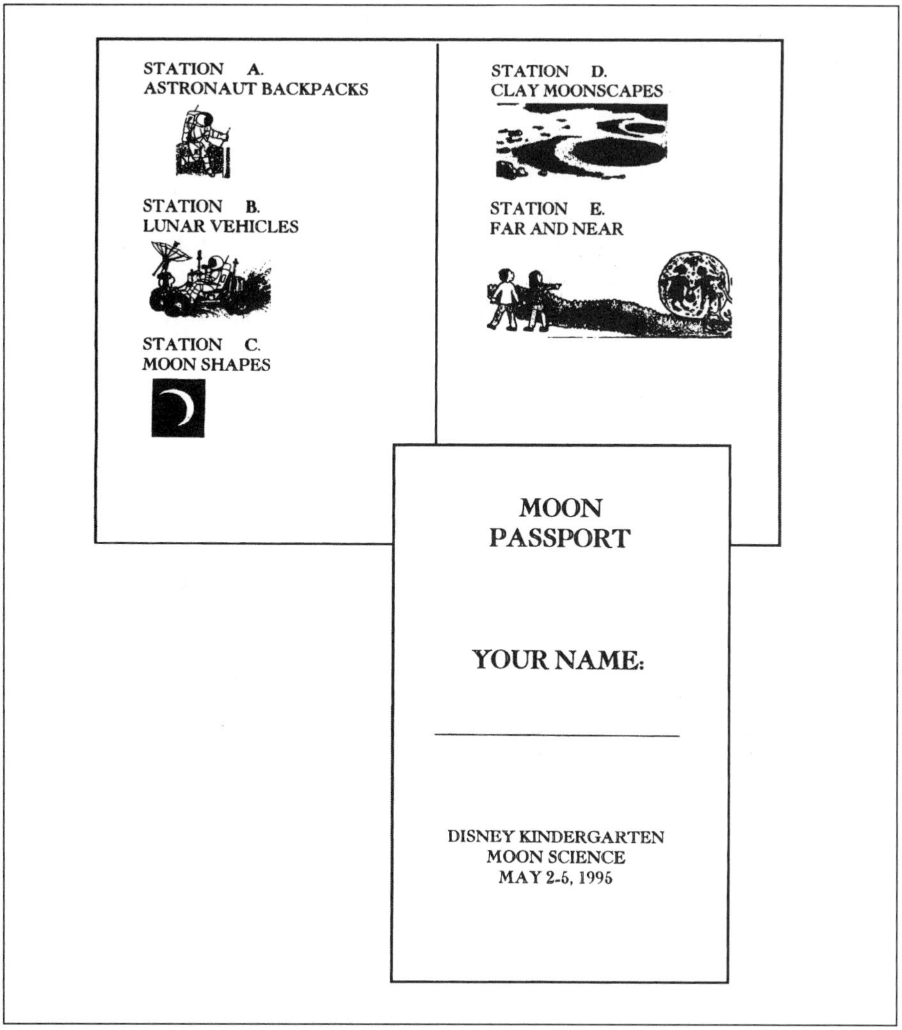

open-ended discussion and teaching techniques, and then put them to work setting up the whole thing!

Here is a more detailed list of the moon centers, with their goals, outcomes, descriptions, and assessments and the name of the teacher who masterminded each one.

Station A: Astronaut Backpacks (Liz Ostman)

■ Goal: To have children select and graph their own preferences from a table of space materials.

- Outcome: Children will write, draw, or dictate reasons for their preferences and answer questions about the graph.
- Description: Children select and pack objects in backpacks and then weigh them with scientific scales to check that the contents are under five pounds. Objects can range from food to supplies to games. Create graphs based on the supplies to show students' preferences. Ask students to tell why they chose each item as it is graphed.
- Assessment: Verbal questioning by a teacher or parent.
- Suggestions: Backpacks should be big. Have parents or teachers help with the center. Use a scale with large numbers.

Station B: Lunar Vehicles (Elizabeth Segiel)
- Goal: To have children be able to identify the correct size of wheels for the lunar vehicle that they will drive on the moon.
- Outcome: Students will be able to correctly identify and pick the correct size wheel on their moon vehicle.
- Description: Prepare two different sizes of wheels for the students to select. Prepare a vehicle base for each student to use to assemble their vehicle. Ask students which size wheel they would select for their moon vehicle and ask why they would choose that particular wheel size. Have students put their selected wheels on their moon vehicle and glue a Styrofoam cup somewhere on the top. Students should put their names on the vehicles and graph the size of wheel they choose to use on their vehicle.
- Assessment: Verbal questioning by a teacher or parent. Ask the students why they chose the specific wheel size and why.
- Suggestions: Students should be versed in the moon's surface and talk about the appropriate shapes for a rocky, cratered, hard surface. Parents or teachers must be at this center.

Station C: Moon Shapes (Carrissa Mazzeffi)
- Goal: To have children identify the different phases of the moon.
- Outcome: Students will identify the different phases of the moon (full, half, and crescent) after a sitting in the box.
- Description: Create a large box for children to sit in and move around in one at a time. Paint the interior of the box black. Cut a circular hole at the top of the box. Provide a Styrofoam ball for the child to use when enclosed in the box. When a child sits in the box, tell her to first hold the ball high, next at shoulder level, and then close to the floor. Tell the child to always focus her attention at the top of the ball. After she has left the box have her draw on a piece of paper what she viewed in the box.

- Assessment: A child should be able to draw three distinct phases of the moon upon exiting the box (full, half, crescent).
- Suggestions: Students should be versed in the moon's phases before participating in this center. The outside of the box should be painted with fluorescent paint and stars could be attached to the interior. A large box is preferable. A teacher or parent must manage this center.

Station D: Clay Moonscapes (Audrey Laufman)
- Goal: To have children know about the surface of the moon.
- Outcome: Students will understand there are craters on the moon and the moon goes through different phases.
- Description: Children should hear stories and see pictures about the moon. Prior to this activity, they were given a particular page for homework that guided them through observing the moon. Clay is set up on a table and children are instructed to form different phases of the moon with craters and rocks on it.
- Assessment: Each child is asked to form a moon with craters and rocks and to show it to a parent or teacher.
- Suggestions: This type of unit takes a lot of work and preparation. Instead of using parent volunteers, we use upper-grade children and work around their schedules. We also need a bigger budget—$60 is not enough for 180 students.

Station E: Far and Near (Joyce Campbell)
- Goal: To have children know about the concepts of near and far in relation to the moon.
- Outcome: Students will understand the difference between far and near in relation to the Earth and moon.
- Description: Six pieces of tape should be placed on the rug. Hanging in the background should be a diagram of what the students are supposed to do in the center. A person should instruct the students that they are going to partake in an activity to learn about *far* and *near*. A Nerf ball and a paper towel tube are needed for the activity. One student should hold the ball and the other student should hold the tube against his eye. As the student with the ball moves, the other student should be asked to describe what is happening to the ball. Both students should take turns doing this, and at the end of the activity they should be instructed to draw what they viewed.
- Assessment: A child is asked to draw what she or he saw when looking through the tube.

■ Suggestions: This center requires either a parent or teacher to aid the students. Also, preparation for the students is needed before they participate in the activity or they will be lost.

Station F: Astronaut Puppets (Linda Wishney)

■ Goal: Giving children an opportunity to have fun doing a culminating activity while improving their small-motor skills and developing their vocabulary.

■ Outcome: To understand that the moon is part of our universe and that astronauts in rocket ships have visited the moon.

■ Description: For this activity, you will need paper bags, glue, crayons, and scissors. Children will color, cut, and paste an astronaut face and body. The face is placed on the part of the bag that folds down on the bottom. The body is pasted on the top of the bag. Children will hold their bags up and tell about something they learned while on the moonscape.

■ Assessment: Children will say three things about the moonscape.

■ Suggestions/Culminating Activity: For this activity, you will need crayons, scissors, glue, and craft sticks. Have the children choose one of the pictures that has been included. They will cut it out and glue a craft stick to the bottom. They may hold up their puppets and tell about something they learned about the moon.

 Literature Circles in Third Grade

THERESA KUBASAK AND HARVEY DANIELS

Every day, in classrooms all across America, almost all students meet in small groups to work on reading. Among these groups are a wide variety of structures, ranging from traditional teacher-dominated, round-robin reading all the way to genuinely collaborative, student-led book discussion groups called literature circles. So what makes a genuine literature circle? What are the distinctive features of this special collaborative structure? While some of the defining ingredients of literature circles may be intentionally omitted when students are first learning the activity or when the group is applying lit circles to some mandated curriculum, authentic literature circles will manifest most or all of these key features:

1. Students *choose* their own reading materials.
2. *Small temporary groups* are formed, based upon book choice.
3. Different groups read *different books*.

4. Groups meet on a *regular, predictable schedule* to discuss their reading.
5. Kids use written or drawn *notes* to guide both their reading and discussion.
6. Discussion *topics come from the students.*
7. Group meetings aim to be *open, natural conversations about books,* so personal connections, digressions, and open-ended questions are welcome.
8. In newly forming groups, students play a rotating assortment of task *roles.*
9. The teacher serves as a *facilitator,* not a group member or instructor.
10. Evaluation is by *teacher observation and student self-evaluation.*
11. A spirit of *playfulness and fun* pervades the room.
12. When books are finished, *readers share with their classmates,* and then *new groups form* around new reading choices.

Obviously, many of these features are different from (even contrary to) the usual reading lessons in school. So the question arises, how can teachers prepare students to join in this welcoming, student-centered, but very different kind of activity? Students who are already veterans of other collaborative group activities or who are accustomed to open-ended book discussions may be able to jump right into lit circles with little formal preparation. But for those who need more background, teachers may want to invest a couple of weeks in showing students how to successfully run their own book groups. To find a model of such careful and thorough training in literature circles, we could do no better than follow Theresa Kubasak into her third-grade classroom.

"I've noticed that one of our literature circle groups has already started meeting," Theresa calls out. "Maybe that's our cue to put the math stuff away in our cubbies and move into our book clubs." Without any further prodding from Theresa or student teacher Erin McCarthy, the kids shift gears smoothly. They gather up the materials from their math work and stack them away, taking out their novels and journals, and regrouping into five book clubs in different corners of the classroom. They set to work, talking about the self-assigned chapters they have read for today, comparing notes from their journals, and running their own lively literary discussions for more than thirty minutes. There are jokes, disagreements, connections, and lots of explicit self-assessment. As you range through the room, you hear kids using language like "I disagree with that because . . . ," "If you look at page 43, you'll see . . . ," "This reminded me of the time when I . . . ," and "Following up on what Trevor just said . . ."

Of course, the kids didn't achieve this degree of autonomy and focus spontaneously. Their ability to operate in peer-led book discussion groups is rooted in two things: the warm community that Theresa has been cultivating since the beginning of the year, and about twenty days of specific literature circle training in September and October.

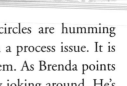

Now it is April, and Theresa's third-grade literature circles are humming along. Near the door, one book club starts its meeting with a process issue. It is Tony's turn to be the Questioner today, and there is a problem. As Brenda points out forthrightly, Tony is always getting the group off task by joking around. He's really amusing, but it's just not useful for the book talk. Tony listens to all this undefensively; he seems to know that his jokester tendencies can be a problem. The other kids nod as Brenda challenges him to really do the job.

"You won't get out of hand?" she asks.

"I'm OK," Tony replies.

"'Cause we gotta stay on the book."

"I feel fine," he assures.

Ms. Kubasak comes by and gets the kids to state the problem. She asks Tony to make a commitment. "What are two things you can do to be a funny guy and still be a good discussion member?"

"I'll be the Questioner," Tony offers, showing a list of notes jotted in his journal.

"Let's all be Passage Pickers," offers Beth.

After Ms. K moves on, leaving them to settle their own group issues, the kids continue negotiating. Tony finally decides he will assume the role of Questioner for the day after all. He suggests that the group begin its work by considering some especially important words from today's reading selection, starting with *scowling*.

Another group is discussing E. B. White's *Stuart Little*, and they notice a pattern of problem/solution, something that Ms. K has talked about at a previous whole-class mini-lesson. They decide to make a list of the problems and solutions:

Problem	Solution
Mom was washing and lost her ring	Stuart's Dad had to lower him down the chair and Stuart got the ring
Stuart got locked in the refrigerator	Mrs. Little finally opened the refrigerator
One key in the piano that stuck drives George crazy	Stuart goes in the piano to make the stuck key go down

Across the room, another group is reading *Hope's Crossing*, a novel set during the American Revolution. There's some initial discussion about the reading assignment itself. Some members think they are reading too few pages each day. The book is interesting and easy, so why not step up the pace and finish the book sooner than they had originally planned? But then they realize Eva has been absent for a few days and is already behind on the reading. Just when they want to jump ahead, it seems they are pulled back. But Eva looks at the calendar and realizes there's a school holiday coming up. "Don't worry, I'll catch up," she promises good-naturedly, and the schedule is readjusted. Now, before plunging into the day's discussion, the kids give Eva a quick summary of the events in today's chapters so she can join the conversation.

Pretty soon a lively debate breaks out about a British attack on the colonists.

Meiko: It was just the mom, the two girls, the baby, and the dogs.

Rachel: I hated it when she got captured and they shot the dogs.

Anna: That was the worst.

Eva: Think about it—dogs? The mom might get killed, the house might get on fire, they might starve. Compare those things to the dogs getting shot. You wouldn't be . . .

Rachel: My dogs are like people to me.

Keegan: Do you think in wartime—you wouldn't be concentrating on dogs.

Eva: They're like my best friends, we play all the time. They do make mistakes.

Anna: I would take my dog with me.

Eva: Dogs to me . . . it would be like if you shot my mom and dad. Anne and Carla in the book . . .

Anna: Both people and dogs can help you. If something really horrible . . .

Meiko: Even though they can't talk, you can communicate.

Eva: I'm not saying you're wrong.

Keegan: Last year my dog Milton was out with my dad. My dog protects me a lot. A guy came in our house at 9:00 at night. He was a burglar. My dad is a rowing coach and he leaves the dog home when he's gone. My dog is really faithful.

Eva: I'm not saying . . .

Meiko: We're just saying our opinion.

Anna: I worry about fire in our apartment house, what could happen to our dogs. I get so scared.

Rachel: We had fires in our neighborhood.

Anna: We had a tornado!

Rachel: OK, let's talk about something else.

Eva: Can we get back to the book? No tornados, please!

Meiko: Well, I would stand up to them [the British].

Keegan: You might get a whuppin'. If you stood up to the British, they have ways of killing you.

Meiko: I'd rather die than have someone . . .

Rachel: It's like that song we sang in the all-school show: "Before I'd be a slave, I'd be buried in my grave."

Meiko: I'd rather die than have someone controlling my life completely.

Today's literature circles session didn't have much of an introduction, and certainly no formal mini-lesson from Theresa. The kids sort of slipped into it spontaneously. But now, as Theresa calls the kids back to the wooden bleachers in the corner of the room, the sharing time will be highly structured—and it will last more than fifteen minutes. Into this stretch of the literature circle lesson, Theresa will gracefully slide mini-lessons on vocabulary building, book selection, and solving group problems; she and her student teacher will also demonstrate how book club members can disagree respectfully.

Some kids are dawdling in arriving at sharing time, so the ones already on the bleachers start singing, to the tune of "Frère Jacques,"

> We are waiting,
> We are waiting,
> Just for you,
> Just for you
> Please come over,
> Please come over
> Tha-ank you,
> Tha-ank you.

They keep singing as classmates straggle in. The singers really get into it, turning it into a round, a quite melodious one at that. Even the latecomers are singing as they arrive and slip into their seats.

Now Theresa simply asks, "OK, what went well today?" And then ensues a whole series of embedded mini-lessons. Some of them come up spontaneously from the kids' comments, and some are drawn from the page of notes Theresa has made while wandering the room for the past half hour, watchful for teachable points and next steps. The lessons go by pretty fast, but these are among today's highlights:

The group with the jokester problem is eager to report. "How'd it go?" Theresa asks. "Was Tony too funny?"

"I think it went perfect," says Joe. "He didn't goof off. It was great."

Tony is happy with his performance, too. He comments sagely, "Well, we did argue a little bit over some words. But eventually we worked it out."

"I noticed two ways that different people were using to figure out words that you didn't know. Like this group came upon the word *Hamlin*. And you read the sentence over to see if you could figure it out. Somebody said, 'It sounds like a place.' Which made sense. Then you also looked it up in the dictionary, and found it really is a place. Those are two really good strategies—try to figure the word out from the sentence, or if that doesn't work, look it up."

"I was worried about Alex a little bit today. He was sitting with some people who really yak a lot, and I was thinking he might not get a word in. You know, some people are just quiet. Like Ms. McCarthy. Did you know that she was nominated as Illinois Student Teacher of the Year? Isn't that great? But she never talked about it, because she's kind of quiet and there are so many other people talking in here."

Alex pipes up, "But I got one, I got a word in today."

Theresa laughs. "Yes, I loved it. You just butted in, and it was so perfect."

"I noticed that sometimes it's hard to disagree with someone when they are your friend. Like Ms. McCarthy and I really disagree about this one character in Harry Potter, don't we?"

"We sure do."

"It's not like we really argue. It's not like we aren't going to hang out together, but we do argue about the book."

"Yeah. I think that this character, Professor Trelawney, is a big hoax. I can't believe Professor Dumbledore was shocked."

"Well, I'm never giving up on this character. I'm going to read some more so I can find some things to change your mind about her."

"Well, you can try."

"Chrissa and Bobby were working on a song about Maniac McGee and Martin Luther King, which they are going to sing for us in a minute. Can you tell us how you made this comparison? It kind of surprised me at first. What do those two people have in common?" While Chrissa and Bobby confer, Theresa quickly sketches a Venn diagram on the flip chart.

"They both got blacks and white together," Chrissa offers.

"They were not respected," says Bobby.

Theresa jots these words in the overlapping section of the Venn diagram.

"I guess you've got something there. They did want to get everyone together." Theresa ponders for a minute. "Can we hear the song?"

Then the kids perform their song about Maniac McGee, all six verses, to the tune of a folk song about Martin Luther King called "Once There Was a Gentle Man." In fact, this is the same song that came up earlier in today's *Hope's Crossing* literature circle, and that the kids had performed in the recent all-school show.

Theresa's classroom is a very special place, and literature circles are not the only special feature. Here, abundance is offered to children, and much is expected of them. In this admittedly advantageous situation, Theresa Kubasak is practicing what we might call "state of the art" literature circles. It starts with tons of really good books, available in multiple copies. Many, but not all, of the books are coordinated with curriculum themes, so that kids can naturally extend their burgeoning interests. There are no official discussion sheets, but Theresa starts the year by teaching explicit lessons on visualizing, questioning, predicting, attending to authors' craft. The classroom culture is highly reflective; everyone understands that certain social and thinking skills are needed for small groups to operate well, and they know how to debrief, hone, and refine these skills every day. The groups set their own schedules, including starting and ending dates. Kids have developed a broad repertoire of response strategies; they can analyze plot structures, make emotional connections, study the words in the text, or take a variety of other approaches. There are no mandated artificial projects at the end of the book, but instead occasional book advertisements like the Maniac McGee song.

In Ms. Kubasak's room, literature circles are not just a way of building lifelong reading habits and nurturing careful thinking, they are also really, really fun. As one of the kids in the *Homer Price* group put it, shaking his head with a grin, "You think you're going to Australia, and then you go to Guatemala. You never know what to expect with books!"

Student Survey Teams: Asking Questions, Seeking Solutions

STEVEN WOLK

About a month ago, near the end of summer, I received a letter from Elizabeth, a seventh-grade student who had been in my class last year. Here is part of her letter, reproduced with her permission:

> Before I came to Burley [School] I really didn't care about what happened in the world. Nobody ever taught me how important it was to know what happened around me. That way I would know how I would be safe and how I wouldn't. I never really knew. But you taught me that we should know how much violence and racism and poverty is going on and destroying our world, and especially our future. At my old school my teacher would never ask me how I felt about these situations. You did. You actually made me think about them.

I do not include Elizabeth's wonderful words to boost my ego, but rather as the sweetest form of authentic assessment a teacher could ever ask for. This article is about one of the projects that our classroom community of seventh graders undertook last year and that contributed to Elizabeth's (and, I believe, the rest of the class's) thinking about social issues like racism, violence, and poverty, among many others. For lack of a better title, I call the project "Social Issue Surveys." The basic idea is to have the class form small groups, choose a social issue that interests them, write a survey about it, give their survey to a selected population, analyze the survey responses, and then communicate their results in some form of visual presentation, usually a graph. Although you could say that this is a math project, you will see that the project was multidisciplinary, or what James Beane (1993) calls "integrative." I also need to emphasize that the ideas and the content presented in this article may appear to apply mainly to older kids, but I consider them to be important and possible for all students—even, as famed kindergarten teacher Vivian Gussin Paley (1992) shows, for five-year-olds. Before we get to the specific project, however, a little background information is necessary.

Throughout my teaching career I have called our classrooms democratic. That's because they are not my classrooms, but rather a physical space, a wide variety of experiences, and a curriculum that is owned and created by all of us, teacher and students together as a community of learners. A democratic classroom, however, is not just about the methods of our learning. It is not just about the underlying concepts of teaching and learning (such as constructivism, developmentalism, collaborative learning, and learning in a social context) that direct my thinking as a teacher and that establish the philosophy of our classroom environment. To me, a democratic classroom is equally about the content (or the knowledge) that children have access to and the knowledge that is made an important part of our classroom experience. The knowledge that Elizabeth wrote about in her letter has its roots in critical theory (Freire [1970] 1993; Giroux 1983; McLaren 1994) and the sociology of knowledge (Berger and Luckman 1967; Bowers 1984), and can lead to what many call *critical literacy*.

Critical literacy means helping children to see the power, the politics, the ideology, and the interests in knowledge, language, and images; it means helping children to be critical readers of text, of society, and of "reality" itself; it means nurturing in children skeptical and questioning habits of mind; it means empowering children to take a lifelong role in what is supposed to be a participatory democracy; it means helping children see that racism, sexism, xenophobia, economics, violence, environmental issues, and politics all affect our lives on a daily basis; and possibly more than anything else, critical literacy continues the vision of John Dewey by promoting the conscious effort to transform our society and our world and to make it better, more humane, more just, and more caring. Critical literacy and transformative pedagogy is a way to realize the hopes and the ideals of a democracy. Patrick Shannon (1995) writes:

A [critical] question-centered approach to education breeds active learners. But to participate actively in civic life, we must become more than active learners. We must approach the social world as a created, transformable reality that was put in place and is maintained according to human interests. If the social world is a human artifact, then it is changeable through the acts of other human beings. This concept is not too abstract for children to comprehend. (108–09)

It is fair to say that Shannon's notion of a "question-centered" approach to schooling is a way of life in our classroom. I believe there are far more questions in life than "answers," so I want to nurture in my students the idea of living a life asking questions and seeking solutions.

It is important to emphasize that the freedom to think for oneself and to share thoughts and knowledge within a critical perspective is not only absent from most classrooms, but actually proscribed by strict, predetermined curriculums designed and written by people who have nothing to do with schools. Such curriculums prescribe "teacher-proof" programmatic materials like textbooks and workbooks, and, as Linda McNeil (1988) has shown, underscore the primary emphasis of school: to maintain order and control. Through our Social Issue Survey project, I hoped to bring "forbidden" issues into our classroom and to empower my students to become agents of change, to live their lives in ways that help make our world a better place for everyone.

Writing and Giving the Surveys

The class first broke into nine self-selected groups of three. After a day or two of group discussion, each of the nine groups had their topic: racism, poverty, the O. J. Simpson trial, women in the armed forces, television, gun control, illegal drugs, freedom of speech, and prejudice. In hindsight, we had too many groups. It wasn't easy finding nine different populations to give the surveys to, so we ended up giving several surveys to the same populations. When I do this project again, I'll either increase the group size to four or five (making five or six groups), or, even better, take the kids outside of school and into the community to find enough populations. Last year, the surveys were given to various classes in our school and to the teachers. When I did the project in a previous year, one group sent their surveys home with students for parents to complete.

In order to write a survey, we first had to look at some surveys, then talk about what a survey is, decide how to create one and what demographic information to ask for, and discuss the issue of anonymity. Some of this information was communicated through mini-lessons—ten-minute presentations I make to the entire class. However, much of this information was either taught or expanded while we did our work. This is a critically important point. Most of our class time is not spent listening to me teach about survey writing and graphing so that students can then go home and write a survey and make their graphs. Rather, the vast majority of our time together is spent learning by doing and learning through spontaneous interaction as a natural part of a highly social classroom environment.

We spent time looking at the difference between open-ended and closed-ended questions, and the strengths and weaknesses of both. There's an enormous difference between asking someone, "Were you ever the victim of prejudice?" and asking someone to "Write about a time you were the victim of prejudice." The surveys took a good deal of time (about two weeks) to draft, revise, edit, and type. It's important for children to learn that creating something of quality takes time, and if we don't practice this in school we're tacitly teaching the exact opposite. Some groups even did research to write their survey. For example, Jaime, Adam, and John wrote a survey on poverty. In order to help them get a better understanding of the issue, I showed them statistics for poverty in an almanac, some of which became a part of their survey (see Figure 4.2). Maria, Javier, and Jose had to research the Constitution for their survey on gun control, as did Nick, A. J., and Pablo for their survey on freedom of speech.

At various times throughout the project we discussed and did journal writing on related topics. We asked critical questions and searched within ourselves for possible answers. Where do our opinions and beliefs come from? Who and what shapes our opinions? (We came up with our family and friends, the media, movies, music, businesses and corporations, religion, and advertising.) How and why do we change our opinions? And, would it be a good thing if we all had the same opinions? This final question was of particular interest. Many of the kids thought that it would be good if we all had the same opinions—as long as the opinions we had were their opinions!

Analyzing the Surveys and Communicating the Results

Just as writing the surveys took time, so did analyzing them. After a few mini-lessons on mathematical computations (such as turning fractions into decimals), different types of graphs, and using a calculator, the students worked together in their groups performing the necessary computations for the four questions of their choice (two open-ended and two closed-ended) that I required each group to analyze. Once again, most of my "teaching" of these math concepts and skills was done in one-on-one or group conferences while everyone was scattered all over the room doing their work. There are two reasons why I keep whole-class instruction to an absolute minimum: first, research and my own experience as a student confirm that listening to a teacher lecture is one of the least successful ways to learn; second, all of the students are at a different developmental place in math, so it only

Figure 4.2: One team's bar graph depicting answers to a survey question.

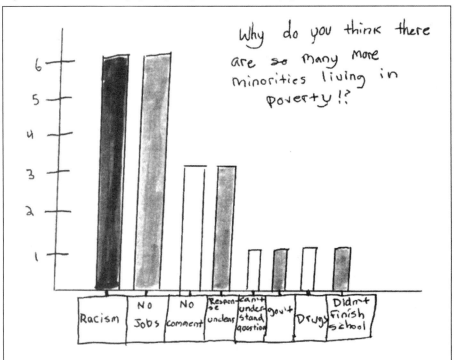

makes good sense to individualize teaching and learning through short conferences. That way I can help students with exactly what they need most. Also,
because we are a true community of learners, I'm not the only teacher in our classroom. The students can teach each other.

One of the most critical issues raised by this project is the subjectivity of surveys and knowledge in general. When we read about a survey in the newspaper or
hear about one on television, it so often has the appearance of truth and objectiv-
ity. Actually, it is anything but. Not only are the responses of surveys open to interpretation, but the original selection of questions, the selection of the respondents,
and the form the survey takes all bias the results. Note that the results are filtered
through and delivered to us from yet another source, such as a newspaper that gave
its own interpretation. In analyzing their surveys, students had to talk in their
groups and make conscious decisions regarding their interpretations of their population's responses. This was especially difficult with the open-ended questions.
When responding in a narrative format, people using different language may
mean the same thing, or using the same language may mean different things. Or
people may use language that's just plain unclear. Throughout the process I tried

to help the kids see how subjective this knowledge is and understand the power survey creators have in bringing "knowledge" to our society that is so often falsely (and subconsciously) accepted as being truth.

If we had had the time, I would have had each group complete a written analysis of their survey, possibly from a demographic perspective. Since all of the surveys asked the respondents their age and gender, it would have been interesting to look at possible patterns of responses. Some of these patterns were obvious and came up in formal and informal discussions. For example, Elizabeth, Pedro, and Andro, who did their survey on women in the armed forces, asked the question, "Do you think women should be included in combat?" and did two graphs comparing the responses of males and females. While only 42 percent of the males responded "yes," 100 percent of the females responded "yes." Comparisons like these led to lively, and at times heated, discussions and brought up yet another important point: the danger of drawing conclusions too quickly, overgeneralizing, or stereotyping.

Before any final graphs were done on posterboard, a draft copy had to be completed and edited on paper. Once the posterboard visuals were finished, each group made a short presentation to the class, explaining them. From beginning to end, the project took about five weeks.

Turning Our Surveys on Ourselves

As a final step in our project, I selected one open-ended question from each survey, typed them on a sheet, handed out copies, and had everyone choose one question and write their response in their journal. I wrote, too. Once finished, we sat in a circle on the floor, and those who wanted to, read aloud what they wrote for open discussion. Andro chose to respond to "If you have ever been a victim of prejudice, write about it":

> I have been a victim of prejudice many times. For example, I was at [a] school playing basketball with an African American kid and then more African American kids came and started calling me "porkchop" because they noticed I was Hispanic. I don't know how they found out. A lot of people don't think I'm Hispanic. But anyway, they started telling me to get off the court because they were going to play basketball. So I did. I was walking out toward the gate and they threw the basketball right at my back, and started laughing, calling me "spic." When I went home I did not tell my mom anything because I thought she would make a big fight about it. And anyway, I didn't want anything to happen to me or anyone.

Toward Meaningful, Integrative, Critical Learning

Was this really a "math" project? It would be difficult for me to say that it was. We certainly spent a lot of time doing math. But we also spent a lot of time discussing and writing about a wide variety of issues affecting our society, which would place the project in social studies (as would the constitutional implications of issues like gun control, freedom of speech, and women in the armed forces). We also did a lot of writing, including drafting, revising, and editing the surveys, as well as journal writing, which would place the project within the scope of writing. The project involved reading, talking, listening, analyzing language, and a host of other activities and ideas that come about as a natural result of spontaneous, self-directed learning in a social context. The answer here should be obvious: this project wasn't really a "math" project at all, but rather a life lesson, where we were presented with a constant stream of overlapping ways to think about and make sense of knowledge and the world.

Aside from that, the real strength of the project was in what Elizabeth wrote. The project helped raise her consciousness of the world. It tacitly communicated to her that these concepts are valuable and that they're just as important to learn and think about as reading, writing, math, and science are. Ideally Elizabeth will apply these ideas to her own life and will become a critical and informed thinker, asking questions, seeking solutions, and, in the words of Maxine Greene (1988), searching for possibilities of what "could be."

Collaborative Digital Storytelling

SARA KAJDER

Stories abound in our classroom community, allowing students to see themselves in our work, to participate within our literacy community and, often, to take huge strides in defining themselves as readers and writers. In a culturally diverse, socio-economically challenged suburban school ten minutes from Washington, D.C., the mix of students is rich and staggering. The thirty-seven students in period two, English 11, were the first to tell me that they were not readers or writers—and their test scores and student files reflected several years of that thinking. I countered that they were. Each time they picked up a manual, jumped on-line to instant message (IM) a friend, or got on the Metro and headed into town, they were readers.

Some culture critics would agree with the kids' declaration of nonliteracy. They worry that today's young people seem captivated not by books, but by the Internet, television, film, and video games. But I believe that these new media support and *promote* reading. Modern students are intensely literate, but not in the ways that might allow them to think like a standardized test.

Recently, I offered a new challenge, designed to evoke students' stories, extend their literacy skills, and provide a collaborative and largely multimedia environment that allowed them to work not only as readers and writers but also as directors, artists, programmers, screenwriters, and designers. They created teamed digital stories that conveyed a three-to-five-minute personal narrative in response to a significant question of each student team's choosing. Some students explored essential questions ranging from "What is an American?" to "What is community?" Others worked to tell stories of their family's immigration or relocation.

The project took two weeks of instructional time and required the development of a sustained community. It was not an easy sell. Students lacked trust, and rarely had space within a classroom that was their own. They all read below level and were used to worksheets as opposed to invitations to be seen. We started with the reality that Adrienne Rich describes: "When someone with the authority of a teacher describes the world and you are not in it, there is a moment of psychic disequilibrium, as if you looked into a mirror and saw nothing." Each student had to look into the mirror and see through different eyes.

Nuts and Bolts

Students were provided with basic tools. No more than three digital cameras were provided, resulting in a ratio of one camera to every eight to ten students. One classroom scanner was used, attached to the single classroom computer. Though it often took some creative approaches and scheduling, every student was provided with access to a computer while the projects were developed in class. These weren't state-of-the-art machines, often requiring that we use PowerPoint or other presentation tools instead of digital video tools like iMovie or Premiere. The bare-bones requirement was simply that students could compile images and their recorded narration, side by side.

Teaming It Up

Students were divided into teams of four, with one student filling the role of director and three assigned to the roles of artist, videographer, and the "techie." Instead of spending valuable class time teaching all students to use the technology tools needed to create their digital stories, I trained only those team members who were assigned the role of "techie." Aware of the responsibility within the role and in response to the "hook" provided by visual, digital media, students met with me during four lunch periods for training in how to use a digital camera or how to

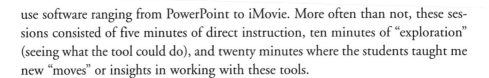

use software ranging from PowerPoint to iMovie. More often than not, these sessions consisted of five minutes of direct instruction, ten minutes of "exploration" (seeing what the tool could do), and twenty minutes where the students taught me new "moves" or insights in working with these tools.

Searching, Writing, and Composing Together

Before sitting down in front of a computer, student teams were required to complete a storyboard. Students were required to map on paper each image, technique, and element of their digital story by constructing a storyboard. This visual story had two dimensions: chronology (what happens and when) and interaction (how audio information interacts with the images) (Lambert 2002, p. 61). Using a template, students arranged and rearranged images that were listed on sticky notes. Another line on the storyboard allowed students to sequence the images that would appear on the screen with the text that would be spoken aloud.

Conventional digital stories involve the writing of a script that is read aloud and recorded in order to provide narration. The most essential component of the scripting and narration process is that it allows for the student's voice to be present in the reading of the print text. Students are present as readers, writers, and thinkers throughout the project, many for the first time. A benefit to writing collaborative stories was that many student voices could be present within a single text.

The artist was responsible for the selection of the images that would be used throughout the digital story. The power of using digital images in this work comes in the students' representations of their worlds. Several students used this as an opportunity to develop their own artwork where others saw it as an invitation to use pictures of the world around them. Many projected themselves into the textual world they created by inserting their own image into the photos they captured from on-line sources.

Every group member contributed to the written script. Students understood that the personal narrative needed to be a window into a moment, a self-contained story set in one particular place and time. They chose to tell rich stories that were about discovery and understanding. Dahabo, an immigrant from Somalia, wrote the story of the first day she wore pants, explaining what freedom and America meant to her and the other three members of her group. Harold, Qui, and Frank wrote about their experiences in a summer Outward Bound program. Though they were all locked into the logistics of writing, each student group submitted a draft of between one and one-and-a-half pages, double-spaced. The required length was short, but packed with precise language that provided an entrance for struggling writers who were intimidated by the blank page. The trick was to develop voice while exercising economy.

Creating the Digital Story

In order to build their digital stories, students needed to import or digitize their photos, add transitions and special effects, record narration, add a sound track, and burn their finished work to a CD. Students had limited time to use the classroom computers but were able to come in after or before school, use computers in the media center, or work from home or the community library. Because several students had better tools at home, several teams built their stories there, bringing in work to meet my "checkpoints" on their progress.

Central to the process was a rule that emphasized content over presentation, setting the balance at 80 percent content and 20 percent effect. Without the rule, students were caught up in zooms, pans, and special effects that showed knowledge of the tool but little control of the story. By putting the story first, students were selective about effects, choosing those that drove the story further as opposed to those that mimicked what might be seen in films or television.

Throughout the construction process, I met regularly with each director, challenging them to provide leadership to the fuller group and to keep the team on task. Videographers and techies worked together with the primary responsibility of compiling the image, sound, and narrated files into a finished, coherent, meaning-packed story. Interestingly, though with many aspects of the work the "roles" blurred into genuine collaborative work, students maintained close responsibility and ownership for those tasks that were a part of their original role description.

Screening

At the close of our work, we screened the finished products, complete with popcorn and student-written responses. Shared responses celebrated students' attempts to reflectively add meaning to past events, and classmates often requested more detail. Other comments focused on technical suggestions for both the presentation and the content, referring to cinematic terms or texts that we read. We had discussed those strategies for reading film that translated well to reading print text. These early conversations marked the start of a collaborative interpretive community that was a safe, supportive structure for talk and interaction as readers and as writers.

The Story Continues

Kylene Beers writes in *When Kids Can't Read, What Teachers Can Do* that she "wants to teach kids how to struggle successfully with a text" (2002, p. 16). I firmly believe that engaging readers is my critical teaching responsibility. While I was working here to help students create published personal narratives, my goals were actually much bigger. I wanted students to struggle with their words and experiences, to work as writers and readers, and to reinvent their understanding of how they functioned within those roles. I wanted them to tap into powerful communication tools to tell their story verbally, visually, and powerfully. By allowing each student to see that "all ways of seeing have their silences and their exuberances" (Myers 1996, p. 134), we reached a starting point from which students began to see a new value in their work as scholars and members of an interpretive community.

 # Centers and Stations: Decentralizing the Classroom, K–12

HARVEY DANIELS

In Chicago, where we work, there are still a few of those depressing, old-style classrooms left, the ones with the desks screwed to the hard oak floor in straight rows. Sometimes there's even a little platform for the teacher, a step up from the student level, which makes the blackboard (and it *is* black, not green or white) more visible to all. Those immobile cast iron desks, frozen in six rows of six each, are exhibits in a museum of passivity, emblems of an era when the pedagogy was as fixed as the furniture. What a profound architectural-educational metaphor. The floor plan screams out, "Sit down. Shut up. Eyes on me. Keep your hands to yourself. Stop fiddling!"

Of course now, in Best Practice classrooms, we *want* students to fiddle around; we want them to get up and go learn something, to engage with materials, touch things, wrestle with ideas, talk to each other, make stuff, and show what they found out. This kind of learning requires variety and flexibility in the ways students, materials, and equipment are deployed around the classroom. In order to teach the Best Practice way, teachers must be able to subdivide and decentralize their space, to create and re-create the learning environment, not just in elementary but also in secondary classrooms.

Spaces for Learning

So what exactly are centers? At Joseph Landis School in Cleveland, Debra Kunze runs a second- and third-grade classroom that has a rich assortment of centers. The last time we visited, she had five stations up and running: (1) a writing center where students could pursue their own writing projects; (2) a math center in the form of a store with many priced items to be purchased and toted up; (3) a measurement center at which students tested various attributes of water, including volume measured by different metric and conventional containers and temperature as measured in Fahrenheit and Celsius; (4) a "geosafari" center where students used a simple computer program to find the location of countries around the world; and (5) a physics center focused on simple machines, with assorted materials for building bridges and then testing their strength. While Ms. Kunze's centers were creative and varied, they were also equipped with mostly makeshift items; Landis is an underfunded inner-city school serving poor kids, and it doesn't have an extra dime for "real" hands-on materials.

The children, well accustomed to the procedures during their daily hour of center time, deployed themselves without fuss to their respective areas. They knew what to do at each station from Debra's orientation earlier in the week. It was quiet in the writing center, as children opened folders and bent to their papers. Elsewhere, kids talked quietly about the work at hand. We were particularly struck by the way the simple machines center had captivated some of the kids, and especially Herbert, who was trying to build a bridge that would support a weight hanging underneath. His brow knitted as he tinkered with different support systems, tested his experiments, watched the bridge collapse, and then started over, trying new structural supports, piling on the weights, watching the bridge go down again, and then starting over with a new design wrinkle.

Jean Piaget would have loved to watch Herbert at work. This center was constructivist learning theory in action. Herbert was in the process of reinventing, and owning for himself, some principles of physics that no lecture, worksheet, or textbook could ever transmit. And he was learning these principles by doing, by playing with real stuff. Well-designed centers like this one are a key way that teachers can make student-centered, hands-on learning come alive.

So here's a more formal definition: Centers or learning stations are special spots in the classroom where the teacher has set up curriculum-related activities that students can pursue autonomously. Usually a classroom has multiple centers, enough so that when thirty kids fan out to them, there are not too many at each— five or six stations is about average among the teachers we've worked with. Centers are used during part of the day; indeed, in many classrooms there's something called "center time" that might occupy an hour of the schedule. Centers are often set up in cycles; that is, the teacher sets up a crop of centers, and the students visit them over a week or two. Then, perhaps after a pause for other activities, the teacher creates another set and the cycle begins again. Rotation is integral to centers (over the cycle, all students are supposed to work their way through all centers, sometimes visiting each one several times). During center time, the teacher is typically supervising, roaming, solving problems, serving as a resource, and when time permits, doing some observational assessment of students at work.

There's tremendous artistry (and lots of teacherly sweat equity) in the design of centers that both embody key curricular concepts and support kid-run inquiry. Centers require the teacher to think up activities, gather (translation: buy or scrounge) the equipment or supplies needed, design an inquiry process, develop kid-friendly instructions, create the necessary charts or handouts, drag everything to school, and hope the janitor helps carry it all in. Because setting up good centers is so demanding, it's not surprising that there are so many poor ones out there: "writing centers" where kids merely copy text, "science centers" where they fill out ordinary worksheets, "math centers" where students do the odd-numbered problems and leave them in an envelope for the teacher to grade. These are not true centers but ambulatory seatwork, and probably not worth the trouble to set them up.

To be worthwhile and genuine, centers must have several key ingredients in place:

- *Something to learn or discover.* Centers are not for review or assessment; they are for learning. Teachers must design stations so that kids can have some kind of "aha" experience there, however modest—like Herbert, with the bridge. Teachers can design centers that are applications or extensions of previously taught concepts, ones that illustrate topics currently being studied during other parts of the school day, or stations that preview upcoming topics, offering the teacher a chance to base future activities on kids' responses to early samples.

- *Some kind of interaction.* Many centers feature tasks that students do individually, though this can mean that students end up waiting while the kid ahead of them finishes the solitary task. One alternative is to design centers so that four to six kids can work simultaneously. Even better, recognizing that kids generally do arrive at centers in groups, and that talking is a good way to externalize one's thinking, the station can incorporate ways for the kids to work and talk together.

- *A tangible outcome.* Learning stations should provide students with something to take away from each stop around the room, whether this is a sketch in their journal, a completed puzzle, or some Web sites bookmarked on the classroom computer. Some centers also ask kids to leave something behind: posting their results from an experiment that becomes part of the station's data, leaving a poem for others to read, or making an entry in a log that stays behind to be read by subsequent visitors.

In order to make centers work, the teacher must choose and put into place management procedures to cover several concerns.

■ *Scheduling students into centers.* In some classrooms, kids simply vote with their feet, going to whatever center they're interested in on a given day. This approach has the advantage of being casual and spontaneous, but can of course lead to clogs in some corners of the room. Other teachers ask kids to sign up in advance—say, the day before—listing their center preferences in priority order, so that overcrowding problems can be worked out beforehand. Still other teachers, often those just beginning with centers or those with rambunctious youngsters, will build a schedule themselves, assigning students to a rotation through the centers. Though this approach deletes a bit of the student voice and responsibility, it can create optimal combinations of kids and prevent off-task groups from traveling through the stations together. Debra Kunze runs a daily center lottery; kids draw from twenty-five Popsicle sticks, five for each station, to guarantee the random (and indisputable) assignment of kids to centers.

■ *Instructions.* Because students are supposed to do centers without the teacher present, the instructions posted at the stations become critically important. More than one teacher has become a human ping-pong ball, with kids crying out for the clarification of unclear steps or procedures from all six centers at once. Like Ms. Kunze, smart teachers make it a habit to walk kids through the centers on the first day they are introduced, previewing the directions for each.

Centers for Older Students

Some people assume that centers are a little-kid activity that's supposed to be phased out as kids move toward adolescence. Wrong! The secondary classroom can benefit from the same spatial flexibility and decentralization that is practiced in the lower grades. Two instructional phenomena have begun to show the teachers of big kids that stations are for them, too. One is collaborative learning: by setting kids to work in collaborative group investigations or peer editing groups, secondary teachers have already started rudimentary centers. And then there's the computer. The arrival of computers in classrooms, not just in labs, has almost forced teachers to invent ways that some kids can be using the computers while others are doing something else. The classroom computer often becomes the first center—now what will the other four or five be? The door to the multitasking secondary classroom is kicked open!

What kinds of centers can you have within and beyond the high school classroom? To begin with, in some classes (science, art, physical education, home economics) centers are already happening. In these subjects, teachers are trained to organize stations where pairs or small groups encounter structured laboratory experiences. Too often, these centers are identical—that is, all six groups in the home economics class are making the same brownies, each in their own little kitchen. If this were elementary school, the centers would probably feature different recipes, with students being invited to create innovations and variations on bar desserts. At Best Practice High School, our physics teacher Arthur Griffin sometimes offers labs where everyone does the same thing, but at other times he sets up multiple stations, where kids work through different aspects of the refraction of light or the nature of waves. Also at Best Practice High School, our colleague Mike Myers makes extensive use of centers in his social studies classroom. In a simulation of the way a bill becomes a law, Mike set up and equipped five centers, assigning several kids to each: the House of Representatives, the Senate, a House-Senate conference committee, the White House, and the Supreme Court. At Stevenson High School, math teacher Noelle Canela scattered kids around five "probability centers" featuring dice, coins, M&M's, playing cards, and Lego toys to start students experimenting with the dynamics of probability.

Secondary centers don't need to be contained within the four walls of a single classroom, nor do they have to be invented and supplied by one lonely classroom teacher. We can assign students to "centers" throughout the building, ones that don't need to be created anew, and that are already supervised by others. These include, of course, the library, the computer lab, the tutoring center—as well as sites like a school telephone where interviews can be conducted, the classroom of another teacher with needed expertise, or an off-campus research site arranged in advance. If students are pursuing a broad and meaty inquiry (perhaps as part of an integrative, interdisciplinary unit), it is natural to think of the school as a building full of centers where they may go to work on different aspects of the inquiry. As with younger kids, there need to be management structures and operational controls in place to answer questions like: Where are you going? Why? With whom? What product will come out of this? When? How long do you expect this segment of the study to take?

At Best Practice High School, we have developed a variant of centers called "choice time," which happens once a week on Wednesday afternoons, after students return from their service internships around the city. During this time the faculty sets up eight to ten learning centers based on student requests, and kids sign up to attend the center of their choice. Lately, some of the popular ones have been chess, singing, drama, computer art, photography, and special help in physics. Each "center" consists of a room in the school, provided with the needed equipment (like chess boards) and one adult who is knowledgeable about the activity at hand.

Even though decentralized classrooms are an important tenet of our school philosophy, the local board of education hasn't been much help equipping them.

When we started BPHS ten years ago, we requested six-person tables and chairs as our baseline furniture, instead of separate student desks. But there weren't any tables to be had in the city's huge school furniture warehouses, because hardly anyone uses tables, because the board buys desks instead. Understand? We didn't, either, but we still needed tables, which we ended up buying out of our measly Chapter 1 funds.

But we spent the money willingly, because the ability to flexibly arrange our students was critically important to our curriculum, both practically and philosophically. Space matters. We have to subdivide the classroom. Kids must multitask. If we cannot set up situations where small groups of kids can meet, sit, lay stuff out, and work through materials, how can we offer an active, experiential curriculum?

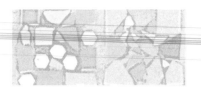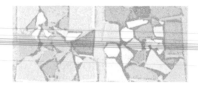

F I V E

CLASSROOM WORKSHOP

One of the most valuable instructional metaphors to emerge in recent years is the idea of the classroom as workshop. In this model, elementary and secondary classrooms are no longer merely locations where information is transmitted. Instead, they become working laboratories or studios, where genuine knowledge is created, real products are made, and authentic inquiry is pursued. The classroom workshop is the pedagogical embodiment of constructivist learning theory; in a workshop, students and teachers together reinvent whatever field of knowledge they are engaged in.

The workshop model is simple and powerful. It derives from the insight that children learn by doing, and that in the past schools have simply failed to provide enough time for doing math, science, reading, writing, art, music, and history. It recognizes that kids need less telling and more showing, that they need more time to *do* learning, and less time hearing about what particular subjects might be like if they ever engaged in them.

The idea of the workshop as an educational institution has centuries of rich tradition. Through much of human history and across the world, the crafts shop, where a master craftsperson coaches and mentors apprentices, has been a traditional and effective mechanism for both schooling young people and producing useful artifacts. In the context of making real stuff, learners observe demonstrations by the master practitioner and try out the trade with feedback and close supervision. The production isn't pretend, it's real—the workshop isn't a separate institution like a modern school, set apart to prepare learners for later entry into the real producing world. Instead, the workshop is part of the real world now, and its participants are immersed in a whole, genuine process. At the same time, we don't need to romanticize the ancient workshop; many of them probably were authoritarian places where apprentices were rigidly controlled and offered precious little "voice and choice" in their education. For us today, the challenge is to translate the most valuable structural features of the workshop method to contemporary education.

Of course, the crafts-shop idea is not entirely new to modern education. Some subject fields like art, science, home economics, physical education, and other "doable" subjects have a long history of workshop learning, although they usually call it the laboratory or studio. Teachers of these subjects know a great deal about the value of modeling versus presentation, about working with real materials, about guiding and coaching students, and even about managing student work in small groups. Too often, though, even in these inviting subjects, the workshop opportunity is squandered when the classroom is harnessed to convergent, right-answer outcomes and low-level exercises, rather than truly exploratory, meaning-creating experiences.

We have to thank language arts teachers, who have been experimenting with the classroom-as-workshop idea over the past twenty-five years, for inventing many of the procedures needed to adapt the workshop model to modern schools. Educators like Donald Graves, Lucy Calkins, and Nancie Atwell helped solve the inherent management problems of workshops by developing new, clear-cut roles for both teachers and students. They created the operating structures and training processes that make a workshop work—and make it easily transferable across subject fields. Following on their accomplishments, teachers in other fields have generated more models, such as *History Workshop* by Karen Jorgensen and *Science Workshop* by Wendy Saul and colleagues.

Thanks to this long history and these creative contributors, we now have a contemporary version of the workshop-style, learning-laboratory classroom, and it looks like this: students in the workshop choose individual or small-group topics for investigation, inquiry, and research using long, regularly scheduled chunks of classroom time for doing the work. They collaborate freely with classmates, keep their own records, and self-evaluate. During workshop time, students take responsibility for the whole learning process, from topic selection all the way through producing and sharing meaningful results with others. Teachers take on new roles, too, modeling their own thinking, investigating, and authoring processes, conferring with students one-to-one, and offering well-timed, compact mini-lessons as students work. In the mature workshop classroom, teachers don't wait around for "teachable moments" to occur—they make them happen every day.

Workshops meet regularly—every day if possible, at least once a week at an absolute minimum. Within the workshop session, time is divided into several key steps. Below is a generic schedule for a single fifty-minute workshop session that could happen in any subject:

- *Five to Fifteen Minutes:* Mini-lesson. The teacher briefly demonstrates one element or ingredient of the kind of work students will be pursuing during the upcoming session.
- *Five Minutes:* Status-of-the-Class Conference. Each student announces in a few words what she has chosen to work on during this session, from a list of approved alternatives.
- *Twenty to Thirty Minutes:* Work Time/Conferences. Students work according to their plan. Depending upon the rules and norms, this may include experimenting, researching, reading, writing, talking or working with other students, going to the library, conducting phone interviews, and using manipulatives or microscopes. The teacher's roles during this time are several. For the first few minutes, the teacher may experiment, read, or write to model her own doing of the subject. Then the teacher may manage for a bit, skimming through the room to solve simple problems and make sure everyone is working productively. Then the teacher shifts to her main workshop activity: conducting individual or small-group conferences with students about their work, either following a preset schedule or based on student sign-ups for that day. The teacher's role in these conferences is as a sounding board, facilitator, and coach—rarely as a critic or instructor.
- *Ten Minutes:* Sharing. In many workshop sessions, teachers save the last few minutes for a few students to discuss or present what they have done that day. Math students may show how they applied a concept to a real-world situation, young scientists demonstrate a chemical reaction, social studies teams report the results of their opinion survey, writers read a piece of work aloud, or readers offer a capsule book review. Alternatively, the teacher can use this after-workshop time to offer a mini-lesson based upon her observation of what worked (and what didn't) during the day's session.

A defining element of the workshop is choice: students choose their own phenomena for investigating, topics for writing, books for reading. They follow a set of carefully inculcated norms for exercising that choice during the workshop period. They understand that all workshop time must be used on some aspect of the inquiry, so when they complete a product, a piece, or a phase, they aren't "done" for the day: instead, students must begin something new, based on an idea from their own running list of tasks and topics, or seek a conference with the teacher. While there are regular, structured opportunities for sharing and collabo-rating in a workshop, students may also spend much time working independently and autonomously.

Teachers who value the workshop ethic often create hybrids that fit their par-ticular settings and curricular parameters. Julia Charlesworth, who teaches English at Lake Forest High School in a suburb of Chicago, has developed an interesting way of combining reading workshop with literature circles. Here is how she explains the process to her students in a handout:

> Reading workshop and literature circles give you the opportunity to *have more choice and control of what we read and study in English class.* Workshop provides significant class time to *just read*—an activity that is an important and valuable part of your education. Literature circles pro-vide significant class time for you to *share books with your peers through dis-cussion* of the literature where the *topics are chosen by you* and your group and *guided and supported by me.* I hope you will find this academic free-dom stimulating and fun, and that you will use the valuable time to explore your interests, expand your horizons, and challenge yourself as a reader, thinker, and writer.
>
> Along with this academic freedom of choice and control comes added responsibilities. Reading workshop and literature circles will be successful only if everyone lives up to the *following responsibilities*:
> - Always have a book to read.
> - Keep the literature circle discussions interesting and fun for you and the group.
> - Use the class time responsibly.
> - Come to the literature circle meetings prepared to discuss and share ideas.
> - Be open to sharing your group's ideas with the rest of the class.

This clever adaptation of the workshop model was implemented within the traditional fifty-minute high school period, and called upon Julia to use every minute carefully. In reflecting on her ambitious undertaking, Julia says that the workshop worked, and that students really did learn to take responsibility for their learning. As she puts it,

> In genuine, student-driven learning situations, high school students begin to discover and develop their own literate and literary vocabulary. They create a pattern of how to approach, read, and understand books. Choice is a very important component in this process, and students can

become very uncooperative when that choice is compromised or threatened in any way by the teacher or by peers. Concrete feedback from the teacher is very important to the process of students learning from and improving performance in literature circles. Feedback needs to be immediate and constant, or students can get off track, not meet expectations, and lose motivation.

In most effective workshops, teachers and students set quotas and due dates. Even as students enjoy the autonomy of self-directed study, they are also accountable for regularly producing work and meeting deadlines. For example, in typical writing workshops, students are encouraged to start many different pieces of writing. But, on a regular schedule (weekly for younger kids, every three weeks for older ones) they are required to select the one most promising piece and take it through a full publication process: careful revision, multiple teacher and student conferences, scrupulous proofreading and polishing, and "publication" of the final draft within the group. Other quotas agreed upon by students and teachers often involve a distribution among genres; while some repetition is permissible, at some time during the year all students are required to produce polished pieces over a specified range of genres: poetry, drama, exposition, argument, and book reviews.

The workshop method is naturally linked with some key assessment practices. Since students are working on different topics, either individually or in teams, the teacher needs a system for recording students' choices and monitoring their day-to-day work. Because conferences are a key ingredient of the workshop, the teacher typically develops a simple system for jotting down the highlights of these conversations. With students working on many different materials at once, generating all kinds of notes, drafts, clippings, and sources, it becomes vital to have folders for storing all the different artifacts as they are created. Later on, ingredients of the folder may also be used for showcasing finished products and looking back to assess a cycle of workshop activity.

Though the workshop model is undeniably powerful and effective, implementing it can be a real challenge for teachers. The structure itself violates the expectations of many students, administrators, and parents; it seems to compete for time with the official curriculum; and it often contradicts teachers' professional training and their own childhood experience in school. Nor do students always take smoothly and effortlessly to the workshop model: on the contrary, implementation can be bumpy, tricky, and slow, even for dedicated teachers in progressive schools. Because the structure is unfamiliar and complex, smart teachers give plenty of time to training. They begin by explaining the structure to students long before commencing the workshop. Joanne Hindley, whose book *In the Company of Children* (1996) provides a superb picture of a workshop-based third-grade classroom in New York, spends one whole month preparing children for workshop. She reports that by the time the month of orientation (and buildup) ends, her students can't wait to write.

When the workshop is first begun, teachers keep the time short—it can always be lengthened later as kids become more independent. To help with the start-up, they may bring in an extra adult or some workshop-savvy upper-grade children from down the hall. In the early days of workshop, teachers keep the structure simple, limiting kids' choices as needed to get the work started. For example, if having a peer conference is an available option right from the first minute of the workshop, some kids will automatically choose to talk with a classmate instead of producing something to conference about. So teachers install temporary rules: "Work by yourself for the first twenty minutes. After 9:15 you can have a kid conference if you want." This and a hundred other adaptations show how teachers move from the promising metaphor of the crafts workshop to the manageable reality of classroom workshop.

All the trouble and training are worth the effort. When the workshop starts to work, it turns the traditional transmission-model classroom upside down: students become active, responsible, self-motivating, and self-evaluating learners, while the teacher drops the talking-head role in favor of more powerful functions as model, coach, and collaborator. The classroom begins to embody the ideals of Best Practice, becoming genuinely (and manageably) student-centered, authentic, collaborative, and challenging.

Into the Classroom

Now we hear from five teachers who are pioneering their own variations of the workshop method. After spending a two-year internship in master teacher Jane Stenson's classroom, Elizabeth Roche, from the Baker Demonstration School, tells us how she started and grew a writing workshop in kindergarten. Next, Christine Paul tells us about a science workshop in third grade where students learn to think like scientists and turn guesses into hypotheses. Using the workshop time for scientific thinking, observing, and writing, students plan and conduct experiments on topics they choose for themselves.

Workshop works for math, too, as Dale Halter explains next. Dale recounts his conscious attempt to transfer the workshop model of Graves, Calkins, and Atwell directly into his sixth-grade mathematics classroom in suburban Des Plaines, Illinois. He shows how mathematical understanding and communication, two aspects of mathematics emphasized by the National Council of Teachers of Mathematics *Curriculum and Instruction Standards*, can be brought to life in a workshop situation. Finally, Harvey and our colleague Steve Zemelman write about conferences, the heart of the workshop. One main reason for setting up the whole workshop structure is to give teachers one-to-one time with learners, and these student-teacher conversations are the key mechanism for mentoring, coaching, guiding, and assessing students' growth.

Further Reading

Allen, Janet, and Kyle Gonzalez. 1998. *There's Room for Me Here: Literacy Workshop in the Middle School*. Portland, ME: Stenhouse.

Anderson, Carl. 2000. *How's It Going? A Practical Guide to Conferring with Student Writers*. Portsmouth, NH: Heinemann.

Atwell, Nancie. 1998. *In the Middle: New Understandings About Writing, Reading, and Learning*. Portsmouth, NH: Boynton/Cook.

Avery, Carol. 1993. *. . . And with a Light Touch: Learning About Reading, Writing, and Teaching with First Graders*. Portsmouth, NH: Heinemann.

Brown, Cynthia Stokes. 1994. *Connecting with the Past: History Workshop in Middle and High Schools*. Portsmouth, NH: Heinemann.

Buis, Kellie. 2004. *Writing Every Day: Reading, Writing, and Conferencing Using Student-Led Language Experiences*. Markham, ON: Pembroke.

Bullock, Richard, ed. 1998. *Why Workshop? Changing Course in 7–12 English*. Portland, ME: Stenhouse.

Cruz, M. Colleen. 2004. *Independent Writing: One Teacher—Thirty-Two Needs, Topics, and Plans*. Portsmouth, NH: Heinemann.

Fay, Kathleen, and Suzanne Whaley. 2004. *Becoming One Community: Reading and Writing with English Language Learners*. Portland, ME: Stenhouse.

Fletcher, Ralph, and JoAnn Portalupi. 1998. *Craft Lessons: Teaching Writing K–8*. Portland, ME: Stenhouse.

———. 2002. *When Students Write* (videotape). Portland, ME: Stenhouse.

Graves, Donald. 1983. *Writing: Teachers and Children at Work*. Portsmouth, NH: Heinemann.

Harwayne, Shelley. 1992. *Lasting Impressions: Weaving Literature into the Writing Workshop*. Portsmouth, NH: Heinemann.

———. 2003. *Learning to Confer: Writing Conferences in Action*. Portsmouth, NH: Heinemann.

Hindley, Joanne. 1996. *In the Company of Children*. Portland, ME: Stenhouse.

Hubbard, Ruth Shagoury. 1996. *A Workshop of the Possible: Nurturing Children's Creative Development*. Portland, ME: Stenhouse.

Jorgensen, Karen. 1993. *History Workshop: Reconstructing the Past with Elementary Students*. Portsmouth, NH: Heinemann.

Ostrow, Jill. 1999. *Making Problems, Creating Solutions: Challenging Young Mathematicians*. Portland, ME: Stenhouse.

Perl, Sondra. 2004. *Felt Sense: Writing with the Body*. Portsmouth, NH: Boynton/Cook.

Ray, Katy Wood, and Lisa B. Cleaveland. 2004. *About the Authors: Writing Workshop with Our Youngest Writers.* Portsmouth, NH: Heinemann.

Rief, Linda. 1992. *Seeking Diversity: Language Arts with Adolescents.* Portsmouth, NH: Heinemann.

Saul, Wendy, Jeanne Rearden, Anne Schmidt, Charles Pearce, Dana Blackwood, and Mary Dickinson Bird. 1993. *Science Workshop: A Whole Language Approach.* Portsmouth, NH: Heinemann.

Tobin, Lad. 2004. *Reading Student Writing: Confessions, Meditations, and Rants.* Portsmouth, NH: Heinemann.

Zemelman, Steven, and Harvey Daniels. 1988. *A Community of Writers: Teaching Writing in the Junior and Senior High School.* Portsmouth, NH: Heinemann.

Writing Workshop in Kindergarten

ELIZABETH ROCHE

It is a celebration. In kindergarten we use any and every reason to celebrate, and today, the tenth day of kindergarten, is a great occasion. It is a milestone, not just because we have survived the first ten days, but because it is the first day the children in my class will be asked to write something besides their name. Lauren proudly shows me the ten carrots she has brought in honor of the tenth day. I smile and ask her to write the word *carrot* on our chart. Lauren looks at me with a mix of skepticism, incredulity, and fear and says, "But I don't know *how* to write." My reply is simply, "You do know how to write, you just don't know how to spell."

This is where we begin creating a writing workshop, a process we'll work on all year long. Now, in September, some children are comfortably writing with invented spelling, others have not yet even considered the act of writing, and many are in between. But for all of them, there is fear that their "kid writing" will no longer be acceptable, and that from now on, since this is school, everything must be perfect. So many are focused on spelling and penmanship, and aren't thinking of writing as a way to share what they actually want to say. The normal range is quite large at this age; it will narrow with time, but for now we have children at all different stages. So we start at the *very* beginning.

In these early weeks, we spend plenty of time working on the mechanics of writing—letter recognition, letter-sound correspondence, and letter formation. But, if we did only that, we would never get children writing in the best and fullest sense of the word. The balance must lean toward the creative expression through writing while not ignoring the necessary mechanics. In kindergarten, this means that we start story dictations very early in the year. The children must start to think of themselves as storytellers early on if they are to grow in both comfort and skills. Because "making up" stories can be daunting for children as well as for adults, I have the children practice storytelling with a story box developed by Jane Stenson. This is a simple, shallow wooden box, painted blue on the inside and filled with white sand and little tchotchkes (human figures, assorted props) to be used as story prompts by the children.

I discuss the components of a story with the children. In simplest terms, I say stories should have characters, a setting, a problem, and a solution. For their dictated first story, children may feel most comfortable retelling a story they already know, such as "The Three Little Pigs" or their favorite storybook. Other children will make up their own story, but it will be short and sweet. David's first story is an example of this type:

Once there was a cat who lived in a house.
My brother pulled his tail.
The cat ran away.

It is short, but it does contain all the elements of a story. In contrast, some children may start with "heaping" the events. These stories are filled with "and then this happened . . . and then this happened . . ." Trying to encourage the child to reduce the number of problems and the rapidity with which they are solved becomes the issue here. But, always, the critical thing is that children are telling stories, and thinking and playing with words and images. Once they have something to write, the mechanics will be much more manageable.

By October, along with individual story dictation, we are writing group stories as well. The "big book of kindergarten stories" is a favorite for the children to take down and read as the year progresses. Shared writing, when the whole class composes a story together with the teacher as a scribe, is a tricky but valuable proposition. When children are still learning how to take turns in conversation, it can be arduous to hear and make sense of all the wonderful ideas being thrown out by children for the story. It is worth the effort to manage, though, not only for the literate processes of writing, reading, speaking, and listening but also for the community of writers that it creates. The children's exuberance as they yell out ideas, get silly with each other, and generally have fun "making a story" is the best incentive to write and a joyous example of learning from and with your peers. These stories are often goofy, but they are also a great indicator of what is on the mind of the classroom community, and as such illustrate and strengthen the need for writing. As a teacher, group story writing is the much-needed reminder of the innate giddiness in any group of young children. But despite the risk of completely losing the kids to the delicious chaos of the moment, I have found that with gentle guidance group authoring is not only possible but one of the most enjoyable activities in my writing program. This is the children's story, and they do take ownership of it. So my part is three-fourths scribe and one-fourth editor. We will go back later to revise the story as a group.

My role, the teacher's role, can be difficult when a story starts going in a direction that I, as an early childhood educator, am not comfortable with. One day, Alex came up to me and asked, "Can we make a story and act it out?" My response was an unequivocal "yes." The children started the story, and by the second sentence it was clear that this was a story about war. My mind started racing. After all, good early childhood teachers don't accept violence in their classrooms, right? Yet, I knew that at this time it was very important for these children to process war in a safe environment. I would figure out later how we were going to act it out, much less how to explain it to the parents. What was exciting was seeing the children use writing (and play) to work through their thoughts. Another reminder of the necessity of words and of writing!

By winter the children are on a roll, and feeling quite comfortable with both the mechanics and the process of writing. They have been writing in their journals, "making" stories together, acting out stories, and dictating their own individual stories. Now the time comes to challenge them anew, by giving them a broad, open-ended topic around which to create stories. Working with artist-in-residence Denise Berry-Hanna, the topic is shoes. Shoes are accessible, understandable, and cool enough to be of interest to the children. We start by thinking about and telling stories we already know about shoes: "Cinderella," "Puss-in-Boots," and so on. But then we begin really *looking* at shoes, and we start from the bottom up. We give the children a wide selection of different shoes, let them choose their favorite, and then make prints of their chosen shoe using the sole as a stamp. But next comes the fun part: the children tell a story about their shoe. These stories start with a prop (the shoe print), or a topic of sorts, but then the children are flying on their own wings. Orli decided to make prints of three shoes right next to one another, and this is the story that went with them:

> Once there was a shoe family. And when the father went to work the mother had to go to work, too. And then the little one was the only one left. So she decided to take a walk and she got lost on the way. She saw a little wolf and a bird. When the father and mother came home, she said, "Where is she?" So, the father said, "She might be up in her room." And when the father went up to her room, the other said, "She's not here." It was a snowy day and the little shoe remembered her tracks. So she followed those tracks and then she found her house. And the father and mommy rushed outside. The father and mother hugged her!

The shoe unit marches on with the children decorating their shoe. This time, they are in charge of making the shoe everything they want it to be. When it comes time to write the story of the shoe, Denise gives the children the opportunity to first write an outline of the "bones of the story." Again, using the basic story structure the children now write their own outline, and begin to think about the details of their story behind the shoe. Some children have begun thinking about the story before they decorated their shoe; others let the shoe come first and then layer the story on top of it. For the final publication of their shoe story, they will dictate to a teacher. Although it is winter, and they are writing for all kinds of reasons, from notes to reminders to signs, the actual process of transcribing a story is too arduous if the integrity of the story is to be maintained. That time is not far off, but if we want stories of any depth now, the children will need to dictate them. They have story structure down by now, and are feeling like wordsmiths and authors.

By spring, everything is shifting in kindergarten. And now comes the time to put it all together, the penmanship, the invented spelling, and the expressive writing. We begin "reading and writing parties" with our first-grade buddies who come to visit once a week. For this half-hour time, the pairs may either read or write together. Most often, they choose to write stories because that allows for more playfulness and interaction. This is a great opportunity for peer mentoring by the great big first graders, and the children do actually work together! Here is an example of a story written over a course of two reading and writing parties:

I Can Read
by Max and Andrea
I can read a little book. I can read a meadyem book. I can read a big book. I can read a chapter book. I can read a story book. I am a reader. I can make books that I can read. I can read my name. I can go to the library and read. The End.

The idea is for the children to experience the writing process, the creative process, with someone else in the community. They may read what they have written to each other or to the whole class, in what is the beginning of peer conferences and final drafts. Just as real writers turn to others for feedback, so do the children in this situation—and from the most important people, their peers! We have now created the kindergarten equivalent of a writers' workshop, complete with cookies at the end of the session.

The children are continuing to grow in taking responsibility for their own learning, and in their skills. The next challenge that awaits them is writing poetry.

If poetry is thoughts and feelings distilled, then there can be no better form for the beginning writer. It is a natural fit. It is the carefully chosen word, thought, and feeling that makes poetry so accessible, yet challenging, for children. Because it is not necessary that poems be lengthy, the children are also able to do all the writing, composing, and transcribing on their own. The children most often follow a poetic form that is introduced in a mini-lesson, though that is not required. If I do give them a format to follow, the creation is all their own.

Although it is spring, we still have children in different stages of skill and comfort with writing, so some of the poems are quite brief, others quite detailed. But the process of writing, revising, and publishing is the same for every child. Here are two examples of first attempts at poetry:

In the Sea
by Alex
In the deep, deep sea there is an octopus
In the deep, deep sea, under the octopus,
There is a sea-horse.

Smelly Socks
by Cole
Smelly socks
Smelly shirts
Smelly pants
I hate smelly clothes.

Both of these poems show children playing with words, images, and ideas while they are writing. Because they have not been forced to write before they are comfortable doing so, they allow themselves the luxury of playing with language as they work. There is no tension about writing any more. They have come to see themselves as competent, responsible learners who can take joy in playing with language and ideas—and that is the beginning for every writer.

In kindergarten, as everywhere else, the hardest part of writing is getting started. In my writing program, I focus on creative expression and know that the mechanics of writing are only strengthened by this approach. If children are given the opportunity to share their stories, images, and ideas from the beginning of their life in school, they will share them forever onward. They need only a little convincing that they are the next great novelists or poets, and they are hooked on the notion that writing, with all its challenges, is important and, even better, fun. The need for words is undisputed; our job is to give children the joy of using them.

A Young Scientist's Workshop

CHRISTINE PAUL

As a third-grade teacher I feel very confident using the writing workshop model developed by Lucy Calkins, Donald Graves, and Nancie Atwell. I start on the first day of school by creating a classroom community that supports a free exchange of ideas, open dialogue, and choice. But after reading *Doing What Scientists Do: Children Learn to Investigate Their World* by Ellen Doris, I realized that the workshop approach need not be limited to reading and writing. Math and science, although they appear on the surface to require a very different method of delivering content, can be taught using a similar workshop structure.

By offering choice, talk, and modeling, I create a community where my young scientists experience the cycle of questioning and investigating much like student writers who write during workshop. Students have natural curiosities about the world and their questions open doors for exploration and authentic hands-on work. The county in which I teach provides engaging hands-on kits that include lesson plans and materials in several core science areas. In the past I relied heavily on the prepackaged lesson plans included with these kits. While using the ready-made lessons was a good place to start, I wanted to take science a step further and make the workshop about being a scientist; to question like a scientist, plan like a scientist, and analyze like a scientist. Where the kit might lead students to one natural conclusion in an area of study, a genuine science workshop would support a free exchange of ideas, model various ways to find an answer, and allow for multiple conclusions after testing.

I initially felt intimidated teaching science, so I began by reviewing each of the five kits my school district provides for third grade. From the kits, I identified the principles that are central to the scientific process. I reminded myself that what we do in writer's workshop is write. Therefore in science we need to *do* science—particularly, experience the cycle of questioning and discovering our world. Here is the list of scientific steps I pulled together from our county kits and Doris's book:

1. observe
2. formulate questions
3. make hypotheses
4. devise a plan, research, test variables, and conduct experiments
5. draw conclusions, and
6. replicate experiments to show reliability

My goal was to merge these steps with the workshop ideology I knew so well. As I recount some of the basic steps I use to set up an authentic science workshop in my classroom, notice how I focus on one step of the workshop at a time, all the while bringing the students through the entire process of science inquiry. Many of my students have experienced reading and writing workshop since kindergarten, so the initial groundwork existed. However, I also recognize that effective workshops have strong classroom communities and I needed to ensure that our safe community would carry over to science time. For the students to grow as scientists they need a community with a free exchange of ideas in an environment that models and supports student thinking.

Workshop Approach

As with any workshop, setting up a classroom environment that is conducive to teaching science is imperative. Before the year begins I open my own mind and eyes to the world around me and collect interesting things that we can keep in our classroom. I begin to live like a scientist much as I live like a writer, by keeping a writer's notebook. I gather things such as interesting leaves, seed pods that have landed on the roof of my car, dead locusts on the sidewalk, and colorful shells. I purchase a few live animals: a fish that survives on the root of a water lily and two mice. I begin to record observations in a science sketchbook and locate blank notebooks for each of the students to keep. These are simply spiral notebooks filled with blank pages where students can record thoughts, sketches, data, and plans. I also use these notebooks to track growth and assess individual understanding of projects being completed. I stock our library with science books and hands-on items to make our room receptive to young scientific minds. I recognize that it isn't just the physical environment that is so important, but what we do inside of it that counts. Placing these items in our room is a foundation for me to then model how to use these items to question and investigate. We all take ownership over these items in our community and begin to use them as real scientists would.

Early in the year we gather as a group and list the work we do during language arts. The students come up with basic things fundamental to every writer's workshop:

- whole-group lesson or reading using an author's writing as an example
- status of the class/how you can use that author to help your writing
- independent writing time
- conferencing, and
- sharing

Whole-Group Mini-Lesson

With this framework established, I ask the students, "What do scientists do?" Their answers are varied and all-encompassing; "study dinosaurs, work with chemicals, look at animals, study nature, do experiments, and work with fun stuff." To show the students the connection to our previous lesson about what we do in a workshop, I check off "whole-group lesson" from our workshop schedule once our brainstorming is complete. This portion of our day didn't last more than ten minutes so that we could spend most of our time doing independent work and exploration.

Status of the Class

I then ask the students to find a comfortable place in the room to independently continue their thinking about science. I dismiss them from the carpet with a science notebook and ask them where they are going in the room and why they chose that space to think about science. Initially the students are unsure as to what to say. They have never thought of our classroom space as a laboratory. They know it as a library and a writing space, but they need to redefine it as a place for science much as I had done as I prepared over the summer. I call on Daniel, who is particularly astute in science. He replies, "I am going to go by the fish because I want to observe how he eats the roots of the plant." His comment has all the students chatting. Can they actually use this time to visit with class pets? Can they simply look out the window at the weather? Can they look at the rocks they filled their pockets with on the way to school? It is a chance for them to take a risk and for me to go out on a limb and let them lead the way to their own definition of science. As the last student leaves the carpet, I ask Kellie to check off "status of the class" to show the similarities between our writing workshop time and the time we are creating together in science workshop.

Independent Time

Beginning any new workshop requires a lot of leading by example. Even though the basic setup of the workshop is old hat, the act of using a portion of science time to write is new to the kids. They are accustomed to the science kits, where an entire experiment's steps are laid out for the students to follow. Oftentimes, materials are given out in sets, partners are chosen, and data collection charts handed out. My students now sit in front of various items in the room with a blank science notebook—daunting for anyone, to say the least. On this first day, I model how to record observations on a large sheet of paper at the front of the room. I use a nearby plant as an item to observe. I sketch the plant, label some of the parts I know, put questions next to parts I don't know, and so on. I notice the students taking my lead as they watch me and then begin to sketch. Some of them begin to write a series of questions in their books and several begin descriptive paragraphs about what they see in front of them. Once a majority of the students are engrossed with their thinking and work, I check off "independent time" and begin to roam around the room to help students who appear to be stuck.

One such student is Sandra. Her sketchbook is open and she has a few sketches of the mice, but nothing is written and she seems to be staring into space for a great length of time. Sandra joined my class as an English language learner who had been in the country for only half of second grade. She is shy but eager to please. She feels very comfortable sketching the mice that she sits in front of but unsure about writing anything on the paper. Before approaching her I speak with Mary, who, like Sandra, speaks Spanish but is not as eager to do work, and ask her to work with Sandra to write questions in their native language. I bring the two girls together:

Mrs. Paul: Sandra, I thought it would be helpful to have Mary work with you during science. You could work as a team to watch the mice and talk about what you see. Have you ever seen a mouse this close before?

Sandra (*in Spanish while Mary translated*): My cousin has a mouse that is like this but it is different because it has black fur.

Mrs. Paul: That's exactly what scientists do! They use what they know, like your cousin's mouse, and compare it with what they see. Can you make a list of how your cousin's mouse and our mouse are the same or different? You can write in Spanish and put it in your notebook next to the sketches you made.

Mary: Can we make a chart like this to record it in? (*draws a T chart*)

Mrs. Paul: Absolutely. Scientists use many different ways to organize their observations so that they can make sense of them later when they are answering their questions.

With over 80 percent of my science class English language learners, it is imperative that I allow the students ample time to talk. Oral language helps these students make sense of new things and cement these ideas in their brains. The best way for the students to learn a new language is to have many opportunities to use the language they are learning. They need to work through the science and experiment with the language to make sense of their emerging understandings as well as the inquiry process. I had seen too many instances when students were excited to do the hands-on work, but then bound by not being able to record or share their discoveries. The county kits limit them to mere exploration, never really allowing them to make concrete conclusions about those hands-on experiences.

Conferring and Sharing

After about twenty minutes I wrap up independent work time by having kids quickly pair up. As I progress through the year, our independent time will increase to nearly an hour, but early in the year the students feel most successful with fifteen to twenty minutes. I share with them one thing Christian said to me during independent time: "Scientists also share what they learn!" I encourage them to share three interesting things they noticed and one question they still had with their partner. Once they do this, we all meet for group sharing. It takes us a while to fine-tune this portion of our workshop time. I am intrigued because many of these same students feel comfortable sharing and responding during writer's workshop; however, in this setting they are unsure of what to say. I wonder if they don't see themselves as scientists and therefore feel uncomfortable responding as a voice of authority on the topic. The children look to me for answers. For example, Robert shares his question with the whole group after looking at the fish eating the roots. "I noticed the fish would swim into the middle of the roots and then stop using its fins to swim—he just hung in the roots. Why didn't he use that time to keep eating, when he was relaxing?" Robert is eager to hear suggestions, but the students sit silently.

It is at this point that I think I can let my group in on a little secret. I explain to them that I majored in English in college and science is not exactly my expertise, either! I will have to learn to be a scientist right along with them. I can help them become scientists, but they will have to ask the questions and we will discover the answers together. Allowing myself to be free of having to "know everything in science" put me at ease to be a better science teacher. I finish by telling the kids that Robert made an observation and asked a follow-up question. What can he do to find the answer? I write the students' ideas down, many of which involve looking in books. Looking in books is one of the hardest habits to change in the science workshop. Many students want to look in books for the *right* answer, and I always redirect them to make a plan that allows them to *do* something to come up with a possible explanation. While finding answers in books is one way of obtaining information, I want them to investigate and come up with their own conclusions based on theories they prove or disprove. I don't want to stop their thinking process.

Ellin Keene once said that when we immediately give kids the answers to their questions we stop their thinking. As an adult I know that in science nothing is concrete because scientists are always trying to disprove a theory. This is a pretty lofty notion but important for the students to develop into authentic scientists. I am still figuring out how to solve this issue but I'm sure that the workshop approach will allow room for such thinking over time. After I explain to the students that finding answers in books is only one way of solving problems, Sang speaks up. "Maybe the fish was just sleeping. We don't eat when we sleep. Too many things at one time to do." Thrilled at such an astute connection, I write it on the board next to the word *hypothesis*. I want them to begin to use the scientific terminology even early in the process. I tell the students that often scientists ask a question and then make a guess as to what they think the answer will be. Then they make a plan to see if their guess is accurate. All of the steps that they did that day are what scientists do every day in their labs.

I finish the lesson, which takes the full math and science block, by having the students cite the specific ways we participated in a workshop like we did in writing. By checking off each step along the way, the students concretely understand how this science workshop will be our way of living like scientists, going through the cycle of questioning and discovering, something we'd return to each day.

Mini-Lessons

Over time we build on the principles that we laid out the first day. It takes nearly three months of doing science workshop three days a week for the kids to move through each step confidently. During each independent work time I take copious notes, making sure to acknowledge the gains made for assessment purposes, but also noting where the class needs to have more guidance. Pulling directly from conferences and observations, I am able to teach mini-lessons that reflect our class's unique science investigations while teaching the scientific process. These lessons focusing on the scientific process take about three months. Some of the lessons include the following:

- How do you observe?
  - Sketches
  - Photographs
  - Labeling
  - Questions
  - Statements
  - Magnifying
  - From various angles
- What makes a good question?
  - What is a question?
  - Open versus closed questioning
  - Questions that require you to do something
  - Questions that require you to research something
  - Generating questions from questions
  - Making a statement into a question
- Making a guess or hypothesis
  - What is a hypothesis?
  - Making sure the guess relates to the question

- ■ Putting thought behind your guess, not random ideas
- ■ Using books to help you make a comparison
- ■ Using a plan
  - ■ Making a plan
  - ■ Being specific in a plan
  - ■ Following a plan
- ■ Making a conclusion
  - ■ Conclusions answer the original question
  - ■ Was your hypothesis correct?
  - ■ Writing conclusions that explain your thinking
  - ■ Sharing your conclusions with other scientists

Independent time gives the students an opportunity to try different stages of the process and also allows the students to watch me work through the entire process so they can see where they are going with their lines of questioning. During this entire time, everyone in the class brings in fascinating things to observe and put on our science table, which is located in the center of the room. The table always has sketching materials and a large paper for students to write questions they come up with while spending time at the table. It is from these questions that I make several mini-lessons. The wonderings from the students come at any part of the day so it is critical that I remain perceptive to what is going on, particularly when I am eager to match a student question with a concept needing to be addressed in the third-grade curriculum.

What Makes Soda Fizz?

One day the class is eating lunch in the classroom after a field trip. Christian is excited about his soda since he usually has milk for lunch. When he opens it, the soda makes a loud hissing noise and fizzes. He thinks aloud to the friends at his table, "I wonder how soda does that?"

I immediately jump in and ask, "How does soda do what?"

"How do they make it get fizzy?" he replies.

Knowing that third graders are required to learn the states of matter, this is an ideal opportunity for several lessons about writing a hypothesis and a plan while addressing an applicable content area. I ask Christian if we can use his question with the entire class to make a science plan and use it as a series of mini-lessons for the next week. He excitedly agrees.

The next day we work as a group to write several guesses to Christian's question.

- ■ They put chemicals inside the bottle.
- ■ Air rushes in when you open it and it bubbles to the top.

- Special ingredients make it fizz.
- When you shake it you get the air all mixed up and it wants to push out.

We then refine these guesses into one hypothesis that reads, "The fizz in soda is created by a chemical reaction when all the ingredients come together in the bottle." It is important that we refine their thinking because my intent with this lesson is to help students go beyond their first and most obvious guess when writing their hypothesis. I had noted several students the previous week spending little time writing a hypothesis. They made simple statements without much thought to the question and what really was happening. I was convinced that many students could make more educated guesses if they put more time into thinking about it. By combining several student guesses in whole-group time, they are able to see that many ideas can be combined to make a concise hypothesis. I encourage them to use their independent work time that day to look back at the most recent hypothesis they made and try to make several guesses and then combine them to make the best possible statement.

The next day we write a plan. Writing a plan proves to be the most difficult stage for students to accomplish independently. First drafts are limited and so short that several steps are left out or assumed. Another person picking up the plan would not be able to complete the experiment. I continuously work on this step, and this is yet another opportunity to write and revise a plan as a whole group. The first version of the soda plan follows:

1. Get a bottle.
2. Get water.
3. Get all the other ingredients.
4. Mix them together.
5. Watch for fizz.
6. Taste it.

As you can see, it isn't nearly as detailed as it needs to be. When I see plans such as these I am often overwhelmed with where to start. I can see so many things wrong. I remind myself on a daily basis that to be a powerful teacher I have to focus on one thing; in this case it was specificity. We leave this first plan as it is after the mini-lesson and I encourage the students to make sure they have a first draft of a plan from their own independent investigations before the next science period. I always invite them to try what we learned in whole group or what I had modeled. This helps make the material concrete and doesn't allow students to become passive during whole-group work. They know I expect them to put into operation the things we learn during this time.

The next day I gather up what is listed in the plan and we follow it exactly. Step number one has us asking questions right away. I read it aloud. "Get a bottle." I turn to Sang and say, "Can you please go get a bottle?"

He looks back at me with a blank grin. "I don't know what kind of bottle," he finally responds.

I add, "Well, I don't know, either, the plan just says get a bottle."

Robert blurts out, "You know, the kind of plastic bottles that soda comes in."

"Should we write it differently in our plan so that Sang knows what to get then?"

"We can write, 'Get a 12 oz. plastic soda bottle.'"

"Oh, Sang, do you think you can get that kind of bottle?" Sang quickly locates a bottle from our sink area. The students soon discover the need to be specific and begin to break down every step in the plan to accommodate our new needs. The first plan simply didn't have enough information to accomplish the task at hand. The second version of the plan read:

1. Get a 12 oz. plastic soda bottle.
2. Read the ingredients label on the side of a Sprite bottle and get all the ingredients.
3. Use a funnel to mix them together one ingredient at a time to see if something happens.
4. Record results in lab book.
5. Put top on bottle and observe the next day.

I could take this a step further and fine-tune several of these steps. I notice that the quantities are missing and it is impossible to get all the actual ingredients from the side of a Sprite bottle. In science workshop, you will see "holes" all the time as the students learn the process. As with any workshop, trying to correct everything is unrealistic. I look to see where I can help the most, what technique or strategy will bring them closer to the ultimate goal of becoming a scientist, and then run with it. We end the lesson trying to revise our own plans during independent time.

Still using the soda fizz experiment as a backdrop, and after meeting two goals of writing revised hypotheses and specific plans, we do the experiment as written. Of course, nothing happens. No fizz. Nothing. We begin to share to figure out what happened. A few of the students say, "We did it wrong. We messed it up." I explain to the kids that nothing in science is wrong; all conclusions lead us to some sort of explanation. In this case we learned that a chemical reaction didn't cause the fizz. We are one step closer to figuring out how the fizz works because now we have eliminated one possible explanation. Some science experiments take several attempts and you will need to revise your hypothesis after having tested the first one. Kellie points out that the fizz didn't appear until after it was opened and thought that it was a reaction with the air. I encourage her to write a new hypothesis based on her observation and try the experiment again. Even though we don't come up with a hard and fast reason as to where the fizz comes from, the students are now beginning to understand how to question, hypothesize, make a plan, and conduct an experiment. Now it is just a matter of making sure the students conduct experiments that encompass the state-mandated curriculum.

Meeting National, State, and County Objectives

The county in which I teach aligns its curriculum closely with that of the national standards in science. Even though there is a lot of material, I am always in awe at how the students' natural curiosity about their world leads them to the very questions that serve as the backbone of our experiments. Sometimes, I add items on the science table that will naturally guide the students to question a certain core topic.

For example, once I placed a tub of water on the floor and some toy boats next to it. One of the questions that week was, "How do boats float?" This was a perfect introduction into the otherwise rarely used kit called Sink and Float. As a class we designed our very own experiment testing objects in various liquids. The students went above and beyond the state requirements and what the kits provided. My students not only learned about the states of matter, but also tested six different materials in three different densities and designed several flotation devices, all the while writing the entire experiment themselves. They performed these experiments in small groups as we documented the entire process piece by piece during mini-lesson time. They went beyond the requirements and made learning about matter more powerful and long-lasting. I was impressed with the ownership they took over the work and the eagerness to ask more follow-up questions.

Evolution of the Workshop

With time, my third graders are able to work on several different small-group investigations at the same time. On any given day you might find explorations on evolution, inclined planes, cricket distance jumping, and volcanoes. They sign up in groups of four next to questions at the science table. New groups are always forming, and I help them set time lines to ensure they cycle through the entire scientific process and share the results with the entire class (and often other grade levels). Having multiple projects going simultaneously requires that I take careful notes about each group and where they are headed, the resources they might need, and the never-ending need for obscure supplies. I also try to make sure the groups always shift members, responsibilities are shared, and English language learners have sufficient support. As the students become immersed in their own projects it becomes important that all students be responsible for all material being learned in the room. The sharing and brainstorming portion of the workshop becomes the most critical time for learning. Students have to teach what they discover and answer questions from students not participating in their group. They have to follow up on questions they may not yet know the answer to and field ideas about things that may have them puzzled. By May, my presence in the circle is merely as assessor. I write their dialogue and just try to keep up with their amazing accomplishments. They have all become scientists in the most authentic way: doing and being.

A Community of Mathematicians

DALE HALTER

Like English, mathematics is a language. People use mathematics to make sense out of the world and to communicate what they think and know. NCTM's *Curriculum and Instruction Standards for School Mathematics* (1989) put heavy emphasis on two particular aspects of mathematical power: understanding and communication. This language-oriented view of mathematics calls for some changes in our vision of teaching and learning. It seems reasonable, then, to look at the best theory and practice already developed for language education and think about applying those principles to our teaching of mathematics.

One method that has been extraordinarily successful in many language arts classrooms is the reading and writing workshop. Many teachers are already familiar with this popular model; Nancie Atwell, Donald Graves, Lucy Calkins, Steven Zemelman, and Harvey Daniels have all written extensively about workshop. In this article, I want to discuss how I have adapted and translated some principles and techniques of workshop to teaching mathematics in my own sixth-grade mathematics classroom.

The following assumptions have guided my explorations of the mathematics workshop. In my own special community of mathematicians:

1. Students learn to use mathematics to create meaning for themselves and others. Rather than learning only about the discrete skills involved in mathematics, specific skills like adding and division are taught in the context of the students making meaning in real-life applications.

2. Students spend time talking and writing about mathematics for real audiences and for real purposes, because understanding and communication are so closely linked. The purpose of mathematics is to understand the world and communicate that understanding; school mathematics must have that same purpose.

3. Students relate the mathematics they use in school to their everyday lives, and to other school subjects (social studies, music, science, physical education, etc.).

4. Students have a great deal of choice in what they study. They confer with the teacher to determine what investigations or reports they will work on, and what mathematical concepts those projects will involve. The teacher and students also decide how the results of the work will be reported, and to what audience (an oral report to the class, a poster in the hall, a letter to the PTA, etc.). Within this context of real mathematics work, the teacher finds opportunities to help students develop the specific skills they need and the curriculum requires.

5. The teacher is a fellow learner and mathematician with the students, as well as an expert resource and coach.

The math workshop encourages students to work together, using mathematics to understand their world. The teacher works alongside the students, encouraging them to become more sophisticated in their mathematical skills and understandings and in their ability to communicate mathematically. This atmosphere is designed to resemble a community of mathematicians dealing with real-life mathematical situations and problems.

With these principles in mind, the teacher's goal is to help students create this community in the classroom. Reaching that goal is a complicated, interesting, and invigorating task; of course, there is no one way to do it. What follows is my own approach to beginning the year in a mathematics workshop. It is not a plan for a whole year of teaching, but rather an example of the kinds of activities that have been used to get one classroom community started.

Beginning the Year: A Survey

I start the year by asking my sixth-grade students to fill out a survey of their attitudes toward and experiences with mathematics (see Figure 5.1). This survey looks very similar to the reading and writing surveys Nancie Atwell published in *In the Middle* (1998). Two purposes are served here: I get to know something about the kids' attitudes and history as math students, and they begin to get a sense that this

Figure 5.1: The math workshop begins by seeking students' mathematical autobiographies.

Mathematics Survey

Name _____

For the first seven questions, circle the number that best shows what you think or feel about the question.

1. Do you like math?
   Not at all   Very much
   0   1   2   3   4   5   6   7   8   9   10
2. How good are you at doing math?
   Not at all   Very much
   0   1   2   3   4   5   6   7   8   9   10
3. Do you get good grades in math?
   Not at all   Very much
   0   1   2   3   4   5   6   7   8   9   10
4. Do you use math outside of school?
   Not at all   Very much
   0   1   2   3   4   5   6   7   8   9   10
5. In school, how often do you learn new things in math?
   Not at all   Very much
   0   1   2   3   4   5   6   7   8   9   10
6. Do you use math in other subjects in school?
   Not at all   Very much
   0   1   2   3   4   5   6   7   8   9   10
7. Outside of math class, is math important?
   Not at all   Very much
   0   1   2   3   4   5   6   7   8   9   10

Please write a brief answer to each of these questions:
8. What does it take to be good in math?

9. What do you do best in math? Why?

10. What kind of math is most difficult for you? Why?

11. When is math the most fun to do? Why?

12. How do teachers know when a student is good at doing math?

13. In general, how do you feel about math?

---

math class is going to be about what they think, that their ideas will have an important place in our classroom.

An Initial Investigation

Our upcoming year of mathematics workshop will be filled with students doing mathematical investigations and reporting their results to the class (and to other audiences when appropriate). In order to help them get prepared for this kind of work, I begin an investigation with the whole class together. One simple project students have found engaging begins with the question, "How long do you think our class would stretch if we lay down in the hallway end to end?" Students work in groups to make an estimate; then they tell their estimate to the class and explain how they reached it. We then go out and lie down in the hallway to see how long we are. This leads to discussion of what an average sixth grader's height is. It also helps students deal with problems involved in adding, multiplying, and dividing using feet and inches (or centimeters and meters).

This first whole-class investigation gives the students a framework for going about similar projects on their own and in groups. This height project can lead into an inquiry in which the class describes the "average sixth grader." Students think of ways to describe themselves, and then each student chooses one attribute (age in days, eye color, distance of home from school, etc.). That student's job is to gather information about that attribute, describe the "average student" in a mathematical way, and present the results to the class. While each student is responsible for a report, students may also work in groups, which act as support and give feedback to the individuals on how their reports are coming. The culminating event for each student is a report to the class, which can include visual and oral presentations of the information (what attribute I studied, what information I got, and how I found the average). My students usually make "average student posters" to hang in the hallway for Parent Orientation night.

A Typical Unit: Measurement

In the math workshop, one unit of study might focus on measurement. Students begin by discussing why and how people measure things. After making a list of their ideas (and the teacher's), students are formed into groups. The students' tasks can be explained as follows:

> **Your Measurement Projects**
> In our last class discussion, we listed many things that people measure. Some of them are listed for you below. If you think of other things people measure, add them to your list. That list can help you decide on projects you want to do.
>
> Things People Measure
> 1. Length (6 inches, 10,000 miles)
> 2. Area of a flat surface (900 square feet)
> 3. Volume (1 quart, 50 cubic feet)

4. Time (three hours, 1/10 of a second, 500 years)
5. Speed (55 miles per hour, 186,000 miles per second)
6. Loudness (25 decibels)
7. Heat (98.6 degrees Fahrenheit, 1 degree Celsius)
8. Work (800 foot-pounds)
9. _____
10. _____

As you work through this unit, your group needs to do the following things:

1. Each member of the group must do an individual measurement project. This project will use one or more types of measurement. You will do the measuring and calculating necessary to describe whatever you have selected, and report to your group (and maybe the whole class) on what you measured and how you did it.
2. Your group will also work together on a group project. This will be like the individual project, but everyone in the group must help do the measuring and calculating. Everyone in the group must also help present the project to the class.
3. During this unit the whole class will work together on some mini-lessons. Every member in the group must participate fully in these lessons. Your participation may include leading lessons for the class, if you wish.

As the students think about possible subjects for individual and group reports, they may need help in the form of suggested topics. While it is ideal for students to come up with their own ideas, it is also natural for mathematicians within a community to ask each other for ideas. Below are some measurement questions that kids have pursued at our school; certainly every school or community presents a wealth of similar possibilities.

1. How many concrete blocks were used to make (our classroom, the gym, etc.), and how much do they weigh?
2. How much air is there in this room (the hallway, etc.)?
3. How much area is there in a (football field, baseball park, tennis court, soccer field, etc.)? Which sports use the largest areas?
4. How much garbage does our lunchroom throw out per (day, week, month, school year)?
5. Develop a rating system to judge the performance of basketball players. Use that system to rate the Chicago Bulls (or your school team) for several of their games.

6. Develop a lesson to teach something about measurement (measuring to the nearest quarter inch; cups, pints, quarts, gallons, etc.). You might choose to teach our class or some other class in the school, such as our first-grade buddies.
7. How big is our playground (perimeter, area)? How much of it is blacktop, grass, stones?
8. How thick is a piece of paper? Are all types of paper the same thickness?
9. How fast do people grow? How tall are students of various ages at Orchard Place School?
10. How does the temperature change as we go from fall into winter?
11. How far would you go if you walked continuously for (one day, one week, one month, one year)?
12. How many stones are there under the swings and slides on our playground?
13. How much work does it take for our class to walk upstairs from the lunchroom?
14. How long does it take for the average person to perform some task?

Organizing the Mathematics Workshop

If the idea of students working on different projects and investigations in a mathematics workshop sounds valuable for students, it can also sound difficult to manage. If you are familiar with workshop in a reading and/or writing context, you will see how I have adapted the familiar structures of a literacy workshop to mathematics. Here are some suggestions of organizing techniques, many of which I've borrowed from colleagues who are running successful reading and writing workshops.

Five Minutes: Status-of-the-Class

Status-of-the-class is a simple procedure teachers can use to make sure that every student has something productive to do. The teacher starts the period by asking each student to say very quickly what they will be working on that day, and where they are in their project. Typical student responses in a mathematics classroom might be "I'm going to measure the hallway so that I can figure out its area" or "I'm finishing the poster about the speed of cars in front of the school" or "I need to talk to you about what I should do next in my project." Status-of-the-class gives the teacher an idea of who is making good progress and who needs immediate attention. It calls on the students to be responsible for determining what they will do and for making progress each day. It also helps students get ideas by hearing about each other's projects, difficulties, and activities.

Five to Ten Minutes: Mini-Lesson

After status-of-the-class, the teacher might lead a short mini-lesson on some topic appropriate to the type of projects the students are currently working on. Typically these take five to ten minutes near the beginning of the period and are used for a wide variety of purposes. The teacher might use mini-lessons to teach about different ways to organize and present data. The teacher (or the students) might teach lessons on a particular kind of computation that is difficult for a number of students.

These mini-lessons provide an important opportunity for the teacher to "deliver the curriculum." If many students are working on games, the teacher might briefly present key concepts about probability. If they are working with measurement, mini-lessons about standard units, margin of error, area, and volume might be appropriate. The students' real-math work helps them grasp the concepts and helps them see why and when basic math skills are used. In general, these mini-lessons can help the classroom community participate in a shared set of experiences and develop a common vocabulary for their mathematical discourse.

Thirty-Plus Minutes: Work Time

After the mini-lesson, students work independently and in small groups. This working time takes up most of the class period. The students use this time to plan investigations and carry out various kinds of research, measurement, and calculation. They organize their results into coherent final presentations (written, oral, or both) for their classmates and other audiences. During work time, the teacher meets with students to guide and advise them and to assess their progress. The teacher might make anecdotal notes about students' progress and difficulties, or use a checklist to record observations. This time provides an excellent opportunity to see exactly what a student needs to learn and to provide specific individual or small-group instruction.

Ten Minutes: Sharing Time

Sharing ideas at the end of a workshop session is important and enjoyable for most kids. During this time, a few students will explain to the class what they have done (finished or in progress), and ask their classmates for feedback. Individual students or groups can tell the whole class what question they are studying, what they have done so far to figure it out, and what they plan to do next. They can also ask for advice on how to go about the work. Feedback from the class is officially limited to what the presenter needs and requests.

Important learning takes place when students share their work this way. Students learn from each other's reports, and the reporters learn, too. I have seen more than a few students work most of the way through a project incorrectly, only to realize their mistake when they prepare to tell their classmates what they have done. Students need a wide array of such "publishing" opportunities, chances to communicate their mathematical ideas. This can be done either through oral presentations in class or in writing, with posters to be hung in the halls, chapters in class magazines, or letters to outside agencies or individuals. A rich assortment of these outlets for sharing provides students with many opportunities for the kind of discourse so highly recommended in the NCTM standards.

Conclusion

Together, the teacher and students in a mathematics workshop can build units around such topics as time, money, games, numbers smaller than one, or anything else of interest to them. As they do this, the teacher will find appropriate places to teach the skills and knowledge the students need—as defined by the district curriculum or the national standards. The key is designing mathematics classes that are about what the students think and know and that respect and use their real-world mathematical experiences and knowledge. Then mathematics learning takes place in a context of real mathematical work.

One very important difference in the workshop approach is that the teacher serves not just as a presenter of mathematics, but as a co-learner, a model, and a side-by-side participant as students work. By joining in investigations alongside our students, we honor their work; we naturally demonstrate how adult learners tackle mathematical questions; we gain firsthand understanding of the rewards and difficulties of the kids' work; and we receive a wealth of teaching opportunities. Best of all, it gives us a chance to celebrate real-life mathematics, to show how math is really a tool for understanding subjects that are important to all of us.

Many of us learned a language like Spanish or French when we were in high school, but have lost that language because we haven't used it since then. Sadly, this is the same experience many people have with mathematics. It becomes a strange, abstract, lost language spoken only in school, and too many students leave it at the door at the end of every school day. In the same way, "school math" can seem so unrelated to things students know in the real world that they leave all their common sense outside the door when they enter math class.

Mathematics workshop is one attempt to bridge this gap, to connect the in-class language of mathematics to the outside world, to everything else our students think, know, and do. It is a way of turning our math classes into communities of active, independent learners and mathematicians.

Conferences: The Core of the Workshop

HARVEY DANIELS AND STEVEN ZEMELMAN

One of the reasons teachers set up workshop-style classrooms is to make room for regular one-to-one conferences with individual kids. These student-teacher conversations are so fundamental that the workshop model itself is sometimes called the "studio-conference method." As master teachers like Donald Graves (1983, 1994) have shown, even teacher-student conferences as short as three minutes and spaced as far apart as two weeks can have a surprisingly strong impact on students' learning. So, while the structure of workshop has many other beneficial effects, it inherently provides a set of norms by which the teacher can hold brief individual conferences while other students work autonomously for extended periods of time. When teachers institute a workshop for forty-five minutes or an hour a day, they are implicitly swapping the low-intensity impact of whole-class instruction for brief but powerful individual lessons embedded in long chunks of orderly practice time.

Why are conferences so valuable? Why are they worth the trouble to set them up? To start with, conferences obviously facilitate the individualization that educators (and parents) always dream of but find so hard to provide in practice. In conferences, we can talk to each child just about what that person needs at that moment, instead of aiming our teaching at "the middle of the group." Teachers also find that students are more comfortable and self-disclosing in private conversation than in the whole-class setting. Many kids "open up" in conferences, showing far more of what they know and what they need. In a very real sense, conferences are a way of opening a whole separate channel of communication between teacher and students, one that is unexploited in classrooms where the talk is predominantly teacher-to-group.

Ironically, once teachers have created time for conferences, they sometimes cannot think of what to say. Teachers new to workshop-style classrooms ask: "How can I be sure I'll say the right thing in conferences?" "What happens if I say the wrong thing?" "How can I plan what to say to many different children in a day?" But these worries reflect a more teacher-as-expert role than conferences really require. Conferences should not be treated as simply another delivery system for teacher presentations; indeed, they are actually quite inefficient mechanisms for distributing information. What conferences do uniquely provide are chances for teachers to take on some very different roles: as model, mentor, and coach.

Instead of delivering facts, teachers can demonstrate patterns of thinking, habits of mind. With virtually any piece of student work on the table before them,

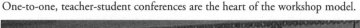

One-to-one, teacher-student conferences are the heart of the workshop model.

teachers can lead students through the stages of reflection and self-assessment. As an experienced learner, the teacher can show how a researcher sifts and winnows information, creates categories, interprets data, resolves discrepancies; or how a writer combs back through the text of a draft, finding places for revision and improvement, editing and polishing.

The ultimate value of conferences lies not just in what goes on during any one three-minute session, but in what develops over a recurrent series of meetings between a teacher and a learner. When conferences are a regular occurrence, teachers can inculcate the habit of stopping to take stock: to pause amid one's efforts, to review the work to date, to identify strengths and weaknesses, to review possible courses of action, to make choices among possible next steps, and to put one's plans to work—and, after not-too-long an interval, to pause and reflect once more.

In other words, conferences are private demonstrations of how to think, how to run your brain, how to monitor your work, how to evaluate your products, how to sustain your efforts. In the best of conferences, the teacher does not step in to solve students' problems or make their decisions, but guides them to decide for themselves, making their own choices and living out the consequences.

Conferences help kids internalize that vital cognitive habit of shifting gears from production to reflection, from immersion to distancing, from doing to assessing. And the key to this cognitive coaching is not advice or information given by teachers, but their presence, patience, and consistency in accompanying students through the process.

Conducting Conferences

Understanding the deep structure of conferences, teachers can relax about what they say in any one conference, and see themselves more as long-term thinking coaches. The process, the regularity, the developing relationship, the habits of mind are most important. There's not one right conference to have, but there are many worthwhile conversations to pursue. With any given child, with any piece of work at hand, and at any particular moment, there will always be several "correct" conferences, many valuable things that a caring, tuned-in adult could say. Of course, some approaches may be better than others, and we could imagine a few that would be ill-timed or even destructive. But by and large, teachers can't go too far wrong as long as they construe the conference as a natural, human conversation between an expert and a novice or apprentice.

Here are some ideas about the mechanics of conferencing, drawn largely from the works of Atwell (1998), Graves (1994), and Zemelman and Daniels (1988).

- Before you start conferences, explain how they will work, so students know what to expect and can come prepared. Because time will be short, kids need to realize that conferences will probably focus on a single issue or topic rather than a comprehensive review of a study, paper, or reading project. Let students know that conferences are for real, back-and-forth talk, and that they should be ready to join in by sharing questions, ideas, plans, or problems. If you think students will have trouble envisioning a conference, act one out in the "fishbowl"—pick one volunteer child, sit in the middle of the room, and have a conference for everyone to hear and discuss.

- Pick the spot for conferences. Some teachers like to have students come to them at their desk. While this can be convenient, it also reinforces the traditional teacher-student power imbalance, and can make it hard to break off a conference when time is up and a student lingers. A neutral spot elsewhere in the room can be a better choice; a table in the back works well, so other kids looking up will not be distracted. Nancie Atwell, who pioneered language arts workshops in the 1980s, opined that a rolling chair should be standard equipment for the conferencing teacher, so you can swoop up to (and away from) students' desks as needed.

- Wherever you locate your conferences, sit on the same side of the table with the student, signaling collaboration rather than opposition. Let the student hold the paper and decide to angle it or hand it to you if she wishes.

- The scheduling of conferences presents a variety of choices, each with advantages and disadvantages. Teachers can allow students to request conferences as they need them, one day or one class at a time, which provides flexibility and maximizes the chance to catch students at their "teachable moments." On the other hand, putting conferences on a regular, recurrent schedule—seeing the same five students every Monday, another five on Tuesdays, and so on—offers the benefit of regularity and predictability. When conferences are held on student demand, the neediest or most dependent students may monopolize the teacher's time, while shier students go days or weeks without conferences. Skillful teachers work around these risks: if their conferences are on a fixed schedule, teachers save ten minutes each day for unscheduled students with immediate needs or "emergencies." If conferences are set up daily by student demand (like a sign-up list on the board), the teacher reserves the right to invite students to conferences herself, especially focusing on those who don't volunteer.

- Ask questions and help students talk, rather than just studying what's on the desk and giving a comment. Opening questions can help the student start off the conference and explain what she is trying to accomplish. "OK, Jill, tell me what your report is about and what part you're working on right now." Questions can signal the teacher's interest in the ideas, draw students out, and encourage them to consider more information: "I didn't realize you could do that on the computer. Do you need some special program or equipment?"

- Ask questions that help students see where they are in their work and how they might proceed: "OK, so you are having troubles with your partner. Tell me how these problems started. How could you two sort this out?" Questions can also encourage students to identify the main idea or structure they are creating: "So what is the main thing you are trying to say with this bar graph?" As we wait while students answer these questions, we are letting them work out what they need to take their next steps or improve their work.

- Search for questions students can answer, rather than questions that put them on the spot. Conferences should encourage students, not just prove the teacher is smarter. If the student thinks their project is perfect even though problems are apparent, ask what it is that gives him the most satisfaction with it, or how he thinks a reader will react to particular parts. This can give you valuable information about what the student is trying to achieve, and what approach might help him understand the difference between his own perception and that of an outside reader.

- Wait after asking a question. Give students a chance to think, and try not to jump in immediately. Silence can be a good sign. Remember, we are using conferences to teach thinking, and we must allow students time to think.

- If the student wants to read a chunk of their journal, log, or draft aloud, simple listening can sometimes be a helpful form of conferring. Not only can you offer a response at the end, but you can notice (and perhaps won't even need to help at) those lovely moments when the student hears an error or thinks of a revision, picks up a pencil, and jots down a correction or a note to herself. This is what it means to be a thinking coach; it is conferencing in action.

- Keep conferences short. Many teachers limit meetings to three or four minutes, which allows them to see a good number of students during each workshop session, often getting to each student once a week. Though at first a three-minute conference can seem almost rudely short, once teachers and students become accustomed to the span and come prepared, both are often surprised how much can be done within these limits. Some teachers can never get comfortable with such short conferences, and so they simply conduct longer ones more infrequently, without reproaching themselves.

- You don't always need to prepare for conferences. At times, it is entirely appropriate to talk with students about work you haven't previously read or reviewed. Indeed, as a coach of the inquiry, research, scientific, or writing process, you don't need lesson plans to ask important procedural questions like: What is this about? What makes you think that? What are your assumptions? What are your problems? What could you do instead? In other words, you can help students stop and reflect without necessarily taking on an expert role.

- Stick to process and thinking issues early in the conference. If you are going to provide information or teach particular skills, do so late in the conference, and limit the amount, so the student will remember those few items clearly.

- Listen and learn from students. Conferences not only help students think, but help the teacher understand how they think, discover what is blocking them, or notice the valuable ideas hidden under surface confusion.

- Tape-record conferences periodically to monitor the process and your own teaching methods. Give your conferencing program some time before judging whether or not it works.

Basic Types of Conferences

Because conferences are brief and must by necessity focus closely on limited tasks, it can be helpful to think about a few of the different jobs teachers and students can tackle in conferences. Each of the following types could be appropriate in any given school subject—indeed, on any given day, a teacher might be having several of these types of conferences with students at different stages in a project or with different needs as learners.

Process Conference

There are lots of great conferences, but this is the basic one, the classic. This conference allows teachers to conduct quick but helpful conversations with students without prereading the work at hand, without preparation, without "teaching" skills, and without offering any advice. Over the course of the conference, the teacher simply asks some version of these three questions: (1) "What are you working on?" (2) "How is it coming?" and (3) "What are you going to do next?" Other than these questions (or your own variations) the teacher doesn't need to say much else except "uh-huh" as the student talks to herself—which is the point. (This interaction is not unlike the sort of psychotherapy in which the therapist does very little talking, compelling the client to take the lead in explaining, probing, and evaluating experiences—with the long-term goal of helping the person become more reflective and self-reliant.) Often in process conferences, teachers find that they will raise one additional question somewhere along the way, something completely contextualized by the student and the topic, something that comes up naturally and unpredictably in the course of the meeting.

Status-of-the-Class Conference

This is a whole-group conference held at the beginning of a workshop session, during which each student says aloud what he will be working on that day ("I'll be running my statistics on the computer." "I'll be making a diagram for my report." "I'll be revising my draft.") In this conference, each kid makes a public commitment to some specific work, while also letting others know what they're doing, so they can work together on common tasks. Some teachers have students run and record the status-of-the-class, saving themselves from the record keeping.

Topic Search Conference

In workshop-style, project-oriented programs where kids actually have a choice of what to pursue, they sometimes need help choosing. The topic search conference focuses on helping the student generate a list of possible interests, and then selecting one promising idea to pursue. Essentially, this is a process of guided brainstorming; the teacher's job is to help the student develop a written list of possible choices. The point is not to struggle toward one idea, but to generate a bunch, a surplus, and then narrow down. The teacher can be the recorder, freeing the child to generate ideas and alternatives, and then handing over the list at the end of the conference. Some teachers bring along another kid or two for more good ideas in topic search conferences.

Read-Aloud Conference

When students are drafting a report, paper, or story, they can read a section or part of the piece aloud to the teacher, as a way of hearing their own work and getting the teacher's reaction and comments. Students are encouraged to pause amid the reading as they notice problems or get new ideas. Teachers wait while kids make notes about what to do later. One common variation is for the teacher to read a section aloud to the student, again pausing for the student to make notes or changes.

Summarizing Conference

One problem that often arises in primary grades is that students want to spend all their conference time reading their work aloud to the teacher. In the secondary version of this phenomenon, students hand papers to teachers, expecting them to use most of the conference silently reading, and then offering a response. As noted above, some of this sharing can be valuable, but there are many other important purposes for conferences. By holding summarizing conferences, the teacher helps students to move beyond the simple hunger for an audience (or for approval) and begin to reflect more broadly on their thinking strategies and work habits. In summarizing conferences, teachers ask students to tell about, summarize, or paraphrase the work they are doing, instead of sharing samples of it. In these conferences, the written work usually stays in the folder or even back at the desk.

Content Conference

Though many of the types of conferences described here focus on thinking and inquiry processes, content does matter—and teachers are often experts in subject matter. So it is entirely appropriate at times to have conversations officially aimed at discussing and developing the ideas, meaning, or content inside a research project, draft, or report. If the teacher is offering information, sources, or authors to be investigated later, notes jotted by the teacher can help a writer remember things to do later, back at their desk.

Dialogue Journal Conference

This is the written version of conferences, in which students and teacher exchange notes about selected chunks of curriculum on a specified schedule. The most common use of written conversation is reading logs, where students regularly record their responses to class readings in the form of an informal note to the teacher. The teacher responds in kind (on a schedule designed to avoid burnout while providing every student with regular personal notes). In addition to being a coaching conversation, dialogue journals are also a powerful reading and writing lesson, since the teacher is creating a personalized text for each student, modeling skillful adult writing in the process.

Editing/Publication Conference

It is fine for some conferences to be devoted to simple, narrow tasks, such as the final proofreading of a draft aimed at a publication or display. Usually, time prevents doing the whole job, so editing conferences amount to a brief stretch where the student and teacher are doing the task together (a paragraph or a page) with the teacher showing how a skilled adult catches and fixes mistakes. A nice version of this for younger kids is the finger-editing conference, useful when the child wants a "perfect" final draft. The kid reads through the piece aloud as the teacher runs her finger under the text. There are three possible outcomes when an error is encountered: (1) The child recognizes it, stops, and makes the correction herself; (2) The student stops but isn't sure what to do, in which case the teacher supplies the information and the student enters the change; (3) the student doesn't notice an error at all, so the teacher stops her, locates the problem, and asks if she knows what is needed. If the student can make the fix, she does so; if not, the teacher supplies the change.

Evaluation Conference

Though many conferences stress the ongoing process of inquiry, searching for revisions and next steps, students also do finish work from time to time. Then, it is appropriate to hold an evaluation conference, with the student and teacher sitting down to review the strengths and weaknesses of a project or piece of finished work. Among the key outcomes of such conferences are specific written goals (entered in the student's course log or folder) for the next project. An important form of evaluation is the portfolio conference, in which student and teacher review a body of work over a span of time. Typically, the student is asked to identify the most successful and most problematic pieces, talking about strengths and weaknesses, and setting plans for future growth. On an even wider scale, teachers with ongoing workshops often schedule quarterly evaluation conferences, which involve students in the grading process. They may ask students to score themselves on a performance rubric, fill out another copy themselves, and then meet in conference to review and reconcile each other's ratings.

Student's Choice Conference

One of the trends we hope to see in workshop classrooms is students taking more ownership and responsibility for all phases of their work, including the focus of conferences. In mature workshops, one often hears teachers starting conferences with a single question: "How can I help you?" or "What do you want to work on today?" Then, the student brings up a particular problem or concern in their work, which becomes the focus of a free-ranging conversation. This kind of kid-driven conference may not immediately work with inexperienced students, who

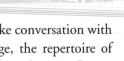

don't yet know how to initiate and carry on a true give-and-take conversation with a teacher. Sometimes they first need to experience the range, the repertoire of choices that they actually enjoy, before they can effectively "run their own" conferences. But after teachers have shown them the choices, kids should be charting the course of most conferences.

Small-Group Conference

While the basic design of workshops calls for individual student conferences, small-group meetings can be an important option, as long as teachers stay in the role of thinking coach. The teacher can meet with three or four kids at once, perhaps ones with a common interest or who are teaming on a project. Small-group conferences can be a way for the teacher to get to more students when there isn't enough time or when classes seem too big. For teachers new to workshopping, small-group conferences may simply feel more comfortable and familiar, since they seem similar to reading groups. The drawback to group conferences, of course, is that the special focus isn't on a single child; on the other hand, in groups children do get a wider audience for their thoughts, and get to hear how other students are thinking and talking about their work.

Peer Conference

Teachers are the main bottleneck in scheduling conferences; the number of meetings is limited by the amount of time the teacher has. The obvious and necessary solution is to work toward student pairs or peer group conferences. Once kids have learned from their own individual teacher conferences what kinds of conversations can be held, they can run their own meetings without the teacher present. Students can eventually conduct any of the above types of conferences: topic searching, editing, process, whatever. As students take more responsibility in this area, teachers will need to shift to coaching groups, making sure students keep to the spirit of the conferences at hand, don't regress to bickering or gossiping, or otherwise get off track. Student-led evaluation conferences can be especially tricky and require some special training so that kids neither wound nor soft-soap each other. Smart teachers prepare kids by having them first practice on "training papers" taken from unknown students outside the class, which helps students hone their critical diplomacy before evaluating each other's work.

■ ■ ■

Conferences, when they are genuine two-way conversations, can develop student responsibility and promote growth. If conferences become teacher-dominated or advice-centered, they can backfire, silencing kids and discouraging involvement.

And make no mistake—it can be tough for teachers to stay in this unfamiliar mentor role. Donald Graves says it well:

> How hard it is for an activist to conduct conferences. Everything is reversed. I have to give up the active, nondelegating, pushing, informing role for another kind of activity, the activity of waiting . . . But the rewards, the new energy as the learner teaches me, keep me going . . . The top teachers, I've found, whether in the center of the city, or a rural school, have an insatiable appetite for learning. When teachers learn, children learn. (1983, pp. 127–28)

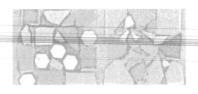

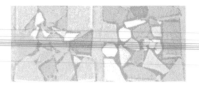

S I X

AUTHENTIC EXPERIENCES

The national curriculum standards that we've quoted throughout this book have an especially strong consensus on one recommendation: school needs to *get real.* For too long it's been a commonplace (and a truth) that kids find school dry, dull, and detached from that thing called "life," which happens somewhere else. From *Leave It to Beaver* to *The Simpsons,* popular media images of school always show teachers droning and students dozing in drab classrooms where desks are in rows and nothing interesting ever happens. However cartoonish, there must be some truth to this amazingly persistent stereotype, or it wouldn't have lasted this long. And plenty of gray-haired thinkers before and after John Dewey have argued for school to be more lifelike, more genuine, more authentic.

Try this experiment: ask any teacher from kindergarten through high school to describe the very best unit they ever taught. You'll probably hear about the kindergarten kids who turned the classroom into a rain forest, the fourth graders who learned about our food supply by growing a vegetable garden outside the school, the eighth graders who visited Washington and returned to school to simulate the three branches of government, or the high school math class that learned about vectors by playing a game of human chess. Come to think of it, if you look back on your own most memorable school experiences as a student yourself, you may find that those kinds of authentic activities stood out for you, too.

For the past four chapters, we have been talking about a special family of teaching methods that can bring Best Practice to life in classrooms. But this next ingredient, *authentic experience*, is not exactly a method, is it? Actually it was not one of the classroom structures we initially identified when we started writing this book. But the more classrooms we visited and the more stories teachers told us and wrote about, the more we recognized that the best teaching always makes kids' experiences tangible, real, or genuine. In so many truly exemplary lessons, students were either engaged outside of the school, or with outside activities brought into the school.

Authentic Experiences Take Many Forms

Authentic experiences can be as simple as writing a letter to a favorite author, or as large as schoolwide projects like planting a garden, setting up a recycling center, or investigating the sources of pollution on a local river. Just as in real life, these experiences are inherently multidisciplinary and often messy; problems need to be identified, complexity needs to be faced, and solutions must be found.

The importance of real-life investigations, both large and small, is recognized by many national subject-matter organizations. The National Academy of Science makes this bold statement: "Inquiry into authentic questions generated from student experiences is the central strategy for teaching science. Teachers focus inquiry predominantly on real phenomena in classrooms, outdoors, or in laboratory settings where students are given investigations or guided toward fashioning investigations that are demanding but within their capabilities" (1996, p. 31).

This thoughtfully written standards document offers many rich classroom examples to support its call for authenticity. In one example, Mrs. F helped her third-grade students learn about collecting data and conducting research when she noticed their fascination with the earthworms living in an empty lot next to the playground. Before ordering some earthworms from a biological supply house, she asked students to prepare a proper habitat for worms. The students spent much time examining the natural habitat of the earthworms in the empty lot before creating a similar environment in a terrarium, away from the sun and filled with soil, leaves, and grass.

The students spent two weeks observing the earthworms and recording their behavior before they began to list the questions they wanted to answer. Among the many questions that the students generated were: How do they have babies? Do they really like the dark? How big can they get? How long do they live? Children formed into small groups to decide together which question they would be most interested in exploring. The small groups were given time to decide how they would conduct their inquiries, and by the following week, the investigations were under way.

The group that chose to study the life cycle of earthworms had found egg cases in the soil, and while they waited for the eggs to hatch, they read some books about earthworms to add to their knowledge base. One group was studying what earthworms like to eat and prepared alternative foods to test. Two groups wondered what kind of environment earthworms preferred, and they experimented by varying moisture, light, and temperature in the classroom habitat.

This authentic scientific inquiry started with the interest and natural curiosity of the students and taught them much more than stuff about earthworms. They became researchers, gathering data, manipulating variables, asking questions, conducting experiments, recording information, discovering answers, and asking more questions. The students worked collaboratively, because in the real world science is a collaborative enterprise, dependent upon the sharing of ideas and discoveries.

This kind of inquiry becomes more possible when the conditions that support Best Practice are already in place. The classroom is a *community*; students are willing and eager to take *responsibility* for hands-on experiential learning; as students learn, they have many opportunities to *express* what they are thinking; they use *technology* to advance their inquiries; and the *diversity* of the class brings different questions, perspectives, and learning styles to the work.

Social studies, like science, is a natural home for authentic school experiences. *Expectations of Excellence: Curriculum Standards for Social Studies*, published by the National Council of Social Studies, asserts that "the social studies are powerful when they are meaningful, integrative, value based, challenging, and active" (1994, p. 162). These qualities emerge when students immerse themselves in real-life thematic inquiries where knowledge is connected and useful both in and out of school. Further, says the NCSS, "Social studies programs should reflect the changing nature of knowledge, fostering entirely new and highly integrated approaches to resolving issues of significance to humanity" (p. 5).

Following this advice means teachers should develop social science experiences around the real issues that people face in the world, helping to immediately connect students to the importance of what they are learning. These authentic connections deepen the learning process and help students construct a personal meaning about their world. The social studies provide many opportunities for this kind of knowledge building. Students can learn about democracy by practicing it in their own classrooms. Whether through writing a class constitution, setting and implementing the classroom rules, or negotiating with teachers what they are interested in learning about, students practice the skills that are necessary for adult participation in the world.

To help students build an understanding of themselves and their place in the world, a promising starting point is the investigation of family history. In their

1999 book, *History Comes Home: Family Stories Across the Curriculum,* Steve Zemelman, Pat Bearden, Yolanda Simmons, and Pete Leki share a form of personal historical investigation that starts by asking students to interview each other and their families about their roots. They begin with very basic questions such as: Where do my ancestors come from outside of America? Where do they come from inside America? and Where does my name come from? These initial questions send students home to interview their parents and grandparents and are the beginning of a sophisticated investigation into their own families and the events in American history that affected their lives.

Students make time lines of their lives and the lives of their ancestors, and they compare these living histories along parallel time lines of our nation's development. For example, students who find that their ancestors were slaves can read to find out what their lives must have been like. Students whose ancestors fought in World War II read to find out how the war affected their families. Just as in science, these real-life investigations, which start with the interests of students, can provide a powerful tool for taking the learning deeper and help kids see the connectedness and importance of all of the disciplines of the social sciences, including history, sociology, political science, and geography.

At our own Best Practice High School, one of the key components of our curriculum is an internship program, which provides service learning and work experience from freshman year onward. These once-a-week placements help young people experience what it means to work, provide them with real-world problems to solve, and open the world of career options for them to explore. When we asked students what they learned from their internships that they would not have gained in "regular school," they reported that they learned how to deal with adults better, to solve problems on their own, and often, to speak to groups. Almost all students had learned to operate at least one new machine or piece of equipment. Some had learned to use big office-type photocopy machines, while others used cameras or video equipment. Perhaps most impressive was our pair of student interns at Chicago's Adler Planetarium, who gradually became trusted to run the five-million-dollar "sky show." Returning to school after one internship morning, these girls bashfully reported that as they switched on the night sky that morning, they had forgotten to "turn off the sun." They were embarrassed, but their teachers were delighted to hear that in their internships, at least some of our students were running the universe.

Opening the Doors to the School

In order to bring learning to life, it is important to get beyond the four walls of the school, using the world as a learning laboratory as well as bringing chunks of the world inside. When students are given the chance to study outside the building, important things can happen. At Washington Irving School in Chicago, principal Madeline Maraldi provides buses and blank checks for each class to visit a bookstore three times a year. In this way, the children participate in building their own classroom libraries. Each student is allowed to select one book, which is placed in their classroom's library with a bookplate saying "Selected for Washington Irving School by _____." Students experience firsthand the wonders of a real bookstore and the joy of purchasing a book of their choice, many for the first time.

But the door to the school swings both ways, and sometimes we can bring equally rewarding authentic experiences into the school. Students in Bonnie Flannigan's second-grade class at Hendricks School in Chicago invited their grandparents to school to be interviewed for an intergenerational unit. Students did a great deal of preparation before the visitors arrived. Interview questions were written, and the students practiced using a video camera to tape the interviews. The grandparents served as expert informants, sharing their stories about growing up and going to school. This authentic experience seemed to be as satisfying and special for the grandparents as it was for the students.

The Chicago Arts Partnerships in Education (CAPE) brings working artists into Chicago schools to help students and teachers find the artist in each of them. Forsaking the residency model of the artist as a transient discipline expert, CAPE artists join with teachers to plan extended, holistic units of study, meeting curriculum standards even as they use the arts as a lever to integrate the curriculum and invite kids' expression. These practicing artists are typically found helping to design and teach units on ecology, community history, or ethnic heritage, working alongside the regular classroom teachers. For students, working and learning with a real dancer, sculptor, or actor helps them know that doing art is a real endeavor that happens both inside and outside the school.

Into the Classroom

Of course, those of us who teach in ordinary schools will still spend plenty of our days in the building, not on field trips, and with only one adult in the room, not a crew of artists. But authentic experiences can be brought to students in many simple ways, as our next group of teacher-authors will share. The key is providing students with activities that have relevance and meaning built right in, whether they occur inside or outside of the classroom.

So let's see how school can "get real," with the guidance of imaginative teachers. One deeply authentic topic for everyone is who we are as human beings. Linda

Bailey tells how her school addresses that most basic issue with something called "Me" portfolios. Using collections of personally significant artifacts, along with a spoken narrative, students start off the school year by setting patterns of sharing. "Me" portfolios challenge both students and teachers to explore themselves, their families, and their places in history—and to open up to others in a safe environment.

Next we enjoy one more visit with Pete Leki, who shares some of the origins of the urban ecology theme at Waters School. In this story, fourth-grade students and their teachers discover that even a dump can be a wonderful place to do science. Next, Jim Tebo asks his middle school students to apply their math skills to the problem of remodeling their bedrooms at home. When this high-interest problem is placed in their laps, kids quickly realize that math can be a very handy problem-solving tool.

John Duffy explains how the study of primary source documents can become a central feature of teaching history, enabling students to find personal meaning in text while making social studies classrooms exciting and dynamic places. John believes that primary sources also help students to develop their own family stories and to find personal connections to the stories of history. Finally, Mike Myers takes us through one of his favorite *simulations*, a role-playing game that brings real social and historical dynamics alive in the classroom. In this example, the students are arbitrarily divided into three social classes, the Shlubbs, the Risers, and the Goldens, and within half an hour, students who have been friends for years are almost at each other's throats. We have to engage students' feelings as well as their minds, Mike says, if learning is going to be real and stick with them.

Further Reading

Bourne, Barbara, ed. 2000. *Taking Inquiry Outdoors: Reading, Writing, and Science Beyond the Classroom Walls.* Portland, ME: Stenhouse.

Burke, Kay. 1999. *How to Assess Authentic Learning.* Arlington Heights, IL: Skylight.

Chancer, Joni, and Gina Rester-Zodrow. 1997. *Moon Journals: Writing, Art, and Inquiry Through Focused Nature Study.* Portsmouth, NH: Heinemann.

Clyde, Jean Anne, and Mark W. F. Condon. 1999. *Get Real: Bringing Kids' Learning Lives into Your Classroom.* Portland, ME: Stenhouse.

Fresch, Eula T. 2004. *Connecting Children with Children, Past and Present: Motivating Students for Inquiry and Action.* Portsmouth, NH: Heinemann.

Horwood, Bert, ed. 1995. *Experience and the Curriculum.* Dubuque, IA: Kendall-Hunt.

Kaplan, Mathew, Susan Perlstein, Robert Tietze, and Linda Winston. 2001. *Grandpartners: Intergenerational Learning and Civic Renewal.* Portsmouth, NH: Heinemann.

Kraft, Richard J., and James Kiesmeier, eds. 1994. *Experiential Learning in Schools and Higher Education.* Boulder, CO: Association for Experiential Education.

London, Peter. 1994. *Step Outside: Community-Based Art Education*. Portsmouth, NH: Heinemann.

Nabhan, Gary, and Steven Trimble. 1995. *The Geography of Childhood: Why Children Need Wild Places*. Boston: Beacon Press.

Primary Source Inc. 2004. *True to Our Native Land: Beginning to 1770. Sourcebook 1.* Portsmouth, NH: Heinemann.

———. 2004. *A Song Full of Hope: 1770–1830. Sourcebook 2.* Portsmouth, NH: Heinemann.

———. 2004. *Lift Ev'ry Voice: 1830–1860. Sourcebook 3.* Portsmouth, NH: Heinemann.

———. 2004. *Our New Day Begun: 1861–1877. Sourcebook 4.* Portsmouth, NH: Heinemann.

———. 2004. *March On Till Victory: 1877–1970. Sourcebook 5.* Portsmouth, NH: Heinemann.

Roberts, Pamela. 2002. *Kids Taking Action: Community Service Learning Projects K–8.* Greenfield, MA: Northeast Foundation for Children.

Saul, Wendy, and Jeanne Reardon, eds. 1996. *Beyond the Science Kit: Inquiry in Action.* Portsmouth, NH: Heinemann.

Stephens, Lillian. 1995. *The Complete Guide to Learning Through Community Service: Grades K–9.* Boston: Allyn and Bacon.

Zemelman, Steve, Patricia Bearden, Yolanda Simmons, and Pete Leki. 1999. *History Comes Home: Family Stories Across the Curriculum.* Portland, ME. Stenhouse.

"Me" Portfolios: The Way to a Classroom's Heart

LINDA BAILEY

Nicky sang. Tony showed his two lucky pennies and photos of his eight brothers and sisters, most of whom still live in another town with his mother. His twin, Tommy, showed photos of the series of family homes where they had lived since they left their grandmother's home five years ago. Leonardo shared a hand-carved key chain that his grandfather had made for him in Guatemala. Even though he was speaking Spanish, even we monolinguals all knew how precious this memento was to him. We also discovered how much scientific knowledge Leonardo had about dinosaurs, as he showed his models and described their diet, habitat, and geological era. Pamela was happy to translate for him *this* time.

Erika demurely displayed a large fan of certificates and awards she had earned over the years in school; her first baby bootie; her First Communion book, carefully protected in plastic, which was her only memory of her great-great-grandmother; her foreign money collection; her favorite mystery book; and a poem of which she was especially proud. Rebeca showed her miniature mask collection, two tiny white teddy bears from "someone special," letters that she saves, and photos of her family.

Erika was a stellar student, destined to be her class's valedictorian. Rebeca often struggled in school. Yet both Erika and Rebeca did a great job of presenting their "Me" portfolios. Erika and Rebeca were equally expert on their topic, had researched it thoroughly, and took genuine pride in their presentation. Each felt good about sharing personal information and artifacts about herself, and each had taken thoughtful care in the selection of each item in her "Me" portfolio. Each knew that the teachers and students with whom she shared her "Me" portfolio were learning more about the real and whole person she was. They were willing to open themselves up because *everyone* in their learning community at Burley School in Chicago, including their teacher, had made a "Me" portfolio.

Paula Saks-Zellhofer, Burley's second-grade teacher, brought photos of her handsome son and her farm in Wisconsin, a stone fragment from the Temple of Jupiter in Athens, and an unidentifiable lump that had melted on her stove (to signify her culinary prowess). Steve Wolk, the seventh-grade teacher, brought photos he had taken and "memory cards" on which he had written a special memory. I brought a sample of the jewelry I make, photos of my husband and children, a toy soldier with the international "no" symbol taped to it, my journals, and a memoir that was published in my local newspaper.

Students presenting their "Me" portfolios found that classmates and teachers were sincerely interested in their personal lives, stories, and interests. Classmates asked questions at the end of each presentation that delved more deeply into one or more aspect of their portfolios and asked them to explain some items more thoroughly. They discovered that their teachers and their classmates were genuinely interested in the story of who they are.

Birth of the Idea

Several years ago, when the Burley faculty sat around four pushed-together tables during the planning days at the end of the school year, we were looking for a really engaging activity to grab the students in September, pull them out of their summer stupor, get them into the dynamics of school, and begin to build a true community of learners. We wanted something that our whole K–8 school could do, that integrated the curriculum, motivated our students, and excited them about returning to school. We decided that a variation of the literacy portfolio idea might just do it. Many of the primary grade teachers already had planned self-exploration as part of their curriculum anyway, and when I raved about the successes my students enjoyed with literacy portfolios the previous year, the whole faculty enthusiastically embraced the idea.

During summer assessment/curriculum planning sessions, we revised and fine-tuned the project to meet the curricular and assessment needs of different grade levels. We wrote parent letters, prepared student handouts, and gave a completed package to all teachers on the first of the preclass institute days.

During the first week of school, the teachers shared their "Me" portfolios with their brand-new classes of students. As Burley's writing specialist, I went to almost all the classes and presented mine as an additional model. The students were receptive and respectful. They were amazed that teachers really had children of their own, and asked all kinds of questions about my two sons. They were surprised that I actually watched *Star Trek* on occasion and were curious about my favorite book. They were eager to start their own portfolios.

Student presentations of the "Me" portfolios began the second week of school. Burley was bustling with excited kids bringing in colorful boxes and bags filled with personal treasures and precious mementos. The children were proud of their portfolios and wanted as much audience as they could get. As I ran into students in the hallway, the lunchroom, or the playground, they would eagerly show me their portfolio container and invite me to see their presentation. Few things have warmed my heart more than seeing a big, burly Burley eighth grader show his cute little bare-bottomed baby picture, or his collection of toy cars with which he still plays. I got a new perspective on the *very* sophisticated young lady, constantly trying to sneak into school wearing makeup, who still sleeps with her held-together-by-a-thread teddy bear and collects trolls with neon-colored hair.

The little ones were impressed that they had the same assignment as their older siblings, and the older sibs were happy to help the younger ones. Parents were engaged in helping their children dig up family and personal history, and many expressed their joy in the memories and feelings that resurfaced during this endeavor. A lasting bond between home and school was forged. The whole school was focused on the same purpose at the same time. It was a powerfully moving time to be a teacher.

Older students did their "Me in the Universe" graphic organizers, to visually place themselves in the greater scheme of things, as well as time lines of their lives. Individual teachers, of course, freely modified the "Me" portfolio plans to suit their instructional needs. For example, the fourth-grade team decided that it matched their curriculum better to have their time lines begin in 1895, the year that Burley was built, and extend five years into the future. The second grade and below brought in five to ten items for the collection, while the fourth grade and above requested ten to twenty items. Each item had to be accompanied by a 4-by-6-inch index card on which the student had written about the object, its origin, and its significance. These were useful in the students' oral presentations, but also served as short, informal, student-centered writing activities. Each portfolio was to include the child's favorite book and, as appropriate, her own favorite piece of writing and artwork. Some classes mounted their items or photos of their items on posterboard, with accompanying descriptor cards. These posterboard displays, placed all around the room and in the hallways, told in no uncertain terms who reigned in this school. These displays were also a big hit at parent Open House Night.

The students understood the value of the project, too. Hugo España said, "It was good to do the 'Me' portfolios at the beginning of the year because we didn't know each other and it helped us to feel comfortable in the class." Alberto Estrella added, "I liked them because we learned about our families and how we were as little children." Jose Luis Gonzalez said, "We learned about each other's lives and the things that are important to them." They also knew that *who they are* was important to their teachers.

Burley teachers felt that the "Me" portfolio experience helped them build friendship and community at the start of the school year. Rusty Burnette, the upper-cycle special education teacher, said, "During 'Me' portfolio presentations, it was evident the bond between everyone in the classroom strengthened. We each had a spotlight to share what makes us tick." Meghan Cunningham, the interme-diate bilingual teacher, added, "I thought it was a wonderful way to build trust and it served as a wonderful introductory assessment/index of their writing [language arts outcomes]." Nancy Laho, the principal, and Mary Beth Groene, the assistant principal, were ardent advocates of this project and even suspended our "no toys in school" policy for the duration of the "Me" portfolio presentations. Ms. Laho plans to continue to start each year with "Me" portfolios. "We are excited about the thought of observing over a period of years the growth and development of our children as manifested in their 'Me' portfolios," Ms. Laho said.

Other Schools Join Us

Since the success of the "Me" portfolio project at Burley, I have shared this proj-ect at a multitude of workshops and schools. Many other schools have imple-mented "Me" portfolio projects, from the tiniest kindergartners to college-level English classes. At Los Niños Heroes Community Academy, the kindergartners presented their "Me" portfolios in the huge multipurpose room (combination auditorium, lunchroom, and whatever-you-need-it-to-be room). Because these lit-tle kids had tiny voices, the teacher provided them with a microphone. They had an audience of other kindergartners, parents, the principal, Gloria Stratton, and other school staff. Their parents presented along with the kindergartners, provid-ing moral support, accurate historical detail, and sometimes a leg to hide behind. But these five-year-olds absolutely shone as the center of attention. They shared their real lives with this big strange kindergarten place, received ear-splitting, enthusiastic applause from the audience, and made a place in this school for themselves. Their wholeness as unique and individual human beings was important to all these strangers. The parents were also enthusiastically drawn into their child's school activities in an authentic and meaningful way. They knew that their contributions were appreciated by the teachers.

With the bigger kids at Niños Heroes, a few classrooms also started out their year with "Me" portfolios. As teacher Miriam Perez said, "The 'Me' portfolio was a wonderful experience for my fifth/sixth bilingual [Spanish] class and me. I made a portfolio. I shared with my students pictures from my school days and my family, as well as many trinkets and tokens of the past that had meaning for me. This opened a line of communication. I believe the students were able to see me as not just as teacher, but a real human being. As a spin-off of the 'Me' portfolio, my students made time lines of their lives from the year they were born to the present, including one item per year. Then they went ten years into the future and fifty years into the past. They had to ask parents and grandparents what happened in their lives during that time period. This was a great learning experience for my students and me!" The school planned to expand the "Me" portfolio project to include the entire school.

George Rogers Clark School also did the portfolios schoolwide with great success. Arthetta Connors, a teacher at Clark, said, "It made children have a better understanding of each other's multicultural differences. One Hispanic student brought in baby shoes and the class was surprised to see how different they were from what they were used to." The Clark principal, Sandy Anast, commented, "I enjoyed it. It worked especially well with our second-grade unit, 'Snapshots.' There were boxes all over the school. Ms. Fisher did a continuation of the 'Me' boxes—three valuable things you'd give to someone from your heart. The art teacher, Marsha Looney, did self-portraits with the children using their favorite colors."

In another Chicago school, Jenner Academy of the Arts, the "Me" portfolio project was first done with the faculty as a whole to build community among the staff, then with the parent group, and finally with individual classrooms across the school, K–8. Joan DeCleene, the reading specialist at Jenner, said that the teachers reported that this project was among the most effective they had ever done.

Worth the Effort

Miriam Perez observed that there is substantial value in inviting the students to see their teachers as real flesh-and-blood human beings with a life beyond the school parking lot. If about half the art of teaching is getting the students' attention, then firsthand knowledge of the teacher-as-true-mortal should help grab that attention. It's harder to turn off to someone who has let you glimpse her soul. If a teacher is serious about conducting writing workshop or any kind of group collaborative or cooperative activities, then building a trusting classroom community of students who can work with each other is certainly crucial. Teachers are always concerned with classroom management. Children who really know each other and have been encouraged to respect and celebrate each other's differences and who have discovered all the surprising similarities they have with their classmates may have less fear and anxiety—and, just maybe, fewer behavior issues.

The "Me" portfolio project also gives teachers a quick response when a student moans, "I don't know what to write about today." The teacher can check her notes and respond, "Why don't you write about that darling blue dress that your grandmother so lovingly crocheted for you when you were a baby?" or "Tell about the day that you won that track medal." With a "Me" portfolio, students will probably *never* run out of real reasons for writing!

Carver's Woods: Science in a Dump

PETE LEKI

They stand in the morning sun. Twenty fourth-grade students. Binoculars pressing into their eye sockets. Sue Friscia points across the baseball field behind the school where a group of the throaty seabirds squat.

"Uhhh. Ring necked gull," one child shouts. Nineteen others chorus the same answer a second later, "Ring necked gull."

Ms. Friscia is a science resource teacher at Carver Primary School in the Altgeld Gardens on Chicago's far South Side. She loves birds and knows them by the merest flash of a tail or faintest call. For her, taking these kids out is a great and apparent pleasure.

"And what's that up on the chimney? What do we often see on the chimney? What's that?"

Binoculars rotate to the pearly western sky.

"What are these things we're standing on?"

"Rocks."

"Rock dove," says one thin voice.

"Rock dove," joins the chorus.

"I can't focus. How you work these things?"

Sue got these binoculars with Carver's discretionary funds. There are enough so that each child can learn to be comfortable with them. One child, Cynthia Barrett, totes Sue's own tripod and telescope, bringing tiny, insignificant species up close so that eye rings, tail stripes, and idiosyncrasies of habit can be seen.

"Look. Over there. Black bird, short tail."

"Crow."

"Crow, crow."

"A crow is a big, big black bird. This one's smaller. Short tail." She waits. "Stars on its chest . . ."

"Starling."

"Starling. Starling."

"European starling. Right."

Shavanna Jackson is the group's secretary. She writes down everything, adding it to the list on the clipboard. Phillip Allen flips through the field guide, finds *starling*, and walks down the line showing the page.

Now, single file, we enter the woods that stand between Carver and the Little Calumet River. In the marshy, wet understory we hear a peculiar cheeping.

"Stop. Hear that? What is that?"

"Frog."

"What kind of frog? What do you call it when people sing together?"

"Fun."

"Music."

"Choir."

"Another word for choir?"

"Chorus."

"Right. Western chorus frogs are singing to us this morning."

The woodland habitat around us is unique to my experience. Besides the scrub wood growth of box elder, maple, poplars, and a few big cottonwood, there are dozens of scattered garbage mounds. And everywhere are TV sets, picture tubes gutted and broken, circuit boards showing garishly through cracked simulated wood exteriors. There are nightstands, tar-paper shingles, plastic hoodinkis, and four million tires. This place has the curious quality of seeming to exude tires from the earth. To these things Sue pays no attention. She is all given up to the birds, the kids, the sounds of the day.

"Kirchee."

"Look. Long tail, black bird. Look at the head. See how iridescent it is."

"Grackle."

"Grackle. Grackle."

"Right."

In the distance just across the river is the Dolton dump. A Caterpillar tractor labors up and down the hill pushing dusty clay over the wasteland.

Sue tells me, "They aren't allowed to expand horizontally anymore. But they can keep piling up vertically. So we'll see how high they go before the whole thing topples over."

Much of this land was subdivided years ago but has remained untenanted. What was supposed to be a strip of lovely riverside lots became undesirable in this abused and neglected corner of the realm. Its neighborhood includes two monster landfills, a steel mill, a Metropolitan Water Reclamation District (MWRD) sludge-drying site, and the tiny isolated community called Altgeld Gardens. Abandonment gave rise to dumping of trash and all the other wasteland dangers, including drug dealing and thuggery. Two human bodies were disposed of here last year, doused with gasoline and burned.

I break from the group when I see an overgrown sidewalk appear and disappear into an overgrown patch of blossoming hawthorn. It ends at an abandoned basement and foundation, now filled halfway up with brown water and hundreds of tires. Through the tires, silver maple saplings shoot up and leaf out. Beyond this ruin are acres of open prairie with hawthorn edges. It is really very beautiful.

Some teachers at Carver are hesitant to visit the site. Children are warned not to enter except as a classroom activity. But they hope to reclaim the land as a nature preserve and wildlife sanctuary, connecting Carver and Altgeld Gardens contiguously to the Beaubien Forest Preserve to the southeast.

Passing through the woodland dump section, we arrive at the bank of the Little Calumet, one of Chicago's neat anomalous morainal drainages. Most rivers catch water from the upland and erode downhill in a dendritic pattern, tiny tributaries linking up to make bigger ones, like the veins in a leaf. But the Calumet area drainage follows long, looping courses parallel to the lake boundaries around sand spurs deposited by successive receding stages of Lake Chicago. We pause here in the shade of a huge overhanging cottonwood to look at the catkins hanging down from a young poplar like ornaments.

The muddy waters are being aerated downstream by a series of man-made waterfalls in an attempt by the MWRD to resuscitate life in the waters fouled by effluents from the sewage treatment plant. Toxic ammonium levels caused by heavy industrial loading at the plant are discharged into the river and oxidized to nitrates, depleting oxygen available to living things. These sidestream elevated pool aeration (SEPA) stations apparently work well, adding another oddity to this manhandled river system and geography.

The rutted trail that runs along the river may be where 135th Street was supposed to go had the development plan worked out. Instead, it traces a path through a wet prairie teeming with life, occasional stereo speakers, lost boots, and tires.

"Flicker!" Sue points to a small stand of poplars ahead.

Cynthia sets the scope. The children mutter, "Where? Where?" and search through the dappled branches. "I see it. It's a woodpecker."

Sue had hopes a few years back that the city or the state or the Department of Conservation or the United Nations might buy up this piece of land, throw a fence around it, patrol it, stop trucks from dumping. It seemed the landholders were saddled with a loser, a tax liability with no future. Then Mayor Daley started making noises about building an airport near the site and hopes for a cheap sell-off vanished. But with the airport project abandoned, and the woods leafing out, and the migrating birds making every day an adventure, hope begins to spring eternal once again.

Carver School has signed up with The Nature Conservancy's Mighty Acorn project, where schoolchildren learn science and ecology through stewardship activities in natural areas. Carver is scheduled to begin work at the Beaubien Forest Preserve.

Diane Reckless, chief Mighty Acorn, agrees with Sue that the abandoned strip has a lot to offer. "Not only as a wonderful habitat for birds and animals and prairie plants, but because it's part of the neighborhood. Part of what we hope to teach is a sense of connection to the land. Part of the Mighty Acorns is about social studies, how and why areas become wastelands, degraded and unavailable to communities. And how they can be reclaimed through stewardship and study."

"Look. Look." Sue points to a bird, whose name I thought my brother had made up for me. "A yellow-bellied sapsucker."

"'Tsa woodpecker."

"I don't see no yellow."

I couldn't see yellow, either.

We cross over a tiny drainage creek and Ms. Jackson, the homeroom teacher, sinks her foot in the mud. "Worse things have happened," she says. "I'll clean it off later."

Sue says she's seen crayfish in this creek and this makes me glad because decapods are not pollution tolerant. I walk into the tall skeletons of last year's goldenrod and poke around in a riffle hoping to see one. The water is clear, with leaf litter along the edges. An isopod scurries away, aquatic cousin of the terrestrial sowbug. Not a decapod, but not a bad sign. Except for the growl from the dump and the background rumble of I-94, it is very peaceful here. I realize that I'm sitting on the rusting carcass of a spring bed frame, thoroughly commingled with the grasses and weeds.

I find out later that Altgeld Gardens and this strip of land was once the dump for Pullman Standard. This woods sits on garbage. Across the river is garbage. Across the highway is garbage. And to the north is sewage. Sue and Cynthia,

Diane, Shavanna, Phillip, and Ms. Jackson are building their hopes on garbage. They are rethinking this place, renaming this garbage dump. Maybe, Carver's Woods and Nature Preserve. The renaming will help envision a different place. Like calling a bird a rock dove where others see only a pigeon.

Home Improvement: Remodeling Mathematically

JIM TEBO

In teaching seventh- and eighth-grade students, one of my goals is to incorporate as many real-life math applications as I possibly can. I find that kids like to learn math when they understand the meaning behind their learning. One of the ways I accomplish this is by assigning a project called "Home Improvement." The kids are given the job of redecorating any one room in their house, just the way they would like to have it done. Each student is given a $2,000 budget and is encouraged to spend as much of it as she possibly can.

My goal is to get the students to use their knowledge of perimeter, area, scale drawings, and budgeting in a genuine, real-life situation. In the redecorating project, students must follow certain criteria, which ensure that they will use each of the key math concepts and calculations this activity is designed to reinforce. They are encouraged to choose any room in the house to decorate, and most kids choose their own bedrooms. They must carpet or tile the floors, wallpaper or panel at least one wall, paint the ceiling and remaining walls, and put up a border or chair rail. After spending the money on these necessary items, they can spend the remaining money on any other items they would like to buy to improve their room.

To get started, the kids are given a list with four steps to follow. First, they must write out a plan sheet. This is generally a one-to-two-page written list of all the possible decorating options the student is considering. The ideas range from the color and style of carpeting to the design of the wallpaper and even to extras like new furniture, if they will have enough money. The purpose of this step is to get the kids to think carefully about what they would like to do and to create a plan that they can follow.

The second step includes a fact sheet and a scale drawing of their room. The fact sheet is a list of room measurements, including every wall and any windows, doors, or closets; the area of the floor; and the perimeter of the room. From this information, the students are to make a scale drawing of their room on graph paper (see Figures 6.1a and b).

Figure 6.1a: Calculations used to determine quantities of materials needed.

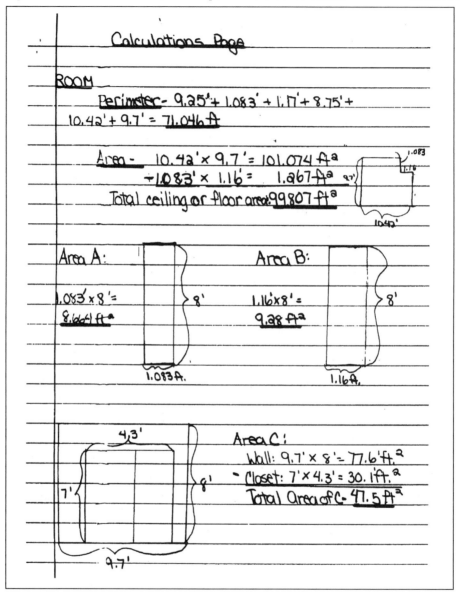

The third step, the price guide, is probably the most challenging and eye-opening experience for the kids (see Figure 6.2). For every item the students wish to purchase, they must find a minimum of two prices. This requires looking in newspaper ads, calling different stores for prices, or actually going out to the businesses to obtain information. This step has the nice side effect of teaching kids about comparative shopping. During this step the kids must also keep an updated

Figure 6.1b: Diagram of one student's room (teddy bear not to scale!).

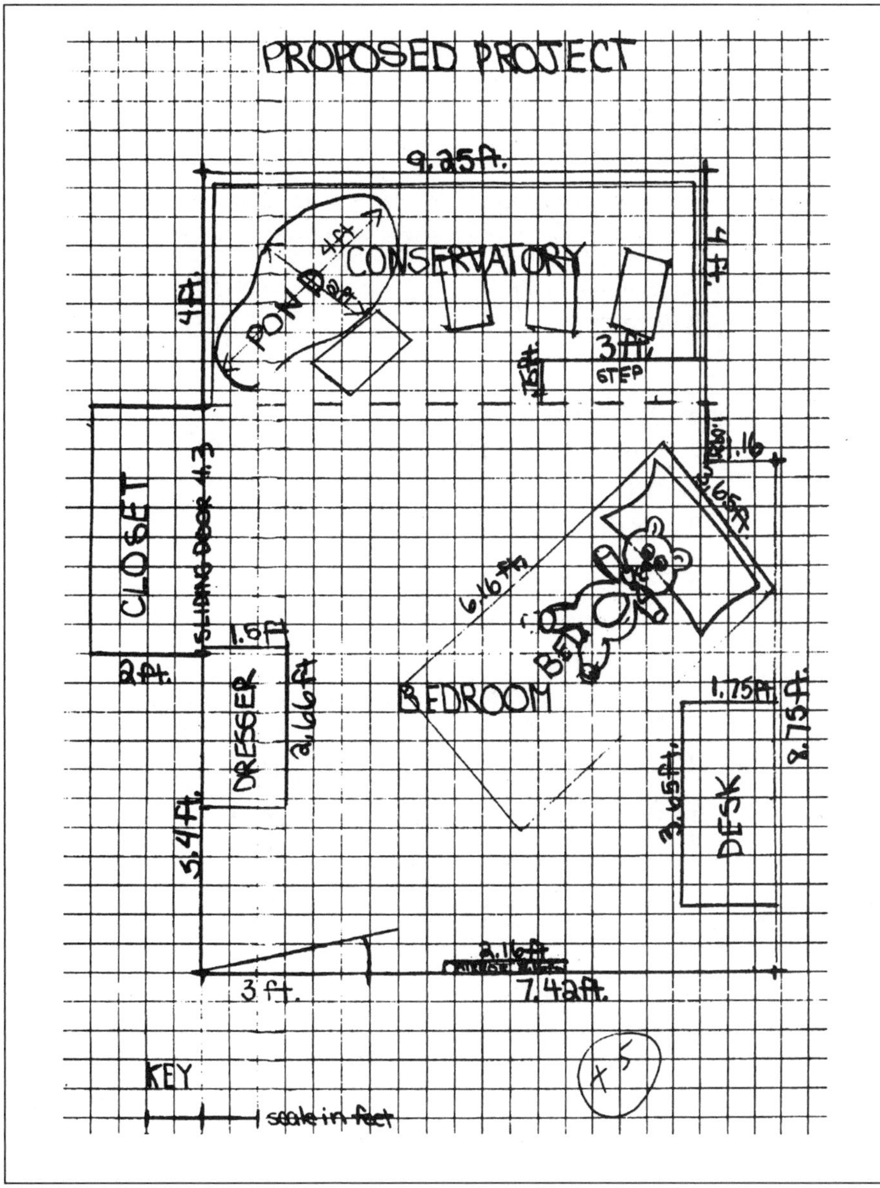

balance of their account. I also ask the kids to cut out any pictures of items they want to purchase. By doing this, the kids, their parents, and the teacher can really get a good look at what the kids have in mind.

The last step is called the closing remarks. Here, the kids write about and describe how their project went. Was it easy or difficult? How much was spent?

Figure 6.2: Shopping list students used to obtain prices from two different suppliers.

SUPPLIES	ESTIMATE 1	ESTIMATE 2
Bedroom	ACE	HANDY ANDY
1. Paint	√$6.79/gal	$18.99/gal.
2. Wallpaper	$40.77/3rolls	$59.98/2rolls
3. Chair-Rail	√$19.35	$29.58/5-9ft. lengths
4. Varnish	$11.49	$7.28/per quart
5. Carpeting	$300.00*	$299.09/8.99sq.yd.
Conservatory		
1. Contractor's Estimate	$8,000.00	—
2. sand→pond	$4.00	$128.39/plastic liner
3. stepping stones→rocks	$3.16/4**	$1.96/4
4. hose	3.77/50ft.**	$9.37/50ft.
Backyard		
1. cement→fence	$47.92/40 lbs. 8bags	$11.96/4 bags 80 lbs.
2. Picket fencing	$219.60/10ft**	$299.80/14.99 set.
3. posts	$56.49/2.69** per post	$51.24/2.49 per post
4. arbor	$199.98	$200.00/100 per cubic
5. paint→flat	$26.47	$65.97/3 gal total
6. sand→pond	$8.00	$238.00/plastic quart liner

Was $2,000 enough money? I ask the students to share their final report with their parents, then write about their parents' reactions. I have had a number of cases where the parents were so impressed with their child's work and effort that they actually allowed their child to do the redecoration.

I really enjoy this project because the kids get so wrapped up in doing it. They love using their imagination and having total control to do whatever they would like to their room of choice. The students use the math skills of measuring, scale drawing, and budgeting for a real-life purpose, and they have a good time in the process. One word of caution: during this period, kids will come to school excited and curious, with an abundance of questions ranging from prices to measurements to budgets. So be prepared for anything and have fun.

Using Primary Sources: Bringing Literature and Students to Center Stage

JOHN W. DUFFY

When I began teaching American history in 1972, I quickly learned how dreadfully inadequate secondary textbooks were. They were poorly written and uninspiring, but most important they failed to address the issues my students encountered in their daily lives. When my African American students complained that our book "only talked about slavery," they sensed the passivity and acceptance that textbooks encouraged from students. Some asked why great leaders like Fred Hampton were not in their textbooks. He was from their neighborhood, had attended our school, and at the age of fifteen led the youth committee of the NAACP in a protest to integrate a segregated community swimming pool. When he was eighteen, he became chairman of the Illinois Black Panther Party. At nineteen his death at the hands of the FBI and Chicago police led to investigations and trials that would radically change Chicago politics and make possible the multiracial coalition that elected Harold Washington as Chicago's first black mayor.

On another occasion, a local businesswoman who was a Crow Indian told our class of the wonderful relationship between the U.S. government and her tribe going back to the nineteenth century. She challenged my students' impression that the history of U.S. and Indian relations had always been one of broken treaties, and the students wondered why voices like hers or other Indians were not part of our text. When some of my female students pointed out the gross inequities in our boys' and girls' athletic programs and challenged male stereotypes of women's roles, the only hint of the long history of women's struggle for equality in our textbook appeared in a single column on the suffrage movement. Incidents like these, together with the historical and aesthetic shortcomings of textbooks, helped me realize that only by finding and sharing real voices from the past might my students begin to see any relevance to studying history.

With a similar goal at just about the same time, the Committee on History in the Classroom was founded. Scholars and teachers who formed the CHC established the twin goals of incorporating primary documents as an alternative to textbooks and placing greater emphasis on developing the art of teaching history. It is my strong belief that these two goals are not linear, but integrated and interdependent. I believe that the use of primary literature should be a central feature of history teaching. However, the use of primary documents as the fundamental texts will make a significant qualitative difference in our classrooms only if we place the literature and students at center stage. Only when students are allowed a variety of ways to find personal meaning in a text, when reading becomes more than responding to teacher-generated questions, when students are able to interact with, re-create, and move beyond texts in a variety of imaginative and critical ways will the use of primary literature begin to make history classrooms exciting, dynamic places for students to be. In short, using primary documents must also be accompanied by a more central and active role for students and a lessened emphasis on the teacher as dispenser of knowledge.

Primary source literature is not just an effective way to enrich lectures or more vividly illustrate mass-marketed textbooks. It is the central ingredient in allowing students to construct historical meaning, to begin to understand the meaning of personal agency, to develop their own stories, to re-create the histories of their families, and to uncover the history of their own neighborhoods and communities. Early and frequent use of primary sources becomes the pathway to the time in my course when students become authentic historians—when a Vietnamese student tells for the first time the narrative of his family's sea escape from Vietnam, and another second-generation Vietnamese American, after reading primary literature on the Vietnam War, takes on the persona of a Viet Cong soldier in a student presentation based on selected readings of oral histories; when a child reads the transcript of his interview with his cousin and breaks down before he can relate the trauma of village battle; when a girl interviews her mother, who tells the stories of her involvement in the student freedom movement and the terrifying night spent in jail in Mississippi; when a panel of civil rights veterans visits our school and a fellow teacher on the panel relates her family's friendship with Medgar Evers; or when world cultures and U.S. history students, after reading student accounts of the freedom movements in South Africa and America, work together to produce a musical drama connecting nonviolent resistance and divestment for an all-school assembly during Black History Month.

Primary Sources in U.S. History

Now, let me share some ways I use primary materials in junior American history classes at Hinsdale Central High School, where I have taught for the last several years. One common feature of all these lessons is teacher support and guidance before students read, while they read, and after they read. Sometimes the entire class reads the same document; sometimes documents are part of a set that everyone reads in common. At other times, students may have a choice or a range of related documents on a common theme. On other occasions small groups of students might read representative samples of related documents on a common theme and then share what they learned with the whole class.

Through the years I have learned several techniques that make the use of primary literature more successful. A key element of my pedagogy is introducing documents in a variety of ways. For example, before reading Columbus's diary accounts of his encounter with the Arawaks, I ask students to compose hypothetical diaries, which we share in class as we explore the concepts of bias and frame of reference. Before studying the struggles of working people during the Industrial Revolution, oral reading from *The Autobiography of Mother Jones*, especially the chapter "The March of the Mill Children," provides students with a feeling for the human impact of the industrial policies of the late nineteenth century.

Prior to reading a set of primary texts on the impact of World War II on American and Japanese citizens, I read the powerful children's picture book *The Faithful Elephants*, by Yukio Tsuchiya. In an informal writing students record their reactions to this story about how Tokyo zookeepers euthanized zoo animals out of fear that they might escape and threaten citizens during the American bombing. Students first share their reactions with one or two other students and then with the entire class. Finally, as students choose from a variety of individual personal accounts of the war, they are motivated and prepared to encounter the agony, courage, and horror the war brought to both Americans and Japanese.

Films like *In Country, Platoon,* or *Letters Home from Vietnam* are excellent methods for raising long lists of questions about the impact of the Vietnam War on American veterans and heightening student interest and curiosity. Personal narratives, both fiction and nonfiction, may also serve as an introduction to a study of a larger set of primary documents. Before reading oral histories of Vietnam, I have read Tim O'Brien's description of a soldier's first encounter with death in *The Things They Carried*. Richard Wright's narrative of growing up in the South in the *Ethics of Living Jim Crow* provides a child's perspective on confronting racist America and helps establish a fuller understanding for reading and discussing authors like DuBois, Washington, and Garvey and exploring which direction the African American freedom movement should have taken in the first decades of the twentieth century. All these strategies allow students to mentally and emotionally transport themselves to the historic ground where they will meet authentic actors of history.

I have used primary literature effectively around the American Revolution in several ways. Simulation and role-playing around policy conflicts and political decisions vis-à-vis England can be enriched by providing students with documents from Frank Moore's *Diary of the American Revolution*. Sets of selected documents from Moore also provide excellent background reading for narrative fictional writing about an imagined character of the revolutionary era. This year students created a radio documentary about the lives of soldiers after reading sets of documents about battles, prisoners of war, and how the war affected people's lives.

Clearly, extended student response is not possible with all primary literature, but providing students with creative options that allow them to work critically with literature in personal and imaginative ways brings a liveliness, challenge, and excitement too often absent from history classrooms.

Before studying Indian issues in the early nineteenth century, students have role-played dialogues between missionaries and Indians, then studied Red Jacket's response to missionaries asking to preach to his people. This activity becomes an introduction to exploring the great debate between Tecumseh and Pushmataha. Before this culminating large-group activity, students read an excerpt from Chief Black Hawk's autobiography. They are asked to keep a reading log that is guided by a few simple questions like identifying Indian perspectives on land, religion, and culture and treaty relations with the United States. The goal here, as it should be when any manageable, well-written documentary reading is assigned, is to encourage students to find their own meaning in texts. Specific questions to guide students are

■ What did you learn about the Sac way of life from Black Hawk?
■ How and why does his attitude toward the United States change?
■ What did you find most amazing, interesting, or disturbing in the reading?

I also ask students to choose a passage or selection that they think has special literary quality worth reading to the class.

In small groups, they read additional short excerpts from Indian speeches found in Tehschick's *To Touch the Earth* and Nabokov's *Native American Testimony* as well as Tecumseh and Pushmataha's speeches, which are found in a wonderful two-volume anthology called *To Serve the Devil* (Jacobs and Landau 1971). Each student then composes a formal statement to be read at tribal council meetings, where the proponents of resistance and the proponents of conciliation make their cases. One chief reads Andrew Jackson's letter to the Choctaws at the beginning of the council meeting. At the end of the debate another student provides a dramatic reading of the beautiful and moving speech by Chief Sealth of the Chinook. The best experiences with this activity, which takes at least one full week of school, is a feeling in my class that we have come as close as humanly possible to understanding the agony and anguish Indians went through in deciding whether to fight or accommodate to further white encroachments.

Crucial themes in social history often receive but brief mention in textbooks. In such cases, well-written chapters or excerpts from secondary sources provide excellent ways into primary literature. For example, students studying abolition have read chapters on African Americans in the North and abolition from *Then Was the Future* by Douglas Miller and selected essays on slavery and abolition from

Lockwood and Harris's *Reasoning with Democratic Values*. They then read original selections from Frederick Douglass, Solomon Northrup, David Walker, and other abolitionists.

A sure way back into time to the Seneca Falls women's rights convention is a fun reading of Anthony Brown's *Piggybook*, a children's picture book that deals with domestic division of labor in contemporary families. A follow-up directed reading of the Seneca resolutions leads to a comparison with gender issues today. Students are then given choices of primary readings about nineteenth-century women who vividly described the conditions of their lives. A seminar structure allows two or three students to choose one of the women, discuss the implications of her character, and then share with the entire class.

Until recent years, there had been little sense among students that perhaps Columbus was not the great American hero. For years I have introduced interpretation, evidence, bias, and frame of reference by having students initially create hypothetical diaries or dramatic skits about the first encounters between Europeans and the Arawaks of the Bahamas. Students then read excerpts from Columbus's diary, compared his accounts with the versions presented in their text, and read critical perspectives on Columbus like that found in Howard Zinn's *A People's History of the United States*. One year, after this exercise, several students looked at the way Columbus is depicted in children's literature. They then created revisionist children's literature that presented a more realistic look at the Arawak Indians and Columbus in a style that was critical yet sensitive to the developmental needs of younger students. Other students examined textbook versions of Columbus and interpretations gleaned from reading Columbus's diary entries. One group of students interviewed people about popular perceptions of Columbus and created a video to share their findings. In addition to responding to primary literature in creative ways, this early look at Columbus helped students become aware of critical concepts relating to historical investigation and also addressed an important political question: In whose interest are textbooks written?

On a regular basis I allow students to respond to primary literature in a varied and personal way. Readings might be guided by a set of general prompts that allow students to personalize their reactions to an author without the constraints long lists of teacher questions place on their enjoyment of reading. Free responses can be kept in individual student journals. I might give students a range of response choices such as these:

- Write a letter to a character.
- Compare a group of individuals.
- Predict the future of the individual.

- Speculate on how that person might react to issues and settings at other times in history.
- Evaluate the choices a person makes in his life.

Most important, regular response writing about primary documents provides a vehicle for students to make connections among the past, the present, and their own lives. They learn firsthand the human drama of history, the constant play of ethical decisions in people's lives, and the importance of individual actions in influencing the world. So a study of the Indian debate on resistance raises questions about just war, then and today. Indian removal and treaty rights become contemporary ethical problems as students examine the Navajo resettlement conflict, Chippewa fishing rights in Wisconsin, and the use of Indian mascots in their own communities. Reading about how women described their lives in the nineteenth century leads to contemporary questions, such as these:

- What are the relationships between men and women in our school, community, and homes?
- Are males and females treated differently in school?
- What experiences have you had with sexual harassment?

Reading Indian perspectives on American history, slave narratives, and abolitionist attacks on slavery brings students face-to-face with a racism that textbooks either omit or gloss over. Primary literature provides the opening to explore racism today. The response prompts now become

- Have you been the victim or witness to similar racist actions in your community?
- Why did this happen?
- What can be done to change this situation?

In these ways, primary documents serve as a rich conduit between the past and the present and provide the opportunity for reflective critical writing, discussion, and (we hope) actions that will make our communities more democratic and just places to live.

Just as students need options in writing responses to reading assignments, they also need ongoing choices in the selection of reading materials. My students, be they remedial or advanced placement, thrive on opportunities for choice in reading material. Obviously, there is a certain body of primary and secondary literature we want all students to read and understand. But we need not look further than our own lives to be reminded of the motivating power of personal choice.

Choice is influenced by curiosity, and the more options we create for students, the more curiosity and desire we will generate in our classrooms. I use a set of oral histories from World War II taken from several anthologies currently available. I start by realizing there are hundreds of fascinating oral histories that my students might read. Why should I make all their final choices? I sometimes provide them with a short excerpt from an account, or at least a description of the person and setting. They choose with great interest and motivation. They now possess the crucial ingredients for learning: curiosity and ownership.

To bring authentic voices into the classroom, to provide time for students to reflect, wonder, imagine, and reconstruct our collective past, their individual pasts, and our collective future, I have made primary literature a major part of teaching and learning in my classroom. Most of all, these strategies seem to be part of that magic combination that says to students, "I can relate to this. It has a personal connection to my life. I am beginning to understand the world better and I am enjoying the process."

Crimes Against Humanity: A Simulation of Prejudice

MIKE MYERS

The juice, the snacks, the flattery, and it was all over. They were Goldens now. With an easy flick of the pedagogical wand, my finicky crew of twenty-plus seniors, whom I had dragged, pushed, and wheedled through their yearlong senior research projects, had metamorphosed into a confident elite, completely and smugly convinced of their manifest superiority, and openly contemptuous of their inferiors.

The unit, an integrated effort put together by our grade-level team of four senior teachers, was "Crimes Against Humanity," and this simulation was our culminating activity. In the two years we've taught this unit, reflections of its key themes have repeatedly appeared on the pages of daily newspapers, underscoring the unit's relevance. We first introduced the unit as the war in Iraq got under way. In 2004, as we studied the Geneva Conventions and other international war crime agreements, the first photos from Iraq's Abu Ghraib prison surfaced, giving rise to one of the worst scandals of the Bush administration and proving that the United States, too, could use its awesome power to torture, humiliate, and abuse foreign prisoners.

The goal of our simulation was to extend the study beyond the historic genocides we had been focusing on in the rest of the unit toward a territory that was potentially both more risky and more productive. We wanted to re-create and help students *feel* the conditions of group hostility—the kind that could lead to hatred and violent conflict—but in a safe, laboratory setting. By interrogating the roots and potential for hatred and violence in our own lives, we hoped that through synthesis and analysis we might better prepare ourselves to identify and abort its origins in real life.

However, simulations about recognizable, real-life problems can be tricky and risky. I remember running successful mock slave auctions when I student-taught classes that were virtually 100 percent Mexican American, but I would never try that in the integrated classrooms I've worked in since then. Using real ethnic divisions or social rifts from the school community is also out of the question. Feelings become too real too fast, threatening to overpower learning objectives with anger, emotion, and pent-up frustration. Hashing out such issues makes for good—maybe necessary—therapy, but it probably means forsaking the original objectives.

Our challenge with the Crimes Against Humanity unit was to create an artificial situation that was at once provocative enough to engage students and realistic enough to show that it wasn't just a game. At the same time, the simulation could not be so realistic as to activate and completely unleash students' real grievances. At the end of the day, *they* would have to return to and cope with their real world. We wouldn't be there with our evaluation sheets, blackboards, and journal notebooks.

We wanted to show how quickly and easily we could get students to generate social prejudice, envy, and contempt on absolutely specious grounds. In the end, we hoped, the experience would vaccinate kids from comparable influences in the real world, creating a reflexive impulse to challenge and analyze simplistic prejudices.

Drawing on a few familiar, elaborate simulations, we synthesized and tinkered with a new scenario until it met our needs. The result was a three-tiered, unequal microculture called Best Practesia, which included the socioeconomic groups the Shlubbs, the Risers, and the Goldens. Besides the initial indoctrination period that established each group's status, most of the action consisted of the groups moving through three rounds of an exchange economy that clearly doled out privileges and punishments according to each group's assigned station in life.

Throughout the simulation, artificial rules, customs, and conditions reinforced group identity in ways that also promoted disregard and hostility toward the other groups. For instance, each group was trained to use Best Practesia hand greetings, but only the Goldens were told that the standard Shlubb greeting ritual signaled crass, lowbrow conduct. In turn, the Shlubbs were discouraged from using the genteel greeting that was standard in Golden circles. Risers learned both, along with the social messages they carried.

So from the start, the Goldens knew their place in this microcosm. They were greeted with snacks and drinks, party hats, name tags, and an upbeat, congratulatory spiel. "Congratulations! You've all made it. You're in this group, so you're obviously all very successful people." They were urged to relax as they listened to the instructions and received far more chits (money tokens) per student than any of the other two groups. Most took the bait with gusto.

The Risers' orientation meeting was less cordial and more Spartan, but peppered with hints that they could better their status through hard work and emulating the behavior of the Goldens. At the other end of the spectrum, meeting in their room, the Shlubbs didn't have it nearly as good: no party hats, no refreshments, and not enough chairs—sorry, budget cutbacks and all. They didn't even get real name tags. Scraps of notebook paper, carefully dulled pencils, and tape had to suffice for the Shlubbs. The Shlubbs also received far fewer chits than the generously endowed Goldens and Risers.

Once the action got under way, all three groups were divided into thirds and sent to one of the three "home" rooms to purchase their required necessities, including clothing cards, All-Purpose Nutrition Balls (doughnut holes), and work supplies. There they would also have a chance to rub elbows with subgroups from the other two status levels.

We teachers reinforced the status system by treating Goldens with first-class respect, greeting them warmly and reserving their places at the front of the line so that they could make their necessary purchases first; Risers were treated with guarded respect; and Shlubbs were closely monitored and contemptuously ordered to stay put in a holding area until it was time to leave. The line order was significant because we had programmed in an element of scarcity. While the instructions required students to purchase the necessities, there just wasn't enough to go around.

After each of the three rounds, groups returned to their homerooms to debrief what had just happened. As discussion leaders, teachers steered students toward "obvious" conclusions and peppered them with talk about group loyalty. My group, the Goldens, were quick and clear about understanding exactly what was going wrong. The Risers and, above all, those darn Shlubbs just didn't know how to behave. They were "ghetto," the cause of all the bad behavior and petty theft, because it certainly wasn't the Goldens! What was wrong with them anyway? Why did *any* of them even have to come into our clean, snack-blessed room in the first place?

Meanwhile, a tide of resentment was building in the Shlubb room. Unlike the Goldens and Risers, they perceived immediately that they were being "treated." Poor supplies, distrust, and harsh words from all the teachers, along with an untenable economic status, swiftly convinced them that the system was stacked against them. Resentment among the Shlubbs evolved into contempt for the other two groups, especially the Goldens. Rebellion broke out in the form of lawlessness. Suspected Shlubb thieves made off with a bottle of pop, some of the merchandise, and Golden party hats. A few unruly malcontents tried to steal chits, cut in line, and break other rules as well.

To the smug Goldens, who had an ample supply of chits, these developments served as further evidence of the Shlubb predilection for crime, violence, and sloth. Really. Goldens—who hadn't existed two hours earlier—believed that they were simply better, calmer, more cultured, and more successful than their peers. A particularly hostile little cabal of male Goldens (in a chilling display of Shlubbism) went as far as to voice their opinion of the underclass by creating a threatening totem comprising Shlubb name tags taped to a ruler.

The Risers, appropriately, took a middle path. While some rebelled, showed resentment of the Goldens, or showed contempt for the Shlubbs, others aspired to a more successful station. They wanted to make it to the top, just like the Goldens, instead of alienating their social betters. A few, collaborating with their gracious benefactors, developed a "Golden in Training" program to certify their progress up the imaginary social ladder.

The simulation ended with an animated, large-group debriefing session following the final round. The opening minutes of the discussion were marked by a lot of finger-pointing and blame. As the evaluations make clear, Goldens tended to cling to the notion that they deserved what they had gotten and earned it fairly through their brief, but successful, tenure in Best Practesia.

How did they feel right now? Eduardo felt like he should "do something" because the "shulbs [sic] and risers are animals. They were rough, no respect for the better race." Various other Goldens felt "Really proud and high and mighty," like "the most power[ful] human" or "good to be on top." Most Goldens also laid the blame for problems squarely at the feet of the lower castes. Trichelle felt that other groups should just "stay w[h]ere you are [and] leave us alone." And Jenny, expressing a common viewpoint, would have liked to "kick out all those who don't know how to act civilized." Several Goldens sternly urged Risers and Shlubbs to work harder and emulate them if they wanted to succeed.

What was especially striking was that the Goldens really bought the line that they had done something—anything at all—to earn their privileged status. Gradually, the Risers and Shlubbs began to disabuse the privileged caste of their illusions with obvious facts. Economic circumstances were entirely contrived and unequal; Shlubbs had been treated poorly and given incomplete information; we had thoroughly stacked the deck against the Shlubbs and Risers. The latter groups also expressed anger and resentment of their Golden betters. Those who had looted food, merchandise, or chits justified their actions as righteous rebellion against an undemocratic hierarchy.

In evaluating the simulation, the senior teachers certainly identified some weak points we could address and features we could adjust if we were to repeat the simulation. But overall, we felt that the activity had worked. By dropping kids into an utterly contrived and relatively simple scenario, students had been pushed to develop a full complement of sentiments about different levels of an artificial caste system. Victims were blamed and scapegoated for their misfortunes and aristocrats were admired. Many of those who had been handed advantage and privilege actually believed they had earned it.

Through the debriefing discussion, students eventually enlightened each other about how the results of the scenario had been preordained by the teacher-deities of Best Practesia, that the grounds for their prejudices were as groundless as could be. The seniors had learned more about how easy it can be to accept unjustified prejudices and how those who most influence society—politicians, the media, educators, advertisers—might manipulate the public, leading them into dangerous directions.

The entire Crimes Against Humanity unit, which had included a reading of Iris Chang's *The Rape of Nanking*, the horrifying account of the Japanese army's eight-week, genocidal rampage through China's former capital in 1937, and other topics and activities had reinforced this lesson in various ways. But the simulation, we hope, had made it more memorable and clear on a gut level. Now, perhaps, if our seniors were to face some future movement that drew its momentum from fear and hatred of a particular ethnicity, race, religion, or social grouping, some of them would see right through it. Perhaps they might recall the feelings that this experience had generated, and understand exactly how to respond.

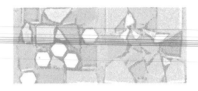

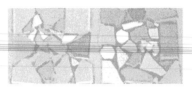

S E V E N

REFLECTIVE ASSESSMENT

In a minute, this chapter will become practical and constructive. Shortly, we will discuss ways to help students become self-monitoring, self-regulating individuals who take charge of their own learning, set ambitious goals, monitor their own progress, keep their own records, adjust their efforts, make good decisions, and become part of a collaborative community that grows by means of healthy and measured mutual feedback. We will introduce six specific methods for monitoring student growth that help teachers to balance assessment in their classrooms.

But first, we must address the toxic role played by certain kinds of assessment in our educational system. We must make a careful distinction between constructive, classroom-rooted, Best Practice forms of student evaluation, and the more prevalent, high-profile standardized tests that are at the center of today's education debates. These standardized measurements are of little use in guiding student learning, they distort our expectations of individual kids, and they frequently lower the standard of teaching as they drag teachers down to their level of gamesmanship and test coaching.

The History of Standardized Testing

All through human history, including the last few thousand years, which we compliment ourselves by referring to as "civilization," people could judge each other's intelligence or capabilities only by what someone said or did. All that really mattered, as we might put it today, was what a person "knew and was able to do." This all changed in 1908 with the invention of mental measurement. Albert Binet introduced the idea, later institutionalized in America's Army Intelligence Tests, that a paper-and-pencil test of assorted multiple-choice questions could determine what people knew or could be expected to do much more quickly than actually observing or knowing someone.

Among the first uses of mental measurement was the ranking of ethnic groups by intelligence. In 1917, Binet tests administered to American immigrants revealed that 83 percent of Jews were "feebleminded," as were 80 percent of Hungarians, 79 percent of Italians, and 87 percent of Russians. As mental testing became more prevalent, the distribution of intelligence among putative "races" was widely established. At the pinnacle were "Nordic" peoples, followed by "Mediterraneans" (Italians and Spaniards being dimmer than Swedes, apparently), on down through Asians, Indians, and finally, at the very bottom, Africans. Early IQ testers also promulgated a kind of lowerarchy of intelligence for "mental defectives," which ranked "morons" in the top slot, down through "imbeciles" to "idiots."

In short, early mental measurement was mainly the exercise of scientized racism, as has been thoroughly "outed" by Stephen Jay Gould in *The Mismeasure of Man* (1981) and by Alan Chase in *The Legacy of Malthus* (1977). As these scholars have shown, early standardized mental tests had no more validity than the "sciences" of phrenology and craniology that they replaced. Among the scientifically indefensible assumptions of early mental measurement were two especially crude ideas: that intelligence is a single trait, and that it is permanently fixed. These deterministic fictions remain at the heart of mental measurement seventy-five years later. As this book is being written, there has just been a flurry of overheated press reports about some scientists who have "mapped the brains" of defective young readers and "proved" what's wrong with their gray matter. We still talk about the construct "IQ" as though it were an actual, inherent, internal feature of human beings. We still run our educational system as though intelligence were a unitary trait, in spite of articulate challenges by people like Howard Gardner (1983). To this day, we screen, track, reward, and segregate people (children and adults alike) using tests rooted in bad science and redolent of bigotry.

Today, the main use of standardized tests in America is to justify the distribution of certain goodies to certain people. This kind of misuse has penetrated our educational system as thoroughly as any branch of society. For example, from the 1950s into the 1980s, the National Teachers Examination was used to grant or renew teaching licenses in many states, despite the fact that testmakers had never shown any correlation between scores and teaching performance. The test was eventually removed from the marketplace by its unrepentant makers only after decades of protest by outside scholars who documented its irrelevance. Right into the 1990s, the Preliminary Scholastic Aptitude Test was used to hand out tens of millions of scholarship dollars disproportionately to male applicants, even though the test's discrimination against females had been documented for decades. The ongoing use of IQ tests to place students in special education or gifted programs, entrance exams to admit freshmen to colleges, and placement tests to select candidates for certain programs continues to be more pseudo than science.

If teachers feel threatened by standardized tests in their own schools or communities (and most American teachers surely do) history warns them to be skeptical but realistic. These tests are clearly here to stay, and very real punishments will be handed out to students and teachers who don't perform well on them. But accommodating the reality of standardized tests doesn't mean being ruled by them, catering to them, or even believing in them. It means giving your students the coaching they need to show their best on the tests—and then returning to the real business of education, which is nurturing the growth of individual students' thinking, over years, across disciplines, and among collaborators. And never forget this: In 1950, contemplating graduate school studies at Boston University, Dr. Martin Luther King took the Graduate Record Exam—like the SATs, another Educational Testing Service product. The man now considered by many to have been the greatest orator of the twentieth century scored in the third quartile on "verbal skills"—below average.

Let Them Eat Tests

The people running our country's educational accountability movement—that is, politicians, state legislators, governors, and blue-ribbon panels of businessmen—don't know or care much about the structures of Best Practice education: workshop, integrative units, or collaborative learning. Indeed, few of them could probably tell a center from a conference. But they do care a lot—a whole lot—about test scores. Indeed, in many states and localities, the only tangible outcomes of two decades' worth of school reform are new layers of standardized tests, with their attendant schedules of penalties for low-scoring kids, teachers, and schools.

As pretense of reform, mass testing is a pretty tempting commodity. Testing is relatively cheap, it sounds tough, and its numerical results are irresistible media fodder. Since most standardized test scores correlate highly with socioeconomic status, any new round of testing will usually reconfirm the unworthiness of the underclasses and comfort the privileged. The predictable test results justify the blaming, shaming, and stigmatizing of low-scoring schools and communities.

After all, why should we spend more money on those people, if they can't even pass the tests?

In Chicago, for example, we currently have scores of schools on probation, a status determined solely through standardized test scores. Virtually all the probation schools serve poor children. The result is that these schools, in addition to facing the daily challenges of working with kids who may live in public housing projects, endure tremendous family stresses, speak other languages, or run with gangs—these schools are also publicly humiliated by their test scores, their teaching staffs are repudiated, their neighborhoods are further disgraced. But in the ultimate zero-sum game that is standardized testing, it has to be this way. Some schools must by definition occupy the bottom half, the lower quartile, the tenth decile in the distribution. And no matter what the test, does anyone seriously expect rich suburban kids, whose "Nordic" neighbors create and sell these tests, to wind up at the bottom?

Amid the hubbub of school reform, teachers are actually receiving a schizophrenic message: teach in creative, innovative, constructive ways, but your students will be tested very differently. Monty Neil and Joe Medinal of FairTest, a testing watchdog organization, argue that the teaching methods that are effective in raising scores on tests of lower-level cognitive skills are nearly the opposite of those strategies that develop complex cognitive learning, problem-solving ability, and creativity. Test scores provide little useful information to improve instruction, and many teachers, in attempting to make sure that their students are prepared for the tests, must abandon the innovative and challenging instruction in which they are engaged in order to dumb down the curriculum to conquer the test.

According to school reform expert Roland Barth (1992), teachers need to be encouraged to take chances where a safety net protects those who may risk and stumble. Many principals encourage, and seem to understand, this kind of classroom risk taking. However, standardized test results often place so much pressure on principals that they pass that pressure right along to their teachers. According to Peter Johnston (1992), each year the average elementary student loses four days of instruction to taking standardized tests, an upper elementary student loses six days, and a junior or senior high school student loses approximately ten days. These numbers don't reflect the days spent preparing for the tests, which grow as we continue adding layers of tests. With all that is known about the importance of instructional time, it is unconscionable to devote such large amounts of time to a procedure that is inconsistent with what we know about good instruction.

Of course there are genuinely ineffective schools in Chicago and elsewhere, which should be identified by some means and promptly improved. Some test scores probably do accurately point toward schools that are doing a lousy job, that are not giving their students "value added," even taking into account the special challenges or difficulties the children there may face. If standardized testing were used mainly to aim massive aid at such failing schools, its negative effects might be counterbalanced with constructive outcomes (although we hardly need more tests to know where to send the massive aid, right now).

But in most of America that's not how testing is used, now that it has become the main ingredient of many "reform" programs. Schools do not receive the resources to raise achievement, only the mandate to measure it more often. There's little or no help for any struggling school or district once the scores are in. Numbers are published in the papers, the lineup of winners and losers is official-ized, and life goes on with no reallocation of resources. Perhaps this is because rais-ing achievement would cost real money and might even (who knows) upset the standard scoring patterns and undermine the advantages currently enjoyed by the children of blue-ribbon businesspeople who sit on panels that prescribe more stan-dardized tests for low-scoring schools.

If this all sounds a bit intemperate and suspicious, perhaps that is because in thirty-five years of working with schools we've come to see large-scale, standard-ized assessments as the force that always messes things up, that derails the best efforts, that keeps genuine reform from taking root, that maintains and perpetu-ates the status quo. Because of the subskills-based items on the citywide reading test, teachers dare not take time to read aloud to students or to let them discuss their own books in literature circles. Because the statewide science exam covers scores of topics, only brave schools like Waters in Chicago let students linger for a whole month at the nearby riverside, studying the ecosystem in depth. Because of the threat of probation, schools give up most of January, February, and March to test coaching for the spring testing season. Instead of reading real books, kids read and fill out sample standardized tests. The tests *literally* become the curriculum. And the test obsession strikes most severely, of course, at the schools that score the lowest, which are most in jeopardy from further low scores. The schools that stand to lose the most, and who have the least chance of actually beating the tests, are the ones that are most ruled and distorted by them. The kids who need Best Practice teaching the most (who need authentic, holistic, developmental experi-ences) are guaranteed not to get it because of standardized tests.

Constructive Assessment

This is all politics—important politics, but politics nevertheless. No matter how the results of standardized tests are used, they offer little help to classroom teach-ers, who must guide and document the learning of individual students 180 days a year. And most of this chapter so far has also been pretty negative, focusing on things that don't work and don't help. So, what does work? What kind of assessment is constructive? What models and procedures can teachers employ to steer kids toward growth? After all, teachers need real structures and strategies to assess and support students' growth inside the day-to-day reality of the classroom, within a close coaching relationship with each individual child.

In a moment, we will talk about the six structures of what might be called "Best Practice assessment." But because we still worry about the toxic legacy of assessment in American education, because these six structures can so easily be corrupted back into the same kind of accountability testing that we are trying to mitigate, we want to be very clear about the principles behind these six key strategies. The following ideas can help us make sure that our new assessment methods really do enact the ideals of Best Practice.

1. *Assessment should reflect, encourage, and become an integral part of good instruction.* While many traditional measures occur separate from or after teaching, the most powerful assessment activities (such as conferences, analytic scoring rubrics, and portfolios) are ingredients of good instruction. When assessment overlaps with instruction in this way, it helps teachers to be more effective in the same amount of instructional time. Ideally, assessment activities should unequivocally reinforce state-of-the-art curriculum and teaching methods. At the very least, the evaluation of student work should never distort or obstruct exemplary classroom practice.

2. *Powerful evaluation efforts focus on the major, whole outcomes valued in the curriculum:* real, complex performances of writing, researching, reading, experimenting, problem solving, creating, speaking, and so on. The new assessment paradigm dares to focus on the higher-order outcomes of education, the real payoffs in which kids orchestrate big chunks of learning in realistic applications.

3. *Most school assessment activities should be formative.* This means that we assess primarily to ensure that students learn better and teachers teach more effectively. Summative evaluation, which involves translating students' growth to some kind of number, score, or grade to be reported outside the classroom, is just one small, narrow, and occasional element of a comprehensive assessment program.

4. *Traditional norm-referenced, competitive measures that rank students against each other (such as letter grades and numerically scored tests) provide little helpful formative assessment and tend to undermine good instruction.* Instead, constructive programs increasingly rely on *self-referenced growth measures*, where the student is compared

with herself. This means teachers must have ways of valuing, tracking, and recording individualized factors such as growth, improvement, quality of work, good faith, insight, risk taking, rate of change, energy, and so on.

5. *A key trait of effective thinkers, writers, problem solvers, readers, researchers, and other learners is that they constantly self-monitor and self-evaluate.* A solid assessment program must consistently help (and require) students to take increasing responsibility for their own record keeping, goal setting and monitoring, portfolio management, metacognitive reflection, and self-assessment.

6. *Skillful and experienced evaluators take a developmental perspective.* They are familiar with the major growth models, both general cognitive stage theories and the models from specific curriculum fields (stages of reading, mathematical thinking, invented spelling, etc.). Rather than checking students against arbitrary age- or grade-level targets, teachers track the story of each child's individual growth through developmental phases.

7. *Teachers need a rich repertoire of assessment strategies to draw from in designing sensitive, appropriate evaluation activities for particular curriculum areas.* Among these broad strategies are anecdotal/observational records, checklists, interviews, portfolios, performance assessment rubrics, and classroom tests.

8. *It is never enough to look at learning events from only one angle; rather, we now use multiple measures, examining students' growth from several different perspectives.* By triangulating assessments, we get a "thick" picture of kids' learning, ensuring that unexpected growth, problems, and side effects are not missed.

9. *Teachers need to reallocate the considerable time that they already spend on assessment, evaluation, record keeping, testing, and grading activities.* They need to spend less time scoring, and more time saving and documenting student work. Instead of creating and justifying long strings of numbers in their grade books, teachers should collect and save samples of kids' original, unscored products. This reallocation of time means that, once they are installed, new assessment procedures don't require any more time of teachers than the old ways—or any less.

10. *Sound evaluation programs provide, where necessary, a database for deriving legitimate, defensible student grades.* However, major national curriculum groups have recommended (and we concur) that competitive, norm-referenced grading should be de-emphasized and replaced by the many richer kinds of assessments that will be outlined further on.

11. *It takes many different people working cooperatively to effectively evaluate student growth and learning.* In every classroom, there should be a balance between external assessment (such as district standardized tests, state assessments, etc.), teacher-run evaluation, student self-evaluation, parent involvement in assessment, and collaborative assessments that involve various contributions of these parties.

12. *The currently available state and national standardized tests yield an exceedingly narrow and unreliable picture of student achievement, are poor indicators of school performance, and encourage archaic instructional practices.* Therefore, professional teachers *avoid teaching to standardized tests.* Instead, they show colleagues, parents, and administrators the more sophisticated, detailed, accurate, and meaningful assessments that they have developed for their own classrooms.

How can these principles be put into manageable and practical use in classrooms? We can see six basic structures of constructive, formative, reflection-oriented assessment that may be used at any grade level, in any subject, with any students.

- Portfolios
- Conferences
- Anecdotal records
- Checklists
- Performance assessment rubrics
- Classroom tests

In order to provide the deepest and widest view of students' growth, these strategies need to be implemented in a balanced, healthful mixture. Below we describe each in a kind of declining order of progressiveness, moving from profoundly formative, student-centered assessment practices like portfolios and conferences, toward more nearly traditional procedures like performance assessment and classroom tests. These structures, especially the first five, have been quite well documented in recent years. Happily, there has been a long-overdue burst of literature about alternative forms of assessment, including many teacher-written books replete with useful models, samples, and stories. The listing of such resources at the end of this chapter will be particularly helpful for teachers looking to implement and troubleshoot some of the more complex and promising assessment structures.

Portfolios

Portfolios represent a diametrical shift from old-style assessments. Where we used to prize strings of numbers and letters in a grade book, symbolizing the outcomes of long-discarded test papers, we now collect and study the raw materials of students' learning. In using portfolios, we invite kids to *collect* samples in working folders; rough and polished; written, drawn, acted, and painted; individual and collaborative. Depending on the subject and grade level, students may include writing samples, videotapes of class performances, findings from experiments, graphs of research results, CDs of reading aloud, photographs of themselves at work, artifacts from projects, comments from partners and parents. From the large collection in their folders, they *select* important pieces to be included in their portfolios. These pieces are chosen for various reasons: their best work, a piece that exhibited growth, a particular genre, the first foray into a new medium, to name a few. The students are then invited to *reflect* on the work that they chose to include in the portfolio. Students use this reflective work to help them set goals for the future.

As an assessment tool, the portfolio provides an exceptionally deep multidimensional record of kids' learning. If a student is struggling with math facts or spelling, evidence of these problems will be evident in the work. But larger strengths and weaknesses will be manifest as well: Can the student conceive and pursue an inquiry? Can he make connections, draw analogies, support a position, notice contrasts? For reporting to parents or school authorities, a well-made student portfolio provides a body of evidence, a basis for decision making, that surpasses the validity of any test score number. And as we ask students to create and regularly review their own portfolios, talking and writing about what they see there, we are inculcating the habits of reflection, self-monitoring, responsibility, and planning. Some teachers have student-led conferences for parents where the students talk their parents through their portfolios, a productive experience for all involved.

Conferences

Conferences are an elegant example of how assessment can actually become one with instruction. In a writing workshop classroom, for example, it is integral to the model that students have regular one-to-one conferences with the teacher to review individual pieces of writing in progress as well as talk about general strengths, weaknesses, trends, and goals in their writing development. In other words, the purpose of the conferences is to help students reflect on their work, from the lowest-level elements, say the impact of one word choice against another, all the way to the most global characteristics, becoming able to step back and think about one's emerging style as an author. Even as conferences teach students to reflect, they also obviously help the teacher to gather much information about what a child knows and needs, and to offer personal, precisely targeted feedback. Providing that the teacher keeps simple notes or records of these meetings, conferences can combine instruction and assessment in a single seamless activity.

Anecdotal Records

Anecdotal records, sometimes called "kidwatching," involve the teacher in making regular, written notes about each child's learning and growth. Some teachers do this by focusing on three to five children per day, carrying a clipboard with these kids' names on it and jotting down, in the seams and intervals of the schedule, what they notice about each child's learning. The teacher's style of note taking may be quite personal and telegraphic: "10:45—Jim helps Marianne use the protractor." Some teachers try to jot the child's own comments: "I don't get these cross-products, Miss K." These notes become part of the teacher's thinking, planning, and cumulative record keeping for each child. They are particularly useful for tracking a student's growth over long periods of time, and provide a strong basis for conversation with students and parents. "I see here that back in October you were confused about cross-products but now you're doing them right most of the time. What helped you figure it out?"

Checklists

While anecdotal records are typically open-ended, *checklists* are a more anchored form of observational assessment. Again, teachers devise some kind of schedule during which they pay special attention to individual children—usually one or just a few at a time. Then they observe using a prepared list of competencies or behaviors, noting the degree of each student's progress. For example, in a first-grade classroom, the teacher might be checking whether each kid "Rarely," "Sometimes," or "Always" makes predictions while reading, adjusts her reading rate to the text, or retells a story accurately. One advantage of checklists is that teachers can create them together with their grade-level teammates—or with students themselves ("Let's make a list of the things that good readers do"). Classroom checklists can also be specifically designed to reflect an official district curriculum, so that teachers can use the instrument to see if their instruction is working as planned. In some schools and districts, the classroom checklist becomes an integral part of the report card, telling parents, in more detail than any "A" or "B" ever could, exactly what their child knows and is able to do.

Performance Assessment Rubrics

While in traditional classrooms teachers have mostly been concerned with tallying the accumulation of subskills (the alleged building blocks of educated behavior), Best Practice directs our attention to larger, higher-order, more complex performances. That is, we want to assess not just whether a child can tell if words are nouns or verbs, but whether the student can craft an original, logical, well-organized piece of writing out of a whole lot of nouns, verbs, and other parts of speech. But assessing so complex a product as a piece of writing (as opposed to a multiple-choice test) requires a new kind of instrument. *Performance assessment rubrics* are just such a tool; they are simply a set of specific criteria for successful performance of a given activity, presented in a scoring guide. Thus, for example, you might determine (as the state of Illinois has) that an effective piece of persuasive writing has four ingredients worth 25 percent each: focus, support, organization, and mechanics. Now, writing teachers across the country might quibble with this formula, but at least it tells students what some of the inarguably necessary ingredients of successful writing are. It invites them (before they write, as they draft, and while they revise) to attend to and balance these features so that the final product will be effective with its audience.

At the very least, performance assessment is a big step ahead of the days when teachers assigned students grades on projects and papers without ever revealing the criteria for assessment. Performance assessment is most meaningful when teachers invite students into the rubric development process, brainstorming together what the formula might be for a well-done lab report, an effectively enacted scene, a well-done geometric proof. Creating this kind of scoring guide thus becomes part of instruction, helping to make curricular goals transparent and explicit. Good performance assessment tools can remind teachers to teach and students to master the elements of successful performance in the field of study at hand. And finally, while performance assessment can genuinely bring students into the process and make the criteria of success more public, it can also be used to generate the kinds of numerical and comparative results so hungrily demanded by many school systems.

Classroom Tests

Classroom tests, of course, are familiar to all teachers and former students. When used formatively to monitor and guide student instruction, teacher-made tests can be one ingredient of a balanced assessment program. There's nothing wrong with the occasional spelling quiz or math test, as long as the items represented and the scoring system used are reasonable measures of what has been studied. In Best Practice classrooms, though, classroom tests tend to look a little different. Since there is much curriculum jigsawing, with student groups studying different chunks of curriculum, it would be a rare occasion when everyone sat for the exact same test, at the same time. Chances are that even the weekly spelling test would be individualized, including some words chosen by each student from their own reading and research, and entered into a personal dictionary for study and mastery. Also, since teachers are most interested in students' higher-order, conceptual understandings, classroom tests would likely try to gauge those learnings and not focus much on disconnected factual recall. Chances are the students would help design any test that was given, would have input on scoring, and would be responsible for fitting their results in with other items in their own self-assessment process.

As we noted at the outset, we've presented structures of classroom assessment in a roughly declining order of student-centeredness: that is, portfolios and conferences seem more harmonious with Best Practice principles of authentic, developmentally minded education than performance assessment or classroom tests. But in the real world, a blend of these different types is undoubtedly realistic and perhaps even healthful for kids. On this matter we tend to be highly pragmatic. If teachers are under the gun to employ some competitive, norm-referenced assessment measures along with the more individualized, student-centered ones, so be it. We think it is fine, as a practical matter, for teachers to average the two together in creating grades and other reports. For example, teachers can assign point values to never-sometimes-always checklists (0, 1, or 2 points) and create tallies that average into grades. Kids can set their own goals in conferences, assess their percentage of attainment ("I conquered 80 percent of my spelling demons"), and plug that into the report card.

Into the Classroom

Now we'll meet some teachers and schools that are working with evaluation in exactly this way, creating balanced assessments that enact Best Practice principles in a complicated, real world. These educators are feeding the grading machine as necessary, while also trying to give kids meaningful, personal, and constructive feedback on their growth. They are trying to turn more responsibility over to students, to help them become more reflective, self-aware, self-guiding people.

Debbie Gurvitz gives us a glimpse of a comprehensive first-grade assessment system in which students collect, select, and reflect on important samples of their own work. Using individual working folders and final portfolios to collect data, Debbie's students make their own report cards and conduct parent conferences three times a year. Luanne Kowalke tells how she teaches the big ideas of reflection and metacognition, helping kids to set goals and monitor their thinking throughout the school year. Luanne opens a window on the kinds of records that can help teachers richly document kids' cognitive growth. Next, Pam Hyde shows how assessment and instruction can be seamlessly woven together when both teacher and students focus on the higher-order outcomes of the curriculum.

Readers may be surprised to see how complex and sophisticated assessment can actually be in third grade, and they may also notice that this long-term performance assessment is highly applicable to teaching at other levels.

Kids are assigned lots of books to read in middle and high school, and teachers often use end-of-the chapter quizzes or end-of-the-book tests to make sure that students did the reading. Nancy Steineke has a better idea: assess the kids by whether they can create a public performance based upon the characters, plot, theme, and setting of the book. Her "skit with narration" activity shows how assessment can be both meaningful and, believe it or not, fun. Finally, George Wood, the principal of Federal Hocking High School, and his faculty share their model for graduation by portfolio. At FHHS, and at many other Coalition of Essential Schools programs, students don't complete high school by taking a prescribed number of courses and earning a certain GPA. Instead, every senior in this small, rural high school must demonstrate what they know to a panel of adults from the community using both written documents and public presentations.

Further Reading

Akhavan, Nancy. 2004. *How to Align Literacy, Instruction, and Standards.* Portsmouth, NH: Heinemann.

Azwell, Tara, and Elizabeth Schmar, eds. 1995. *Report Card on Report Cards: Alternatives to Consider.* Portsmouth, NH: Heinemann.

Cambourne, Brian, and Jan Turbill, eds. 1994. *Responsive Evaluation: Making Valid Judgments About Student Literacy.* Portsmouth, NH: Heinemann.

Costa, Arthur L., and Bena Kallick, eds. 2000. *Assessing and Reporting on Habits of Mind.* Alexandria, VA: Association for Supervision and Curriculum Development.

Falk, Beverly. 2000. *The Heart of the Matter: Using Standards and Assessment to Learn.* Portsmouth, NH: Heinemann.

Freeman, Ann, and Eric Paulson. 2003. *Insight from the Eyes: The Science of Effective Reading Instruction.* Portsmouth, NH: Heinemann.

Graves, Donald H. 2002. *Testing Is Not Teaching: What Should Count in Education.* Portsmouth, NH: Heinemann.

Harris Stefanakis, Evangeline. 2003. *Multiple Intelligences and Portfolios: A Window into the Learner's Mind.* Portsmouth, NH: Heinemann.

Hill, Bonnie Campbell, and Cynthia Ruptic. 1994. *Practical Aspects of Authentic Assessment: Putting the Pieces Together.* Norwood, MA: Christopher-Gordon.

Johnston, Peter H. 1997. *Knowing Literacy: Constructive Literacy Assessment.* Portland, ME: Stenhouse.

Mahoney, Jim. 2002. *Power and Portfolios: Best Practices for High School Classrooms.* Portsmouth, NH: Heinemann.

Murphy, Sandra, and Mary Ann Smith. 2001. *A Bridge from Teaching to Assessment.* Portsmouth, NH: Heinemann.

Porter, Carol, and Janell Cleland. 1995. *The Portfolio as a Learning Strategy.* Portsmouth, NH: Boynton/Cook.

Rhodes, Lynn K., ed. 1993. *Literacy Assessment: A Handbook of Instruments.* Portsmouth, NH: Heinemann.

Rhodes, Lynn K., and Nancy Shanklin. 1993. *Windows into Literacy: Assessing Learners K–8.* Portsmouth, NH: Heinemann.

Sunstein, Bonnie S., and Jonathan Lovell, eds. 2000. *The Portfolio Standard: How Students Can Show Us What They Know and Are Able to Do.* Portsmouth, NH: Heinemann.

Wiggins, Grant P., and Jay McTighe. 1998. *Understanding by Design.* Alexandria, VA: Association for Supervision and Curriculum Development.

Woodward, Helen. 1994. *Negotiated Evaluation: Involving Children and Parents in the Process.* Portsmouth, NH: Heinemann.

Reflective Assessment in First Grade

DEBBIE GURVITZ

At Lyon School in Glenview, Illinois, we have a student portfolio system that informs everything we do in the primary grades. Beginning in kindergarten, we ask students to reflect on their learning, their strengths and weaknesses, their goals for the future, and the ways they learn best. In a very real sense, these young children are becoming metacognitive, even before they know what that big word means. In everything we do, we insist that students are partners in the learning process, always taking responsibility for their learning.

For their portfolios, the children *collect* materials in a working folder, *select* pieces that are especially important to be placed in their portfolios, and *reflect* upon why they chose each piece and what it demonstrates about them as writers, readers, and thinkers. These portfolios travel with the kids through the three grades they are with us and the collection finally goes home at the end of second grade.

The portfolios are an important way of informing and involving parents. When student work goes home with the children, parents are periodically asked to help select a piece to return to school, accompanied by a written reflection about what that sample demonstrates about their child. Students use the portfolios as a way of assessing how they are doing and are always pleased to see the progress they make. Starting in kindergarten drawing pictures and graduating from second grade as a fluent writer is "way cool."

The portfolios provide us teachers with a tangible way to watch students grow and take a personal look at each child's progress. By the time kids get to the end of first grade, they are pretty adept at thinking about their thinking. Figures 7.1

Figure 7.1: Emma's early-in-the-year reflections.

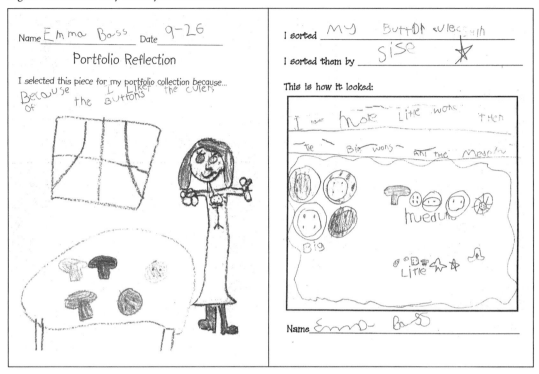

and 7.2 show reflections that Emma wrote in Ms. Aronow's class, two at the beginning of first grade and one at the end. It's not hard to see how much Emma learned in first grade.

Also in Emma's first-grade portfolio is a compact disc containing her PowerPoint research presentation on lions. Each of the students chose a subject they were passionate about. Emma focused on lions. Most of the students gave oral presentations, but a few did their reports on PowerPoint. After her experience with this high-tech art form, Emma has some suggestions for future users:

> My edvice would be to lisen to the directions carfully or if you could not understand raise your hand and a teacher will help you or I can tell what to click on or problems solve or I can click for you.

When asked if she thought that PowerPoint was a good way to share information, she wrote:

> I likt it because it is much eser to click then to stand up get your cards and put the mike on and start to talk

Figure 7.2: Emma's end-of-year reflections.

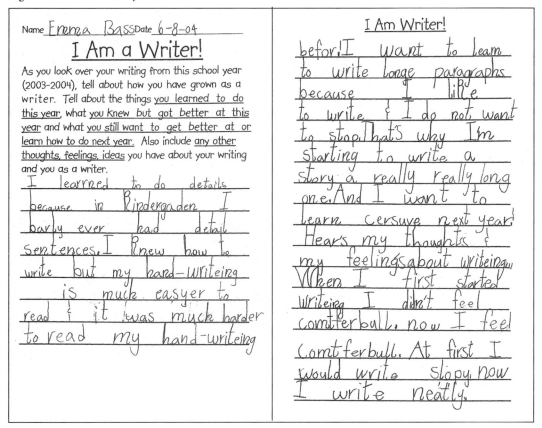

Name Emma Bass Date 6-8-04

I Am a Writer!

As you look over your writing from this school year (2003-2004), tell about how you have grown as a writer. Tell about the things you learned to do this year, what you knew but got better at this year and what you still want to get better at or learn how to do next year. Also include any other thoughts, feelings, ideas you have about your writing and you as a writer.

I learrned to do details because in Kindergaden I barly ever had detail sentences. I knew how to write but my hand-writeing is much easyer to read & it was much harder to read my hand-writeing

I Am Writer!

befor! I want to learn to write longe paragraphs because I like to write & I do not want to stop. Thats why I'm starting to write a story a really really long one. And I want to learn cersuve next year. Hear's my thoughts & my feelings about writeing. When I first started writeing I didn't feel comfterbull. now I feel comfterbull. At first I would write slopy now I write neatly.

Emma's portfolio shows us a lot about what she can do at age six; she reads, writes, draws, reflects, and uses technology as a tool for learning.

Writing

All of us at Lyon School put a big emphasis on writing as a way of learning to read and as a way of demonstrating learning. In Illinois, third graders face a tough standardized writing exam, and that means all the third-grade teachers in the state are stressed out trying to meet the writing standards. Of course, this high-stakes test doesn't measure just third-grade instruction, but all the writing skills that have developed from K–3. In order to help the primary kids get ready for the test, the whole faculty looked at the state's third-grade standards. We matched them up with high, middle, and low samples of first-grade writing and developed our own rubrics for first graders. Now, we use the rubric to look at student writing (and guide our instruction) three times a year.

Figure 7.3: Fall writing sample.

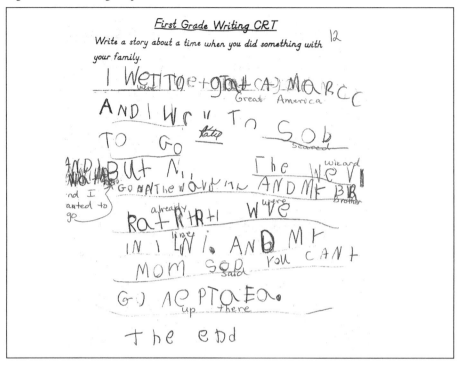

Figure 7.4: Spring writing sample.

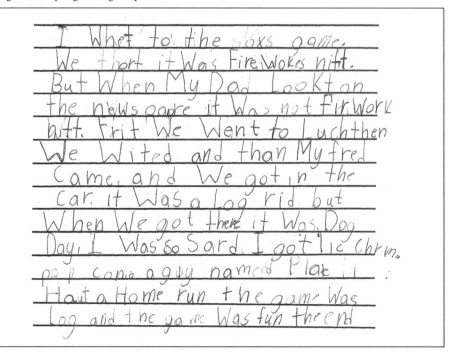

Amy wrote the pieces shown in Figures 7.3 and 7.4 in November and June of first grade. Using our adapted scoring system, we estimated that Amy scored one-third higher after all she experienced in first grade. In both examples, Amy has a lot to tell us about her life, from Great America to the Sox game. But between November and June, Amy also acquired the skills to write so that more readers can understand the stories she wants to tell.

Dialogue Journals

Three times a year, all the teachers spend a week in written conversations with our children. Often, students will later select some of these dialogue journals to go into their portfolios as favorite examples. I love these weeks and take great pleasure in having personal conversations with each of my kids. My instructions are simple: I just ask students to answer my questions, pay attention to spelling, and use the word wall if they need help. These written dialogues teach me a lot about what each child knows about language, reading, writing, and life (see Figure 7.5).

Figure 7.5: Written teacher-student conversations.

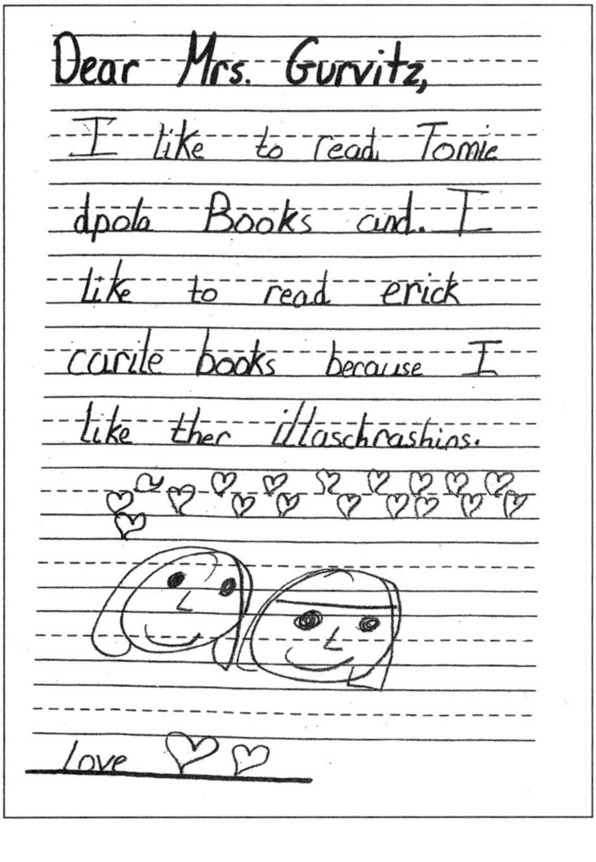
Dear Mrs. Gurvitz,
I like to read Tomie dpola Books and. I like to read erick carile books because I like ther illaschrashins.
Love

Here is some more of the dialogue I had with Betty in February:

Dear Betty,
Guess what? I like the illustrations that Tomie dePaola and Eric Carle use in their books, too.
What are your favorite Eric Carle and Tomie DePaola books? I think I like Strega stories the best. What do you think about that?
Love,
Mrs. Gurvitz

Dear Mrs. Gurvitz,
I think I like Schregnona to and Erick carle and now Im thinking abot marc brown. I like moust of the caricters I forgot some of the caricters names but I purnela Arthur buster brain bincky
Sinerly,
Betty

Dear Betty,

Which Marc Brown character is your favorite? I think I like DW best. She is funny and sometimes she is annoying. That reminds me of when I was little and my sister was annoying. Does that ever happen to you?

Write back.

Love,

Mrs. Gurvitz

Dear Mrs. Gurvitz,

I think I like muffy because sum times my sister is snotey and shes also snotey when Im chring to have fun! and Im in my room and I don't like it at all.

Love,

Betty

Dear Betty,

What do you do when your sister gets snotty? Are you ever like Muffy? Which Marc Brown character reminds you of yourself?

I hope I don't remind anyone that I am like Mr. Ratburn.

I have had fun writing to you.

Love,

Mrs. Gurvitz

Betty's dialogue journal shows me a lot. I know that she understands much about how language works, including consonants and vowels, her basic spelling is good, she uses good strategies to figure out words that she doesn't know how to spell, and she is good at printing. Betty's journals also tell me that she loves to read, and has strong opinions about some of the authors we have studied this year.

Actually, these weeklong written conversations are very personal and individualized reading lessons. I ask questions about topics that are meaningful to each student, and in my letters back to them, I model writing, spelling, and comprehension. When kids write back to me, I often ask them to read their responses aloud to me, as we sit side by side, so that our journaling becomes an even more powerful reading and writing experience.

Problem-Based Learning

Each year we spend some time investigating the topic of "critters," meaning common and sometimes pesky animals like squirrels, spiders, raccoons, and the like. As a class, we examine the many aspects of critters; their life cycles, habitats, adap-

Figure 7.6: Critter assessment.

Critter Assessment

My cousin bought a new house in a new development. The builders cut down a forest and built 10 houses. My cousin was so excited to have a new house. He planted a flower and vegetable garden in his back yard. But all his flowers and vegetables were eaten. And his trees had the bark stripped off. He looked out his window and saw 5 deer in his yard.

Tell what is happening and why.

The 5 deer are eating the vegetables and flowers because they don't have to much of Food. The cousin shouldn't have planted a flower and vegetable garden because he should have known that the forest was cut down and the 5 deer would have nothing to eat they would come to eat the flowers and vegetables. The 5 deer ate the Flowers and vegetables because they were hungry.

Critter Assessment

My cousin bought a new house in a new development. The builders cut down a forest and built 10 houses. My cousin was so excited to have a new house. He planted a flower and vegetable garden in his back yard. But all his flowers and vegetables were eaten. And his trees had the bark stripped off. He looked out his window and saw 5 deer in his yard.

Tell what is happening and why.

The Cousin bought the house. But Animals keep bothering him? The deer Wants to eat the flowrs. the stripped off bark was a beave tacking the Wood to make it's home. I think he Shod Wose a fence to keep the animals away.

tations, and how we get rid of critters humanely when necessary. We read a lot of good nonfiction about critters, and we take several "critter walks" around the neighborhood to spot each species. For the final project, the children work in small groups to present a chosen critter to the class. This way, the children learn about their own critter as well as the ones that other groups present.

I am always curious what students remember from the critter project, whether they retain information and can apply their learning to a new situation. So about a month later I give a little assessment (see Figure 7.6). It is great to see that all this critter stuff really has some staying power. When students dig down into content they choose for themselves and take responsibility for their learning, they truly remember information.

Report Cards and Conferences

Report cards and parent conferences are required by our district three times a year. We teachers really enjoy this because we have designed a student-driven process that draws from kids' portfolios, reflections, and their self-ratings in math, language arts, and behavior. Before the big night when the parents come, students assess themselves on forms like the one in Figure 7.7 and get their portfolios ready.

Figure 7.7: Student report card, first quarter.

My L.A. Report Card

Name: Anisha   Date: 12-1-03

Put a circle around the word that shows how you feel.

I like reading fiction (made-up) books:
(By myself)
(With a helper partner)
With the teacher

I like reading non-fiction (true) books:
(By myself)
(With a helper partner)
With the teacher

When I am spelling for my journal I use:
The word wall
(Word families)
Sound it out

I feel my handwriting is:
(Pretty good)
Okay
I wish it was neater

When I am reading I feel:
(Very good)   Okay
Good   (Not So Good)

Why do you feel this way? because it makes me learn

When I am writing I feel:
(Very good)   Okay
Good   (Not So Good)

Why do you feel this way? because I keep getting distractid

One thing I feel is hard for me in Language Arts is:
Thinking for ideas

One thing I would like to improve in Language Arts is:
learn to write and read more.

At Lyon School, our kids keep demonstrating that they are our partners in both learning and in assessment. They constantly surprise us with what they can do and what they know about themselves as learners. Assessment is not a separate topic at our school because it is embedded in instruction. We always think first about how kids can show us what they know. Every activity has a built-in assessment component, and the learning portfolio reflects the process. When young children are given the chance, they can teach themselves—and us—a great deal about learning.

Reflection and Metacognition: Thinking About Our Thinking

LUANNE KOWALKE

To help children become intelligent, insightful, educated human beings, we teachers must help them become conscious of their own learning and thought processes. Instead of teaching students *what* to think, we need to teach them *how* to think, and how to think for themselves. In other words, we must teach metacognition. But what does this term mean in everyday classrooms?

Put simply, metacognition is thinking about your thinking and knowing what you know. For many people, this is simply called reflection. When we reflect, mull, muse, weigh, contemplate, meditate, speculate, or express carefully considered thoughts about our own thinking, we are involved in metacognition. Metacognition is an important kind of reflective thinking that people use, often unconsciously, to help themselves in the learning process, by recognizing and understanding what they know and don't know, and by making decisions about this knowledge. People are metacognitively involved when they plan, monitor, and evaluate their own actions and thought processes.

We can help our students become intelligent thinkers by addressing their needs in the areas of planning, monitoring, and evaluating. In the planning and monitoring stages, we can encourage students to set and reach for their own goals. In the evaluating stage, we can ask students to self-assess their learning. To nurture all three, we can provide students with the daily classroom time they need to think about their thinking as they participate in discussions and activities.

Goal Setting

Each morning I model goal setting for my fourth graders as we begin our school day. "Today, our most important goal is to finish our writer's workshop revisions. Our other goals include on-line voting for the MayaQuest expedition, finishing our bulletin board, and allowing time for literature circles. If we have time after that, we'll tackle some spring cleaning and e-mail our buddies. If not, we'll take care of those things tomorrow" is how I model short-term goal setting for my students.

Then, I expect my students to set goals for themselves, too, write them down, and check in with me periodically to report how they are doing. I ask the kids to set social, personal, and educational goals. One of Chris's goals is "to keep my desk neater. I will put my papers in clearly marked folders so I don't have to search all over tarnation for them." Jenny's is "trying to work better in cooperative groups. I know I've improved over last quarter, but I still need to get better." Min-Ho, Mito, and Yoon-Tae want, respectively, "to be a better writer and reader," to be "less shy," and to "understand linking verbs like *have* or *has*."

These are all personal goals chosen by the students. At times, I will also request that they set a goal for a particular assignment. Under these circumstances I usually set a few parameters and ask for a formal, written proposal. An example of this would be the following:

Tell me:

1. your topic
2. how you will cover your material
3. how you plan to present the information to the class
4. on what criteria you wish to be evaluated.

These parameters can be changed to meet the needs of the situation and of each individual student. The important thing I try to remember is not to become too restrictive. The purpose of goal setting is for the students not to "fill in the blanks" I have left for them, but to truly have an opportunity to set, reach for, and attain goals they have chosen for themselves. Goals should be authentic, student generated, and individualized to meet the needs of each student. Teachers can facilitate goal setting by modeling different types of goals themselves and by using student-made goals in the evaluation process.

The following are student goals for group science projects about the topic of light. Each group wrote what their topic would be, how they would cover the material, and how they would like to be evaluated.

Dear Ms. Kowalke,

We will be doing a talk show and Katie will be the host. We want to be graded on organization, drama, and the amount of information. The three visitors will be John, Neal, and Lauren. It will be about how light bounces off different objects.

Lauren, John, Katie, and Neal

Dear Ms. Kowalke,

Our project is going to be a mural. We are going to draw a laboratory of people studying light. The thing we would like you to grade us on is drawing, effort, and information.

Sincerely,

Kristin, Abby, Patrick, and Chris

Dear Ms. Kowalke,

Our project is the oral report. We would like to be graded on how well we work together, and how our report is tied into the chapter, and how creative our project is. The report will be about Isaac Newton and how the prism changes colors.

Sincerely,

Sarah, Alex, and Jenny

Self-Assessment

One purpose of assessment should be for students to become self-evaluating. I often ask my students to stop for a moment and assess their accomplishments. This is a difficult yet fulfilling process. In the words of one student, "This is so hard because it makes me really use my brain!" Amazingly, student self-assessments and my own evaluations of them are often mirror images.

When I ask students to self-evaluate, I make sure that I have not made judgmental remarks about that particular assignment. For example, I would not mark a piece of writing for the grade book and discuss positives and negatives of the piece with the student, then ask them to self-evaluate. Instead, I would ask students to do their evaluation of the piece first, then complete my own evaluation without looking at theirs. What I find when I later compare the two evaluations is startling: about 85 percent of the time, our evaluations are extremely close.

Students put so much thought and effort into their self-assessments that I take them very seriously. They really don't rush through a self-assessment when it is meaningful and relevant. In fact, it can take my fourth-grade students forty-five minutes to complete a thorough self-evaluation. In most cases, both my evaluation and the students' carry equal weight in the grade book (unfortunately, report cards are still the reality in our school, so grades are necessary).

At the beginning of the year, I photocopy the "Social and Study Skills" portion of our report card, enough for every student to have their own copy. At the end of each quarter, I give each student the checklist and ask them to reflect on their progress for the marking period. As we move through the year, I give the students their reflections from past quarters to review. Each student completes the checklist thoughtfully, then answers the following questions:

1. What area do you feel showed your greatest improvement this quarter?
2. What area do you feel still needs improvement?
3. What goals would you like to set for next quarter?
4. What would you like me to discuss with your parents during conferences?

I always share report cards with students before they are sent home to parents. At that time, I give each student my copy of the report card, their copy of the checklist, and their reflections. The only thing I request of students is that they find a quiet, private place to look over their report cards. It is wonderful to see what happens next. Students look cursorily for a letter grade in the various subject areas, and then their attention is drawn to the check marks rating their behavior growth and skills.

Before I began using this self-assessment technique a few years ago, students would look at their letter grade in each subject and then hand their report card back to me; it took them about thirty seconds to find out what they wanted to know—their grade. Now, I block out a full thirty minutes for students to look at their report cards, because most take at least fifteen to twenty minutes to look over the check marks, comparing each one with their own assessment. If there is a discrepancy between my evaluation and the student's, we will discuss it. I do make changes if necessary, but this rarely happens because the two evaluations are usually so close. I am always sure to ask students if there were "any surprises" on their report card (this would mean that one of us had a very different point of view from the other, and I would want to find out why). In two years, four grading periods each, I have had only two students answer "Yes" to that question, and one of those students received a higher grade from me than they expected.

Figures 7.8a and 7.8b show checklists filled out by Lauren and me. Below is a sample of her first- and second-quarter reflections. Lauren shows particular growth in her self-perceptiveness from first to second quarter.

Lauren's First-Quarter Reflections

1. I improved on math like I learned how to do multiplacation tricks.
2. I need improvement on science skills. It's a little hard for me.
3. I think you should talk to my parents about what I'm good at and what I need to improve on. You should also talk to them about how I do in other classes like p.e. or music or something.

Lauren's Second-Quarter Reflections

1. I feel I've improved on a lot of things this quarter. I've improved on math because I used to get late slips pretty much. This quarter I think I only got one. I like having my work in on time. I also improved on making good use of my time. I work neatly now and go a little faster on my work. I used to write not so good, but now I have fun writing and try to write the best I can.
2. I think I need to improve on listening a little bit more carefully. Sometimes I'm trying to listen but I get all mixed up. I usually understand what the teacher is saying. I also need to organize the things in my desk better. At home I organize things very well.
3. Two or three goals I will try to reach next quarter are to have things I will need in my desk to be ready and right there when I need them. I will try to clean out my desk and put things that belong together like a math page goes in my math folder. Next quarter I will try to remember more things.

Figure 7.8a: Lauren's rubric.

Social and Study Skills	1				2			
	Needs More Time to Acquire Skill	Improving	Making Acceptable Progress	Consistently Does Well	Needs More Time to Acquire Skill	Improving	Making Acceptable Progress	Consistently Does Well
Assumes responsibility for own actions and words			✓					✓
Relates well to others				✓				✓
Is courteous and respectful toward others				✓				✓
Respects the rights and property of others				✓				✓
Listens while others speak			✓					✓
Accepts correction				✓				✓
Follows school rules				✓				✓
Organizes work and materials			✓					✓
Listens carefully			✓					✓
Follows directions				✓			✓	
Works independently			✓				✓	
Works quietly	✓						✓	
Makes good use of time			✓				✓	✓
Participates in discussions				✓			✓	✓
Works cooperatively in group activities				✓		✓	✓	✓

This kind of self-assessment takes time for students to do well. They need time to process their thoughts, but it is well worth the effort. Students become more invested in the work they are doing, and they are truly honest about how hard they worked on a particular assignment. In this way, student and teacher become partners in evaluation, instead of the teacher dictating a grade. Students become self-evaluators—and isn't that the ultimate goal of assessment?

Figure 7.8b: Ms. Kowalke's rubric.

Social and Study Skills	1				2			
	Needs More Time to Acquire Skill	Improving	Making Acceptable Progress	Consistently Does Well	Needs More Time to Acquire Skill	Improving	Making Acceptable Progress	Consistently Does Well
Assumes responsibility for own actions and words			✓					✓
Relates well to others				✓				✓
Is courteous and respectful toward others		✓				✓		
Respects the rights and property of others				✓				✓
Listens while others speak		✓				✓		
Accepts correction		✓				✓		
Follows school rules				✓				✓
Organizes work and materials		✓				✓		
Listens carefully			✓				✓	
Follows directions			✓				✓	
Works independently			✓				✓	
Works quietly		✓						✓
Makes good use of time				✓			✓	
Participates in discussions				✓			✓	
Works cooperatively in group activities				✓				✓

Two Case Studies

Now let me tell you how two specific children grew, over a year's time, as self-assessors. I've picked Jan and Alan to discuss, because at the start of the year I was concerned about their ability to reflect on their work.

Jan is highly regarded by her past teachers. She writes neatly, displays confidence in her abilities, enjoys artwork, works quietly, and gets the correct answers on assignments. An only child, she is used to getting lots of attention at home, and always likes to be right. In the eyes of a traditional teacher, Jan might be described as "the perfect student."

As you already know, as part of our thinking curriculum, I regularly ask the students to reflect, predict, infer, and evaluate. Jan had a hard time doing any of these things. This was evident from her earliest reflections and her research report reflections about working with a partner. At first glance, they look well written; Jan always likes to do a perfect job. On closer inspection, however, one realizes that she isn't saying anything very soul-searching, or reflective.

For example, in her rubric reflections, Jan gives herself the highest mark in "Responses are well thought out," because "I thought my responses were well thought out." She gives herself a 3 for effort because "I felt I didn't really do my best on it. All though I did do a good job on it."

In her reflections about working with a partner on a research report, she says that what she learned about working with a partner is that "you can get more work done. You could split the report in half and you can do a half and your partner can do a half . . . If your partner makes a mistake, you can point it out to them and correct them." So much for teamwork.

Periodically I would talk to Jan about looking a little deeper when she was writing her reflections and participating in class and group discussions. I was not seeing metacognitive growth during discussions, and I wondered if perhaps the Piagetian research I read was right—that metacognition can't be fostered in some children before the age of twelve. Slowly, very slowly, as I pushed Jan to look deeper, I began to see small improvements in her written reflections. At the end of second quarter, Jan's comments about the areas in which she had shown the most growth emphasized cooperation and following directions.

> I feel that I have improved on working cooperatively with my classmates.
> I still need to work more on that, but I know I did better than last time.
> I also feel that I have improved on following directions. I listen carefully,
> and I give whoever's speaking eye contact.

The goal she sets for herself for third quarter is to put all her papers into folders so her desk won't get so messy. Although not earth-shattering, this was definitely an improvement over first quarter. As third quarter rolled around, I was still not seeing any signs of reflective growth during class and group discussions. When we did some reflecting at the end of third quarter, however, I was quite pleased with her thoughtful responses.

For example, Jan now wants to learn "how to be creative, and express you're feelings and imagination . . . I also want to learn more about history, and geogrefy . . . I suddenly have a sudden interest in those subjects." Jan also talks about our read-aloud lessons being helpful to her. She comments, "Read-aloud has helped me become a better thinker, by using my imagination, and to picture what Ms. Kowalke is saying, it has also helped my sense of humor!—Alot!"

Jan still needs to work on being able to verbalize her self-assessments—in that area, she's shown little growth since the beginning of the year. Nevertheless, her improvement in written reflections shows that she is indeed capable of deeper thought. I hope she will continue to stretch herself in this area.

Alan is quite a different story. He is outgoing, slightly eccentric, and quite sloppy in his work. He has an easy smile, is eager to please, and was very unsure of himself when he entered my class in the fall. At the beginning of the year, Alan literally could not complete any task independently. He would approach me seventeen to twenty times daily to ask for clarification (Yes, I really mean seventeen to twenty; I counted!) on any and all tasks. There seemed to be three reasons for these check-ins. First was his eagerness to please; he wanted to do everything just right. Second, Alan was unsure of himself, and needed assurance that he was doing things correctly. And further, Alan was just a bit impulsive, and it was easier to let someone else do the thinking than to take the time and do it himself.

Alan needed reassurance and support, but he also needed to learn to stand on his own two feet. I let him know very quickly that I would not answer questions he could easily answer for himself with a little effort. Then we began to work on the others. Some substantive questions I would answer for him. For others, I would send him checking with his peers, and still others, we would work through together, with me questioning him instead of him questioning me. An example of this would be the following:

A: I don't get it.
LK: What don't you get?
A: I don't get the directions.
LK: What don't you get about them?
A: I don't know.
LK: Well, what do they say?
A: (*reads directions out loud*)
LK: All right, now what does that mean?
A: It means I'm supposed to . . . Oh, I get it!
LK: So, you understand now?
A: Yeah. Thank you.
LK: Alan, who really answered your question?
A: I guess I did (*flashes a quick smile*).
LK: Right (*smiles back*).

As time went by, I began asking Alan to use the strategies he was learning to answer his own questions and to think for himself. Eventually, Alan's requests for help lessened to ten per day, then to five, then to days when he would not request help at all. Once in awhile he would relapse; on about his third trip to me we would flash each other knowing smiles, and he would return to his desk to figure out the problem for himself.

Alan's few lingering requests for help became much more valid than they used to be. One day, Alan approached me with a page from a book he was reading in his spare time. "I can't make this make sense. Can you help me?" he asked. Looking at the book, it took me a moment to figure out what was wrong with the page as well. It turned out that four lines of text were completely out of order— no ordinary typographical error here! It is hard for children to comprehend that books can have mistakes, and he had found a huge one. In the past, Alan might have skipped over the passage; instead, he used all the strategies he knew to make sense of the passage. When that didn't work, he knew it was time to get help. That's progress.

Alan started out the year with about as much skill in reflecting as he had in answering his own questions—very little. When asked what he did well on his verb book, he wrote, "The thing I did well on was my pictures. I think I did well on them was that I tryed my best on them." What would he do differently next time? "I would have maken the words neatlyer so that people can tell what I'm say easlier."

Considering we had already talked several times about careful reflection at this point in the year, I was a little worried about Alan's seeming lack of metacognitive awareness. In his first-quarter reflection he said simply, "I improved on not getting any more late slips. I need improvement on not doing my spelling on the last minute. I sort of improved on science. Like I like to listen about an atom is made out of H_2O."

By second quarter, Alan had made a bit of headway, commenting that he felt he had improved on "getting my homework done. I get my homework done by getting into my room and not wath TV . . . I think on need improvement on my cursive in the morning." As future goals for third quarter, Alan wanted to improve by using "cursive in the morning. My plan is to write it down in my assignment note book. My second goal is to keep all of my D.O.L. papers. My plan is to put them in the same folder." These comments were more specific and thoughtful than first quarter's, but I still hoped for more from Alan.

As third quarter drew to a close, I again asked students to reflect on a variety of topics. When asked what they had learned about themselves this year, Alan wrote, "I have learned that I can think better than I thought I could." Alan also commented that what he would like to learn about learning is "how you now

[know] exactly know when you are learning about learning. I would lik to know how the brain works." Alan made many metacognitive advancements throughout the year. He began using a variety of strategies to answer his own questions, pondering more thoughtfully to answer reflective questions and reminding himself to stop and think before giving in to impulse.

Alan and Jan began fourth grade with very little "instinctive" metacognitive ability. Through discussion, coaching, and practice, both developed a greater sense of their reflective selves. It is my hope that they will continue this growth, not only in fourth grade, but throughout the rest of their lives. It is a skill that will serve them well.

Understanding Mathematical Concepts Through Performance Assessment

PAMELA R. HYDE

I want the assessment of my students' mathematical thinking and understanding to be authentic and valid. There are many new concepts to learn in math in third grade, and because of the added pressure to have most of them understood by the middle of March in order to do well on the state math assessment tests, I want to make sure my teaching is efficient and complete. I need to know exactly what my students understand, how they conceptualize the content, and if that conceptualization is consistent with the cognitive model I am trying to convey. If there is a breakdown in understanding, I want to know where that breakdown occurs and some indication of what direction I should take in helping my students fully understand the problem before them. I feel, as most teachers do, that I have no time to waste. I want to integrate assessment into the curriculum and have it function as an instructional, as well as an assessment, tool.

As a student, I experienced frustration with instructional methods and especially with the assessments traditionally used in mathematics classrooms. I have been in the situation where the tests I have taken have not demonstrated what I knew, where anxiety has devastated test scores. I feel a strong commitment to my students to enable them to be capable of learning math concepts and to feel confident about themselves in this area. I want to alleviate "test and math anxiety" so that I can accurately view their depth of understanding instead of having to wonder what went wrong on a paper-and-pencil test. Some of the assessments I used were done independently by the students, and a product was the result. Sometimes the product was a written explanation, sometimes a picture or a model made with manipulatives. I will quote some of their responses exactly as they were given to me. Some of the assessments were my observations that I wrote down, others were interviews with children. Their oral responses will be verbatim.

In the beginning of the school year I want to find out which students need a quick review of the concepts covered in math in second grade, and which ones need to have more extensive reteaching. This way I know what I can build on conceptually. The first assessment addressed concepts that traditionally have been covered in second grade.

Colors in a Jar

In this task I was assessing their ability to estimate, adding three two-digit numbers together and using carrying. The usual method of evaluation for this concept is to give students three numbers that don't refer to anything, already set up in the algorithmic form of two columns. There is no counting or thinking involved; they merely manipulate numbers. I wanted to make it a broader task involving objects they were familiar with. I wanted to be able to evaluate the thinking it takes to solve the problem. I filled a jar with cubes of three different colors: 18 white, 14 blue, 13 red. Students were told to look at the jar and first estimate, without counting, how many cubes were in the jar, then determine which color they saw most, and which color they saw least. These questions were used to help them really look at what was in the jar. Then they were asked to pour the objects into a shoe box lid and figure out how many cubes there were of each color. Then they were to find out how many cubes there were altogether. Finally, they were asked to show their work on paper, and to write an explanation of how they reached their answer.

While I watched them working on this task, I realized that many of them had no idea how to set the problem up, had a hazy idea of place value, and had even less knowledge of base 10 and how to carry one 10 into the tens column. For example, one student counted all the colors individually in such a way that he counted a few cubes twice and got the wrong numbers for each color. He then started all over again, counting one by one to find the total number of cubes. When I asked him if he could think of another way to do it he said he couldn't. I prompted his thinking by asking how many reds he had, how many whites, and how many blues. He had not written those numbers down when he counted the cubes, so he counted again. I asked if those numbers could help him in any way. He said no. When he wrote his explanation on how he found his answer, he simply wrote, "I cownted."

This example was typical for four of my students. It told me that they did not see the problem as a whole but as segmented parts. They did not see the connection of counting the individual colors, and combining those numbers to get the

Assessment can be part of good instruction in mathematics.

total. They started over again, using a one-to-one correspondence in counting, and some were not even able to do that correctly. They were at a primitive level of cognitive development in number sense.

The majority of my class was in a middle range on this task. For example, one student counted the individual colors and wrote, "There are 18 white one. There are 14 blue ones and 13 red one. I couted them up. There are 45 objects in the jar." Another midlevel response said, "I figured it out by counting by twos. ther are 44 cubes. there are 14 blues there are 13 reds there are 18 whites." Even though they had the right number of the individual colors, they didn't see that adding the three numbers would get them the answer.

Compare these to some typical high responses: "18 + 14 + 13 = 45 I first counted the wite then the blue and then the red. then I added them together." "14 blue 13 red 18 wight 45 all togather 27 + 18 = 45 How I did it. First I counted each color by its self. then I added them togather." These higher responses not only saw right away that the three numbers should be added together to find the total, but they added correctly, remembering to carry the 10 from the ones column.

Perimeter

I have come to believe that the different strands of mathematics should be taught and assessed in an integrated fashion. Perimeter is one of those concepts that has been taught as a separate entity when it is probably one of the richer vehicles available to connect to other concepts. After many hands-on activities, and lots of discussion among the students and between the students and me, it was time to check their level of understanding for information that would direct my instruction. I wanted to evaluate the students' ability to understand both metric and customary measurement, how they use measurement tools (especially when the measurements were larger than the measurement tools themselves), the concept of perimeter, and a continuation of adding numbers requiring carrying. I also wanted it to be an experience where they were actively "doing mathematics" in a real-world situation.

The students were put into cooperative groups of four to five to encourage them to make sense collaboratively of the mathematics involved and to communicate their mathematical ideas to one another. The instructions were to find the perimeter of the front chalkboard, the front face of the heater, the project table, a handwriting book, and the entire room. They had to label the dimensions of each object and show the math involved in solving each problem. They were each given a sheet of paper with the objects to be measured listed next to small drawings that were the approximate shapes of the objects. They were all rectangles and all but one was a large object. I provided them with various tools including meter sticks and measuring tapes and rulers with metric and customary measurements on them. This part of the assessment was to be done in the metric system, but I purposely had tools with both measurements on them so that students would have to distinguish between them. They would repeat the activity using customary measurements on another day.

They started at different parts of the room so they were not in each other's way. While they measured the objects, I walked around taking notes on what I observed. This activity took more than one class period to complete. I could see that some of the students had a hard time distinguishing centimeters from inches. Since it was a group activity and I encouraged them to discuss their strategies with each other, the ones who had a problem were helped by their group members. Some students had not experienced using measuring tools other than what we had done in the classroom when I had introduced measurement. I noticed that the less experienced students were not careful when lining up the end point of the ruler to the end point of the object they were measuring. The experienced students in their group pointed that out to them by explaining, "Put it edge to edge or we'll get the wrong number."

When they had to measure the perimeter of the really large objects, such as the front chalkboard or the room itself, they had various ways of marking off the measurements. One group used five meter sticks laid end to end, picking up the first and placing it at the end of the fifth one, then the second one they used after the sixth one, and so on. Others used only one meter stick, marked the carpet or chalkboard with chalk at the end of the stick, then put it down at their mark, and repeated the process to the end of the room or chalkboard. Some used one meter stick and their fingers to mark where it ended, others used the tape measure and their fingers to mark where it ended to see where the tape should be laid next. That group counted the whole room in centimeters instead of meters. It was very interesting to hear all of the groups reason which was the most efficient way to accomplish the task and note the level of sophistication with which many of them measured.

This assessment was very broad, and I wanted to be open to discovering as much as possible about several areas addressed by this activity. Several issues became apparent to me. The first issue was measurement. I was looking for answers that were reasonable as opposed to being exact. Most of the students were able to come very close to the actual dimensions. Of the few who did not, the reasons varied. For example, one student added 99 many times to calculate his dimensions. He was using a meter stick, which is 100 centimeters long but the last number printed on the sticks is 99. That last centimeter ending at the edge of the stick is not labeled. His problem stemmed from improper use of the tool. When I asked him how many centimeters were in a meter, he knew. When he looked closely at the meter stick, he realized his mistake. A few children made the mistake of labeling the longer sides of the rectangle with the measurement of the shorter sides. While they understood the concept of perimeter, they did not understand the situation well enough to use the drawings effectively and did not realize that the dimensions did not make sense in the real-world setting.

The second issue I looked at in this assessment was conceptual. There were a couple of cases of incomplete conceptual knowledge of perimeter itself. For example, one student had four dimensions labeled, but had the measurement of only one of the sides as the total perimeter. I saw that he was still not conceiving of perimeter as the complete outside measurement of the object. Another student who had the perimeter of the chalkboard significantly bigger than the perimeter of the entire classroom showed me that she was not really thinking about the situation. She was relying on her knowledge of the procedure for finding perimeter rather than the conceptual model I was trying to elicit.

The third issue addressed by this assessment was computation. I was pleased to find that there were relatively few errors in this area, but due to the fact that many of the students had been introduced to addition with carrying only recently, it was something I wanted to follow carefully. For instance, some students had the numbers set up in the wrong columns and added incorrectly. This showed a problem in understanding place value as well as not knowing addition combinations. One student showed a sophisticated computation strategy for a third grader in finding the perimeter of the classroom. He added one long side of the rectangle to one short side, then added that total twice. This shows a higher level of computational reasoning as well as a more abstract understanding of perimeter. This had never been taught; he inferred it on his own. This assessment allowed me to see this capability.

After I examined these papers, I gave the class a chance to revise their answers. I wanted this to be a valid learning activity as well as an assessment activity. Giving them a second chance to work on a product alleviates anxiety about tests and math in general, which is one of my goals. I have not found that it makes them less careful in their original work, because they know they will have to do the work correctly at some point. I compare it to writing, where your best work has been thought through and revised.

Student writing in mathematics can help teachers obtain more insight into the conceptual models a student has. I asked the class to write a few sentences in response to three questions about perimeter. The first question dealt with the concept of perimeter, the second question dealt with the procedure used to find perimeter, and the third with the application of perimeter in a real-world setting. This activity showed that I had quite a wide range in the classroom. In a high-level response, one student answered:

> What is perimeter? "The outside measurement of any object."
> How do you find perimeter? "Measure the sides of the object and add them together."
> When would you ever need to know the perimeter of a space? "When you're going to fence a yard you need to know how much fence you need."

In dramatic contrast, one of my students wrote:

> What is perimeter? "Sq. yard."
> How do you find perimeter? "You add all of the numbers and put it down on the paper."
> When would you ever need to know the perimeter of a space? "To find out how long the building or house is."

Comparing these two papers, it is easy to see that the high-level response has a good understanding of the concept of perimeter. He explains the procedure used to find the answer and has a good real-life situation in which perimeter would be used, putting a fence around a yard. He even says that it would tell you how much fence you need to buy. In contrast, the lower-level paper shows little grasp of the concept of perimeter. He shows he is confused between perimeter and area when he refers to "Sq. yard." His understanding of the procedure is restricted to knowing that the operation used is addition. His idea of the application of perimeter is rather superficial. From this piece I could see that his learning in this area was minimal, and I would literally have to start from the beginning with my instruction. Luckily there were very few students in the class who were at this level of understanding. Besides being a valuable assessment tool, writing in mathematics also enables students to learn to communicate using mathematical language, which is a goal of the NCTM standards. It was another way of uncovering misconceptions. Knowing what needed to be done for whom, I was able to tailor my instruction to meet the needs of my students.

Reflections

Not only did I find these assessments relatively easy and natural to do, but my students actually enjoyed them, found them less anxiety producing than traditional tests, and thought they learned more. In sharp contrast to conventional assessments, these activities gave me specific information about the extent of knowledge my students had so that I could determine what direction I should take with each child to build their understanding. It helped me identify (and therefore dispel) any misconceptions they might have had and give them more meaningful feedback. It allowed me to watch the evolution and development of their ideas and strategies, instead of being keyed into the "correct answer" only. Encouraging students to revise their work helped them develop persistence, thereby gaining self-confidence in their math ability when they were able to be successful. It also showed them that their work was valued and something to be proud of, something worth making right or "polishing." Finally, the collaborative and interactive nature of these assessment activities mirrors the regular instructional activities in my classroom, with which students are familiar.

Using multiple representations enabled me to get at different aspects of each mathematical concept. It allowed students to clarify and elaborate on their original conception of the idea. In order to draw a picture of or write an expository paragraph about a concept, students have to think about it differently from the way they do when they maneuver numbers in an algorithm. They have to use metacognitive skills to check their thinking when they have to explain something in writing. Their inadequate conceptualization was obvious to them when they realized they could not explain something they thought they understood. I could see the gradations of conceptualization more clearly through these multiple representations. Using multiple representations also allowed for different modalities of learning, which gave my students with learning disabilities more opportunity to succeed.

Authentic assessment uses broader tasks, so I could assess (and teach) several different concepts from the curriculum at one time. This efficiency makes up for the fact that designing and evaluating this type of assessment takes more time. My assessment activities were also invaluable when conference time rolled around. I shared my findings with parents, showing them exactly where their children's strengths and weaknesses were. This information gave parents a clearer picture of what they could do at home to support learning and to help their children grow as mathematical thinkers.

Skit with Narration

NANCY STEINEKE

If you are teaching well in middle or high school (at least, according to me) your kids will be reading lots of books. And that means more than just subject-matter textbooks and the novels required in English. They'll be reading lots of current trade nonfiction titles, young adult novels, and more. And they'll probably be discussing their reading in well-structured book clubs, literature circles, or other small-group structures (see pages 130–36).

But using these decentralized, peer-led classroom structures, how does the teacher know what the kids are getting out of the books? How can we get them to "show what they know"? Yeah, you can always give 'em a test or assign a paper, but where's the fun in that? Instead of, or in addition to, those other assignments, have the kids get together and put on a show. A skit is a great way to get students to review a book, discuss it more deeply, and further probe their imaginations.

For a skit, students need to figure out how to intertwine their own personal explanation of story events with actual story quotes. Rather than patterning the skit after a play, actors pantomime while off-stage narrators read the lines. This makes the assignment a little easier since the actors don't have to memorize any parts. The most important things students need to remember as they plan their script is that the skit has to be understandable to any audience member, even those who have not read the book being portrayed.

The problem with any performance project is that quality will run the gamut. There will be some really good ones, some average ones, and at least one that is "almost too painful to watch." However, every performance offers students a learning experience, particularly if you videotape the skits and play them back for self-assessment. As students recognize what works and what doesn't, the skits get better because the kids do genuinely want to entertain each other.

The other important part of videotaping is that when you've got a winner, you can show it to classes for years to come. One prime example from my classroom was a skit based on the book *The Eye of the Needle* by Ken Follet, one of the books used in our World War II literature circles. This skit group consisted of four guys and one girl. When it came time to perform, the audience's first surprise was that the parts of Mrs. Garden and Lucy were not portrayed by the lone girl in the group but by Ron, sashaying around in a dress he must have dug up from his sister's closet when she wasn't looking. The next surprise was that Mike, the kid who played the spy/murderer, portrayed the role with icy precision. Man, when he knocked someone off with this imaginary stiletto, we were all glad it wasn't one of us. But the biggest surprise of the performance was when Mike, playing the spy, tackled Tony, who was playing a cripple in a wheelchair. Obviously, Mike's years of football experience played into his performance. When he took the wheelchair guy down, he took him down! Thank goodness Tony was also a football star because if he hadn't known how to take a hit, we might have been calling for an ambulance rather than encores. And since Tony is a bit of a big-shot around school, seeing him toppled from that chair offered a bit of catharsis for the rest of the class.

Below is the script used for this legendary performance. Notice that the students combined their own original narration along with lines directly taken from the book. While the three boys did the acting, the two remaining group members did the narration. The ellipsis in the text quotes indicate that lines have been cut. In creating the script, students are encouraged to create the most dramatic script from the text rather than copying paragraphs word for word. The parts of the script in italics describe the accompanying pantomime.

Sample Script

Introduction

The Eye of the Needle by Ken Follet (1982) is the story of Faber, a German spy in England who discovers a secret invasion plan of the Allies that will destroy the Third Reich if the Allies succeed. Whenever Faber's mission is in danger of discovery, he quickly murders his witnesses with his razor-sharp stiletto, earning him the nickname "Die Nadel." However, once Faber's path crosses that of a young Englishwoman by the name of Lucy, his steely resolution wavers momentarily.

Scene 1:

Narrator: While Faber is reporting information back to Germany, his landlady, Mrs. Garden, barges into his room. Drunk and flirtatious, she startles Faber, who must act quickly in order to conceal his true identity.

Actors: (*Faber fiddles with his radio while Mrs. Garden enters unannounced. Faber tries to hide the radio.*)

Narrator: "If she'd waited another minute he would have had the radio transmitter back in its case and the code books in the drawer and there would have been no need for her to die . . . He tightened his hold on her jaw, kept her head still by jamming it against the door, and brought the stiletto around." (p. 10)

Actors: (*Faber grabs Mrs. Garden and pushes her against the wall, stabbing her, letting her body fall to the floor. He squats beside the body, trying to think what to do next.*)

Narrator: This is the first of many murders Faber commits as he works to gather secrets and transmit them to the Third Reich.

Scene 2:

Narrator: Wed just that afternoon, David and Lucy are speeding toward their honeymoon retreat. More than a little drunk yet always the fearless fighter pilot, David takes a hill's blind curve too fast with tragic results.

Actors: (*David and Lucy sit beside each other in chairs, pretending to be in a car. David drives recklessly as they both lean in unison from side to side as if they were speeding through tight turns.*)

Narrator: "Lucy heard the distant roar of an approaching truck.

"The MG's tires squealed as David raced around the bends. 'I think you're going too fast,' Lucy said mildly.

". . . There was a sharp right-hand curve, and David lost the back . . . The little car slid sideways and turned through 180 degrees, so that it was going backwards, then continued to turn in the same direction.

"'David!' Lucy screamed.

"There was just room to pass the truck if David could regain control of the car. He heaved the steering wheel over and touched the accelerator. It was a mistake.

"The car and truck collided head-on." (pp. 32–33)

Actors: (*Lucy looks concerned and grabs David's arm. David tries to steer the car back into his control as Lucy throws her arms up in fright. Then David steps on the gas pedal and both actors mime a crash, arms thrown up as they're thrown forward and then fall back, unconscious.*)

Narrator: Though Lucy and David survive the accident, David is permanently crippled, unable to pursue his career in the air force. Looking for a quiet place to convalesce, David moves with Lucy to a remote island located in the North Sea. While Lucy maintains her optimism despite David's severe injuries, David reacts with bitterness and depression. Little do they know that this sparsely populated island will bring them face to face with "Die Nadle."

Actors: (*Lucy moves her chair aside while David sits up in his, as though it were in a wheelchair. Lucy stands behind David as though she were pushing it. Lucy smiles optimistically while David folds his arms and frowns.*)

Scene 3:

Narrator: Armed with secrets that would completely derail the Allies' invasion of Normandy, Faber attempts to rendezvous with a U-505 submarine during an intense storm. Before the meeting can take place, Faber's boat is capsized, yet he manages to swim ashore and find shelter with Lucy and David.

Actors: (*Faber sits in a chair and mimes rowing a boat while viewing the sub with binoculars. He is jostled as the water becomes rough, falls in, swims to shore, and collapses where Lucy finds him.*)

Narrator: While Lucy and Faber develop a "relationship," David remains suspicious.

Actors: (*Lucy and Faber stand close together while David sits in his wheelchair [chair], arms folded, looking suspiciously at Faber.*)

Narrator: Combing through Faber's personal items, David finally finds the proof he needs that shows Faber is a spy.

Actors: (*Lucy and Faber turn their backs to David. David picks up a jacket from the floor [prop] and starts going through the pockets. He eventually finds a film canister. He holds the canister up and has an "aha, now I've got you" expression on his face.*)

Narrator: "Taking matters into his own hands, he attempts to kill Faber but ends up dying himself.

"Faber crashed into the wheelchair, overturning it . . . He . . . looked around in dazed puzzlement.

"'Here.'

"The voice came from over the cliff. David had one hand suspended around the stem of a bush . . . he hung suspended.

"'Pull me up, for God's sake.'

"'Tell me about the film . . . Where are the negatives now?'

"'In my pocket.'

"Faber lay flat on his stomach and reached down . . . He sighed in relief as he reached the film can and carefully withdrew it.

"[Then] he took hold of the bush David was clinging to and uprooted it with a savage jerk.

"'No! It's not fair!' David screamed." (pp. 280–81)

Actors: (*David sits in his wheelchair trying to get away. Faber lunges toward David, knocking him out of the chair. David lies behind the chair, one hand clinging over the top as if he were clenching the bush. Faber reaches over, grabs the film canister, and rips the imaginary bush out. David's hand tries to gain a hold, but he falls back.*)

Scene 4:

Narrator: Even though Lucy discovers Faber's true identity and the fact that he killed her husband, he still doesn't kill her. Instead he tries to escape to the shore where he will again attempt to meet the German sub. As he scrabbles down the face of the cliff, Lucy grabs a rock and takes aim.

Actors: (*Lucy stands on a chair while Faber crouches below, pretending to climb down the cliff. Lucy pretends to pick up a rock. She hesitates and then hurls it with all her might.*)

Narrator: "The rock passed within a few inches of his head and hit his left shoulder . . . He seemed to be losing his grip . . . Then he appeared to lean out away from the face of the rock, arms windmilling, until his feet slipped from their narrow ledge . . . and he finally dropped like a rock to the stones below." (p. 359)

Actors: (*Lucy stands on the chair nervously watching her handiwork. Faber makes a grab toward her as he loses his grip, then windmills his arms as he falls backward toward the base of the cliff.*)

Conclusion

Though Die Nadel gets it in the end, this book has lots of twists and turns that we didn't tell you about. *The Eye of the Needle* also made us think about how important spying really is in any war, so we highly recommend you *pick up a copy today and start reading!*

 Graduation by Portfolio

GEORGE WOOD, KIZZI ELMORE-CLARK, AND THE FACULTY OF FEDERAL HOCKING HIGH SCHOOL

Dear Seniors:

With the assistance of the senior class, the faculty of Federal Hocking High School has worked to revise the options for the Graduation Portfolios. We think this new plan will provide you with the flexibility to both meet school standards and make sure the portfolio represents what you value about your high school experience. As you go through the process, please provide us with any feedback on the portfolio so we can continue to improve it.

There are two goals for the Graduation Portfolio. The first is to enable the faculty of FHHS to review each graduate's readiness to enter the world after high school. The second and perhaps more important goal is to enable each student to reflect on his or her education and how prepared he or she is for the responsibilities of democratic citizenship, the world of work, and a life of learning. The Graduation Portfolio provides you with ways to self-assess your development as a citizen, a worker, and a learner. Each potential graduate will take his or her own approach to the task. We look forward to the presentations of these portfolios on May 21.

Portfolio Presentation Notes

For the past several years the faculty has observed that while students spend a great deal of time preparing their presentation, that presentation does not always deal directly with the portfolio itself. So, this year's presentation rubric will focus more carefully on the presentation of your work to your panel. While you are encouraged to take whatever approach you want to the presentation, please be advised that you are expected to present and discuss the work in the portfolio with the panel. The faculty feels that this places the emphasis on your accomplishments and work, rather than on your presentation skills.

To help you prepare for this presentation, you will be asked to write reflections on the portfolio to be included with your other work. These reflections will help you prepare your presentation. You will be given time to work on these reflections through the Advisory program.

As is our tradition, soon you will be asked to identify a portfolio presentation chairperson. You will take your completed portfolio from your adviser to your chair no later than May 7, and together you will prepare your presentation. You will receive written notice when it is time to select your chairperson.

The Federal Hocking High School Portfolio

The FHHS Graduation Portfolio is made up of three parts, or folios, demonstrating each graduate's readiness to go into a career, take on the role of active citizenship, and continue learning after high school. Each folio is described below. All FHHS graduates will take their own approach to the portfolio and we encourage you to make the portfolio your own.

Folio 1: The Career Readiness Folio

This part of the Skills Demonstration Portfolio includes items that demonstrate your readiness to leave Federal Hocking High School and your preparedness for life after high school. The items included show that you have planned the beginnings of your career and have taken steps to enter your chosen field.

1. An up-to-date resume. You have prepared a resume either in class or Advisory. Now make sure it is updated to reflect your most recent school work and experiences. Your adviser, the guidance counselor, principal, or any faculty member can assist you with this.

2. An application for college, military enlistment, or employment. This is not to be an application that you fill out just for the portfolio. Rather it should be a copy of the application that you filled out in your search for what you will do after high school or if you have received an acceptance letter or acknowledgment of your application, which should be included.

3. Up-to-date reference letters (minimum of two). Don't wait on these. You know you need them, and you know that the entire faculty will be overwhelmed with requests for these near the end of the year. You can use letters from faculty, former employers, internship supervisors, or others. It is not a good idea to get one from a family member; these are not usually seen as good sources for references. You may use letters that you have already received for job or college applications.

4. Career or college-related materials. Here you should include anything else you have done to prepare yourself to get into college or a career. For example, records from your internship, summer camps, or schools that you have attended; jobs you have held; volunteer work in the area; college visits you have taken; or job interviews you have had. Simply put, this should be anything that you have done to prepare yourself for the world after high school as you see it.

5. Reflections. To prepare yourself for your presentation, you should include a one-to-two-page reflection piece that you write on your readiness to take on the world after high school. How have these experiences prepared you, what do you intend to do, what do you hope for or worry about, and are you ready for life after Federal Hocking? This should be typed and included in the portfolio.

Folio 2: The Democratic Citizenship Folio

This part of the Skills Demonstration Portfolio provides you with the opportunity to demonstrate your readiness to take on the highest office in our culture, that of citizen. Upon leaving FHHS you will be (or will soon be) a fully enfranchised citizen simply by virtue of turning eighteen years old. You will be able to vote to choose our leaders, amend our Constitution, set tax rates, and make decisions about the future of our country and community. How well you are prepared to take on the rights and responsibilities of a citizen is displayed in this folio.

1. Demonstrations of active citizenship in the school or greater community. Here you should include explanations of two ways in which you have been involved in the *political processes* of the school or greater community. There are a variety of ways to demonstrate this, including, but not limited to, playing a role in some part of school governance, assisting with some effort in the community such as registering people to vote or working at the polls, being involved in a campaign, registering to vote and voting, being involved in the school's site-based committee, serving on the School Improvement Committee, being an officer in a club, working on the First Amendment Committee, and so on. If you are having trouble thinking about what you have done, check in with any of the social studies staff or get busy and do something.

2. Taking a stand. Citizens in our democracy have the right to take a stand on issues and have their voice heard. However, they also have the responsibility of making sure their voice is informed by facts and reasoning. Include here any evidence you have of taking a stand on an issue that demonstrates your ability to make sure your stand is based on evidence and not just emotion. This could include a paper you have written in school, a letter to the editor of the school paper or local newspaper, a proposal you have made to change something at the school or in your community, sometime when you intervened to stop something you knew was wrong or dangerous, or some other time you "took a stand."

3. Community involvement. Our communities benefit from the volunteer activities of each citizen. We know that you often volunteer in ways of which we are not aware. List them here, including what you did, who you did it for, and any artifacts from that experience (such as letters of thanks, recognition, or notes).

4. Other (optional). You may have ways you have demonstrated citizenship skills that are not reflected in any of the above areas. Simply include those things here.

5. Reflections. Now think about who you are as a citizen and how ready you are to take on the role of citizen. In an essay of one to two pages, reflect on

how these experiences have prepared you to be a citizen and include it in the portfolio. This may prove to be a valuable resource when you present your portfolio.

Folio 3: Skills for Lifelong Learning Folio

In this part of the Skills Demonstration Portfolio you can demonstrate how you are prepared for a life of learning after high school. You will include your work from high school that shows how you have advanced as a learner during your time in high school. There are plenty of ways to show this, and we hope you take whatever path makes the most sense to you.

1. Demonstration of your best work or your competence in *each* of the following areas—Writing, Math, and Science skills. Often the only thing that counts in demonstrating your skills in these areas are scores on standardized tests. That is one way to do this—submit your highest scores on a test of any of these areas that demonstrates your readiness to do work beyond high school. But another, and perhaps more interesting, approach would be to include a piece of work (or maybe a photograph of something three-dimensional) that demonstrates your best work in each of these three areas. You and your advisor can choose what is best for you.

2. Demonstration of your best work or your competence in *one* or more of the following areas—the Arts, Business or Computers, Agricultural Sciences, Second Language, Physical Fitness, Consumer Sciences, or extracurricular areas. This is a chance for you to show off your best skills in an area that has been important to you. You may do as many areas as you want and we encourage you to be creative in what you include. Don't worry if it does not fit in the binder; with our computer technology we can help you put it into a form that will fit. But make whatever it is something you care about.

3. An annotated bibliography of books (or other works) you have read over the past four years that were important to you. One of the things you have done at FHHS is read. Now we want you to tell us what you have read that was the most important to you. Select the top books (or other materials) you have read (a minimum of three) either inside or outside of school and create a bibliography (use the format you learned in Senior English) of those works. Then annotate the list—that is, tell us why this book mattered to you: what did you learn by reading, how did it impact you, and what will you remember from the work?

4. Other (optional). Any other things you have done to prepare yourself for a life of learning or that demonstrate your academic skills. This could include

activities in or out of school, additional courses you took at college or in the summer, or additional readings.

5. Reflections. Now sum all this up by telling us who you are as a learner; in your mind, where are your strengths, what will you be able to do to pursue your own learning agenda, what things do you have yet to develop in order to be successful after high school? This should be a minimum of two typed pages and included in the portfolio.

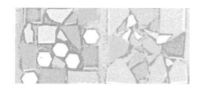

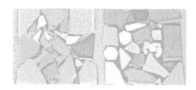

E I G H T

INTEGRATIVE UNITS

Welcome to Integrative Units, the seventh and arguably most complex of the Methods That Matter. We truly feel that we have saved the best for last. Here we show how great teachers put it all together, blending the other six methods into days or weeks of rich, cross-disciplinary investigations driven by student interest and scaffolded by teachers who model, coach, and manage the inquiry process. With integrative units, teachers step emphatically out of single-subject instruction and lead their students into inquiries as complex and multidisciplinary as the real-world issues grown-ups face as workers, parents, and citizens.

Back in the 1990s, when all those professional organizations we cited in Chapter 1 began developing the national curriculum standards documents, they dutifully stayed inside the traditional subject-field boundaries. The National Council of Teachers of Mathematics talked about good teaching and learning in mathematics only, the International Reading Association kept to issues of literacy, the American Association for the Advancement of Science limited itself to recommendations about biology, chemistry, and physics, and so forth. Each group talked about good teaching in terms of the instructional methods, structures, and strategies to be increased or decreased within its own discipline. At one level, there's nothing to apologize for in this. All American educators have inherited a professional world in which knowledge is generated and reported within certain long-established fields. Indeed, these national curriculum organizations themselves are built on those traditional subject-matter separations.

The trouble is, the separate-subjects approach too often leaves students with a disconnected view of knowledge and fails to reflect the way that people attack real problems in the real world. When knowledge and learning are compartmentalized, kids get no view of the big picture. What's the sense of separating mathematics from science, when one is such a powerful set of tools for solving problems in the other? Why separate reading from writing, history from art, literature from science, or, for that matter, natural language from mathematics? Life is holistic. The real world presents us, both kids and adults, with complex events that aren't divided into neat subject areas or forty-minute periods. Real living requires us to draw on many domains of knowledge, multiple strategies of thinking, and diverse ways of knowing.

So now, thoughtful teachers are seeking coherence by crossing the old subject boundaries, translating models from one field into another, applying promising procedures from other subjects, designing cross-curricular investigations, and developing rich thematic units that involve students in long-term, deep, sophisticated inquiry. They believe that students can learn subject matter (including mandated content and "basic skills") amid holistic, integrated experiences, and not just through separate and sequential lessons. These teachers are supported by some national curriculum integration models: problem or project-based learning, interdisciplinary studies, the middle school movement, the Coalition of Essential Schools, the Responsive Classroom. Indeed, many of the nation's most promising school reform models break down rigid subject-matter boundaries and promote some vision of curriculum integration. The most prominent, or at least most costly, of these is the billion-dollar project of the Bill and Melinda Gates Foundation, which has one nonnegotiable tenet: learning must be authentic and tied to real-life situations.

This trend doesn't mean that traditional subject-matter fields are disrespected or abandoned as the curriculum becomes more integrated. On the contrary, as our colleague James Beane (1995) points out, the disciplines of knowledge are the "useful and necessary ally" of curriculum integration. In Beane's view, curriculum should come out of problems, issues, and concerns that are posed by life, with the disciplines of knowledge being called upon to support student investigation and study:

> (I)n order to define curriculum integration, there must be reference to knowledge. How could there not be? If we are to broaden and deepen understandings about ourselves and our world, we must come to know "stuff" and to do that we must be skilled in ways of knowing and understanding. As it turns out, the disciplines of knowledge include much (but not all) of what we know about ourselves and our world and about ways

of making and communicating meaning. Thus authentic curriculum integration, involving as it does the search for self and social meaning, must take the disciplines of knowledge seriously—though again, more is involved than just the correlation of knowledge from various disciplines. (p. 100)

If students experience well-designed curriculum integration, they will enter, draw upon, operate within, and become knowledgeable about the content of many subject-matter fields.

Marilyn: Recently, I was able to observe curriculum integration close-up at an innovative summer institute for Chicago students and teachers supported by the DeWitt Wallace–Reader's Digest Fund. In one memorable classroom, the teachers and kids were working with the consultants to integrate reading, writing, and the arts. The students had been reading Gary Paulsen's novel *Sisters*, about two teenage girls growing up in very different circumstances, one amid privilege and the other facing great challenges. The consultant in residence, artist Cynthia Weiss, was there to help the kids and teachers tap the connection between the visual arts and reading and writing.

Cynthia began by asking what a "portrait" was, and accepted a wide range of responses as students offered definitions. Then she broadened the students' conceptions a bit, explaining that portraits can come in various forms, and that they would shortly be doing portraits of the two young women in the book. Students brainstormed different ways that the characters could be represented by their faces, their homes, their feelings, their families, or by specific events and experiences. Cynthia passed out black construction paper and brightly colored chalks and invited the students to draw on the paper just to get comfortable with the medium. Next she showed pages from several picture books to provide examples of how other artists had revealed aspects of characters in their illustrations. When the students were ready, Cynthia gave out new pieces of black paper and invited them to divide the paper in half and open up their minds to what they wanted to say about the two young women.

The results were immediate. Students jumped right in and began creating portraits, many talking quietly to each other as they put chalk to paper. As I walked through the room watching and listening, it was obvious that this art experience was fun and energizing. But were the portraits really helping the kids to dig deeper into the meaning of the novel? I went around to the students, who were seated at tables of four, and asked them to talk about their portraits and about the book. In each group I approached, the students were eager to explain their drawings and talk about the sections of the book that had moved them to do their art. One girl told me that doing the portrait had helped her to think about the two young women, and how close her own experiences were to that of one of the characters. She said that she knew that she would have to work hard to avoid similar pitfalls in her own life. I left the classroom feeling that this small experiment with curriculum integration, simply bringing together the fields of art and literacy, allowed students to act upon their thinking in an especially powerful and energized way.

Integration from Primary Grades to High School

Curriculum integration can take many different shapes at different grade levels. Primary teachers have long practiced integration by building units around topics such as dinosaurs, apples, Japan, the solar system, insects, or grandparents. In such classrooms, students might read books about grandparents, interview their own grandparents, study family photos and artifacts, trace immigration patterns on world and U.S. maps, bring grandparents in as classroom "experts," and write and draw in response to all these experiences. Many intermediate-grade teachers integrate literature and history by having students read historical novels that connect to the social studies topics being studied: westward expansion, the Civil War, the Industrial Revolution. Reading *Little House on the Prairie* or *Sign of the Beaver* can bring a texture to the study of the pioneer experience that few textbooks can provide, and can help ignite curiosity that leads students to explore other historical sources. The integration of literature and history is one way to show students that learning is connected and that history is composed of multiple stories about real people.

Some of the most sophisticated integration work comes out of the middle school movement, which makes integration the centerpiece of curriculum and supports it with block scheduling and teacher teaming. While in some middle schools, interdisciplinary instruction is mainly harnessed to teacher-chosen themes that retain the separate identities of each subject, Jim Beane (1991) has developed a variation he calls "negotiated curriculum," in which the curriculum is designed around real concerns students have about themselves and their world. This negotiation, which you'll read about on pages 291–97, begins with a series of brainstorming and listing activities that elicit students' questions and issues. From these lists of topics, units of the curriculum are collaboratively developed by teachers and students. Teachers can "back-map" from students' genuine questions to many of the mandated ingredients in district or state curriculum guides. If young people say they want to study diseases (as they often do) teachers can plug in plenty of biology, math, and history, along with reading, writing, researching, and representing.

Curriculum integration often seems hardest to achieve at the secondary level, where subject-area boundaries are guarded by bell schedules, departmentalization, course requirements, and state mandates. Our own Best Practice High School was designed to breach these barriers about ten weeks a year. Some days, BPHS looks a lot like regular high school, with students studying physics, art, or algebra separately. But four times a year, students switch to extended interdisciplinary studies that blend all the city- and state-mandated subjects into broad, negotiated, thematic, integrated units. Students enjoy a cycle of integration during which all kinds of thinking are intertwined, with teachers serving not as subject specialists but more as inquiry coaches. Then, everyone shifts back to traditional organization and scheduling for a few more weeks. And so on.

When we opened BPHS in 1996 with 140 freshmen, our first integrated unit was called "Here We Are." Since all of us were coming from the four corners of Chicago to a neighborhood and a building that few of us knew well, it seemed natural to investigate this particular spot, a latitude and longitude in North America, a natural habitat, a place in the city, a part of the history of Chicago, a waypoint in the migration of different peoples, an example of the transformation of the prairie. After taking a neighborhood walking tour and some reading of local history, teachers helped students brainstorm possible areas of investigation about this special corner of Chicago. The kids eventually identified eight inquiry topics, including the architecture of the building, the ethnic history of the neighborhood, and the achievements of the past graduates of the school. The students each selected their favorite topic and, over parts of the next couple of months, worked with one teacher who had volunteered to coordinate that particular study. In order to achieve this, we had to create a variable class schedule, with teachers dropping their discipline-specific lessons for a day here and a week there so that we could regroup by topics. Toward the end of the project, we set up exhibitions, performances, and publications through which students shared the results of their inquiries. Community residents, school alumni, and other students provided us with real audiences and feedback.

Our first integrated unit had some highlights. Kids had to take responsibility for their own work, and teachers got the opportunity to coach them as researchers, thinkers, and communicators. The students needed to gather information, sift and winnow it, and somehow make it their own. Everyone learned some urban and social history. Many kids made good use of computers in recording and displaying their findings, and art was infused through many of the projects. And we all had to laugh when, during the Q and A session at our alumni gathering, one senior asked an eighty-five-year-old gentleman, "Were you having sex when you went to this school?"

There were worse problems with this unit than bad manners. Both teachers and kids thought the unit dragged on too long, losing energy as curriculum integration alternated with separate-subject work over weeks and weeks. Another problem was that students' interest wasn't deeply engaged in this topic from the start. "Here We Are" had been the teachers' idea: a logical idea, to be sure. But the problem was, the kids didn't really care enough about this old building or its neighborhood to sustain weeks of investigation. They all lived somewhere else, in neighborhoods across the city, connected by Chicago Transit Authority. Now, we can compare the tepid response to the "Here We Are" unit to the more recent and galvanizing "Gentrification" unit in which kids studied how and why their own families were being driven out of the old neighborhood. Ooops.

For our next cycle of integration, we wanted to try a more modest and limited project that would offer kids real ownership while still "covering" some required subject-matter material. Three teachers (of geography, English, and art) got together and quickly discovered some integratable interests. In geography, students needed to learn about the major landforms (mountains, deserts, plateaus, rivers, harbors) and their impact on human development. In art, students were scheduled to study several computer graphic and illustration programs, as well as to continue their yearlong exploration of artistic media. In English, the curriculum guide called for more practice of reading and writing in nonfiction genres.

Aiko, Peter, and Kathy created a two-week unit culminating in a "Design Your Own Island Nation" project, which required every student to (1) create and map a plausible country containing a variety of landforms and posit patterns of economic and human development that were congruent with those geophysical attributes; (2) represent some aspect of the country in an appropriate art form (drawing, Web site, sculpture, fabric art); and (3) write an extended piece about the country in an appropriate nonfiction genre (a constitution, a set of laws, a historical record). Raquel Torres, whose country featured a snowcapped mountain area, figured that a ski resort would be a key economic development, so she selected a stockholders' annual report as her nonfiction genre (Figures 8.1a and 8.1b).

Raquel's report orchestrates a good deal of subject-matter knowledge as well as process skills. She's learned about integrating geophysical forms and economic principles; computing, charting, and graphing statistics; composing and editing within a highly structured nonfiction genre; and using computer desktop publishing, illustration, and text programs to enhance a product. Though not all the students' efforts were quite as polished as Raquel's, the island nation unit generated a feeling of energy and ownership. Kids stitched needlepoint topographical maps of their countries, designed and sewed national flags, and wrote extended histories—at least one of which mysteriously involved members of the Beatles at every key

Figure 8.1a: Raquel Torres's imaginary island nation of "New Einel" featured a profitable ski resort.

1 9 9 7

ANNUAL

R E P O R T

Message To Our Stockholders

We are pleased to report that Shifter Valley Ski Resort, Inc. achieved adequate earnings for the financial year ending October 30. Net income increased to $1,786,000, as compared to $1,071,600 last year.

Shifter Valley's improvement was a result of increased attendance and lower expenses as a percentage of sales. In winter 1996, over 15 million people took to the slopes in Shifter Valley. Earnings also increased by encouraging additional customer spending at the recently completed lodges, restaurants, and pro shops located near the ski area.

In conclusion, we remain optimistic about Shifter Valley's future growth opportunities as we continue to expand. We have acquired adjacent property, which will enable us to double the number of ski runs by this winter. By making our increased size the centerpiece of our marketing, we hope to increase attendance even further.

Thank you for your continued confidence and support as we work diligently to enhance this resort. With your support, we hope to exceed our recent phenomenal growth in the next financial year.

Raquel Torres
Chief Executive Officer
December 15, 1997

Shifter Valley Ski Resort, Inc.

juncture. This project, a brief and modest spurt of integration, evoked kids' sense of playfulness and exploration as well as their commitment to create something valuable. For the faculty, this was an important step ahead of the "Here We Are" unit, probably because it was smaller and certainly because we had learned a lot from our first attempt.

Now, at the end of each year at BPHS, we set aside a few days to plan with students what the next year's curriculum might look like. Students work with facilitators in small groups to identify concerns they have about themselves and their

Figure 8.1b: *(continued)*

Table 1: Statement of Income

	fiscal Year		
	1995	1996	1997
Net sales	$7,352,100	$9,802,800	$16,338,000
Cost of goods sold	4,382,550	5,843,400	9,739,000
Gross profit	2,668,650	3,858,200	6,597,000
General and administrative expenses	1,496,700	1,997,600	3,326,000
Operating income	1,471,950	1,962,600	3,271,000
Interest expense	85,050	113,400	189,000
Provision for income taxes	582,300	776,400	1,294,000
Net income	$803,700	$1,071,600	$1,786,000
Net income per common share	0.13	0.17	0.29
Weighted average shares outstanding	2,717,550	3,623,400	6,039,000

Summary of Results

The financial year ending October 31 was the most successful in the history of Shifter Valley Ski Resort, Inc. As shown in Table 1 above, the end of year results for Net Sales ($16.4 million), Gross Profit ($6.6 million), and Net Income ($1.8 million) were AVSRI records.

Exceptional snowfall boosted attendance, particularly during the holiday season. More important, however, was the return on substantial investments in facilities (eg. skating rinks, lodges) and intra-resort transport (lifts, gondola). Together, these make Shifter Valley New Einal's finest.

Particularly impressive is the year to year growth. Sales jumped by over 60% versus last year, and more than doubled over FY 1995. Gross profits increased by 69% over last year, while net income growth reached nearly 75%.

Despite sluggish regional economic growth, AVSRI performance excelled based on two principal factors.

Gross Profit ($000)

Gross profits rose by 69% over last year and 145% since 1995.

December 15, 1997　　　　　　　　　　*Shifter Valley Ski Resort, Inc.*

world. Though the student body at BPHS is a very heterogeneous mix of city kids, their "self" concerns are not much different from those of young teenagers anywhere: facing issues of identity, trying to envision the future, getting into college, choosing careers, getting married and having families, dealing with peer pressure (gangs), coping with pressure to take drugs, staying healthy, getting along with others. When students look out at the world, they find themselves wondering about racism (will people of different races ever learn to get along?), immigration, violence, pollution and the environment, war, and the effects of technology on the

Figure 8.2: The BPHS model for establishing curriculum units follows these seven steps.

**Negotiating Curriculum
BPHS Model**

The goal of this process is to develop several student-chosen themes that can become curriculum units to be investigated. The students identify questions and concerns about themselves and about the world. These questions and concerns eventually lead to themes.

Step 1.   The facilitator explains to the group of students that we are interested in their questions because we want to build a curriculum around subjects of interest to them.

Step 2.   Students are seated at tables and are asked to take about five minutes to individually jot down questions and concerns they have about themselves. The facilitator may model some questions such as "Will I go to college?" and "What will my job be when I grow up?"

Step 3.   In groups of four or five, students are asked to share their "self" questions and concerns for about fifteen to twenty minutes to find topics they have in common. The students are looking for those questions that are most common. The facilitators go around the room helping students arrive at a consensus. In some cases, the facilitators help students see that different questions are about the same issue. For example, "Will I have kids" and "Will I get married" are questions about family.

Step 4.   The group appoints a recorder to list their common concerns on pieces of chart paper, which are hung around the room.

Step 5.   The students circulate through the room for about five minutes looking at the lists.

Step 6.   The spokesperson from each group shares their chart with the whole class.

Step 7.   The facilitator helps the students combine common concerns into a more comprehensive one. For example, if one group asks if a cure for cancer will be found and another group wonders whethe there will be a cure for AIDS, the facilitator helps them find a more inclusive question, such as, "Will we ever find cures for all the deadly diseases?"

These steps are followed a second time to find students' concerns about the world. Out of these two sets of student concerns come the themes or issues to be investigated throughout the year.

---

future. The BPHS model for establishing curriculum units follows the seven steps in Figure 8.2.

Now we have been doing integrative units for nine years at BPHS. When we finish the negotiating process in the spring, the teachers can look carefully at the lists of student concerns spread around the room on chart paper, and see how the themes raised by kids can guide big chunks of next year's curriculum. Often, we can coordinate separate-subject teaching with several integrated units, block-scheduled and spread across the year. In these studies on cultures, "isms," family history, fast food, the environment, gentrification, plagues, vectors, and violence, teachers abandon the boundaries of their disciplines and work with groups of students to generate inquiry, allowing the students' questions and concerns to lead the way. The products of these inquiries have been varied, from reports, petitions, and presentations to videotapes and art exhibits to leafleting and social action. Students work together with teachers to develop rubrics for what makes an effective demonstration of knowledge and competence in the different types of projects. We believe that students' participation in planning and pursuing these units from the ground up is one reason our kids stay in school, finish school, go to college, and do well.

Crossing Boundaries Requires Teachers to Change Roles

The separate-subject tradition is powerful and enduring, and crossing curriculum boundaries is not just tinkering with the curriculum. At Best Practice High School, our first-year forays into integration were clumsy, and neither students nor teachers were completely comfortable with letting go of their traditional views of how schools work. We discovered that this kind of learning requires big blocks of concentrated time, and that both teachers and students need to change their roles. Students can no longer be viewed as cognitive living rooms into which the furniture of knowledge is moved and arranged, and teachers cannot act solely as subject-matter experts. Now teachers need to be generalists, researchers, and learners alongside their students. In classrooms where students are helping to plan and negotiate the curriculum, teachers need to ask their own authentic questions right along with the kids and pursue ideas that are new to them, just like everyone else.

Teachers who are learning in their own classrooms are very often working at the edge of their professional comfort zones. But by taking this risk they contribute something rare and vital: direct modeling of how a resourceful and curious adult thinks, and how she encounters and deals with new information. Too often in school, teachers simply relay ideas that they themselves long ago encountered and digested. With negotiated and integrated curriculum, teachers are in on the exploration, too. These teachers are showing kids how to think and are exemplifying the principles that learning never ends, that even teachers have room to grow, and that students have knowledge to be shared and valued.

At Addison Trails High School, Katy Smith, with her partners Ralph Feese and Robert Hartwig, worked with high school students on a yearlong curriculum that integrates English, social studies, and science. In their class, students helped decide not only what they were going to learn but also how they were going to learn it and how they could demonstrate their learning. These role changes were not always comfortable. According to Katy, "At times our role did seem to have shifted from 'disseminator of information' to 'collator of note cards.' More than once we questioned whether we were on the right track, and there were times when we inwardly agreed with the student who said that 'it would be a lot easier if you two just taught and we just obeyed and learned!' Easier? Probably. Better? We thought not" (Smith 1993, p. 37).

Into the Classroom

Now we'll hear how ten teachers plan and manage several curriculum integration models. We begin with Terrie Bridgman's first graders at Baker Demonstration School, who spend a month each year studying Lake Michigan, which is just three blocks from their school. In this thematic, teacher-planned unit, children read, write, observe, and conduct experiments with the lake and its creatures. To culminate the unit, they turn Terrie's classroom into a magical underwater environment. Linda Weide, Eleanor Nayvelt, Donna Mandel, and Cynthia Weiss developed an ambitious yearlong, cross-school, arts-intensive, multicultural curriculum with African American, Hispanic, and Russian immigrant children. Over the course of this experience, children challenged their own preconceptions about other ethnic groups and made important personal connections through the arts.

From Wisconsin, James Beane, Gary Weilbacher, and Barbara Brodhagen explain how they plan a curriculum with young people on a perennially favorite topic: money. Their story shows how smart teachers can back-map kid-driven curriculum to any state or local standards, while working on questions students pose themselves. Jim's book, *A Middle School Curriculum: From Rhetoric to Reality*, is the gold standard for curriculum integration at any grade level.

Our colleague and media maven Scott Sullivan shows us how his high school students critically examined big business and its media representations from a critical point of view. When students begin to understand the power of their expenditures for shoes, CDs, or clothes, they become more selective when they "vote" with their dollars. Our last story comes from Best Practice High School, where Matt Feldman shares an integrative unit about fast food, diet, and nutrition. In this ambitious cross-curricular study taught by four teachers, students began by reading the nonfiction best-seller *Fast Food Nation* by Eric Schlosser, and ended four weeks later taking social action to inform the community about the dangers of junk food.

Further Reading

Allemen, Janet, and Jere Brophy. 2001. *Social Studies Excursions, K–3: Book One: Powerful Units on Food, Clothing, and Shelter.* Portsmouth, NH: Heinemann.
Beane, James. 1993. *A Middle School Curriculum from Rhetoric to Reality.* Columbus, OH: National Middle School Association.

_____. 1997. *Curriculum Integration: Designing the Core of Democratic Education.* New York: Teachers College Press.

Boomer, Garth, Nancy Lester, Cynthia Onore, and Jon Cook, eds. 1992. *Negotiating the Curriculum.* London: Falmer Press.

Davies, Ann, Colleen Politano, and Caren Cameron. 1993. *Making Themes Work.* Winnipeg: Peguis.

Doda, Nancy, and Sue Carol Thompson. 2002. *Transforming Ourselves, Transforming Schools: Middle School Change.* Westerville, OH: National Middle School Association.

Five, Cora Lee, and Marie Dionisio. 1995. *Bridging the Gap: Integrating Curriculum in Upper Elementary and Middle Schools.* Portsmouth, NH: Heinemann.

Lake, Jo-Anne. 2000. *Literature and Science Breakthroughs: Connecting Language and Science Skills in the Elementary Classroom.* Markham, ON: Pembroke.

Lindquist, Tarry, and Douglas Selwyn. 2000. *Social Studies at the Center: Integrating Kids, Content, and Literacy.* Portsmouth, NH: Heinemann.

Manning, Maryann, Gary Manning, and Roberta Long. 1994. *Theme Immersion: Inquiry-Based Curriculum in Elementary and Middle Schools.* Portsmouth, NH: Heinemann.

McCallem, Richard D., and Robert Whitlow. 2001. *Linking Math and Language.* Portsmouth, NH: Heinemann.

Short, Kathy G., Jean Schroeder, Julie Laird, Gloria Kauffman, Margaret J. Ferguson, and Kathleen Marie Crawford. 1996. *Learning Together Through Inquiry: From Columbus to Integrated Curriculum.* Portland, ME: Stenhouse.

Springer, Mark. 1994. *Watershed: A Successful Voyage into Integrative Learning.* Columbus, OH: National Middle School Association.

Steffey, Stephanie, and Wendy J. Hood, eds. 1994. *If This Is Social Studies, Why Isn't It Boring?* Portland, ME: Stenhouse.

Stevenson, Chris, and Judy Carr. 1993. *Integrated Studies in the Middle Grades: Dancing Through Walls.* New York: Teachers College Press.

Stice, Carole F., and Nancy P. Bertrand. 2002. *Good Teaching: An Integrated Approach to Language, Literacy, and Learning.* Portsmouth, NH: Heinemann.

Tchudi, Steven, and Stephen Lafer. 1996. *The Interdisciplinary Teacher's Handbook: Integrated Teaching Across the Curriculum.* Portsmouth, NH: Boynton/Cook.

Thier, Marlene, and Bennett Daviss. 2002. *The New Science Literacy: Using Language Skills to Help Students Learn Science.* Portsmouth, NH: Heinemann.

Vars, Gordon. 1993. *Interdisciplinary Teaching in the Middle Grades: Why and How.* Westerville, OH: National Middle School Association.

Under Lake Michigan

TERRIE BRIDGMAN

I currently teach first grade at Baker Demonstration School in Evanston, Illinois, which is just three blocks from Lake Michigan. The lakefront is a well-groomed, accessible resource that is an important part of my students' lives. Almost all the kids spend time swimming, playing, boating, and camping at the lake with their families. When they join my class, we spend the entire spring quarter weaving our curriculum around Lake Michigan and its ecosystem. This is the story of how my six- and seven-year-olds roll up their sleeves and use a variety of lenses to look at our beautiful blue neighbor, Lake Michigan.

When I first designed this unit several years ago, I drew a curriculum web. The key elements of the web were all the academic subjects that we would include in our exploration. Before we had thoroughly studied Lake Michigan, I knew my students needed multiple experiences in a variety of content areas. My web contained the obvious discipline—science. But of equal importance were reading, writing, social studies, the arts, mathematics, and play. I also believed that if I provided plenty of learning choices along the way, all the different talents and intelligences my students bring would be well served.

At the start of the Lake Michigan study, I bind together twenty-five notebooks of construction paper in which my students can draw during each of our multiple visits to Lake Michigan. Because we have access to a long coastline, we study a different spot each time we visit the lake. At the start of each trip to the beach, the children sit quietly and simply observe the lake for two to three minutes. After their observation, they sketch what they see using colored pencils. Each child's depiction of his or her lake observation is unique. I am consistently surprised by how, while sitting in the same spot, my students "see" so many different aspects of the lake and its ecosystems. Each picture has the personal touch of its artist!

We undertake a myriad of hands-on science activities to advance our study of Lake Michigan. One of the students' favorite tasks is to study the host of animals that live in Lake Michigan. They observe, describe, count, draw, and study these creatures. We examine the habits, features, and anatomy of a variety of fish that range from alewives to coho salmon. There are also numerous children's books that provide interesting and accurate information about fish, including color illustrations of the various species indigenous to the Great Lakes.

Our class's fish "expert" is Bill Roberts, the owner of a local fish market. He invites us to his shop each spring for a lecture about Lake Michigan's inhabitants and the "how-tos" of fishing. As a self-appointed gourmet chef, Mr. Roberts always prepares a delicious tasting of the lake's bounty for us. He also sends us back to school with some fish specimens that we can examine and dissect. At this point in our study, my students are far beyond squeamish reactions to a cut-up fish. All of their senses are involved as they inspect the innards of these amazing creatures.

The water from Lake Michigan is the key to an unseen world that is visible only with the aid of a microscope. I prepare my students for using a microscope by reading *The New True Book of Microscopes* and *Gregory's Microscope*. Next, our middle school science teacher comes to set up some microscopes and show us how to use them. Then we place some good old Lake Michigan water on a slide, with all the many life forms alive in there. A first grader's initial sighting of a living and moving organism through a microscope is always a momentous event. We hear a lot of "Oooohs" and "Yucks" when they see the crablike critters that live in lake water. Following up on our microscope lessons, we also experiment with other properties of water, including surface tension, water absorption, and the different forms that water takes.

This investigation also lends itself to lessons that help students understand how water is related to human activities. We visit a number of sites along the shore that serve the people who live around the lake. The kids' favorite places to study are the water purification plant and Coast Guard Station. The personnel at each site go out of their way to be informative and cordial to the children. After visiting the water plant, we all appreciate the work that goes into producing a sparkling glass of water. The kids always leave the Coast Guard Station feeling secure because these professionals are patrolling our waters. After tours of the station and the boat's equipment, one can't imagine an emergency that these experts can't handle.

During the spring quarter, our math work focuses heavily on measurement, which dovetails nicely with our Lake Michigan investigation. The children use an assortment of containers to measure water from Lake Michigan a number of times. For linear measurement, we use fish, shells, sticks, and a big long pier. I am always amazed at how quickly children learn to measure when their work is for an authentic purpose and feels important to them.

Throughout our study we read fiction, nonfiction, and poetry books that pertain to Lake Michigan, water, fish, ecology, and related topics. By the end of our project, my students are familiar with the special features that make up a nonfiction book. They can also make good predictions about what may happen in a fictitious story, especially when the plot has a connection to our lake investigation. When we read poetry about aquatic elements and creatures it is always good watery fun.

I have always felt that the school year should end in a celebration. Cleaning and packing up the classroom does not help my students rejoice and reflect on what they have learned during the year. So my students engage in a weeklong closing project: we turn our classroom into Lake Michigan!

The weekend before the project begins, parent volunteers help me ready the room. First, we take down everything on the walls and empty the classroom of all furniture. Then we cover every inch of the room with blue. Rolls of blue paper cover the walls, blue plastic wrap covers the windows, and blue sheets cover the floor.

On Monday morning my students arrive with their work clothes on, ready to start on our mystery project. We enter the room together, as we will each morning this week, and sit in the middle of our room. The only light that we see in the room is the blue light filtered through the windows. The only noise we hear is the sound of waves crashing on a shore, being played on a CD. After we sit a bit, someone usually exclaims that he or she feels as though we are in water. And with that statement the magic begins! I tell the children that they can use any art material (already placed on the back counter) on any surface in the room that is covered with blue. I don't directly tell them to use the materials to transform the room into the lake. But after spending ten weeks studying Lake Michigan, I know it will happen.

Soon the empty walls are covered with delightful pictures of lake fish, seaweed, zebra mussels, and many other creatures found in Lake Michigan. Piers and docks are constructed and painted for boats and canoes that are also being built. The floor is eventually landscaped with shiny shells, glittery rocks, and beautiful underwater trees. When our work is complete it is always a unique, incredible interpretation of what the world is like under Lake Michigan.

As a final performance, we stage the Japanese folktale "Urashima Taro" in our underwater classroom. This story tells how a boy falls into misfortune when he doesn't obey the rules upon entering an underwater kingdom. The children make all of their own props and costumes for their production. We present our play for parents and other guests on the very last day of school. The children leave first grade with this wonderful sensory experience in their memory. They often return in later years to make sure that I keep the tradition of the Lake Michigan project alive, which I have for thirteen years.

Immigration and Family History Through the Arts: A Story in Many Voices

LINDA WEIDE, ELEANOR NAYVELT, CYNTHIA WEISS, AND DONNA MANDEL

Linda: It is mid-March. Darkness has fallen outside my classroom window. This is my last parent-teacher-student conference of the day. From my chair I watch with great emotion as Brandi and her mother move, dipping, swaying, and twirling in perfect sync, two graceful birds joyfully trying out their wings on the first spring breezes, sharing how Brandi had brought school home, teaching her mother and the members of her church to story dance—or, as they called it, "worship dance."

My teaching path has led me from schools in Chicago's Humboldt Park, with a Latino and African American population, to an international school on a Caribbean island, to a Lincoln Park school integrated by thirds—African American, Latino, and white. In each of these diverse settings, I have felt challenged to create community where children separated themselves by ethnic difference. One step was for me to live by the adage that "children do as we do." By sharing with them my own diverse friendships and family (African American father, German mother, Panamanian uncle, German Turkish cousins) I showed my classes that not everyone sees difference as a cause for division.

Then I came to Washington Irving three years ago. We are an inner-city school on the West Side of Chicago, about half African American and half Latino, with a few white and Asian children. I soon learned that many of my students viewed whites as people who either have no problems, or are all racists and are all the same. We also had rifts in the classroom between the Latino and the African American children. Of course these conflicts are found schoolwide and throughout the community at large. I know African Americans and Latinos who are so overwhelmed by perceived differences between themselves and white Americans, whom they haven't been exposed to until adulthood, that they limit themselves professionally to avoid working with whites. I wanted my students to begin meeting and getting along with people from outside of their own community before they, too, became isolated and fearful.

Meanwhile, my old friend and colleague Eleanor Nayvelt was teaching third grade across town at Clinton School, where she worked with recent Russian immigrant children in a special bilingual program. Because we were both concerned about our students' ethnic separateness and lack of contact with other groups, we wanted to find a way to work together. Years before, when we had been students at the University of Illinois, Eleanor and I had developed an interdisciplinary curriculum we called the "Chicago-Leningrad Connection," which was designed to help young American and Russian children learn about each other's culture, history, and arts.

Now we realized there was a chance to bring that "dream" curriculum to life. We agreed that an arts-integrated, multicultural, cross-school project would be our aim, with language arts playing a strong role. In this way, we could develop children's critical thinking through a project-based curriculum, complexly interwoven with opportunities for them to interpret their world and express themselves through different art forms. As Charles Fowler says in his book *Strong Arts, Strong Schools: The Promising Potential and Shortsighted Disregard of the Arts in American Schooling* (1996), "The subject matter of the arts is as broad as life itself, and therefore the arts easily relate to aspects of almost everything else that is taught . . . They tell us about people: how they thought and felt and what they valued. They help us define ourselves, as well as other people and other times" (p. 48).

In our interdisciplinary history unit, we wanted to include forms of communication that weren't dependent on verbal ability or English competence, so that children whose strengths lie in other areas would have chances to develop their intelligences. The arts seemed the ideal, nonthreatening vehicle to bring students together and help us all examine ourselves and each other. We planned an engaging but rigorous study that would offer all the children opportunities to assimilate information from different sources and to create a rounded picture of their world. We hoped that by using the arts to develop pride in their own ethnic contributions, our students would become more tolerant, empathetic human beings who would learn to go beyond stereotypes.

Eleanor: I started teaching at Clinton School immediately after graduation. It was important for me to teach the "Russian children." I made it my personal goal to help them in the assimilation process, to ease the culture and language shock. From my own experience I know that this shock is not easily overcome. I came to Chicago at the age of thirteen from the former Soviet Union and studied at a small, private Jewish day school, where no bilingual or ESL program was offered. While I remember my experiences there fondly in many ways, my transition into the "American system" was rather painful, although eventually successful. At first I really wanted to belong and would do anything to sit at the same lunch table with my American classmates. But I was different and not readily accepted. I wore dresses while they all wore jeans. I ate different foods and was not familiar with the current soap operas. I decided to use my pride in my culture as a defense mechanism, as a shield. I decided to remain Russian, and I gave up trying to belong.

With this personal history, one of my goals was to support the pride that the Russian children have in their culture, and use it as a positive vehicle in their assimilation. In contrast to using cultural identity as a shield, I wanted my students to bring their pride to the table with other children in this country, as equals, as a means for growth and mutual respect. I wanted them to enter into relationships with other children based upon their own strong sense of identity. I wanted my Russian students to add a flavor to the American pie and bring home other flavors for their families to taste. I dreamed that they could become both self-respecting and tolerant, and not grow up to partake in the racism that exists here.

Linda and Eleanor: In the fall, we began to assemble the resources and plan the specific activities of our extended collaboration. We got mini-grants from the Oppenheimer Family Fund and the DeWitt Wallace–Reader's Digest Chicago Students at the Center project to cover the costs of art supplies, buses for field trips, and the services of artist Cynthia Weiss, history consultant Roger Passman, and dancer Donna Mandel.

The relationship between our two classes officially began when our students wrote letters to each other, which we used to pair them off. (This is why, throughout the year, the Irving students continued to refer to the project as "our Russian pen pals.") After the exchange of correspondence, we gathered in person for the first time, joining in a "getting to know you" activity with artist Cynthia Weiss. On the appointed day, the Irving students arrived at Clinton School, and found Eleanor's class sitting upstairs in the library. The twenty-eight Clinton students were all seated with empty chairs beside them, which were systematically filled by the twenty-five Irving students. The atmosphere was charged with the discomfort and excitement of the children as they looked at each other for the first time. Cynthia welcomed the children, explaining that in a few minutes they would be making portraits of each other.

Cynthia: First I had the children get the feel of the possibilities of the chalks they would use by having them look carefully at their own skin tones and practice blending colors to create the ranges of dark and light browns that prevailed in one class to the paler tones more prevalent in the other. Then they blended the color of their partner's skin. Next I quickly demonstrated drawing a portrait using a child as a model. Now the children were confronted with the difficult task of looking each other in the face. While children worked on these drawings, conversation was flowing.

From the bright-colored chalks on black paper emerged representations of the faces in the room. Each student wrote their own name and the name of their partner on their artwork. The portraits read "Brandi, by Vitaly" and "Vitaly, by Brandi." The portrait process gave them a safe structure during their first meeting to observe each other, first with curiosity and then with respect. Following a lively discussion of the work and the activity, we broke for a meal that included ethnic foods: Russian pastries, chips with salsa, Spanish and Southern rice, guacamole, and chocolate cake. Despite having to go down four floors for the bathroom, some shyness, a couple of small arguments among the boys, and a sense of herding cattle as we moved fifty-three children around, it was a good beginning.

Once our students had become acquainted with their "pals," we arranged a number of field trips to help them share new experiences together outside of the classroom. Our first trip was to the Museum of Contemporary Art to see its special retrospective exhibit of Chicago artists. The Clinton and Irving students were partnered with their pen pals as a docent led us to the first piece in the show. There we were, adults and children, standing before a huge color photograph of the back of someone's head. Against a neutral background, the sleek, blond, pageboy haircut left the image with an ambiguous gender.

The docent said to Eldorado, "If I were to ask you what you are, you would say you are [pause] a boy, right?" she prompted.

Then she turned to his partner, Natalia, and asked her, "If I were to ask you what you are, you would say, 'I am . . .'"

"A girl," Natalia responded to the pattern presented.

"But I don't understand why you say this," Dima cried emphatically. "If someone asked me, I would say I am a human being!"

His intuition about image, and about the artist's intentions, certainly surpassed the docent's explanation. As we walked through the exhibit, Dima continued, despite his limited English, to express other insights. I whispered to Linda, "It's amazing how hard he struggles with the language to find the right words for his thoughts." Linda responded, "Well, my students are going through that same struggle themselves." Then we looked at each other and thought the same thought: "Aren't we all?" It is a continual search to pin down our ideas and make them clear to the world, whether in our own language or in a new one we are acquiring.

Our tour moved on to the Black Light room, a re-creation of an artist's exhibit from the 1970s. The kids ran through the room laughing in delight to see their white shirts and shoelaces glow in the dark. We admired the way some children's brown skin became velvety black, and how all the children's white teeth shone like the Cheshire Cat's. Eugene, a Russian boy, was wearing gray from head to toe. Unclear on the workings of a black light, he tugged on my sleeve and said, "Miss, please, why am I not changing?" We found a small white tag on the back of his shirt and showed it to him. He ripped it out to see it better. He held on to this glowing white square like it was a talisman containing the magic of the museum. Linda, Eleanor, and I were delighted by how fresh this contemporary, conceptual art became, seen through the eyes of the children.

Linda and Eleanor: We also took our groups to an innovative dance performance in the Cultural Center, where the dancers involved the children. One of the dancers was from the Ukraine and spoke alternately in Russian and English. The Russian kids squealed with delight as he swooped around the dance floor, with Virgillia laughing on his back, a bird in flight, an airplane, telling the story of his journey to the United States. The dance performance directly tied into our plan to have children write stories about their families' migrations to Chicago, eventually choosing one story from each culture to represent in dance. At Clinton School, this project would fit into the required third-grade study of Chicago history, while at Irving the activity would satisfy fourth-grade Illinois history mandates.

Linda: To help discover their own immigration stories, students needed to use family members as primary sources. One memorable source was Brandi's great-aunt, a member of the African American Genealogical Society, who came in freezing weather to tell us about seven generations of her family tree and history. After I modeled asking questions, helping to translate her responses to the students, they pursued their own questions. Even my most difficult students quietly listened until it came time to ask questions, and then joined enthusiastically in the conversation. By the time she left we all had a pretty good understanding of how different life in rural Mississippi in the early 1900s was from the way we live today in Chicago.

Linda and Eleanor: By delving into their family stories, the children build a foundation for examining history and seeing themselves as part of it. Brandi now knows that World War II presented opportunities for African Americans to migrate from Mississippi to Chicago, just as her great-aunt moved here in 1944 to work in a munitions factory. Yelena understands that her family is a part of the continuing exodus of Russian Jews from the Soviet Union in a climate of renewed nationalism, anti-Semitism, and economic decay. James now knows that his relatives are among many Chinese immigrants drawn to work in America's health care professions. Armando realizes that his story, like that of many other Mexicans in the class, is that the United States offers his parents work opportunities that are lacking in Mexico. To collect these stories, we developed questions that all of the children used to interview the oldest available member of their family. This is much like the authentic work historians do when they use primary sources like interviews, journals, letters, and newspaper accounts to piece together a picture of what happened in the past.

Eleanor: You could not hear a sound or a movement. All of the children were listening with great intensity. I saw the whole gamut of emotions on the faces of my third graders: sorrow, fear, empathy, understanding, sadness, and joy. We were listening to a tape recording of Dima's grandfather, interviewed by his grandson. He told about experiences, worries, and concerns similar to those of most of the other families that have immigrated from the former Soviet Union. Dima asked careful questions, and if the answer did not immediately make sense, he probed until his grandfather's responses became clear. We were all moved. Perhaps for the first time, the children had the opportunity to hear the emotional side of why their families made the fateful decision to immigrate. Admiring his skillful and sensitive questioning, I could not help but wonder if Dima might become a reporter someday.

Cynthia: I visited the children again, this time to help them study the art of Marc Chagall, Romare Bearden, and Frida Kahlo. The children viewed these Russian,

African American, and Mexican artists as exciting, different, but equally valuable models on which to base their own work. The students spent a long time looking at and discussing slides of paintings by Marc Chagall. Chagall's nostalgic paintings of his Russian hometown, outside of Vitebsk, were filled with his memories of roosters and moons, dancers and fiddlers on the roof. Some of the Russian children had lived near Vitebsk themselves, and all of them knew firsthand about a longing for things left behind.

But it was the Irving School children, African American, Mexican American, and Chinese, who seemed the most intrigued by Chagall's dreamlike imagery. They filled their drawing papers with upside-down houses and floating figures, to represent their own early childhood stories. Chagall's icons, tied to a specific time and place, provided a universal language that all the students could embrace. These images were pieced together in several panels where shapes and colors overlapped and images blended together to tell stories of who we were as a group.

The students then studied the work of Romare Bearden, an African American painter who was active in the Harlem Renaissance, and read *The Block*, a collection of poems by Langston Hughes. Each student made a collage of their own home with photographs and patterned paper. They could choose to show either their Chicago home or a past home in another city. Donald, a wonderful artist in Linda's class, suggested that we take the individual collages and make a "composite" block of our own. Rather than have the adults create the composition, we asked the children to decide how to put the block together. This task, like a choreographer's in dance, involved higher-order thinking skills. The students had to create an overall design that connected the parts in a meaningful way. They had a heated discussion about their options and took a vote. We had two groups of students composing the work; both groups decided to put the Atlantic Ocean in the center of the composition to show the water that the Russian children had crossed to come to America.

One of the groups also created a place in their design for Chicago homes, and their families' earlier homes in places like Mexico and Mississippi, with a collage train track connecting the bottom and top of the picture. The students brought their personal experiences and the knowledge of their families' histories to their discussion on spatial relationships. As they composed the collage, they acknowledged each other's immigration and migration stories. The beautiful finished work represented the realities of the students' lives. Finally, the children examined the Mexican artist Frida Kahlo, particularly her series of self-portraits. In this style the children created self-portraits with oil pastels, weaving things of personal importance into the backgrounds and borders. During discussions of this work students seemed to demonstrate a deepening understanding of self and community.

Linda: A parent, Brenda Kneedly, invited my class to participate in an African American History Month poetry performance at Cook County Hospital where she works. Brenda is a poet herself and came to recite some of her poems at a schoolwide poetry recital. Both classes wrote poems topical to our project. Alongside the poetry and artwork, our classes met with Donna Mandel, a choreographer and dance consultant, whose Fluid Measure Performance Company creates performances that tell personal stories through dance, theater, visual arts, and music.

Donna: First, I introduced children to the choreographic tools of shape, levels in space, and energy or dynamic quality in dance. While one group did their artwork in a classroom, the other met with me to choreograph dances of selected family histories in a performance space. To begin, I led the students in the creation of movements to represent words. Each story was divided into three parts and small groups of children from both classes were assigned a piece of the story to choreograph. Once they were done, I had them create a choreographic score by drawing pictures and symbols that would remind them of the chosen movements. Their movements were put to music from the culture represented by the piece. This melding of movement with music was difficult but helped to flesh out its identity. I infused traditional moves from dances in the same culture to smooth transitions. The kicking of feet from a Russian troika signaled the beginning and ending of Yelena's story. Floating butterflylike, a "crane dance" from the Chinese "Animal Frolics" framed James's family's immigration story. Brandi's migration story included a very cool slide and a group twirl; a variation on a lindy hop move framed its beginning and end. Following this lead, the children also included movements that they had learned elsewhere. A "strike-a-pose" move from the song, "Vogue," was woven into Armando's immigration story. Alternate meetings at both schools provided opportunities to finish the artwork and rehearse the dance pieces.

Linda and Eleanor: At Irving, our project culminated in a major show with dances, poetry, and the discussion of our artwork, which appeared on a backdrop behind the stage. At Clinton, kids presented dances coupled with slides of their artwork in an International Festival. At the end of the year, students at both schools received a copy of the book with their poems, artwork, and family stories. As the project came to a close, we felt it was important to celebrate and spend some social time together. So we went on a picnic to a lakeside park, where we viewed mosaic benches that depict events from Chicago history, created by our own partner Cynthia Weiss and other artists. Afterward we ate and played together. At first each class started their own games, then slowly children from the other class joined in until there was no division, just groups of joyful children playing soccer, Frisbee, ball, Red Rover, and a Russian game similar to Duck, Duck, Goose called Hide the Handkerchief.

We felt that this project was a success both academically and socially. As Charles Fowler says:

> Because the arts often express a sense of community and ethnicity, they are one of the main ways in which humans define who they are. Because the arts convey the spirit of the people who create them, they can help young people acquire inter- and intracultural understanding. The arts are not just multicultural, they are transcultural, inviting cross-cultural communication and understanding and teaching openness toward those who are different from us. (1996, p. 52)

This transcultural connection was one of the highlights for us. All the children learned about the contributions of each other's ethnic groups to our collective interpretation of the world. They reveled in the invitation to understand and express themselves in a range of styles. As they worked together, each contributing a piece, an understanding, a skill, an experience, or an idea to a work of art, they grew to see their own and each other's value.

In this unit, we managed to briefly bypass the ethnic segregation that decades of court decisions and mandates have not been able to resolve in Chicago. We are not saying that this limited exposure was a solution, but we do believe that all cross-group experiences are precious and worthwhile. The modeling of teachers is also important. As schoolteachers, our friendship—as a Russian immigrant, a German-speaking African American, and a diverse group of working artists—showed our students that relationships can transcend ethnic differences when they are based on the informed self-respect and openness to difference. The contributions of everyone who collaborated on this project demonstrated what could happen when people—different, diverse, various, and disparate people—work together.

Show Me the Money

JAMES BEANE, BARBARA BRODHAGEN, AND GARY WEILBACHER

For a number of years we have worked with middle school students to create a curriculum that is intended to be democratic and integrative. Our way of doing things is based upon a number of ideas, including the following:

- Schools in a democratic society ought to have a curriculum that promotes democracy and the democratic way of life.
- Regardless of their age, young people are citizens in a democracy and have a right to have a say in what happens at school.
- The way to "learn" democracy is to live the democratic way.
- Participation in planning is only part of teaching the democratic way; the form and content of the curriculum must also embody democratic living.
- Democracy needs a curriculum with a social conscience and a focus on significant self and social issues.
- Knowledge is not simply a cultural decoration; it is an instrument for understanding self and world as well as for resolving social issues.

Making a Plan

The groups we have worked with most recently have included around fifty heterogeneously grouped students assigned to a two-person team for a four-hour block. A given year typically starts with a few weeks of community-building during which students and teachers come to know about each other through a variety of activities like surveys, discussions, peer interviewing, and ethnic/cultural background maps. In addition the group creates a "Constitution" describing the norms and rules that will guide their time together and their work.

Toward the end of that time we engage the students in a collaborative planning process aimed at creating a curriculum linked to the ideas mentioned above. This planning process was developed as one way to carry out the curriculum proposal made by James Beane in *A Middle School Curriculum from Rhetoric to Reality* (1993). It has been used by teachers interested in curriculum integration, democratic curriculum, thematic teaching, and other teaching forms. While it has sometimes been seen simply as a way to increase student interest and engagement, it is actually intended to create a particular kind of curriculum with student participation. With relatively minor differences, it has worked well with groups of varying numbers and ages at all school levels. We begin by asking the students to do some self-reflection: *"We would like you to begin by thinking about yourself. Who are you? What are you like? What are your interests, aspirations? Please make a list of words or phrases you would use if asked to tell about yourself."*

Next we raise the first of the two major questions: *"Still thinking about yourself and looking at the list you have made, now please list questions or concerns you have about yourself."* After sufficient time has passed for the students to list questions individually, we form small groups of five or six people and ask them to search for shared questions, which are recorded on newsprint: *"Are there questions or concerns that were expressed by several or all members of your group? If so, what are they? No one is required to show their personal list or to share anything from it unless they choose to do so."*

Once the group's self questions and concerns are recorded, we turn to the second of the two major questions: *"Now we would like you to look outside yourself at the world you live in, from the close parts (family, friends, school, cultures, our community, and so on) to the more distant parts (your state, your nation, the global world). We would like you to think about that world—both near and far—and list questions or concerns you have about that world. What questions do you have about the world you live in?"* Again, after having sufficient time to record individual questions and concerns, the students are placed in their small groups and asked to find shared "world" questions and concerns (with the same right to remain silent).

Next we ask the small groups to look at their self and world questions to identify themes for the curriculum: *"Are there any cases where there are connections between self and world questions (such as questions about conflict in school and conflict in the larger world)? If so, what are some words or phrases you might use to name the connections (such as* conflict*)?"* In groups of sixty or less we have also done this by posting all questions from small groups in a central location and asking the large group to find themes.

Next, the lists of themes from the small groups are posted and the large group reaches consensus on a single list. A vote is then taken to select the first theme for the year (with the rest of the themes to be addressed later). Having selected an opening theme, the small groups are reconvened to identify questions and concerns from their lists that they would include within the first theme: *"What are specific self and world questions and concerns we might want to answer within this theme? Be sure to indicate which questions are of interest to all or most of the group and which to one or two since there will be room for both large- and small-group activities."* (For this task we have also used a steering committee with a representative from each small group.)

Finally, we ask the students to identify possible activities the group might do and resources they might use to answer the questions for the theme. We do this in one of several ways: small groups rotating through stations where one or two questions are posted, large-group discussion, or dividing the group in half. This process completed, the teachers proceed to organize and expand the activities, develop a calendar for activities and projects, and so on. The teachers and students also create a web for the unit as a visual organizer.

The Unit Emerges

Over the years the themes that have emerged from this planning have held fairly constant and have consistently involved significant self and social topics and questions. This is not surprising, since students are real people living in the real world and besides, asking for questions about self and world is not likely to elicit simplistic themes. Some of the themes that have repeatedly made the group list include the following:

Living in the Future
Protecting the Environment
Conflict and Violence
Drugs and Diseases
Government and Politics
Jobs, Money, Careers
Cultures

Students have given such themes creative names over the years. One unit that emerged from a large number of questions about currency and the economy was given the title "Show Me the Money." The web in Figure 8.3 shows the big ideas and concepts addressed throughout the unit. Again, the theme as well as the big ideas were not predetermined, but rather grew out of questions raised in our planning process. Following are examples of questions that formed the big ideas in the "money" unit.

History
Who invented money?
Why was money invented?
What things are/were used for money?
When and why did bills replace coins?
What is Confederate money worth?

Distribution of Wealth
Will one person ever control all the money?
Will there ever be a time when no one is poor?
How much money does the U.S. president control?
Who is the richest person in the world?
Will there ever be no homeless people?

Global Economy
Will money always exist?
How do currency exchanges work?
Will the world run out of money?
How are prices set?

Figure 8.3: Concept web on money.

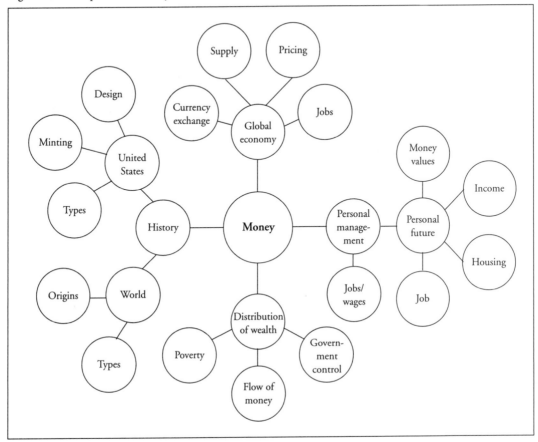

Money Management

Will I have enough money?

Will I be greedy?

What is a minimum wage job?

What jobs bring more income?

Will I own a big house?

As mentioned in the description of our planning process, students and teachers also work together to think about possible activities to answer the questions included in the theme. While a premium is placed on projects, discussion, debate, and other lively activities, both students and teachers also look for opportunities to read, research, write, reflect, and so on. Also, in finalizing ideas for activities we look for ones that respond to several questions simultaneously as well as addressing some of the content and skill standards required at the state and district levels. In the case of "Show Me the Money," some of the activities we did were as follows:

- Questions students had about personal money futures were partly addressed through an activity that began with naming career aspirations. Selecting one career area, students conducted research on requirements and expected incomes. They then did job shadows with people in those careers. Using projected income figures and information about money management they created rough budgets for living costs and discretionary income their "career" might involve. Most students were shocked to discover standard costs of living and how little discretionary income is available in most occupations. With those figures in mind, the group looked at housing types and opportunities, using a city map that showed neighborhood average incomes, housing costs, and other economic features.

- Questions about the history and evolution of money began with a study of how ancient civilizations conducted trade as well as types of currency systems across different cultures, regions, and countries. The whole group then invented its own currency system and used it to trade goods and services over a few weeks. Toward the end of the unit students brought in unwanted items for a "white elephant" auction with buying and selling based on their own currency.

- Questions about the global economy were partly addressed through research involving students' personal possessions. In this case, each student identified their favorite clothing items and then looked to see where those items were made. Not surprisingly, few were produced in the United States. Combining individual lists, a group list of countries was created. Small groups then selected countries for further research and short presentations about the country's political and economic system, per capita income, and any information about what workers would be paid in the garment industry. Discoveries about income and working conditions led to discussions and debates about "sweatshop" labor, child labor, and moral issues involved in clothing choices.

- In addition to larger types of activities, book groups and writing assignments were used to consider questions about personal choices, greed, and wealth distribution. Books and stories included Roald Dahl's *The Wonderful World of Henry Sugar*, Gloria Miklowitz's *War Between the Classes*, and John Steinbeck's *The Pearl*. Movies like *Trading Places* also led to considerable discussion of moral and class issues in the economy.

- Current information gathered from newspapers and other sources was used for daily short discussions about topics like the job market, consumer trends, and product advertising.

■ The unit culminated with students focusing on questions of personal or small-group interest through final projects. These included things like tracing a product from manufacture to market; visiting local merchants to find out how prices and profits are determined; researching how money is portrayed in songs, movies, and other popular culture venues; and staging a debate over income equity comparing professional athletes and more typical occupations.

The Integrative Way

With this unit, as with others, it is important to note that since each activity involved knowledge from a variety of sources, the students proceeded from one project or activity to another during the team's daily block of time. Time slots within the block were thus identified by activity rather than by one subject or another. As always, we also tried to continue the idea of democratic and integrative education throughout. For example, assessment procedures focused heavily on self-assessment, and students helped develop rubrics for various projects and assignments. Regarding concerns about standards and subject-based content, two actions were taken. During and after the unit the teachers "back-mapped" the unit to state and district standards to keep a record of which ones were addressed. Second, to answer questions parents and other adults might ask about school, the students and teachers did a subject map at the end of the unit, identifying which parts of their work could be related to one or another subject. And as always, when the "money" unit ended, the group moved on to their next theme, pulling out the relevant questions from the original planning and creating ways to respond to them.

Voting with Your Wallet: Media Literacy in the Modern Age

SCOTT SULLIVAN

Addressing media and advertising issues in the classroom may at first seem tangential to current educational trends. Why bother? Does No Child Left Behind legislation test media literacy concepts? Is understanding advertising going to appear on a state-mandated graduation test? And what use is it, after all, since most of us teachers have never had media literacy education and we somehow turned out OK, right? So why do we need to cover yet another topic that isn't even going to be nationally evaluated? What purpose would this serve?

I would argue that the main focus of all education, and media education in particular, is to prepare an informed citizenry for future participation in our democracy. As of this writing, a national election looms on the horizon, and the candidates are slugging it out in television ads, well-constructed photo ops, and concise sound bites that drive home complex messages in simple packages—hardly a way for students, or adults for that matter, to understand in depth the issues that confront our nation. Ironically, all of this important activity is carried out in the forum of a commercial media whose economic interests frequently outweigh the needs of democratic discourse.

But if our mission really is to create informed citizens, how do we make kids more aware of the world around them? What steps do we need to take in order to help them become more engaged, curious, and looking beyond those typical issues of the school-age years: Do I look good? Am I cool? Do my friends really like me? How can I get more money to spend? That last question, I would argue, is one way in, a gateway through which we can begin helping students think about what simple things like buying a pair of shoes, or a soccer ball, or a hooded sweatshirt means when examined through the lens of global capitalism.

Targeting Young Consumers

Kids can spend money. Boy, can they. Recent research shows high school–aged kids spend upward of ninety-four billion dollars a year. Yes, $94,000,000,000— that's quite a lot. It's no wonder that advertisers, in pursuit of this lucrative demographic, inundate the teen world with advertising.

No space is sacred anymore when it comes to plastering advertising messages wherever kids can be forced to see them. Channel One, an advertising-supported broadcast network that gives AV equipment to cash-strapped school districts in return for access to captive school audiences for twelve minutes a day, is currently in 12,000 schools, reaching eight million students and 400,000 educators. Soft drink corporations sponsor scoreboards, athletic shoe companies buy naming rights to gymnasiums, and all the while, kids keep spending and spending.

Students are so used to being advertised to, to being seen as the "prime demographic" that most movies, television, music, and video games are being marketed to, that most of them can't remember a time when they weren't constantly bombarded with advertising. Today's young people have never known a world without designer jeans, status labels on all articles of clothing, and basketball shoes that cost a hundred and fifty bucks. To them, there's nothing unusual about a world, seemingly beyond the pale in hypercommercialism, where kids are bombarded with advertising from birth (think Baby Gap), to their teen years and beyond.

But while the problem seems clear, school's response to it is less so. It would seem logical, wouldn't it, for schools to make education about media and advertising mandatory for our students? Making the media and advertising a focus of curriculum enables schools to

- answer the eternal question, "why do we have to learn this?";
- allow students to use popular media texts in classrooms, making the connection between school and the world beyond the school walls;
- begin to build bridges with students between the popular culture texts of today and the "classics" schools traditionally teach, which were, after all, the popular culture texts of their own time. Shakespeare was for entertainment, not simply dry, academic study; and
- become a place where students work to become not only interested but also critical consumers of the culture around them.

Studying Consumerism and Advertising

During senior year at Evanston Township High School students can take a class called Critical Thinking in the Modern Age. Our aim in designing this course was to examine the media and its role in the world, its impact on the lives of teens, and its ability to define our culture. One of the units in the course focuses on consumerism and advertising and asks students to answer one simple question: How should you spend your "ethical dollars"? Before I get into the project that shows how students make those decisions, let me first give you a bit of background on the experiences that help them answer that question.

We read, view, and listen to a variety of texts in class. Most of them deal with consumer culture, the ubiquity of advertising, the strategic plans of marketers, and the growing network of activists who monitor and protest the actions of transnational corporations. Students are initially uninterested in the machinations of media and advertisers, until they see a video called "The Merchants of Cool," a PBS *Frontline* special hosted by Douglas Rushkoff that takes an in-depth look at "cool hunting," focus groups, brand re-imaging, and marketing to teens (www.pbs.org/wgbh/pages/frontline/shows/cool/). The sheer crassness and greed of marketers begin to irritate students, though many of them do recognize that this has been happening to them their entire lives. This film bridges our classroom discussions between other texts we've been reading, Naomi Klein's *No Logo*, James Twitchell's *Carnival Culture* and *Adcult USA*, and others that outline the effects of branding and marketing in the lives of citizens.

While reading and viewing, we also complete two simple but effective assignments. First, the class pledges to avoid all forms of media for an entire weekend, from the end of school on Friday till first bell on Monday. No radio, no TV, no books, no music, no cell phones, nothing. Now, obvious issues arise—"Is a giant ad on the side of a bus a form of media? And if so, how can I avoid that if I'm driving in the car with my mom and she won't turn down a side street so I can miss it?" Obviously, the assignment has limits, but the spirit is to make one's self as media-free as possible. After the media-free weekend (I often send a letter home to make sure parents help monitor compliance), we journal and discuss the experience. Who cheated? Why? What did you do instead of engaging with media? What did you learn about yourself and your media consumption habits from this exercise? Most kids see that media is always there for them, giving them whatever they want, whenever they want it. Need to watch a movie at three in the morning? No problem. Want to talk instantly with your friends while surfing the Web? Done. The speed and individual nature of media delivery systems respond perfectly to the lives of students. They can immerse themselves in an entire culture that caters to their desires and no one else's. It's the ultimate social cocoon. This assignment's main purpose is to help students realize the casual, habitual nature of media usage in their lives.

The second exercise we do during this unit is to count the number of "advertising-related encounters" they have each day. That may seem a bulky term, but the point is to recognize the ubiquity of advertising, the veritable sea of market-speak that we swim in all day, every day, for our entire lives. Some topics that typically come up through this exploration are the predominance of clothing labels, the way all public space has been colonized by marketers, and the seemingly hopeless task we all have of trying to make sense of this advertising-saturated world. Even schools previously thought to be advertising-free zones have become victims of shrinking tax bases and expanding budget needs and have opened the doors to corporate advertisers who pay top dollar to deliver their message to a school's captive audience. Again, what we're after is raising student awareness to the prevalence of media and advertising in their lives.

The culminating project of the unit is aimed toward empowering students to go beyond understanding advertising and marketing ploys and begin, as participants in a democratic society, to "vote" with their pocketbooks and wallets. While boycotts are one time-tested way for activists to pressure companies into changing some sort of policy or practice, they are frequently seen as a weapon of zealots or ideologues who want simply to have changes made that satisfy themselves but not the world at large. An example is the establishment of the Parents' Music Resource Center, or PMRC, founded by former presidential candidate Al Gore's wife, Tipper, in response to what she saw as unacceptable language in recorded music.

Researching Responsible Corporations

Voting with your dollars isn't a form of censorship, as the PMRC advocated, but it is a way for the individual consumer to take power in his or her relationship with multinational corporations whose practices or policies are unacceptable. The assignment was deceptively simple and can be summed up in a sentence: "What company deserves your money?" Some would argue that no companies ever deserve money and the United States has followed the wrong path into capitalism and we should teach students to overthrow that system. Part of me agrees with that assessment, but in the eyes of students, that's a no-win proposition. The world is the way it is, so how can we help kids live with what they've got, while always keeping an eye toward change in the future? The assignment, then, is to investigate one company from whom you consume—Nike, McDonald's, Best Buy, Wal-Mart, the list goes on and on—and determine whether they deserve your "ethical dollars." Does this corporation earn your "vote," your money—do you approve of the way the company does business, cares for its workers, and serves as a steward for our environment?

After picking the company they want to research (always a tough choice for students), the class begins to look into the labor practices, marketing strategies, and environmental impact of the corporation's policies. It doesn't take long for kids to begin to bring back stories: "Did you know they use child labor?" or "A worker in the maquiladora [the manufacturing zones established in Mexico as a result of NAFTA] makes only eighty cents a day, but the jeans they're making sell for eighty-five bucks a pair!" These are just a few of the things that students find relatively easily, researching on the Internet. In the past, consumer information wasn't so easy to find. If an organization or group of people wanted to protest the policies of a corporation, chances are nothing much happened. But with the growth of the Web, which interestingly coincides with the growth of global trade, information is, literally, at the fingertips of students.

Students unearthed some startling facts during this project. One major corporation, known primarily for its chocolate treats, is being held accountable for promoting baby formula over breast milk to the detriment of third-world mothers and their children's immune systems; a shoe manufacturer "greenwashes" its images, making its products and advertising seem more ecologically friendly and financially ethical than they actually are; an oil company sponsors a private militia that drives indigenous peoples from their homelands.

It's easy to argue that the corporations are merely doing what they have to do in order to survive in the capitalist world as it exists. It's not hard to see the race to the bottom line, where jobs are moved around the globe in pursuit of a few more pennies of profit per item sold. Initially kids don't understand that purchasing decisions, which seem so small and insignificant one at a time, can really add up to social action. It's easy to beat up on corporations; they are faceless entities that seem far more powerful than any one individual. But what if we asked students to turn the equation around? What would corporations be without us, the consumers? How would *that* impact their decisions and the way they treat workers, resources, and our planet?

Some kids will choose corporations to study that have a good track record on these controversial issues. The Body Shop, Patagonia, Ben and Jerry's, and others have dedicated themselves to programs of social responsibility. These companies and others have made a concerted effort at good corporate citizenship, and may be worthy of the ethical dollar. In an odd twist, given my own bias against violence in all forms, some students found that the gunmaker Smith and Wesson is one of the most people-friendly corporations. They provide many benefits to workers, they concentrate on environmental issues, and keep their jobs in America. Whatever corporation they chose to study, most kids found themselves questioning their purchases, and, in some cases, they pledged to adjust their spending as a result.

Examining the advertising and messages a corporation sends about itself is one small way to begin helping students read the world around them. If we are truly committed to nurturing young people who will become democratic citizens, then helping them understand the implications of their commercial choices is a small step toward making the world, and their role in it, more known to them.

You Want Fries with That?

MATT FELDMAN

"On your note card, write what you care about in this book so far. What do you want to hear more about, or what has struck you so far as particularly important or interesting?" With these directions, twenty-five seniors begin to write. We've been reading *Fast Food Nation* for a week, and there have been mixed reviews. Some students aren't interested, some are personally affronted by what they perceive as a direct challenge to their lifestyle, and others have had their senses of curiosity and justice turned on. A few kids stare into space, thinking how to respond to the prompt, but most cover one side of the note card in hasty writing. I invite students to share their responses, which come in a wide variety.

Brandon thinks it's plain wrong to market so heavily to children. He points out the fact that advertisements for McDonald's are almost indistinguishable from the Saturday morning cartoons alongside which they air. Marisa comments on the way fast food restaurants exploit their employees with low pay and bad conditions. "On top of that," Marisa says, "I can't believe how many of these fast food workers get killed every year. More than police officers! That just seems wrong." Shade is interested in the success story of Ray Kroc. "He turned this thing into McDonald's from nothing! That's impressive."

The teacher team for the senior class at Best Practice High School picked *Fast Food Nation* for our fall integrated unit because of the many ways it looks at the fast food industry and its effects on our world: nutritional, economic, social, geographic, medical, and more. And we hoped that this variety of connections would entice students into the inquiry. As the month of November unfolded with a variety of activities and experiences, nearly every student did find something to get fired up about.

Background

We do integrated units four times a year, some based on negotiating the curriculum with students (see pages 291–97) and others designed by the faculty. Each summer we look at the themes from the past year, upgrade the successes, and replace ones that didn't work with new ones. We tend to look for units based on ideas that students will be able to hook into. If we *start* with something that seems exciting to students, it can help to avoid the problem of the 10 percent of kids who mentally check out before a unit even begins (the "judging a book by its cover" syndrome) and the additional 10 percent we lose a few days later (the "man . . . this is boring" syndrome).

A few years ago, we started talking about the muckraking best-seller *Fast Food Nation* by Eric Schlosser. It seemed perfect. It was nonfiction written for a broad audience (it spent time on nearly every best-seller list), and it addressed issues that could easily be covered in English, history, and science classes. And it was centered around a topic—burgers and fries—that seventeen-year-olds could definitely sink their teeth into. We felt this was an opportunity not to be missed.

In a series of meetings, the team sketched a skeleton of the unit. We made a reading schedule, an idea for a final project, and a "hook" activity to introduce the text, and identified some issues that the other, non-English classes could address. History would address labor practices, slaughterhouses, and animal rights; science classes would examine the issue of factory farms and nutrition; and English class would do general discussion, some reading workshop–type stuff, and handle the final project, where kids would do some service to the community concerning food and nutrition.

The Video

We weren't sure that giving students the books and telling them to start reading was the best way to begin. Our students are good readers and generally curious, but we knew we could lose many of them if they didn't know why they were doing this or why they should care. Among the four teachers in the senior team we had Mike Myers and me (vegetarians), Sonja Kosanovic (massage therapist/health nut), and Peter Thomas (also a healthy guy but one who doesn't worry too much about what he eats). We decided if we could get the students to laugh at us (not really a difficult task), that could be an in for the unit.

We quickly scripted, shot, and edited a five-minute video. The plot: The four of us are eating lunch in the staff lounge and discussing *Fast Food Nation*, wondering how we are going to get students interested. Three of us are eating pretentious super-healthful meals, and Peter comes in with a Big Mac, fries, and a Coke. Mike, Sonja, and I, of course, rib him mercilessly, but Peter defends his choice. We make arguments using key quotes from the book, which Peter rebuffs with everyman common sense. Then the bell rings and we all rush out of the lounge. A moment later, the door opens and Mike Myers, the most sanctimonious of us all, sneaks back into the empty lounge and takes a huge bite of Peter's leftover Big Mac. OK, it doesn't sound hilarious; you had to be there. The key, for us, was to be silly and allow students a chance to laugh at us while being introduced to many of the key arguments the book makes, as well as their devil's advocate counterparts.

Students responded. They watched the video the day the books were handed out, laughed at us teachers, and were hooked.

We were lucky enough to get a grant to buy copies of *Fast Food Nation*, and so students were in the unusual situation of owning their own books. This opened the door for note taking in a way they were not used to—on the pages of their books. Students were required to mark the text, using either the coding system we provided for them or one of their own design.

In addition, students were to respond with a bookmark for each week's reading, including general response, questions, key statistics, and an important quote they found along the way. Figure 8.4 details the instructions for creating these bookmarks. Some questions students came up with on their bookmarks are as follows:

Why don't people fight to raise minimum wage?

Why do people mess up their lives trying to get revenge on their former employers?

What does McD's have to do with globalization?

Why can't they make fries taste good without adding chemicals?

How can supervisors let workers get hurt at the slaughterhouse and act like it's OK?

Figure 8.4: Bookmark ingredients and instructions.

What to Do While You Read

You already know how to do bookmarks. You do them very well. Let's do them some more.

The bookmarks will be a little different for this book, since it's nonfiction. As with the last unit, a bookmark will be due for each reading assignment.

Response: In this section, write your reaction to what you read. You could connect, agree, disagree, analyze, whatever.

Questions: Write some questions that you had while you read: something that is not answered or a topic for further exploration.

Important passage: In this section, find a part of the text that stands out for you in some way (interesting, disturbing, funny, sad, etc.). Copy it in here and include a citation.

Important statistics: Schlosser really likes to use numbers to prove his points. Write some of those numbers that are striking to you here. Include citations.

Marking the text: Good readers write in their books as they read. You can't write a lot in the book; there isn't much space for it. So you need a system. Here's ours. You can use your own, but it must include these four components. Provide a key on the inside cover if you design your own.

*   A star means that you find the information important.
!   An exclamation point means that your socks have been knocked off by what you just read.
?   Huh? This means you are unsure of what you just read.
E. coli   Any words that you don't know should be boxed. We will do some work with these words shortly.

These assignments were turned in for English class, and were used to drive whole-class discussions. But these responses were also used in each of the three classes for discussion and research. As seen in the examples of questions above, students came up, with little prodding, with questions that were subtle and rich with possibility for inquiry.

Through this type of reader-response work, students in English class were able to bring up issues of import and interest, whether related to Schlosser's style of writing (English class), important sociological and historical points (history class), or nutrition and agriculture issues (science class). So the work we did in English class turned my class into a hub for the unit, where ideas came up that were later addressed in other classes, and where ideas came in from other classes to be applied toward the final project.

Students *get* this kind of integration. It really brings together the subject areas for them, and helps them see school as creating a whole instead of disjointed sets of activities amounting to nothing more than a set of subskills. On the subject, senior James Douglas says:

> When we're studying the same book in three classes, it works better. I feel like I'm in the groove, instead of having to go to one class for fifty minutes, and then going to my next class, and having to get into a whole different mind frame for what we're doing there. Instead, I got going on *Fast Food Nation*, and could really focus on that for a good part of the day.

Service Project

We went back and forth as a team for a while about what a final assessment should be. Finally, we decided that students should apply what they learned in their reading/research with a service project. In groups, students identified an issue/idea that they found particularly significant, and designed a service that they would actually perform. This service could not be done inside the senior class, but could be with younger students, as well as out of school. Kids came up with some truly great ideas. Common ones included a letter-writing campaign to a legislator about raising the minimum wage, teaching a class of elementary school kids about ethical treatment of animals, designing a packet of research materials about vegetarianism/veganism, and passing out pamphlets in school or on the street.

Of course, results were mixed. Shade and Tanarra stood in thirty-five-degree weather to hand out anti-fast-food pamphlets at a nearby McDonald's and found that almost no one wanted to stop and talk to them. They made a video of their ordeal, and instead of making believe it had been a success, they shared the video with us, as well as their thoughts about why people didn't want to stop. "People don't want to know what they're eating," Shade commented. "They'd rather just eat it, because they think it tastes good and is convenient. They don't really want to think about it, and if they're going to be educated on it, we need to have better ways to approach them than 'Hey, take a pamphlet.'" I couldn't have been happier about this response. These students failed in their mission to educate the masses, but very sharply identified and were reflective about the reasons why.

Sean, Jeanette, and Jennifer created a picture book about the artificial nature of many of the foods at McDonald's. They visited a second-grade class in the elementary school downstairs to read the book and talk about how foods that look and taste good are often not what they appear.

The week these projects were due, each group reported in class about their work, and their successes or failures, and very often gave insight into how these types of service can be more effective in the future. These kids got practice in citizenship and democracy while learning content and working on skills.

For our final segment of the unit, we had students write letters in the interest of getting real-world response from experts and those with the power to solve the problems raised in *Fast Food Nation*. They wrote to Senator Dick Durbin, the Occupational Safety and Health Administration (OSHA), People for the Ethical Treatment of Animals (PETA), or the author himself, Eric Schlosser. We thought this would be a good final assessment, as it would demonstrate reflection in an authentic context, rather than writing for ourselves "what I learned from this unit." As it turns out, we got a little greedy in seeking to extend the unit that extra little bit. The letters were slow in coming in, lukewarm, and sometimes just poorly written. The lesson for us teachers: remember to get out while students are still excited.

This unit, like all others that the senior team at BPHS puts together, is a combination of success story and cautionary tale. Each time we finish one, we look back with pride at some of the great things that happened and with shrugged shoulders and furrowed brows at the things that were less successful. On the fast food project, one of the remarkable outcomes was that many students actually changed their eating habits as a result of what they had read—some for a few days, and some all the way through graduation and (we hope) beyond. That's an example of why we believe that the benefits of this sort of integrative curriculum far outweigh the difficulties.

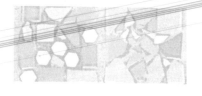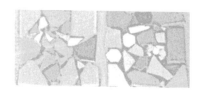

EPILOGUE

Harvey: A few years ago, my daughter and I took a half-day cruise on the *Inland Seas,* an eighty-foot schooner that sails Lake Michigan with the mission of educating passengers about the complex and fragile ecology of the Great Lakes. From mid-April through October, the boat sails with two shiploads a day, mostly students and their teachers, with occasional charters for teacher-educators and environmental groups. Marny and I boarded the school ship at Harbor Springs on a drizzly July morning with thirty other passengers and were a bit surprised when Captain Tom Kelly began the cruise by asking us to form into groups of five or six and to assign ourselves a nautical name. Hooking up with a fun-loving retired couple and another gentleman, we dubbed our team the Keelhaulers.

Next, the crew handed us a learning log in which, they explained, we would be recording our experiences, findings, and impressions of the trip. Before boarding, we were given a safety briefing and invited to sign the official ship's manifest. And then we cast off—the newly formed Keelhaulers, the Sharks, the Pirates, the Barracudas, and the Landlubbers—along with the ship's energetic crew of naturalists and sailors. For the next three and a half hours, we studied Lake Michigan in a dozen hands-on ways. We worked, we tested, we sampled, we experimented, we observed, we recorded, we discussed, we questioned, we laughed a lot, and we even sang a few sea chanteys along the way.

For the first hour, we anchored just offshore and alternated between whole-group and team activities. Our onboard limnologist (lake scientist), Mark Mitchell, demonstrated how to take a variety of weather readings, including wind direction and velocity, cloud types and coverages, air temperature, barometric pressure, and wave height, which we recorded in our logs and compared with other groups. Mark then used a thermometer on a measured string to locate the thermocline, a shifting spot deep in the water where the temperature drops off suddenly, and where fish tend to congregate. That day, the water temperature was 67 degrees at the surface, 60 degrees at thirty feet, and dropped to 49 degrees at forty feet.

Next, each team was given the equipment to test water transparency two ways: with the traditional black-and-white secchi disc, which is lowered into the water on a measured rope, and (even more fun) by dropping colored peanut M&M's into the water (really) and timing the interval until they disappeared. According to the Keelhaulers' group data chart, our red M&M disappeared fastest, within twenty-two seconds, while the green one windmilled visibly through the depths for thirty-seven seconds. This dramatized for us the way water splits the spectrum of light, causing the different-colored candies to remain visible for different lengths of time as they sink. (Yes, fish eat leftover M&M's. Presumably the milk chocolate melts in their mouths, not on their fins.)

Next, we tested water samples for temperature, pH, and dissolved oxygen, which led us to an intense discussion about acid rain. Some of us were worried that we could lose our beloved Michigan lakes to this chemical peril. We learned that the fine limestone marl on the bottom of many midwestern lakes protects them by trapping the acidity that has killed off some rocky-bottomed lakes in New England. Finally, deploying the same kind of equipment used by marine researchers, we collected samples of the water from the bottom to the surface, a scoop of bottom sediment, and an assortment of fish from the trawling net that was dragged behind the ship as we motored for a few minutes.

Then it was time to turn off the engine and put up the sails, all of which was accomplished by the greenhorn crew under the command of sailmaster Remy Champt. Mainsail, foresail, staysail, and jib, up and filled in twenty knots apparent wind. The ship seemed to leap toward the far shore, and Captain Kelly called for five minutes of quiet time, so people could focus on the sensory experience of sailing. We all welcomed this order. Each person found a spot on deck, sat and breathed deeply, drinking in the wind, the spray, and the view of hills above the bay. In the creak of the hull, the flap of the sails, and the splash of the bow wave, you could suddenly feel a kinship with the sailors of old, the explorers of these lakes. It was a sweet moment.

For the next hour and a quarter, our teams rotated through five learning stations set up around the ship, using the samples we had collected to study different aspects of lake ecology. At one station, we worked with the sediment sample, in which we found everything from midge fly larvae, to side-swimming mini-shrimp called amphipods, to wood chips dumped by logging operations of one hundred years ago. At a second station, we studied the fish that had been collected and temporarily placed in tanks. We reviewed the physiology of fish, using charts to determine the species we had caught: brook stickleback, johnny darter, spottail shiner, mottled sculpin, crayfish, and clumps of zebra mussels. Climbing down the gangway into the cabin, we came to the plankton station, where under the microscope our water sample came startlingly alive. As a person who has lived on freshwater lakes his whole life, I was stunned. I thought that plankton was for the ocean. But there they were: our Lake Michigan water was teeming with countless creepy, magnified, crablike critters. Of course! What did I ever think the little fish ate?

Next we moved to the navigation station, where we identified our position on a chart, talked about shipping routes, studied paths taken by immigrating species (like the zebra mussels invading Lake Michigan), and learned about watershed boundaries. We looked at all the different equipment used to guide the boat, from the traditional compass to the latest global positioning system (GPS) receiver. Finally, we reached the seamanship station, where each person got a chance to steer the boat and chat with the captain. He explained the principles by which the ship captures the wind's power and turns it into motion, showing how the different lines control the sails. Some of us immediately noticed the large digital speedometer conspicuously mounted above the cabin, and a jolly rivalry broke out among the unreconstructed competitors among us. Who could drive the boat fastest when their turn at the wheel came? "Jeff!" I heard myself shouting from the helm to a friend on board, "You only had it going 8.76—but now we're over 8.9!"

Now we are sailing back to port, the crew leading us in more chanteys. Our minds are awhirl with information; we feel connected to the water and the wind; we understand in our bones so much about how the ecosystem called a lake works. Above all, we are simply amazed, dazzled by the miraculous complexity and interrelatedness of the lake's ingredients. As we fill out our evaluation forms at the dock, we can't find enough superlatives to thank the crew for this marvelous experience. The trip is too short; the lake we thought we knew all our lives will never be the same. We want to go right back out there.

Sounds like an exhilarating and powerful learning experience, doesn't it? Did you also notice that the *Inland Seas* crew was using all seven structures in our formula for exemplary teaching and learning? That's what dawned on Marny and me as we drove back home from the dock. Wow, we laughed, we just took a cruise on the SS *Best Practice*!

The whole voyage constituted an ambitious *integrative unit* on the ecology of the Great Lakes. We spent much of the morning in collaborative *small groups*, working through five carefully designed learning centers. *Strategic reading* was needed at every station on board; we had to read the text in the safety briefing, the wind on the water, the charts of fish species, the six instrument readouts on the bridge, and the tables we created ourselves as we investigated water transparency. We were constantly *representing-to-learn* as we kept logs of our findings, reactions, and questions. The whole ship took a *workshop* approach, where masters of each "trade" (limnology, navigation, seamanship) demonstrated their craft and then apprenticed us to them, immediately allowing us beginners to try the whole thing (raising the anchor, reading the secchi disc) with careful guidance and coaching. We used several forms of *reflective assessment*, recording findings, comparing them with those of other groups, trying to resolve discrepancies, and speculating on what might have caused them. We reflected on our own learning in our logs, and at the end of the voyage we wrote an evaluation of the program and the instructors—an assessment that the ship's crew uses to revise and plan future programs.

The overarching uniqueness of the school ship, of course, was the *authentic experience* it provided. We spent the whole day working with real stuff—sails, water, air, bottom sediment, fish, plant life, and countless scientific tools. When you looked at your own water sample on the microscope's video monitor and saw the screen fill with wriggling, tentacle-studded phyto- and zooplankton, it was *really* real. When you took your turn guiding the huge wheel of that forty-one-ton boat, feeling the power of the steel-hulled ship striding over three-foot waves, it was real—real fun.

When I later phoned Captain Tom Kelly to compliment him on his shipboard pedagogy and its unwitting adherence to Best Practice principles, he just laughed. "We're just trying to teach the stuff so the kids remember it," he said. But, as Captain Kelly went on to explain, "The ship's program has been very carefully thought out. We believe that people can learn more about ecology by doing rather than reading or hearing someone talk about it. Comprehension and retention are so much greater." Tom also knows how different the *Inland Seas* feels to kids from their regular classroom. "The experience kids have aboard our school ship is like a mountain on the plain of their everyday school experience."

Reading about the school ship as an exemplar of Best Practice education, the reader might be tempted to rejoin: "Well, glad you had a nice sail, but we can't very well take America's sixty million schoolchildren out on an ecology boat every day, now, can we?" Well, yes and no. Of course, the *Inland Seas* offers an extraordinary, rare, and relatively costly form of learning, but every kid should take a few trips like this, whatever it costs. We should make no apology for funding these kind of paradigm-busting, mind-expanding, life-changing, out-of-school experiences (let's even say it—adventures) for children. The people who work in outdoor education have long been arguing, and often proving, that such programs can have profound effects on children, whose imagination, self-esteem, and even career ambitions can be permanently fired by a single day in the real world. As Gary Nabhan and Stephen Trimble have written in *The Geography of Childhood* (1995), all young people need "wild places" to grow by, lakes or woods where they can make their individual connection to the natural world, grounding their sense of belonging on the planet. We would argue that it is not only wild places that children need, but all kinds of authentic places. Every setting is a chance to reinvent yourself and see what happens when you act upon your surroundings.

Still, no matter how passionate our call for adding more real-world, school-ship-type experiences to every child's curriculum, American students will continue to spend most of their time "at sea" in public schools. But our classrooms needn't be barren shores. If the crew of the *Inland Seas* can implement the seven key structures of Best Practice teaching out on the water, then so can those of us back on land. We can arrange time, space, and materials to create powerful, transformative voyages of learning—where every kid takes a turn at the wheel. We can give students voice, choice, responsibility, expression, and connection in their school lives.

We possess the tools and structures to make powerful learning happen; we just have to put them to work. That's what this book has been about.

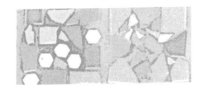

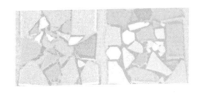

CONTRIBUTORS

Linda Bailey is a reading specialist who works with many different schools in Chicago, helping to improve literacy instruction in all subject areas. Before becoming a classroom consultant, Linda taught many elementary grade levels and spent five years with the Center for City Schools at National-Louis University.

James Beane splits his time between teaching at National-Louis University and serving as a reform coach at Sherman Middle School in Madison, Wisconsin. Jim has written extensively on issues of democracy, integrative instruction, and negotiated curriculum. His book *Democratic Schools*, written with Michael Apple, has been translated into ten languages and has sold more than a million copies worldwide.

Terrie Bridgman received her doctorate in reading and language in 1999. She shares her considerable expertise with the first graders at Baker Demonstration School, the laboratory school of National-Louis University. When she is not teaching "Under Lake Michigan," Terrie consults with teachers around the country.

Barbara Brodhagen is the learning coordinator at Sherman Middle School in Madison, Wisconsin, where she helps students and teachers to stretch the limits of curriculum integration. Barb has worked with fellow contributor James Beane on a variety of middle-level and staff development projects, including the video *Doing Curriculum Integration*.

John Duffy teaches student historians and coaches learning-styles strategies at Hinsdale Central High School. John lives with his wife, Pat, and their six children in Oak Park, Illinois, where he gardens and cheers on his children's field hockey, soccer, and baseball teams.

Kizzi Elmore-Clark teaches at Federal Hocking High School in Stewart, Ohio, where she also helps coordinate the school's staff development program. Over the past two years, she has organized and chaperoned Harvey Daniels and Marilyn Bizar when they guest-taught at FHHS.

Kathleen Fay has more than ten years' classroom experience teaching English language learners. She is currently a Title I teacher and Reading Recovery teacher working alongside teachers and students in classrooms at Bailey's Elementary School for the Arts and Sciences in Fairfax County, Virginia. She is coauthor of *Becoming One Community: Reading and Writing with English Language Learners*.

Matt Feldman teaches English on the senior team at Best Practice High School, a teacher-led school on the West Side of Chicago. Matt has been the spark plug of many an integrative unit, and is much admired as the faculty's chief historian and documenter.

Debbie Gurvitz has taught kindergarten and first grade at Lyon School in Glenview, Illinois, for many years. Now she helps other teachers to implement workshop, literature circles, and reflective assessment in their classrooms. Debbie earned her doctorate in reading and language in 2004.

Dale Halter teaches gifted students in grades 2–6 in Des Plaines, Illinois, concentrating on developing creativity and problem-solving skills. He has learned a great deal from his wife, Beata, and from his parents, all of whom are teachers.

Pamela P. Hyde taught at various grade levels in Illinois and Pennsylvania, seeking authentic ways to teach and assess mathematical thinking. With Arthur Hyde, she co-authored *Mathwise*, and she now serves as an elementary principal in River Forest, Illinois.

Sara Kajder taught middle and high school English in the Montgomery County (Maryland) Public School system. She was selected by the National Council of Teachers of English for a National Technology Leadership Initiative fellowship in 2002. She is currently a graduate fellow in the Center for Technology and Teacher Education at the University of Virginia and author of *The Tech-Savvy English Classroom*.

Connie Kieffer is currently an assistant professor in the secondary education department at National-Louis University, after serving many years at Highland Park High School as chair of the arts department. Connie's passion is helping to find and restore New Deal murals in Chicago-area schools.

Luanne Kowalke teaches at Greenbriar School in Northbrook and holds a master's degree in curriculum and instruction. She enjoys incorporating small-group work, negotiated curriculum, alternative assessment, student self-evaluation, and technology into the daily routine of her bustling fourth-grade class.

Theresa Kubasak taught at Baker Demonstration School in Evanston, Illinois, where she won the Kohl-McCormick Early Childhood Teaching Award for her yearlong curriculum based on the music of Woody Guthrie. Theresa now teaches in New York city.

Pete Leki's work is focused at Waters School, where he has helped students, parents, and community members develop a comprehensive K–8 curriculum of ecology, literacy, and the arts. Pete serves as the parent consultant for the Center for City Schools, is a coauthor of *History Comes Home*, and is the music and adventure director of the Walloon Institute.

Kim Lubeke is new to the field of teaching. She was a science illustrator who received her master of arts in teaching in 2003. Kim is now on the faculty at Adlai Stevenson High School in Buffalo Grove, Illinois, where she uses art to stimulate scientific thinking.

Donna Mandel is artistic codirector of Fluid Measure Performance Company and has served as a dance and arts-integration specialist and in Chicago schools for over twenty years.

Mike Myers teaches social studies at Best Practice High School, where he has developed many simulations that engage students' hearts and minds in the study of historical movements and ideas. Next year, Mike will be teaching at the Young Women's Leadership Charter School in Chicago.

Eleanor Nayvelt has a master's degree in education and teaches third grade in a Russian bilingual program at DeWitt Clinton Elementary School in Chicago. Her interests include her husband and her daughter and translating and editing Russian literature and poetry.

Donna M. Ogle is a professor at National-Louis University in the Department of Reading and Language. Donna is well known for her publications on literacy, including the current best-seller *Reading Comprehension*, written with Camille Blachowicz. She was the original developer of the widely used K-W-L strategy, and served as president of the International Reading Association in 2002.

Christine Paul worked hard to facilitate an authentic classroom community and learning laboratory while teaching at Bailey's Elementary School for the Arts and Sciences in Fairfax County, Virginia. Third and fourth graders created a safe learning environment that was diverse, inclusive, collaborative, and supportive. Christine is currently enjoying her maternity leave by creating a mini-lab at home with her new son, Dylan, and husband, Eddie.

Elizabeth Roche was teaching at the Baker Demonstration School of National-Louis University when she wrote this article. She now teaches at the University of Chicago Laboratory School.

Franki Sibberson has spent the last fourteen years teaching elementary children in Dublin City Schools in Ohio, where she is currently Teacher on Special Assignment in K–8 literacy programs. Franki is coauthor of *Beyond Leveled Books* and *Still Learning to Read*, presents regularly at conferences and workshops, and serves as an adjunct professor at Ashland University.

Nancy Steineke is the author of *Reading and Writing Together: Collaborative Literacy in Action*, which describes the yearlong community-building process in her high school classroom in Tinley Park, Illinois. Nancy has taught at the Walloon Institute for the past nine years, sharing her knowledge with teachers from around the country. Her latest book, written with Harvey Daniels, is *Mini-Lessons for Literature Circles*.

Scott Sullivan is an assistant professor of secondary education at National-Louis University, where he teaches career-changing adults who want to become high school teachers. Scott taught English at Evanston High School, where he developed and taught elective courses in media literacy. Scott also serves as coeditor of the venerable journal *Democracy in Education*.

Jim Tebo teaches seventh- and eighth-grade math at Lincoln Middle School in Park Ridge, Illinois. He received a master of education degree nine years ago, and continues working to integrate and innovate with mathematics instruction.

David Wartik teaches at Hubbard Woods School in Winnetka, Illinois, honored as one of America's "Schools That Work." Always involved in the media, David is also known as the voice of Northwestern University women's basketball team, doing the PA work for all home games.

Linda Weide teaches third grade at the Laboratory School of the University of Chicago, where she continues to design and teach arts-integrated units for her students.

Gary Weilbacher teaches at Illinois State University. He and Barb Brodhagen were teaching partners at Sherman Middle School in Madison, Wisconsin, where they pioneered the process of bringing students' questions and concerns to center stage. Their "negotiating the curriculum" model, documented with James Beane, has since influenced thousands of teachers around the world.

Cynthia Weiss is a painter, mosaicist, public artist, and arts educator. In her own pieces, she works in a style she calls "domestic magical realism." In some of her public work, Cynthia helps teachers develop integrated curriculum through the arts. Cynthia has a master of fine arts degree and has directed numerous large-scale public art projects throughout Chicago.

Steven Wolk now teaches at Northeastern Illinois University in Chicago. He earlier worked at Foundations School, an innovative K–8 whole-language school on Chicago's West Side. Steve is the author of *Being Good: Rethinking Classroom Management and Student Discipline* and *A Democratic Classroom*.

George Wood is a founding member of the Institute for Democracy in Education at Ohio University, where he was a professor of education. George is now the principal of Federal Hocking High School in Stewart, Ohio, where he, the faculty, and students have created a model small high school for others to learn from. George's books, *Schools That Work, A Time To Learn,* and *Many Children Left Behind* are must-reads for all teachers and principals.

Steven Zemelman is the director of the Illinois Writing Project and project manager at Leadership for a Quality Education (LQE), where he brings his knowledge of school reform to new charter, contract, and public schools. He has written many books, the most recent of which is *Subjects Matter: Every Teacher's Guide to Content-Area Reading*, with Harvey Daniels.

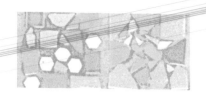

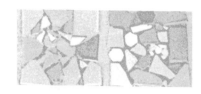

REFERENCES

Akhavan, N. 2004. *How to Align Literacy, Instruction, and Standards.* Portsmouth, NH: Heinemann.

Allen, D., and T. Blythe. 2004. *The Facilitator's Book of Questions: Tools for Looking Together at Student Work.* New York: Teachers College Press.

Allen, J. 2000. *Yellow Brick Roads: Shared and Guided Paths to Independent Reading 4–12.* Portland, ME: Stenhouse.

———. 2004. *Tools for Teaching Content Literacy.* Portland, ME: Stenhouse.

Allen, J., and K. Gonzalez. 1998. *There's Room for Me Here: Literacy Workshop in the Middle School.* Portland, ME: Stenhouse.

Allington, R. L. 2000. *What Really Matters for Struggling Readers: Designing Research-Based Programs.* New York: Addison-Wesley Longman.

———. 2002. "You Can't Learn Much from Books You Can't Read." *Educational Leadership* 60, 3.

Allington, R. L., and P. H. Johnston. 2002. "Integrated Instruction in Exemplary Fourth-Grade Classrooms." In R. L. Allington and P. H. Johnston, eds., *Reading to Learn: Lessons from Exemplary Fourth-Grade Classrooms.* New York: Guilford.

Anderson, Carl. 2000. *How's It Going? A Practical Guide to Conferring with Student Writers.* Portsmouth, NH: Heinemann.

Anson, Chris, and Richard Beach. 1995. *Journals in the Classroom: Writing to Learn.* Norwood, MA: Christopher-Gordon.

Apple, M. W., and J. A. Beane, eds. 1995. *Democratic Schools.* Alexandria, VA: Association for Supervision and Curriculum Development.

Atwell, N. 1998. *In the Middle: New Understandings About Writing, Reading, and Learning.* Portsmouth, NH: Boynton/Cook.

Avery, Carol. 1993. *. . . And with a Light Touch: Learning About Reading, Writing, and Teaching with First Graders.* Portsmouth, NH: Heinemann.

Azwell, T., and E. Schmar, eds. 1995. *Report Card on Report Cards: Alternatives to Consider.* Portsmouth, NH: Heinemann.

Barth, R. 1992. *Improving Schools from Within: Teachers, Parents, and Principals Can Make the Difference.* San Francisco: Jossey-Bass.

Beane, J. A. 1991. "The Middle School: The Natural Home of the Integrated Curriculum." *Educational Leadership* (October): 9–13.

———. 1993. *A Middle School Curriculum from Rhetoric to Reality.* Columbus, OH: National Middle School Association.

———. 1995. "Curriculum Integration and the Disciplines of Knowledge." *Phi Delta Kappan* (April): 100–06.

———. 1997. *Curriculum Integration: Designing the Core of Democratic Education.* New York: Teachers College Press.

Becker, H. 2002. *Art for the People: The Rediscovery and Preservation of Progressive and WPA-era Murals in the Chicago Public Schools: 1904–1943.* San Francisco: Chronicle.

Beers, K. 2002. *When Kids Can't Read, What Teachers Can Do: A Guide for Teachers 6–12.* Portsmouth, NH: Heinemann.

Berger, P. L., and T. Luckman. 1967. *The Social Construction of Reality: A Treatis in the Sociology of Knowledge.* New York: Anchor.

Blachowicz, C., and P. Fisher. 1996. *Teaching Vocabulary in All Classrooms.* Englewood Cliffs, NJ: Merrill.

Blachowicz, C., and D. Ogle. 2001. *Reading Comprehension: Strategies for Independent Learners.* New York: Guilford.

Blecher, S., and K. Jaffee. 1998. *Weaving in the Arts: Widening the Learning Circle.* Portsmouth, NH: Heinemann.

Boomer, G., N. Lester, C. Onore, and J. Cook, eds. 1992. *Negotiating the Curriculum: Educating for the Twenty-First Century.* London: Falmer Press.

Bourne, B., ed. 2000. *Taking Inquiry Outdoors: Reading, Writing and Science Beyond the Classroom Walls.* Portland, ME: Stenhouse.

Bowers, C. A. 1984. *The Promise of Theory: Education and the Politics of Cultural Change.* New York: Longman.

Bradley, James. 2000. *Flags of Our Fathers.* New York: Bantam.

Brodhagen, B. 1995. "The Situation Made Us Special." In M. Apple and J. A. Beane, eds. *Democratic Schools.* Alexandria, VA: Association for Supervision and Curriculum Development.

Brown, C. S. 1994. *Connecting with the Past: History Workshop in Middle and High Schools.* Portsmouth, NH: Heinemann.

Buck, P. S. 1986. *The Big Wave.* New York: HarperTrophy.

Buis, K. 2004. *Writing Every Day: Reading, Writing, and Conferencing Using Student-Led Language Experiences.* Markham, ON: Pembroke.

Bullock, R., ed. 1998. *Why Workshop? Changing Course in 7–12 English.* Portland, ME: Stenhouse.

Burke, K. 2000. *What to Do with the Kid Who . . . Developing Cooperation, Self-Discipline, and Responsibility in the Classroom.* Palatine, IL: IRI/Skylight.

Burke, J. 2000. *Reading Reminders: Tools, Tips, and Techniques.* Portsmouth, NH: Boynton/Cook.

Calkins, L. 1986. *The Art of Teaching Writing.* Portsmouth, NH: Heinemann.

———. 1990. *Living Between the Lines.* Portsmouth, NH: Heinemann.

———. 2000. *The Art of Teaching Reading.* New York: Allyn and Bacon.

Carr, E., and D. Ogle. 1987. "A Strategy for Comprehension and Summarization." *Journal of Reading* 30: 626–31.

Chancer, J., and G. Rester-Zodrow. 1997. *Moon Journals: Writing, Art, and Inquiry Through Focused Nature Study.* Portsmouth, NH: Heinemann.

Chase, A. 1977. *The Legacy of Malthus: The Social Costs of the New Scientific Racism.* New York: Knopf.

Claggett, F., and J. Brown. 1992. *Drawing Your Own Conclusions: Graphic Strategies for Reading, Writing, and Thinking.* Portsmouth, NH: Boynton/Cook.

Clyde, J. A., and M. W. F. Condon. 1999. *Get Real: Bringing Kids' Learning Lives into Your Classroom.* Portland, ME: Stenhouse.

Cohen, E. 1986. *Designing Groupwork: Strategies for the Heterogeneous Classroom.* New York: Teachers College Press.

Cohen, E. P., and R. S. Gainer. 1995. *Art: Another Language for Learning.* 3rd ed. Portsmouth, NH: Heinemann.

Costa, A. L. 1984. "Mediating the Metacognitive." *Educational Leadership,* 57–62.

———. 1991. *The School as a Home for the Mind: A Collection of Articles.* Palatine, IL: IRI/SkyLight.

Costa, A. L., and B. Kallick, eds. 2000. *Assessing and Reporting on Habits of Mind.* Alexandria, VA: Association for Supervision and Curriculum Development.

Countryman, J. 1992. *Writing to Learn Mathematics: Strategies That Work, K–12.* Portsmouth, NH: Heinemann.

Cruz, M. C. 2004. *Independent Writing: One Teacher—Thirty-Two Needs, Topics, and Plans.* Portsmouth, NH: Heinemann.

Daniels, H. 2002. *Literature Circles: Voice and Choice in Book Clubs and Reading Groups.* 2nd ed. Portland, ME: Stenhouse.

Daniels, H., M. Bizar, and S. Zemelman. 2001. *Rethinking High School: Best Practice in Teaching, Learning, and Leadership.* Portsmouth, NH: Heinemann.

Daniels, H., and N. Steineke. 2004. *Mini-Lessons for Literature Circles.* Portsmouth NH: Heinemann.

Daniels, H., and S. Zemelman. 2004. *Subjects Matter: Every Teacher's Guide to Content-Area Reading.* Portsmouth, NH: Heinemann.

Davidson, J., and D. Koppenhaver. 1993. *Adolescent Literacy: What Works and Why.* New York: Garland.

Dewey, J. [1916] 1944. *Democracy and Education: An Introduction to the Philosophy of Education.* New York: Free Press.

———. [1938] 1963. *Experience and Education.* New York: Macmillan.

Diller, D. 2003. *Literacy Work Stations: Making Centers Work.* Portland, ME: Stenhouse.

Edwards, B. 1979. *Drawing on the Right Side of the Brain.* Los Angeles: Tarcher.

Ehrenworth, M. 2003. *Looking to Write: Students Writing Through the Visual Arts.* Portsmouth, NH: Heinemann.

Elbow, P. 1973. *Writing Without Teachers.* New York: Oxford University Press.

Ernst, K. 1997. *A Teacher's Sketch Journal: Observations on Learning and Teaching.* Portsmouth, NH: Heinemann.

Fay, K., and S. Whaley. 2004. *Becoming One Community: Reading and Writing with English Language Learners.* Portland, ME: Stenhouse.

Ferrara, J. 1996. *Peer Mediation: Finding a Way to Care.* Portland, ME: Stenhouse.

Fineberg, Carol. 2004. *Creating Islands of Excellence: Arts Education as a Partner in School Reform.* Portsmouth, NH: Heinemann.

Fletcher, R. 1993. *What a Writer Needs.* Portsmouth, NH: Heinemann.

———. 1996. *A Writer's Notebook: Unlocking the Writer Within You.* New York: Avon.

Fletcher, R., and J. Portalupi. 1998. *Craft Lessons: Teaching Writing K–8.* Portland, ME: Stenhouse.

———. 2002. *When Students Write* (videotape). Portland, ME: Stenhouse.

Flippo, R. F. 2003. *Assessing Readers: Qualitative Diagnosis and Instruction.* Portsmouth, NH: Heinemann.

Fogarty, R., D. Perkins, and J. Barrell. 1992. *The Mindful School: How to Teach for Metacognitive Reflection.* Palatine, IL: IRI/Skylight.

Follett, K. 1982. *The Eye of the Needle.* New York: Signet.

Fountas, I. C., and G. S. Pinnell. 1996. *Guided Reading: Good First Teaching for All Children.* Portsmouth, NH: Heinemann.

———. 2001. *Guided Readers and Writers (Grades 3–6): Teaching Comprehension, Genre, and Content Literacy.* Portsmouth, NH: Heinemann.

Fowler, C. 1996. *Strong Arts, Strong Schools: The Promising Potential and Shortsighted Disregard of the Arts in American Schooling.* New York: Oxford University Press.

Freire, P. [1970] 1993. *Pedagogy of the Oppressed.* New York: Continuum.

Fresch, E. T. 2004. *Connecting Children with Children, Past and Present: Motivating Students for Inquiry and Action.* Portsmouth, NH: Heinemann.

Fulwiler, T., ed. 1987. *The Journal Book.* Portsmouth, NH: Boynton/Cook.

Gaiman, Neil. 2002. *Coraline.* New York: HarperCollins.

Gardner, H. 1983. *Frames of Mind.* New York: Basic Books.

———. 2000. *Intelligence Reframed: Multiple Intelligences for the Twenty-First Century.* New York: Basic Books.

Gee, K. 1999. *Visual Arts as a Way of Knowing.* Portland, ME: Stenhouse.

Gibbs, J. 2001. *Tribes: A New Way of Learning and Being Together.* Santa Rosa, CA: Center Source Publications.

Gilmore, B. 1999. *Creative Writing Through the Visual and Performing Arts.* Portsmouth, NH: Heinemann.

Giroux, H. 1983. *Theory and Resistance in Education.* South Hadley, MA: Bergin and Garvey.

Glasser, W. 1986. *Control Theory in the Classroom.* New York: Harper and Row.

Gould, S. J. 1981. *The Mismeasure of Man.* New York: Norton.

Graves, D. H. 1983. *Writing: Teachers and Children at Work.* Portsmouth, NH: Heinemann.

———. 1991. *Build a Literate Classroom.* Portsmouth, NH: Heinemann

———. 1994. *A Fresh Look at Writing.* Portsmouth, NH: Heinemann.

———. 2002. *Testing Is Not Teaching: What Should Count in Education.* Portsmouth, NH: Heinemann.

Greene, M. 1988. *The Dialectic of Freedom.* New York: Teachers College Press.

Haddix, M. P. 2001. *Takeoffs and Landings.* New York: Simon and Schuster.

Harvey, S. 1998. *Nonfiction Matters: Reading, Writing, and Research in Grades 3–8.* Portland, ME: Stenhouse.

Harvey, S., and A. Goudvis. 2000. *Strategies That Work: Teaching Comprehension to Enhance Understanding.* Portland, ME: Stenhouse.

———. 2004. *Strategic Thinking: Reading and Responding, Grades 4–8* (videotape). Portland, ME: Stenhouse.

Harwayne, S. 1992. *Lasting Impressions: Weaving Literature into the Writing Workshop.* Portsmouth, NH: Heinemann.

———. 2003. *Learning to Confer: Writing Conferences in Action.* Portsmouth, NH: Heinemann.

Heaton, R. M. 2000. *Teaching Mathematics to the New Standards: Relearning the Dance.* New York: Teachers College Press.

Heller, P. G. 1995. *Drama as a Way of Knowing.* Portland, ME: Stenhouse.

Herman, J., P. Aschbacher, and L. Winters. 1992. *A Practical Guide to Alternative Assessment.* Alexandria, VA: Association for Supervision and Curriculum Development.

Hill, B. C., and C. Ruptic. 1994. *Practical Aspects of Authentic Assessment: Putting the Pieces Together.* Norwood, MA: Christopher-Gordon.

Hill, S., and T. Hill. 1990. *The Collaborative Classroom: A Guide to Cooperative Learning.* Portsmouth, NH: Heinemann.

Hindley, J. 1996. *In the Company of Children.* Portland, ME: Stenhouse.

Hirsch, E. D., Jr. 1996. *The Schools We Need and Why We Don't Have Them.* New York: Doubleday.

Horwood, B., ed. 1995. *Experience and the Curriculum.* Dubuque, IA: Kendall-Hunt.

Hoverstein, N. Doda, and J. Lounsbury. 1998. *Treasure Chest: A Teacher Advisory Sourcebook.* Westerville, OH: National Middle School Association.

Hubbard, R. S. 1996. *A Workshop of the Possible: Nurturing Children's Creative Development.* Portland, ME: Stenhouse.

Hubbard, R. S., and K. Ernst. 1996. *New Entries: Learning by Writing and Drawing.* Portsmouth, NH: Heinemann.

Hyde, A., and M. Bizar. 1989. *Thinking in Context: Teaching Cognitive Processes Across the Elementary School Curriculum.* New York: Longman.

Hyde, A., and P. R. Hyde. 1991. *Mathwise: Teaching Mathematical Thinking and Problem Solving.* Portsmouth, NH: Heinemann.

Isaacs, Judith Ann, and Janine Brodine. 1994. *Journals in the Classroom: A Complete Guide for the Elementary Teacher.* Winnipeg: Peguis.

Jacobs, P., and S. Landau. 1971. *To Serve the Devil.* New York: Random House.

Jago, C. 2004. *Classics in the Classroom: Designing Accessible Literature Lessons.* Portsmouth, NH: Heinemann.

James, C. 1969. *Young Lives at Stake.* London: Collins.

Jarden, J. 2001. *Down by the Sea.* Port Melbourne, Australia: Rigby.

Johnson, D., R. Johnson, E. Holubec, and P. Roy. 1991. *Cooperation in the Classroom.* Edina, MN: Interaction Book.

Johnston, P. H. 1992. *Constructive Evaluation of Literate Activity.* New York: Longman.

———. 1997. *Knowing Literacy: Constructive Literacy Assessment.* Portland, ME: Stenhouse.

Jones, M. 1969. *The Autobiography of Mother Jones.* New York: Arno.

Jorgensen, K. L. 1993. *History Workshop: Reconstructing the Past with Elementary Students.* Portsmouth, NH: Heinemann.

Kajder, S. B. 2003. *The Tech-Savy English Classroom.* Portland, ME. Stenhouse.

Keene, E. O., and S. Zimmermann. 1997. *Mosaic of Thought: Teaching Reading Comprehension in a Reader's Workshop.* Portsmouth, NH: Heinemann.

Kieffer, C. 2000. "New Deal Murals: A Legacy for Today's Public Art and Art Education." March. *Art Education.*

Kohn, A. 1995. *Punished by Rewards: The Trouble with Gold Stars, Incentive Plans, A's, Praise, and Other Bribes.* Boston: Houghton Mifflin.

Kordalewski, J. 2000. *Standards in the Classroom: How Teachers and Students Negotiate Learning.* New York: Teachers College Press.

Kraft, R. J., and J. Kiesmeier, eds. 1994. *Experiential Learning in Schools and Higher Education.* Boulder, CO: Association for Experiential Education.

Lake, J. A. 2000. *Literature and Science Breakthroughs: Connecting Language and Science Skills in the Elementary Classroom.* Markham, ON: Pembroke.

Lambert, J. 2002. *Digital Storytelling: Capturing Lives, Creating Community.* Berkeley: Digital Diner.

Lappan, G., and P. Schram. 1989. *Communication and Reasoning: Critical Dimensions of Sense-Making in Mathematics.* Yearbook of Mathematics Instruction. Reston, VA: National Council of Teachers of Mathematics.

Liber, C. M. 2002. *Partners in Learning: From Conflict to Collaboration in Secondary Classrooms.* Cambridge, MA: Educators for Social Responsibility.

Lindquist, T. 1995. *Seeing the Whole Through Social Studies.* Portsmouth, NH: Heinemann.

Lipman, M. 1987. *Teaching Thinking Skills: Theory into Practice.* New York: Freeman.

Lockwood, A., and D. Harris. 1985. *Reasoning with Democratic Values: Ethical Problems in United States History.* New York: Teachers College Press.

London, P. 1994. *Step Outside: Community-Based Art Education.* Portsmouth, NH: Heinemann.

Manning, M. L., and K. T. Bucher. 2003. *Teaching in the Middle School.* Columbus, OH: National Middle School Association.

Mantione, R. D., and S. Smead. 2003. *Weaving Through Words: Using the Arts to Teach Reading Comprehension Strategies.* Newark, DE: International Reading Association.

McLaren, P. 1994. *Life in Schools: An Introduction to Critical Pedagogy in the Foundations of Education.* New York: Longman.

McNeil, L. M. 1988. *Contradictions of Control: School Structure and School Knowledge.* New York: Rutledge.

McTighe, J., and G. Wiggins. 2000. *Understanding by Design.* New York: Prentice Hall.

McVey, V. 1989. *The Sierra Club Wayfinding Book.* Boston: Little, Brown.

Meier, D. 2002. *The Power of Their Ideas: Lessons for America from a Small School in Harlem.* Boston: Beacon Press.

———. 2003. *In Schools We Trust: Creating Learning Communities in an Era of Testing and Standardization.* Boston: Beacon Press.

Mikaelsen, B. 2001. *Touching Spirit Bear.* New York: HarperCollins.

Miller, C. S., and J. Saxton. 2004. *Into the Story: Language in Action Through Drama.* Portsmouth, NH: Heinemann.

Miller, D. 2002. *Reading with Meaning: Teaching Comprehension in the Primary Grades.* Portland, ME: Stenhouse

Miller, D. 1973. *Then Was the Future.* New York: Knopf.

Moline, S. 1995. *I See What You Mean: Children at Work with Visual Information.* Portland, ME: Stenhouse.

Monroe, B. 2004. *Crossing the Digital Divide: Race, Writing and Technology in the Classroom.* New York: Teachers College Press.

Moore, F. 1969. *Diary of the American Revolution: From Newspapers and Original Documents.* New York: Washington Square Press.

Myers, M. 1996. *Changing Our Minds: Negotiating English and Literacy.* Urbana, IL: National Council of Teachers of English.

Nabhan, G., and S. Trimble. 1995. *The Geography of Childhood: Why Children Need Wild Places.* Boston: Beacon Press.

Nabokov, P. 1978. *Native American Testimony: A Chronicle of Indian-White Relations from Prophecy to the Present, 1492–1992.* New York: Crowell.

National Academy of Science. 1996. *National Science Education Standards.* Washington, DC: National Academy Press.

National Council of Social Studies. 1994. *Expectations of Excellence: Curriculum Standards for Social Studies.* Washington, DC: National Council of Social Studies.

National Council of Teachers of Mathematics. 1989. *Curriculum and Instruction Standards for School Mathematics.* Reston, VA: National Council of Teachers of Mathematics.

Newmann, F. 1996. *Authentic Achievement.* San Franscisco: Jossey-Bass.

Newmann, F., A. Bryk, and J. Nagaoka. 2001. *Authentic Intellectual Work and Standardized Tests: Conflict or Coexistence?* Chicago: Consortium on Chicago Schools Research.

Noguera, P. 2004. *City Schools and the American Dream: Reclaiming the Promise of Public Education.* New York: Teachers College Press.

Noppi Brandon, Gail. 2004. *Finding Your Voice: A Methodology for Enhancing Literacy Through Re-Writing and Re-Acting.* Portsmouth, NH: Heinemann.

O'Brien, T. 1990. *The Things They Carried.* Boston: Houghton Mifflin.

Ogle, D. M. 1986. "K-W-L: A Teaching Model That Develops Active Reading of Expository Text." *Reading Teacher* 39: 564–70.

Olson, J. L. 1992. *Envisioning Writing: Toward an Integration of Drawing and Writing.* Portsmouth, NH: Heinemann.

Ostrow, J. 1999. *Making Problems, Creating Solutions: Challenging Young Mathematicians.* Portland, ME: Stenhouse.

Owocki, G., and Y. M. Goodman. 2002. *Kidwatching: Documenting Children's Literacy Development.* Portsmouth, NH: Heinemann.

Page, N. 1996. *Music as a Way of Knowing.* Portland, ME: Stenhouse.

Paley, V. G. 1992. *You Can't Say You Can't Play.* Cambridge, MA: Harvard University Press.

Parsons, L. 1994. *Expanding Response Journals in All Subject Areas.* Portsmouth, NH: Heinemann.

Pearson, P. D., J. A. Dole, G. G. Duffy, and L. R. Roehler. 1992. "Developing Expertise in Reading Comprehension: What Should Be Taught and How Should It Be Taught?" In J. Farstup and S. J. Samuels, eds., *What Research Has to Say to the Teacher of Reading.* 2nd ed. Newark, DE: International Reading Association.

Perl, S. 2004. *Felt Sense: Writing with the Body.* Portsmouth, NH: Boynton/Cook.

Polman, J. L. 2000. *Designing Project Based Science: Connecting Learners Through Guided Inquiry.* New York: Teachers College Press.

Randell, B. 1994a. *A Friend for Little White Rabbit.* Port Melbourne, Australia: Rigby.

———. 1994b. *Mushrooms for Dinner.* Port Melbourne, Australia: Rigby.

Ray, K. W., and L. B. Cleaveland. 2004. *About the Authors: Writing Workshop with Our Youngest Writers.* Portsmouth, NH: Heinemann.

Reynolds, M. 2004. *I Won't Read and You Can't Make Me: Reaching Reluctant Teen Readers.* Portsmouth, NH: Heinemann.

Rich, A. 1979. *On Lies, Secrets, and Silence: Selected Prose.* Chicago: W. W. Norton.

Rico, G. 1985. *Writing the Natural Way.* Los Angeles: Tarcher.

Roberts, P. 2002. *Kids Taking Action: Community Service Learning Projects K–8.* Greenfield, MA: Northeast Foundation for Children.

Robinson, G. 1996. *Sketch-Books: Explore and Store.* Portsmouth, NH: Heinemann.

Rodriguez, L. 1993. *Always Running: La Vida Loca: Gang Days in L. A.* East Haven, CT: Curbstone.

Rogers, C., and H. J. Freiberg. 1994. *Freedom to Learn.* New York: Macmillan.

Romano, Tom. 2000. *Blending Genre, Altering Style: Writing Multigenre Papers.* Portsmouth, NH: Boynton/Cook.

Saul, W., and J. Reardon, eds. 1996. *Beyond the Science Kit: Inquiry in Action.* Portsmouth, NH: Heinemann.

Saul, W., J. Reardon, A. Schmidt, C. Pearce, D. Blackwood, and M. Dickinson Bird. 1993. *Science Workshop: A Whole Language Approach.* Portsmouth, NH: Heinemann.

Schlosser, E. 2002. *Fast Food Nation: The Dark Side of the All-American Meal.* New York: Perennial.

Schmuck, R. A., and P. A. Schmuck. *Group Processes in the Classroom.* New York: McGraw-Hill.

Serafini, F. 2004. *Lessons in Comprehension: Explicit Instruction in the Reading Workshop.* Portsmouth, NH: Heinemann.

Shannon, P. 1995. *Text, Lies, and Videotape: Stories About Life, Literacy, and Learning.* Portsmouth, NH: Heinemann.

Shor, I. 1987. *Freire for the Classroom: A Sourcebook for Laboratory Teaching.* Portsmouth, NH: Boynton/Cook.

Sibberson, F., and K. Szymusiak. 2003. *Still Learning to Read: Teaching Students in Grades 3–6.* Portland, ME: Stenhouse.

Smith, J., V. Lee, and F. Newmann. 2002. *Instruction and Achievement in Chicago Elementary Schools.* Chicago: Consortium on Chicago School Research.

Smith, K. 1993. "Becoming the 'Guide on the Side.'" *Educational Leadership* 51, 2: 35–37.

Smith, M., and J. Wilhelm. 2002. *Reading Don't Fix No Chevys: Literacy Lives of Young Men.* Portsmouth, NH: Heinemann.

Spandel, V. 2000. *Creating Writers through the 6-Trait Writing and Assessment.* Boston: Allyn and Bacon.

Spivak, D. 1997. *Grass Sandals: The Travels of Basho.* New York: Atheneum.

Stefanikis, A. H. 2002. *Multiple Intelligences and Portfolios: A Window into the Learner's Mind.* Portsmouth, NH: Heinemann.

Steffey, S., and W. J. Hood, eds. 1994. *If This Is Social Studies, Why Isn't It Boring?* Portland, ME: Stenhouse.

Steineke, N. 2002. *Reading and Writing Together: Collaborative Literacy in Action.* Portsmouth, NH: Heinemann.

Stephan, W., and W. P. Vogt, eds. 2004. *Education Programs for Improving Intergroup Relations: Theory, Research, and Practice.* New York: Teachers College Press.

Stephens, L. 1995. *The Complete Guide to Learning Through Community Service: Grades K–9.* Boston: Allyn and Bacon.

Stevenson, C., and J. Carr. 1993. *Integrated Studies in the Middle Grades: Dancing Through Walls.* New York: Teachers College Press.

Swartz, Larry. 2002. *The New Dramathemes.* Markham, ON: Pembroke.

Szymusiak, K., and F. Sibberson. 2001. *Beyond Leveled Books: Supporting Transitional Readers in Grades 2–5.* Portland, ME: Stenhouse.

Tchudi, S., and S. Lafer. 1996. *The Interdisciplinary Teacher's Handbook: Integrated Teaching Across the Curriculum.* Portsmouth, NH: Boynton/Cook.

Tehschick, J. 1971. *To Touch the Earth.* New York: Outerbridge and Diensffrey.

Thelan, H. 1967. *Education and the Human Quest.* New York: Wiley.

Tobin, L. 2004. *Reading Student Writing: Confessions, Meditations and Rants.* Portsmouth, NH: Heinemann.

Tovani, C. 2000. *I Read It, but I Don't Get It: Comprehension Strategies for Adolescent Readers.* Portland, ME: Stenhouse.

———. 2004. *Do I Really Have to Teach Reading? Content Comprehension, Grades 6–12.* Portland, ME: Stenhouse.

Vopat, J. 1994. *The Parent Project: A Workshop Approach to Parent Involvement.* Portland, ME: Stenhouse.

Walker, B. 2003. *Supporting Struggling Readers.* Portsmouth, NH: Heinemann.

Whitin, P. 1996. *Sketching Stories, Stretching Minds: Responding Visually to Literature.* Portsmouth, NH: Heinemann.

Wigginton, E. 1985. *Sometimes a Shining Moment: The Foxfire Experience.* Garden City, NY: Anchor Press/Doubleday.

Wilhelm, J. 1997. *You Gotta Be the Book.* Portsmouth, NH: Heinemann.

Wilhelm, J. D., T. N. Baker, and J. Dube. 2001. *Strategic Reading: Guiding Students to Lifelong Literacy 6–12.* Portsmouth: NH: Heinemann.

Wolk, S. 1994. "Project-Based Learning: Pursuits with a Purpose." *Educational Leadership* 52, 3: 42–45.

Wood, G. H. 1993. *Schools that Work: America's Most Innovative Public Education Programs.* New York: Plume.

Wood, J. M. 2004. *Literacy Online: New Tools for Struggling Readers and Writers.* Portsmouth, NH: Heinemann.

Worsley, D., and B. Mayer. 1989. *The Art of Science Writing.* New York: Teachers and Writers Collaborative.

Zakkai, J. 1997. *Dance as a Way of Knowing.* Portland, ME: Stenhouse.

Zemelman, S., and H. Daniels. 1988. *A Community of Writers: Teaching Writing in the Junior and Senior High School.* Portsmouth, NH: Heinemann.

Zemelman, S., H. Daniels, and M. Bizar. 1999. "Sixty Years of Research—but Who's Listening?" *Phi Delta Kappan* 80 (March) 9.

Zemelman, S., H. Daniels, and A. Hyde. 1998. *Best Practice: New Standards for Teaching and Learning in America's Schools.* Portsmouth, NH: Heinemann.

Zemelman, S., P. Bearden, Y. Simmons, and P. Leki. 1999. *History Comes Home: Family Stories Across the Curriculum.* Portland, ME: Stenhouse.

Zinn, H. 1980. *A People's History of the United States.* New York: Harper and Row.

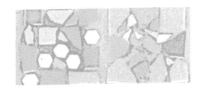  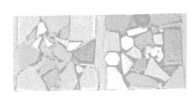

INDEX